POLITICS
OF
NOVA
SCOTIA

DISCARD

Volume Two
Murray-Buchanan
1896-1988

J. Murray Beck

Acknowledgements

The publisher wishes to express his appreciation for the generous
financial support of the **Nova Scotia Department of Culture Recreation
and Fitness** and the **Canada Council.**

Richard Rogers, Publisher

FOUR EAST PUBLICATIONS
P.O. Box 29
Tantallon, Nova Scotia B0J 3J0

1st edition November 1988

edited by Douglas Beall
layout by Desmond M. Trim
printed by McCurdy Printing & Typesetting Limited

This book is printed with acid free paper that should neither yellow with
age, nor become brittle.

Canadian Cataloguing in Publication Data
Beck, J. Murray (James Murray), 1914 -
   Politics of Nova Scotia

Includes index.
Partial contents: v. 2. Murray-Buchanan,
1896-1988.
ISBN 0-920427-16-2 (v. 2)

1. Nova Scotia — Politics and government.
I. Title.

FC2311.B39 1985   971.6   C85-099843-3
F1038.B39 1985

To Evelyn

Preface

This book, like its predecessor, does not fall within the rubric of political science; it simply attempts to recount ninety-two years of Nova Scotia's political history, beginning in 1896. My primary intention was to provide Nova Scotians with a knowledge of their political past in the twentieth century. I have thus depicted the playing of the game of politics within a political culture which has changed in some important respects since the Second World War.

One serious difficulty for any political historian of the period results from the decision of George Murray, premier for more than a quarter of a century, not to have his papers preserved. The personal papers of Robert Stanfield as they apply to his premiership also appear to have disappeared, although not at his bidding. Another problem stems from the abandonment after 1916 of the synoptic reporting of the legislative debates which dated back to the 1850s. This meant that, until the institution of a genuine Hansard in 1952, reliance had to be placed on the reports of debates in the Halifax daily newspapers, a problem magnified by the disappearance of the *Chronicle* at the end of 1948.

Full use has been made of the papers of Fielding, Armstrong, Rhodes, and MacMillan in their varying degrees of completeness. Of inestimable value have been the papers of Angus L. Macdonald as they relate to provincial politics, which have been used with the permission of his son, Mr. Justice Angus L. Macdonald. Highly useful, too, have been the papers of former premier Henry D. Hicks in the Public Archives of Nova Scotia. The essays and opinions of students in Political Science 3212/

5212, my course on the politics and government of Nova Scotia, also made a valuable contribution.

As usual I am more than grateful to Mr. Carman Carroll and to the entire staff at the Public Archives of Nova Scotia for their unfailing courtesy and helpfulness. Year after year this institution provides an invaluable service. I have benefited greatly from the wide knowledge of Nova Scotia politics possessed by my former student, Mr. Allan Dunlop, the associate provincial archivist. And no one could have been more congenial and helpful than publisher Richard Rogers.

I have tried to avoid definitive judgments about those still engaged in provincial politics. I am acutely aware that the opinions of others about events in contemporary politics may differ markedly from my own.

William Stevens Fielding   1884-1896

Contents

Preface   2
Chapter
 1. George Murray: The Early Years   7
 2. Murray: The Middle Years 25
 3. Murray: The Later Years 53
 4. Armstrong and the Liberal Débacle 83
 5. Rhodes and Harrington: A Conservative Interlude 115
 6. Angus L. Macdonald: The Development of a Mystique . . 153
 7. MacMillan: The Gap Filler 187
 8. "Angus L. is Back" 205
 9. The Problems of Transition: Connolly and Hicks 239
 10. Stanfield: A Conservative Establishes Himself 255
 11. Smith and IEL: A Two-Edged Sword 299
 12. Regan: The Fading of Dreams 321
 13. Buchanan: No Cuts in Services despite Deficits 347
 14. Ninety-Two Years of Politics 375
      Epilogue 391
      Endnotes 395
      Appendices 418
      Index 429

CHAPTER 1

George Murray: The Early Years

The night of June 23, 1896 was one of ecstasy for Nova Scotia's Liberals. That day they had helped to defeat federal Toryism, their primary target for eighteen years, and to make Wilfrid Laurier the prime minister of Canada. Yet victory left difficult questions in its wake. Who would be the province's chief political leaders in Ottawa and Halifax? For some time Laurier had tried to induce Nova Scotia's long-time premier, William Stevens Fielding, to become a member of his team, but after much hesitancy Fielding had decided not to run in the 1896 federal election. Part of the reason was financial; on occasions like this he was reminded how unfortunate it was to be poor.

The election over, Fielding told Laurier to choose the province's cabinet ministers as he thought best. Always considerate and self-depreciating, he worried that his appointment would offend some of the province's Liberal MPs. He even went out of his way to tell D.C. Fraser, the member for Pictou, that he "recognized the claims and rights of those who were more directly engaged in Dominion affairs" than himself. However, because of his close rapport with Laurier, he must have realized that he would not be excluded and in short order he was made minister of finance. A second Nova Scotian, Frederick Borden of Kings, became minister of militia and defence. Just as Fielding had feared, A.G. Jones of Halifax and D.C. Fraser were bitterly disappointed. Jones, the leading federal Liberal in Nova Scotia since Confederation, even chided Laurier for regarding Fielding as "a little *Tin God on Wheels.*"[1]

Reconstructing the provincial government caused even greater difficulties. In April 1896, when Fielding had been thinking of entering federal politics, he had sought the opinion of his caucus on a possible successor to himself. The largest number favoured James Wilberforce Longley; the next largest, George Henry Murray; the rest, half a dozen others. Longley, attorney general since 1886, had once written for *The Week* and *Acadian Recorder* and for a time was managing editor of the *Chronicle*. His stand on the province's external relations had been erratic. At first dubious of secession from Canada, he had later supported it. Still later he had favoured commercial union with the United States and even flirted with political union on the ground that membership in the Canadian federation was destroying the province's natural trade channels which God had put in place. He was also something of an intellectual, one of the few Nova Scotian politicians to be elected a fellow of the Royal Society of Canada, and was later a biographer of Howe and Tupper (admittedly without resort to primary sources).

Longley also had a weakness calculated to harm himself and his party. Possessed of the gift of sarcasm — indeed, a master of ridicule — he "never, in private or public, could deny himself the pleasure of saying a sharp and biting thing." Once he told an old political friend in Yarmouth that he never ate at night. When his host replied that he always did, Longley could not forbear a typical rejoinder: "Quite so, some animals, notably the hog, can eat till they are replete and then lie down and sleep." On another occasion he asked lawyer Benjamin Russell who had a better chance to become prime minister than he. When Russell suggested Fielding, Longley replied: "Fielding! . . . [he] is one of your Great Little Men."[2]

Perhaps Fielding was unaware of Longley's appraisal of him, but in any case he preferred George Murray, a man much in his own mould. None had rendered more unselfish service to his party than Murray. As a lawyer in North Sydney, Murray had fought the Liberals' battles in industrializing Cape Breton County when the Conservatives' National Policy put his party at a serious disadvantage. At age twenty-five he was an unsuccessful candidate in the repeal election of 1886, although not as a repealer; a year later he lost federally again. Fielding rewarded him with a legislative councillorship in 1889, but

Murray again sacrificed himself in the federal election of 1891 against impossible odds in Cape Breton County. This time Fielding not only reappointed him to the legislative council but made him the government leader in that body and an executive councillor as well.

For five years Murray remained where he was while far-reaching changes were occurring in Cape Breton County. In 1893 the Fielding government concluded an agreement with the Whitney Syndicate which led to the establishment of the Dominion Coal Company. Liberals now expected the county would become fertile ground for them, but in the short run that was not to be. Fielding had hoped that the manager of the company would have no connection with Nova Scotia politics, but the appointment went nonetheless to David McKeen, the Conservative MP for Cape Breton County. It was he who, in January 1896, resigned his seat to give way to Sir Charles Tupper as the latter made a last desperate effort to save the Conservative government at Ottawa, and it was George Murray who again answered his party's call by contesting the by-election against Tupper.

Even in defeat Murray's candidature served him well. As Tupper's opponent, he was exposed to "a swarm of correspondents from coast to coast" who made his name known throughout Canada. Subsequently, at a testimonial dinner in Halifax, he was described as "the most popular man in Cape Breton." However, most significant of all was Fielding's wish to play a role in determining Murray's future. A federal general election being imminent, Fielding asked him directly whether he intended to run again for the Commons or was disposed to become more active in provincial politics. Offering more advice than he usually did, Fielding added that unless Murray had good expectations of winning federally — and Fielding could see none — he ought not to sacrifice himself further. "You have had a fair share of defeats and might reasonably think that . . . you should [now] be allowed to participate in something that offered a better prospect of success."[3] As a result, Murray let Tupper defeat someone else in the general election of 1896.

Having decided to go to Ottawa, Fielding met his caucus on July 10th to discuss the reorganization of the provincial cabinet. Delightedly, the *Herald* reported "the bitterest kind of feeling,"

and it may have been right because eight days were needed to
reach a decision. If J.W. Longley had not run federally and not
been defeated in Annapolis, it might have been difficult to
overlook him. Certainly Longley's recent defeat made Fielding's
recommendation of Murray as his successor all the easier, even
though Murray had himself suffered four electoral defeats and
never won a personal victory. It was a decision which Fielding
would later describe as the best he had ever made for Nova Scotia
and one which was to set the tone of provincial politics for more
than a quarter of a century. No premier ever started out more
auspiciously. Fielding had left the provincial Liberals
organizationally sound, and the province was entering a long
economic boom.[4] Highly cautious, Murray made a minimum
number of changes in the cabinet. He succeeded Fielding as
provincial secretary, retained Longley as attorney general,
unassuming but competent Charles Church as commissioner of
public works and mines, and appointed three new ministers
without portfolio to succeed those who had entered federal
politics. In mid-August his party won all of six by-elections and
he had his first personal success in Victoria County, a seat he
would hold for twenty-six years.

A little later the Conservative national leader, Sir Charles
Tupper, arrived in Halifax hoping to put his party in fighting
trim and to perfect its organization. The outcome, in October,
was the setting up of the Liberal-Conservative Union of Nova
Scotia, named after its British counterpart, the National Union.
Industrialist John F. Stairs, a former executive councillor and
MP, became its president and the apparent party leader; Dr.
William MacKay, the Conservative house leader became the
Union's vice-president. The meeting also took steps towards the
creation of county associations where they had been non-
existent.

When Murray appeared in the assembly for the first time in
1897, he was something of a mystery man. Even today he
remains an enigmatic figure because he chose not to have his
personal papers preserved. The result has been to compound the
difficulty of recounting the province's political history for over
a quarter of a century. The speech from the throne in 1897 was
an optimistic document which presented a picture of general
prosperity, including the largest coal output to date. Typical of

the man, Murray made no attempt to exercise a dominant influence in the assembly; indeed, Longley did more to defend the government than he. Reflecting his caution, the premier proposed a miniscule legislative programme. Thus the most important government bill of the session did nothing more than simplify the procedures and reduce the costs in the probate court. Much more significant was the passage of a government backbencher's bill which extended the life of general assemblies from four to five years.

The legislation the Conservatives proposed was highly political in character. Once again they sought to repeal the law which prevented most Dominion officials from voting in provincial elections, a product of the bitter Confederation era. However, the Liberals declined to put themselves in a false position, so they said, and refused to adopt this proposal so soon after their party had taken office in Ottawa. The Conservatives also sought to abolish the legislative council through the offer of three years of sessional indemnities to its members, a proposal not unexpectedly rejected by the upper house. Murray, playing the same game as Fielding in pre-election sessions, responded with a bill of his own which made abolition contingent on the approval of the voters at the next election. None knew better than he that the council would summarily reject a bill of this nature, if initiated in the assembly, as a violation of its privileges, but he could at least tell the voters that he had done what he could to effect abolition.

As provincial secretary and hence provincial treasurer, Murray's principal task was to present, first, the financial returns and, later, the estimates or budget. Because coal royalties were below expectations, he had to report a deficit of $13,000 for 1896 despite an unexpected windfall from the sale of Nova Scotia's pre-Confederation postage stamps on the simple condition that their number not be divulged. Allegedly the buyers made a killing, but these were days when unexpected government revenues of only $18,000 still constituted "a most agreeable surprise." For the forthcoming year Murray forecast a surplus of $4,000, based on the expectation that coal royalties would reach an unprecedented $288,000.

As usual, the main opposition attacks, both in the assembly and the *Herald,* were on the government's financial record. After the election of 1894 Dr. William MacKay of Reserve Mines had become Conservative house leader for a second time, but neither he nor any of his followers possessed expertise in political give-and-take. That situation altered dramatically when Charles E. Tanner won a by-election in Pictou. For days he flayed the government's estimates in the style that had characterized the attacks of the *Herald* for a decade. As usual, the parties disagreed on the reason for the increase in provincial revenues. Dr. MacKay attributed it to the federal Conservatives' National Policy and more specifically to the import duty which had permitted Nova Scotian coal to be shipped up the St. Lawrence River. Murray gave the credit to Fielding's agreement with the Whitney Syndicate, the consequent export of substantial quantities of coal to the United States, and an increase in royalty rates. This debate would go on for years.

Only in one instance had the government's major expectations not materialized. Except for thirteen miles of the Coast Railway from Yarmouth towards Shelburne, railway construction had been meagre. All other omens being propitious, Murray followed the course of most premiers in his position: at session's end he had the assembly dissolved to seek his own mandate. Characteristically, he issued a manifesto which, while listing everything that could be said for the government, was far less detailed than those of Fielding had been. The manifesto of Stairs, like those of his two predecessors, was largely a repetition of *Herald* editorials with a special emphasis on financial concerns.

Using this manifesto as their source, Conservative campaigners argued that much of the provincial debt had been incurred unnecessarily; that the government had borrowed immense sums, supposedly for roads and bridges, but actually to keep itself in power, and in the process had reduced materially the municipalities' road moneys; and that in assuming direct control of the Victoria General Hospital it had created "the reprehensible and injurious state" in which that institution existed. Ten days before the election, in a last desperate move, Stairs issued a shorter, second manifesto which appealed to the voters' moral sensibilities. Year after year, it said, the government had made public funds a source of "shameless corruption," even so far as to induce people to "palter with the sacred obligations of an oath." Did Nova Scotians want to continue this "course of political profligacy"?[5]

In defending themselves the Liberals posed such questions as: Had they not incurred the public debt largely for productive public works such as railroads, roads, and bridges? Did the electors approve of "ghoul-like attacks" upon humane institutions which most people regarded as a credit to the province? Although the *Herald* found it difficult to attack Murray because his premiership had been so brief, the *Chronicle* had a field day with Stairs. As an executive councillor between 1879 and 1882 had his record not been so negative that people had forgotten about him? As an MP had he not voted for "a short line" through Maine that damaged the port of Halifax? Had he not agreed to whitewash the misdeeds of Langevin and Caron at Ottawa? Had he not strongly supported the "odious" National Policy and especially the duties protecting the cordage combine in which he had a personal interest?

As the election approached, the *Chronicle* declared that the Conservatives had not a single safe seat. As propitious omens, it pointed to the subdued tone of the *Herald* and the Liberals' winning of two seats in Shelburne by acclamation. Its prophecies were correct and the Liberal victory on April 20th was so one-sided that the *Chronicle* did not content itself with displaying just one rooster the day after the election but instead flaunted three of them. Although the Conservatives' popular vote fell only from 47.3 to 44.4 per cent, their defeat was a veritable disaster. Failing to carry a single county, they elected only three members: Charles S. Wilcox, who was second in Hants; M.H. Fitzpatrick, who ran third in Pictou; and T.G. McMullen, who headed the poll in Colchester, but only by a mere five votes. Stairs lost badly in Halifax as did Conservative house leader MacKay in Cape Breton County. Charles Tanner, who had assumed the house leadership *de facto,* ran fifth among the six candidates in Pictou. In a very real sense the Conservatives were even worse off than in 1867, for in that year they had elected Hiram Blanchard, who could hold his own with anyone. This time none of their members had true leadership potential.

The *Herald* blamed the defeat on the wholesale bribery of a comparatively small, "loose section" of the population which fell prey to "human devices." For the third election in a row it had actually believed that the Conservatives could win over the electorate with tales of financial mismanagement. However, it was folly to think that in relatively prosperous times a government which had steadily improved public services and successfully promoted economic development without resortin to increased taxation could be defeated. The Fielding legacy had been the major determinant of the election.

The Thirty-First General Assembly (1897-1901)[6] witnessed as great a period of optimism as Nova Scotia has ever experienced in the post-Confederation period. In early 1898 the *Chronicle* went into raptures over the province's prospects, much of it based on the rising demand in New England for Cape Breton coal and the likely establishment of a major steel industry.

By 1899 even George Murray had become a little infected. That year saw the incorporation of the Dominion Iron and Steel Company by Henry M. Whitney, the founder of the Dominion Coal Company. Whitney told Murray that he had ᴐent more than $6 million to equip the Cape Breton mines and increase their annual output from 700,000 to 1,200,000 tons, that he had recently bought equipment in Britain to set up a coke and gas company which would consume Nova Scotia slack coal, and that all the ingredients were at hand — coal, iron ore, limestone, and cheap water transportation — to enable Cape Breton steel to compete in the markets of the world. To assist him he aᴗ.ed for a five-year remission of the royalty on coal used in the production of steel. The cautious Murray responded by offering a rebate of one-half the royalty for eight years to any company setting up a substantial steel plant within two years. He had visions that Whitney's undertaking might lead to a score of kindred interests capable of supporting "a population equal to that of one of the great iron centres"; he hoped, too, for the repatriation of young Nova Scotians who had gone to the "Boston States" because of lack of opportunity at home.[7]

On New year's Day, 1900 the *Chronicle* was in a state of euphoria. Nova Scotia, it declared, was finally awakening from its long lethargy. The improved economic conditions made it easy for Murray to handle provincial finances. He turned a deficit of $23,000 in 1898 into a surplus of $6,000 the next year and budgeted for another surplus in 1900. Nova Scotia, he boasted, was fortunate because, unlike other provinces, it did not have to rely on a static source of revenue like federal subsidies but could use a more flexible and steadily increasing source — royalties on coal. Hence it had not needed to use corporation taxes or licence fees. Was it not fortuitous, he asked, that "the affairs of the province were in the hands of men who placed a true value upon our great mineral resources?" A frustrated *Herald* replied, as usual, that the increase in revenues was due primarily to the Conservatives' National Policy and that the surplus was merely a bookkeeping one and a sham as long as the provincial debt was increasing by leaps and bounds. To many Nova Scotians this must have seemed like sour grapes.

In 1900 Murray could say that, barring unforeseen circumstances, he would have the pleasant duty next year to announce that coal royalties had supplanted federal subsidies as the largest single source of provincial revenue. In 1901, when the total revenues exceeded $1 million for the first time since Confederation, he boasted again that the provinces could at last properly maintain its educational services, its public charities, and its roads and bridges: "You will find that perhaps nowhere in the civilized world are such services more generously treated." He was equally pleased that Nova Scotia did not get its revenues directly from the people: "We alone . . . remain practically where we started at confederation on the question of taxation, the only exception being the introduction of succession duties, and even this . . . is on a more moderate basis than that of our neighbours."[8]

Partly because of its small size and partly because of the buoyant times, the opposition had immense difficulties in these years. In 1898, perhaps for the first time, it let the address in reply to the speech from the throne be adopted without criticism or dissent. The session was largely a housekeeping one, in which the government's major proposals were to reduce the size of grand juries and to provide for the distribution of insolvents' assets much as Ontario had done. As in other provinces, the most notable feature of the legislative mill was the growing number of local and private bills. Municipal governments, limited severely by the statute which created them, sought the power to do specific things beyond their normal domain. Companies, new and old, requested the right to initiate activities or extend old ones in all sorts of directions. An unhappy *Herald* declared that the main task of the session had been to "pass special measures for the personal benefit of Grit partisans in and out of the house."

The 1899 session was more of the same. None of the government's bills — to set up an agricultural college, to provide extended training in natural sciences and laboratory work at the normal college, and to regulate inland fishing to accord with a decision of the Judicial Committee — was controversial. Perhaps the most interesting event of the session occurred when Murray, the quiet man, decided, as he did now and then, to put his sometimes domineering attorney general in his place. Longley, after describing the carnage being wrought by partridge, sought to have the closed season repealed. "The marvellous story" which the attorney general brought from Annapolis might be true, said Murray, but "it filled him with considerable wonder" and he had no trouble having the proposal rejected. The only highly partisan debate occurred on Longley's resolution relating to the Conservative-dominated Senate, which was causing the Laurier government no little trouble. The attorney general proposed that deadlocks be broken by joint meetings of the Senate and Commons. However, Charles Wilcox, who led the small opposition, objected to making the Nova Scotia assembly an arena for the discussion of federal issues; in his view, Longley's proposal, if adopted, would cause the Senate to "occupy the same position that the tail does to a dog."

During 1900 the Nova Scotia press focussed its main attention on the Boer War and the federal scene. Great was the rejoicing of the *Herald* at the relief of Ladysmith and the taking of Bloemfontein, loud was its denunciation of the alleged wrongdoing of the Laurier government — scandals in the Yukon, unprincipled gerrymandering, and a "Carnival of Spending." As the provincial legislators assembled for the session, this newspaper expressed the hope, "May they do but little harm," and thus outraged the *Chronicle* which saw the *Herald* as trying to bring the assembly into public contempt. This year Wilcox had found his feet and was unrestrained in his criticism. He contended that twenty years of Liberal rule had not brought development befitting the province's resources and, becoming highly moral, he demanded changes in the independence of the assembly act and the election laws generally. Murray, content as usual to let sleeping dogs lie, simply replied that few assembly men ever received as much as a dollar from the treasury.

In his new forcefulness Wilcox ran afoul of Longley. When he objected to the borrowing of $300,000 for culverts and small bridges, the attorney general found it utterly distasteful to have "the word 'debt' dinned into his ears until he could hardly sleep at night. . . . It was debt, debt, debt, like the patter of rain on a roof." He reacted much the same way when Wilcox lambasted the Crown lands policy which he administered. A year earlier the decision had been taken to lease rather than grant the lands, but for Wilcox the change had come much too late. "We have a kingdom in extent and value given for little more than the price of a horse." In eighteen years, he contended, 701,268 acres worth $4 an acre were granted for 40 cents an acre, a loss to the province of $2,650,761. So "absurd" an evaluation almost caused Longley to lose control of himself. Few, he said, would pay as much as 40 cents.[9]

This year the government's major proposals were to provide a sanitorium for tubercular patients; to establish — unsuccessfully, as it turned out — an agricultural and technical college for the Maritime Provinces; and to grant relief to injured workmen. Illustrating the caution of the Murray régime, it introduced the Employers' Liability for Injuries Act, which like the English act of 1880 provided compensation only where an injury had resulted from the negligence of an employer or one of his supervisors. Obviously it chose to ignore the much more liberal English Workmen's Compensation for Injuries Act of 1897.

Before the legislature met again, a federal general election took place on November 7, 1900. In Nova Scotia Fielding was the hero as he toured the province exulting in the success of his British preferential tariff and scorning Sir Charles Tupper's proposals for Imperial preferential trade as "still-born." It must have come as a shock to Nova Scotians to find the *Chronicle* outdoing the *Herald* in flag-waving. The *Chronicle* even suggested that if Tupper had been prime minister not a single Canadian would have fought the empire's battles in South Africa. It displayed the Union Jack prominently, sometimes two or three Union Jacks, and came out with headlines such as "Empire Interests Call for the Return of the Laurier Government" and "British We Are, and British We Shall Remain, Says Sir Wilfrid Laurier." It also declared that Tupper was "too old for the political 'trick-riding' which he is now attempting." Yet "decrepit and out of date" though he was, the *Chronicle* found him superior to Hugh John Macdonald, son of Sir John A., whom the Conservatives were supposedly hoping to make "a new Moses," but who impressed no one "as a man of even average intellect."

In contrast, the *Herald* had to fight a rearguard action, the more so because of the euphoria produced by Canada's first great economic boom. Day after day, the *Chronicle* kept referring to the "coming landslide," and so it was. Nova Scotia followed the national trend even though the Conservatives took 48.3 per cent of its vote. The Liberals won fifteen of the twenty seats and inflicted upon Tupper his first personal defeat in almost fifty years of politics. Calling his loss a "public calamity," the *Herald* declared that the electors seemed to like "humbug, bad faith, deception, extravagance, corruption, French race cries, and misgovernment generally." All it had to rejoice about was the re-election of Robert Laird Borden in Halifax, a man for whom even the *Chronicle* had great respect.[10]

Marking the assembly's opening in 1901 were a guard of honour composed entirely of Canadians for the first time and a speech from the throne which, for at least the second time, had been given to the *Chronicle* a day in advance. Because it was likely to be a pre-election session, the newspapers debated the value of the lower house and its members. The *Herald* called them "a public nuisance and serious evil"; the *Chronicle* was certain that "more can be done here to advance or retard the vital interests of Nova Scotia than at the Federal Capital." In evaluating the opposition members the *Chronicle* was sometimes laudatory but mostly critical: Fitzpatrick and McMullen seemed to "cherish decided aversions to unnecessary airing of their eloquence"; Wilcox, though not fond of speaking, performed well when he did; Charles Tanner, victor in a by-election, said much that was "justifiable . . . from the standpoint of party," but generally he was on "all fours with . . . the good dog 'Towser'," which "had to climb a tree," because "the bear was right after him." In utter disagreement, the *Herald* declared that Tanner's readiness of speech and sound judgment let the opposition take on new life.[11]

Certainly Tanner quickly made finance the focus of the Conservatives' attack. How, they wondered, could Murray report a surplus when the provincial debt had gone up by $200,000 to more than $4 million? "The increased revenues [might be] in evidence in the blue books, but the increased public benefits [were] in evidence nowhere." How long would the road funds continue to be divided between the government and the municipalities with a consequent frittering away of public moneys? How long, unlike other provinces, would Nova Scotia be without an independent auditor? Murray would go no further than to appoint an auditor to examine the accounts which he designated.

In one financial matter the Liberals could hardly stop gloating over their opponents. After the Eastern Extension from New Glasgow to the Strait of Canso had become part of the federal Intercolonial Railway (ICR), Nova Scotia Liberal governments demanded the return of their grants towards its construction only to be spurned by Conservative governments at Ottawa. With Fielding as minister of finance the situation had altered and Murray could finally announce the recovery of $671,000 and the "triumph of Liberal principles."

As usual, the Conservatives beat their heads against a stone in trying to effect changes in the political institutions — Tanner, to improve the election law; and Wilcox, to introduce universal suffrage. Once again Longley argued that the well-being of society depended upon having a line drawn "by which certain classes in the community should not be permitted to exercise the right of government." When Liberal backbencher D.D. McKenzie sought to repeal the disfranchisement of Dominion officials in provincial elections, the *Chronicle* told him that it would be "bad politics, bad Liberalism." He replied indignantly that it was never bad liberalism to extend the franchise, but to no avail.

With an early election likely, the government played its usual game with the legislative council. By this time the only surviving Conservative councillors were George Whitman and W.H. Owen, and all the Liberals except the aging president, Sir

Robert Boak, were pledged to abolition. Strangely the council found a defendant in the *Chronicle*, which called it a "jewel of great worth," not to be disturbed at a time when the assembly was "too directly amenable to mob impulses, too easily swayed by public passions." Even the premier was equivocal, declaring that the movement for abolition had arisen because of a financial stringency which no longer existed and that the council did no harm and some good. Nevertheless, he had an abolition bill introduced in the upper house by government leader and former premier W.T. Pipes, hoping to avoid the charge that the initiation of the bill in the assembly would violate the council's privileges. However, the council had ample protective machinery. Using the opinion of distinguished legal counsel in 1894 that pledges to support abolition were unconstitutional and a breach of parliamentary privilege, Boak refused to allow even the first reading of the bill. Murray could again tell the electorate that he had fought the good fight and lost.

Murray wanted even more to look good on railways. His government had overseen the completion of the easily built Midland Railway from Windsor to Truro and the near-completion of the Inverness and Richmond Railway between Port Hastings and Broad Cove, intended especially to open up the coal mines of Inverness County. However, the Coast Railway running from Yarmouth towards Lockeport and Halifax had got only as far as Barrington Passage and seemed destined to go no further. This meant that 80,000 people along the South Shore, who had helped pay for railways elsewhere, were still without similar facilities. Clearly the normal provincial subsidy of $3,200 a mile would not attract a suitable builder. Accordingly, Murray proposed instead a loan of $10,000 a mile at interest no greater that 3.5 per cent, the province to hold a first mortgage. Together with the federal subsidy, it meant that $13,500 a mile would be available to an entrepreneur. To the *Herald* the proposal had "all the appearance of having been contrived for public deception." Clearly it would be useful to the government in the general election.

By not going immediately to the polls, Murray lured his opponents into a state of lethargy. Actually there was some unfinished business to complete. Late August saw the appointment to the Senate of Charles Church, Tancook Island's contribution to provincial politics and a quiet, efficient minister with portfolio since 1882. Succeeding him was Arthur Drysdale of Hants, who was abrupt, discourteous, and fond of horseplay — a pleasantry of his was to "seize a companion by the shirt collar and pull collar and tie off" — but also clear thinking, hard-headed, and decisive. About the same time the government signed a contract with Mackenzie and Mann to build the Halifax and South Western from Halifax to Barrington Passage. Clearly the auspices were favourable and Murray announced a dissolution on September 3rd.

His manifesto was not so much a harbinger of things to come as a reminder, through specific illustrations, that Liberal times had been good times and were likely to remain so — the receipt of $671,000 for the Eastern Extension claims; a contract to build the Halifax and South Western and likelihood of a railway for the Eastern Shore; the maintenance of the province's credit at a high rating; the expenditure of the largest sums on record for the public services; the setting up of the Dominion Coal Company, whose annual output had increased from 700,000 to 3 million tons since 1894; and the establishment of the Dominion Iron and Steel Company, which was likely to use a million tons of coal yearly.

As the campaign progressed, the *Chronicle* became more and more ebullient: "The popular torrent in favour of the Local government sweeps irresistibly on." Gloatingly it eulogized the "spotless" and "admirably positive character" of the nineteen-year-old administration. Fielding came from Ottawa to join in the campaigning, but he was not needed. This time the *Chronicle* concentrated on damaging the image of the Conservatives. What it wanted was "a nice neutral name . . . mild, inoffensive, unhistoric, and . . . just sufficiently meaningless and yet suggestive to suit them to perfection." By mid-July it had concocted one to its satisfaction, and so throughout the election its opponents became the "Whity-Brown party" and the *Herald* "the Whity-Brown organ."[12]

Again the Conservatives faced impossible odds. If John F. Stairs was their leader, as he apparently was, he did little or no lending. To improve his chances of winning, he ran in

Colchester rather than Halifax. He issued no manifesto and C.H. Cahan, the Conservative house leader from 1891 to 1894, managed the party's campaign in Halifax and, to some extent, elsewhere as well. The *Herald* set the tone for the party, but having to contend with unprecedented prosperity and a highly creditable government performance, its criticism seemed once more of the sour-grapes variety. Of what use, it wondered, was the Eastern Extension refund when the government had already spent five times that amount in corruption and mismanagement? Did the increased coal output and enhanced provincial revenue not result from the National Policy, "for which no grit is entitled to any credit whatever"? Already it was raising the cry it would use in the next five elections: "It's time we had a change. Vote out the old, vote in the new."

Nomination day provided an inkling of what was to come. The Liberals won Antigonish and Yarmouth by acclamation, and since their only opposition in Shelburne came from an independent Liberal who was not a serious candidate, they started out, in effect, with six seats. The *Chronicle* thought that the Conservatives might be totally destroyed and it turned out almost that way, for on October 2nd Nova Scotia came its closest ever to a one-party assembly. Of the two Conservatives elected, Charles Tanner ran third in Pictou, only twenty-nine votes ahead of the lowest Liberal, and although Daniel J. McLeod was first in Cumberland he led the second Liberal by only thirteen votes. A switch in parties by twenty-two voters would have produced an assembly of thirty-eight Liberals. Admittedly the one-sided distribution in seats largely reflected the vagaries of the electoral system since the Conservatives actually polled 41.7 per cent of the vote.

Upon Robert Borden, who had succeeded Tupper as the national Conservative leader, the *Chronicle* heaped scorn for participating in an election that he had been warned to shun: "He would have found it much more profitable to devote himself to duck-shooting." The *Herald* had a threefold explanation of its party's rout: the unexpected calling of the election and an unprepared organization; the need to fight two governments at the same time; and something it called the "resources of civilization," an apparent reference to the large amounts of government largesse.[13] Perhaps the most surprising thing about the outcome was the little attention or credit given to Murray. Quiet and largely non-controversial, he had not yet begun to win recognition even in his own party for qualities which would help the Liberals retain office for many years.

CHAPTER 2

Murray: The Middle Years

During the Thirty-Second General Assembly (1901-1906) Nova Scotia's good times continued at unprecedented levels. Premier Murray, showing signs of "gloominess, depression, want of confidence in himself," went to the United States to recuperate in 1902, but Attorney General Longley wrote a speech from the throne which was exuberance itself. Coal royalties of $437,000, he boasted, had finally exceeded the federal subsidy of $432,000. Restored to health in 1903, Murray exulted to find that the province was sharing in the national economic boom, as coal royalties of $487,900 and a budgetary surplus of $32,800 attested. So the boom continued in 1904 with royalties of $619,000 and a surplus of $66,000. Buoyant revenues meant expanding services: the agricultural college at Truro, so long in the works, was nearing completion; the tuberculosis sanitorium at Kentville was well advanced; and railway construction was proceeding on three fronts. Dominion Iron and Steel and Nova Scotia Steel and Coal (formerly Nova Scotia Iron and Steel), which had been established earlier by provincial entrepreneurs at New Glasgow, had become so productive that the government had had to refund $52,184 of the royalties on coal used in the production of steel.

In the legislature Tanner's opponents warned him that his "humiliating position" arose from his propensity to criticize for criticism's sake. However, if Tanner heard he did not respond and he continued almost *ad nauseam* his negative, hackneyed attacks. By 1903, however, even he had little criticism of railway development. Thirty miles of the Halifax and South Western were under construction; work was under way on the line from Middleton to Victoria Beach; a contract had been signed to build a line from the ICR at Orangedale to Mabou; and another was likely to serve the Eastern Shore, the last major area without railways.

Elsewhere Tanner found little that was good. The province, he feared, was not securing adequate returns for the great privileges which it had conferred on the Whitney Syndicate. "What was the pittance of royalties that these gentlemen were called upon to pay in comparison with the enormous profits they were making?" Nor should the Liberals take credit for the development of the steel industry, which was primarily due to natural factors and the National Policy. Had not Nova Scotians launched the pioneer Canadian steel company, Nova Scotia Iron and Steel, even before Dominion Iron and Steel had come into existence? Murray replied that the National Policy had not made possible the annual export of 750,000 tons of coal to New England, and that steel-making began in Sydney only because the provincial government had facilitated the consolidation of mines by the Dominion Coal Company. Responding to Tanner's demands for an independent provincial auditor, he pointed out that, whereas in other provinces the departments disbursed public moneys directly, in Nova Scotia "every dollar . . . was paid out by the provincial cashier and by him only." What was the need for a "useless official drawing a large salary"?[1]

Tanner further damaged his credibility by flailing out in all directions. Was the Provincial Exhibition of any use, he wondered. "If the horse races and the fakirs and the advertisers were taken away there would be very little . . . left." He joined the *Herald* in resorting to a guilt-by-association doctrine. After delving into the notorious Gamey affair in Ontario, both concluded that all Grit governments existed by "corruption and crime." Though supported only by McLeod, he did not hesitate to divide the assembly following the expulsion from Province House of a woman who complained loudly in its corridors about an alleged grievance. When the government proposed a bill to protect the house's servants from liability in similar incidents, Tanner feared that an official might "take a respectable citizen by the throat and throw him out on the street" with impunity. But the bill, though enacted, proved unnecessary because the Supreme Court of Canada declared that access to legislative precincts was a privilege which could be denied to preserve order or decorum.[2]

Again, in 1904, Tanner could find little fault with the progress on railways: ninety-seven miles under construction on the Halifax and South Western and twenty-two between New Germany and Caledonia; the opening of the line from Point Tupper to St. Peter's; and continued work on the Victoria Beach line. Elsewhere, however, Tanner behaved much as usual with minor variations. The government should not take credit for a prosperity that was worldwide; it should not exult in the absence of direct taxes since it had imposed marriage licence fees and succession duties ("a tax which the living had to pay for the dead"); it ought not to boast of its financial prowess since, if capital expenditures were taken into account, the result would be a deficit of $932,911, not a surplus of $66,250. He took special aim at a bill which required bridges costing more that $500 to be built of permanent materials by the provincial government. Since the interest would be deducted from the municipal road moneys, was it not dangerous to reduce grants which had already fallen from $124,106 in 1883 to $73,552 in 1903? To him it was simply another step towards the province's taking over complete control of the road service.

A mélange of less usual concerns occupied the assembly between 1902 and 1904. In all three years it sought to repeal the disfranchisement of federal officials in provincial elections only to be thwarted by the legislative council. Both the *Herald* and the *Chronicle* denounced the continuing deluge of private and local bills. To the *Chronicle* they were "bills incorporating Tom, Dick or Harry as soft soap-boilers, maple-molasses compounders and sticky-fly-paper compilers . . . bills to incorporate ambitious 'church-yards.'"[3]

Already interlaced with partisan overtones was the temperance question, which would be highly contentious for three decades. From the beginning the *Chronicle* was suspicious of temperance advocates who sought to restrict people's liberties. In 1902 it lambasted a clergyman who warned the government to move towards prohibition or face the prospect of losing his denomination's support. Surely "we are past the days when the Church . . . could assume to dictate to the State in such matters."[4] In 1904 it laughed at the "grotesque ludicrousness" of twenty-nine persons setting up the Nova Scotia Temperance Alliance and appointing a committee to watch the thirty-eight assemblymen — a "first tottering step" towards "absurd dictation."

A federal election being likely, 1904 was a year of intense political activity. The Conservatives met in convention in March, officially recognized Tanner as their leader in the assembly, and strengthened their county organizations. Meanwhile Fielding and Murray worked as a team to ensure their party's health both federally and provincially. Frederick Borden, the other federal minister, seems to have deferred largely to Fielding in the determination of strategy and the disposition of major offices. Sometimes Fielding's wide knowledge of Nova Scotia's politicians led him to make proposals which looked like unabashed meddling in the provincial field. "I am merely giving my own opinion," he would say, and he would get away with it. To fill two vacancies on the Supreme Court in 1904 he suggested changes which would have altered radically the face of Nova Scotia politics. Benjamin Russell, who had impeccable legal attainments to supplement his useful political contribution, would get one of the judgeships. The other beneficiary, he hoped, would be Attorney General Longley despite earlier objections from Liberal lawyers. Arthur Drysdale would go to the attorney generalship; T.R. Black, a veteran MLA from Cumberland, to the Senate; and W.T. Pipes, the government leader in the legislative council and former premier, for whom Fielding always had a soft spot, would contest Black's assembly seat and assume Drysdale's former portfolio. Finally, Jason M. Mack, an ex-MLA for Queens who assisted Fielding in his constituency work — a grumbler, but "no one of us is perfect" — would become leader in the upper house.[5] When Murray agreed, Russell and Black got their appointments, but the basic part of the elaborate scheme faltered because of the unrelenting opposition to making Longley a judge.

The major issue in Nova Scotia in the November federal election was railways. As part of Laurier's "grandiose conception of Canada unlimited," the Liberals proposed a second transcontinental line starting in Moncton — the Grand Trunk Pacific, essentially an adjunct of the Grand Trunk. To the Conservatives this meant tying the trade of the West to the Grand Trunk system and benefiting its eastern terminus, Portland, Maine, rather than Halifax. However, the Conservative proposal — use of the ICR as part of a new, publicly owned and operated transcontinental line — was equally flawed since not a single mile of railway would be built east of Montreal.

Actually prosperity and its declared architect Fielding — not railways — determined the outcome in Nova Scotia. On November 3rd it returned eighteen Liberals and no Conservatives. Only in two seats, Hants and Cape Breton North and Victoria, were the results at all close. As usual, a bitter *Herald* attributed it to "criminal tactics and methods imported from Ontario," charging that Halifax had been "deluged . . . with cold cash" in order to defeat Borden, "one of the best men who ever sat" in Parliament. In provincial by-elections in December, most of them to fill the seats of assemblymen who had run federally, the Liberals won all seven. Clearly they had reached a peak federally and provincially. However, even after his greatest victory, Fielding was told that seven-eighths of the bar was opposed to his recommending Longley for a judgeship. He felt in fairness that "if the hostility to him is as serious [as his correspondent stated] Mr. Longley should be undeceived,"[6] but once again he had no choice but to drop his plans.

When Murray had little new to propose in 1905, the *Chronicle* declared that a "temporary slackening off can be contemplated with equanimity." This year Tanner committed something the Liberals considered close to *lèse-majesté* when he declared that "there was not one matter of constructive statesmanship to be credited to the Hon. Mr. Fielding." Although Murray advised him to give the assembly "the benefit of some advice instead of always playing the part of the mere politician,"[7] he remained the Tanner of old. He found it "a pretty cheeky thing . . . for even a Grit premier" to claim a surplus of $33,299 when, if capital expenditures were included, a deficit of $1,157,830 had occurred. He also had harsh words for the government's railway policy, even though the Halifax and South Western was operating as far west as Liverpool and the Victoria Beach line was almost completed. Why, he wondered, did the government show such "warm sympathy" for the Mackenzie and Mann interests by lending them money at 3.5 per cent to buy the Barrington to Yarmouth and Victoria Beach lines when it did so little for the Eastern Shore?

Of even more concern than railways to Tanner in 1905 was the "Big Lease, "which granted over half a million acres of Crown lands in Victoria and Inverness counties to Americans for ninety-nine years, allegedly without proper safeguards. Longley told him, unconvincingly, that one condition was the erection of a pulp mill. Much in evidence, too, was Tanner the moralist. He wanted Nova Scotia to adopt the Dominion practice which permitted a member to be unseated for a corrupt practice of one of his agents committed without his knowledge, only to be told by Longley that "you could not make a people moral by any paternal or tinkering acts of legislation whatever." He also called for an independence of the legislature act, again to have Longley insist that the dignity of the legislature could not be secured by "paltry and tinkering legislation."[8] Finally, he pressed for prohibition, impelled in part by the growing temperance movement. Sixteen of eighteen counties had chosen to be under the federal Canada Temperance (Scott) Act, which banned the sale but not the consumption of alcohol. The outcome had been a steadily increasing shipment of liquor from wet to dry counties. Politically astute George Murray sought the favour of the temperance forces by supporting a backbencher's bill which banned this export and import only to raise suspicions that he had instigated its later rejection by the legislative council because of its alleged unenforceability.

The session over, Fielding ignored the objections of Liberal lawyers and had Longley appointed to the bench. This permitted the carrying out of all his earlier suggestions although Pipes waited for the next election before moving to the assembly. Fielding also made clear his philosophy relating to patronage, especially his feeling that elected members should serve the party for some time before receiving major appointments. Accordingly, he warned MPs F.A. Laurence, D.D. McKenzie, and Duncan Finlayson "not to expect to be retired soon."[9]

Though at a low ebb, the Conservatives outlined their position periodically throughout 1905 in letters signed "Nova

Scotia" appearing in the Pictou *Colonial Standard* and the *Halifax Herald* and *Evening Mail*. The picture was that of a Liberal party machine directing a veritable army of office-holders whose principal function was to serve political interests. In December the party drew up a set of resolutions, apparently designed as an election manifesto, and including the promise of a plebiscite or prohibition. It had not had to fight an election in 1905 after Murray had decided to let the General Assembly go into its fifth year. Even the speech from the throne in 1906 did not seem oriented towards an election. As usual, Tanner reacted with one of his "blue ruin" speeches, prophesying that "the country was going generally to the dogs."

He had good reason to be outraged against an act of the previous session. To a minor bill relating to the swearing in of presiding officers and poll clerks, the legislative council, while in committee, had added an amendment that repealed the provision barring most Dominion officials from voting in provincial elections. In Tanner's absence the bill passed both houses without publicity. Both Tanner and the *Herald* protested an "utterly vicious method of surreptitious legislation," the more so because it violated the assembly's privileges by having a franchise bill introduced in the non-elective chamber. Reluctantly, Murray admitted to being a conspirator in the proceedings, as he had agreed to have Pipes introduce the amendment in the upper house.[10] If, as stated, Pipes and the attorney general had explained the amendment in both houses, they must have chosen circumstances in which it would attract little attention. In any case one of the last relics of the Confederation period had disappeared. The debate on temperance was at a reduced level in 1906 although the legislature did act to prohibit licence holders in wet counties from shipping liquor to dry counties if they had reason to believe it was destined for sale. The *Chronicle* rejoiced when Liberal O.T. Daniels won a by-election in Annapolis over a prohibitionist supported by the Conservatives. The result at least stilled the temperance advocates for a while.

On the financial returns Murray became as effusive as he ever did. Since 1898, he pointed out, surpluses totalled $282,432, and although the provincial debt had reached $8 million, most had been incurred for productive public works. Revenues of $1.4

million resulting from the Whitney Syndicate had permitted vastly improved services without resort to direct taxation. As a result, "instead of deserted villages we have prosperous cities and towns. . . . Instead of a decreased output, we have an output increasing by leaps and bounds." Besides, the government had provided well for the comfort and education of miners through relief associations and mining schools. Also, a railway system which in 1896 had only five lines with 169 miles of track would, with the completion of the Halifax and South Western, have seven lines and 617 miles. Tanner's response was typical: "There might be some good things in the government, but . . . it would require a strong magnifying glass to discover them."[11]

In this pre-election session Murray did not seek to abolish the legislative council, an indication that the public had lost interest in the question. However, he did have positive proposals to present. To encourage the building of an Eastern Shore railway and a branch line from Country Harbour to a point on the ICR, he proposed a loan of $10,000 per mile with interest no greater than 3.5 per cent. He also sponsored three bills to improve education. One, based on a Manitoba act, set up a board of educational experts to advise the superintendent of education. A second restored teachers' grants to their 1887 level, but — indicative of his caution — only if the province received an increase in federal subsidies. A third, to introduce a teachers' pension scheme of sorts, did not follow the teachers' request for one based partly on their own contributions. To Murray that was "a little too arduous" to implement and so his bill simply provided that veteran teachers would continue to receive the annual government grants on their retirement, little more than a pittance. Tanner contended that the teachers did not want charity but rather a genuine contributory scheme over which they had some control. The *Herald* declared that if the premier wanted something which served his election purposes, cost little, and was of small value to the teachers he had found it.

When Murray chose June 20th for the election, Fielding hoped that it augured well: "It was on that day in 1882 that our Liberal party won its great and lasting victory in Nova Scotia."[12] Because of pressures at Ottawa, Laurier did not want him to go to Nova Scotia, but he would try to come if he were needed. He was not needed. At long last Nova Scotia Liberals had begun to appreciate the asset which they had in Murray. A year earlier the *Chronicle* had pointed out that this "unostentatious man" had not "once 'tooted his own horn'" even after presenting seven surpluses in a row and building more miles of railway in a year than Joseph Howe had done *in toto*. He is no coiner of showy phrases, no oratorical pyrotechnist, but he is a master of debate as well as of affairs. He has as thorough a knowledge of the men as of the conditions of his native Province, and he is as profoundly politic as he is broadly and sincerely patriotic."[13] Not surprisingly, the principal Liberal slogan in 1906 was: "For Murray, Victory, and a Greater Nova Scotia."

The premier's manifesto, elaborate for him, catalogued his government's accomplishments and asked: "What more could have been done?" While the *Chronicle* boasted that Murray had "wrought miracles," the *Herald* showed little enthusiasm for Tanner. Typically his manifesto chronicled the government's iniquities, especially the mounting of the province's debt and the failure to secure a proper audit or to enact measures to deal adequately with corrupt election practices and the independence of the legislature. Had it not restored the vote to Dominion officials much as a thief returned stolen goods? Day after day the *Herald* carried below its masthead Murray's criticism of the eighteen-year-old federal Conservative government in 1896: "Long holding of office has brought about its inevitable consequences — corruption and jobbery in every branch of the public service."[14] As the campaign progressed, leadership came more and more to the fore. Scornfully the *Chronicle* compared Tanner, "whom his own party will not acknowledge as their leader," with Murray, who was generally held in great respect by both parties. Some might consider his caution as a fault, but more would regard it as a virtue. "It might be more brilliant to plunge blindly and recklessly ahead. But the wise man looks before he leaps, and makes sure of the ground upon which he is to alight. . . . Mr. Murray is safe, in every sense of the word."[15]

Few expected the Conservatives to mount much of a challenge. They gave up the four seats in Antigonish and Pictou without a contest, and in Kings they supported the Unity Reform candidates, one of whom was elected. But elsewhere they ran well and overall they polled 42.1 per cent of the vote.

Tanner headed the poll in Pictou and his party elected five members instead of two, defeating ministers without portfolio George Patterson in Pictou and H.H. Wickwire in Kings. The *Chronicle* could flaunt its rooster again, but the *Herald* also exulted that the voters were beginning to move . . . in the right direction''; next time they might install a new, clean government.

The first session of the Thirty-Third General Assembly had barely opened in 1907 when the Conservatives lost an unofficial leader, J.J. Stewart, who died of burns following the overturning of an oil stove. Editor of the *Herald* since 1877, he had done much to guide the party for three decades. Whether because of his loss or the buoyancy of the financial returns — a surplus of $16,000 and royalties of $643,000, the largest on record — the Conservatives paid less attention than usual to finance. Two measures of consequence reflected the province's strong financial position. Pipes having become attorney general, it was the new Commissioner of Public Works and Mines C.P. Chisholm who sponsored a bill giving the provincial government full responsibility for the roads and bridges outside the towns and cities. After the rural municipalities assumed the primary control over the service in 1879, they had generally performed badly and had suffered a slow but steady erosion of their powers. Though change was long overdue, it appeared to require an act of political courage. Astutely, Murray made it in the first session after an election. Surprisingly, the response was minimal even though the rural municipalities had to collect a provincial highway tax through a levy of between 30 and 50 cents per $100 on real and personal property and a poll tax ranging between $1 and $2.

Technical education was to be the second avenue of new expenditure. The Nova Scotia Technical College would offer training in metallurgical, civil, mining, mechanical, chemical, and electrical engineering and conduct scientific research. Subsidiary schools were to be established in industrial centres and the long-established mining schools were to be enlarged. Though the legislation was clearly progressive, Murray was doing no more than responding to needs evident in the Nova Scotia of the day. A director of technical education would be principal of the college and supervise the entire technical education system. F.H. Sexton assumed the duties after the session and served in that capacity for many years. Because Murray believed that the province badly needed more people, he also secured authority to appoint a secretary of industries and immigration.

This year the opposition centred its criticism on minor bills, especially one which raised the salaries of ministers with portfolio to $5,000 and of Murray to $6,000. When Tanner complained that businessmen did equally important work for smaller salaries, Murray replied that after being premier for ten years at great personal loss, all he expected was half the salary of the premier of Ontario. The session saw Dr. A.S. Kendall of Cape Breton County emerge as the social conscience of the Liberal party, a role he would continue throughout this General Assembly. As was indicated earlier, the government had accepted the provisions of an earlier English compensation act, but not those of the more liberal Workmen's Compensation for Injuries Act of 1897. British Columbia had now adopted the latter and Quebec was considering them. Surely, said Kendall, if they worked in old, conservative Britain, they would do so in Nova Scotia. In 1907, however, he sought no more than to make them better known.

The government having indicated that it would not ban the liquor traffic, Tanner moved non-confidence. Murray's answer was that the Canada Temperance Act was operative in all counties but Halifax and Richmond; that only one licence existed in the latter county and few in the former outside of the city; and that it would be meaningless to adopt a prohibition law for the city where public opinion would render it unenforceable. Hence the most fruitful course would be to strengthen the previous year's act which restricted the export of liquor from wet to dry counties. However, the opposition rightly dismissed as of dubious merit an amendment which put the onus on the shipper of alcohol to show that it was being sent to a legal receiver.

Optimism continued in 1908 despite a deficit of $100,000, partly the result of an unfavourable money market which necessitated higher interest payments and partly the result of a severe winter which had prevented the banking of coal at the pithead and hence its shipment up the St. Lawrence. Counter-balancing it positively, the Nova Scotia Technical College would be operating by year's end, the Department of Industries and Immigration was publicizing the province abroad, a contract for an eastern shore railway appeared likely, and an increased federal subsidy would be forthcoming following an amendment to the British North America (BNA) Act. Only now did the cautious Murray restore in full the teachers' grants which had been reduced in 1887.

Though controversial or exciting legislation was lacking, the first of two significant bills provided for the complete registration of the province's vital statistics. If ever there was a belated measure, this was it. Since 1877 the statistics relating to births and deaths had not been compiled, partly because of a jurisdictional disagreement with Ottawa, partly because of Parliament's failure to appropriate money. A second bill related to old age pensions. Although an earlier commission had reported against any general scheme, it had recommended a plan for aged or disabled miners. Accordingly Murray took action to appoint an Old Age Pension Board to formulate a plan providing old age and disability pensions to members of the Colliery Workers' Provident Society branches, the funds to come from the miners, the coal companies, and the government. Fearful that the proposal would be regarded as socialistic, the *Chronicle* explained that, although the bill might be a pioneering one in America, it was "founded not on the theories of visionaries, but on the sober . . . recommendations of a most responsible and competent Commission."[16] The government also appointed a royal commission to inquire into the effect of an eight-hour day on provincial industries. Apparently the leaven of Dr. Kendall was beginning to work.

However, Kendall won little favour when, in support of a railway from St. Peter's to Arichat, he pointed out that the province had paid out $6,065,000 in subsidies and interest for railway construction on the mainland compared with only $474,000 in Cape Breton, a ratio of 12.25 to 1. An indignant Murray wondered how anyone could believe that he had a prejudice against Cape Breton. Another Liberal backbencher, E.H. Armstrong, suggested the federal acquisition of other railways, especially those of western Nova Scotia, as feeders for the ICR. Murray had no objections, but was skeptical. In contrast with other provinces, he said, no one was seeking railway franchises in Nova Scotia, where they had never been money-makers. Personally he had "given more . . . attention to [railways] than to any other problem" and had become convinced that the remaining provincial railways would not be built unless the government assumed practically the whole responsibility. "When he heard the word 'promoter' he shuddered."[17]

This year the premier had a new temperance opponent, Rev. H.R. Grant, secretary of the Nova Scotia Temperance Alliance, who would contend with him for the rest of his premiership. When Grant argued that the Halifax City Council and the liquor dealers were "shamelessly violating" the Halifax Licence Act, Murray replied that provincial prohibition could never be effective until Parliament amended the Canada Temperance Act to ban the importation or manufacture of alcohol. The assembly accepted Tanner's resolution along these lines, but not his attempt to have offences against the Scott Act prosecuted in counties to which liquor was shipped rather than the county of shipment. The debate was bitter, but less so than on the proposal to increase members' indemnities from $500 to $700 at a total cost of $11,000. Tanner argued that the length of the session was not a justification since it could have been completed in six weeks rather than nine if the government had prepared its business properly. The *Herald* blamed it on Murray's "hungry followers" who, it said, were determined to get more whatever the consequences.

The autumn of 1908 saw Nova Scotia immersed in a nauseous federal election in which the muckrakers had a field day. Borden had a positive programme to offer: a "new national policy," which included the continuance of Macdonald's policy of protection, a national system of telephones and telegraphs, and the restoration of public lands to Alberta and Saskatchewan. However, most of its sixteen articles denounced the government for its scandalous conduct, especially its gross resort to patronage in the purchase of supplies, the sale of lands, and the award of public franchises. For the Liberals the basic slogan was: "Let Laurier finish his work." His only project of substance, however, was the Hudson's Bay Railway and, in the hindsight of time, his government had clearly passed its zenith.

None surpassed the *Halifax Herald* in muckraking. Why should Nova Scotians give the government of a hundred scandals another five years to plunder? Was Laurier's talk of an unlimited Canada anything more than "the braggadocia of a vainglorious old man"? Was the "great spendthrift" Fielding actually a "nation smasher" rather than a "nation builder"? The *Chronicle* stood for the continuation of twelve years of "magnificent progress and prosperity" which would make Halifax the "Long Wharf" of the Dominion and a leading entrepôt of the continent. Could any man be "half so virtuous as Mr. Borden talks"? Had he not forgotten the recent by-election in Colchester during which an agent of Conservative John Stanfield had distributed whisky under the label of "choice tomatoes"?

As usual, Fielding worried about his riding of Queens and Shelburne, which needed "someone to keep the ball rolling." Accordingly he asked Murray to find a Haligonian to organize and canvass for him, promising to meet any expenses of "a legitimate character." Actually he easily won re-election, but the Liberal slippage in Nova Scotia had begun since the "Solid Eighteen" of 1904 was reduced to a dozen. Borden headed the poll in Halifax and although his party won only six seats, it secured 49.0 per cent of the vote. The *Herald* called the results "a prelude to victory next time"; a disappointed *Chronicle* declared it "not an unusual thing" for the miners of Cumberland and Cape Breton to "stab their friends in the back."

The federal election produced a significant change in the provincial legislature in 1909. Charles Tanner had run and lost and then lost again in trying to regain his provincial seat. The *Chronicle* did not regret the absence of a carping critic whose record was "as barren as that of any man who ever sat in the House." Once again the Conservatives resorted to the game of musical chairs which they had been playing since 1890 and turned to Charles Wilcox as their house leader. He had three demands. He wanted abolition of the legislative council — "the fire of life burns low as men drift into extreme age" — but Murray was content to let sleeping dogs be. Wilcox also asked for a redistribution of assembly seats, something not done since

1867. Murray agreed in principle but, cautious as ever, insisted that, when effected, no county should lose seats. Most of all, Wilcox demanded a change in the "evil and vicious system" of supplying goods to government institutions. However, though C.P. Chisholm, the commissioner of public works and mines, conceded grudgingly the existence of a patronage list, he refused to change his *modus operandi* — whenever goods were of the same price and quality, "he would go to his political supporter," and he would sacrifice his seat rather than change his position.[18]

At long last, however, Wilcox had his party's demands for an independent auditor accepted. As some expenditures were no longer being made through the Provincial Cashier, Murray agreed in the interest of public confidence to have a provincial auditor who would be an officer of the legislature removable only by a joint address and generally accorded the status of those in other provinces.[19] However, a provision to set up a provincial treasury board similar to that at Ottawa long remained a dead letter on the statute book.

Overshadowing other bills in 1909 was one to establish a public utilities board. Previous legislation had allowed a grievance against a telephone company to be taken to the governor in council. As Murray found it a "poor body" to settle this kind of dispute, he decided to adopt a practice of the western American states and appoint a board to accept or alter telephone, light, water, and power rates "as the justice of the case may require." The *Chronicle* exulted that Nova Scotia had "taken its place in the forefront of modern progress" by becoming the first province to regulate public utilities in this way. Admittedly innovative, the change fitted in nicely with Murray's philosophy of avoiding personal responsibility by shifting it to non-elective officials.

Once again the government boasted of the growth of the steel industry when it returned $65,294 in coal royalties to the companies in the form of rebates. But, as the *Chronicle* indicated, "Coal is still King in Nova Scotia" and royalties of $681,000 had helped to produce a surplus of $86,590. One dark cloud loomed on the horizon, the steady invasion of the Quebec market by American coal, which could be mined more cheaply than Nova Scotian. This year, socially conscious Dr. Kendall wanted an investigation into public health as it related to tuberculosis, ventilation, and milk supplies. Murray agreed to consider it but, despite the buoyant revenues, warned that the public must be told in advance of additional taxation if action was to be taken. Demands came again for a provincial prohibitory law from the government's most active lobby, the Nova Scotia Temperance Alliance, supported strongly by Wilcox and the Unity Reform member, C.A. Campbell. Murray indicated that, although his ultimate goal was prohibition, his short-term aim was to make the existing legislation effective, and he expressed pleasure that the federal government had accepted the principle of controlling the importation of liquor into Scott Act counties.

By session's end Murray had served as Nova Scotian premier longer than anyone before him. However, even as his personal prestige continued to increase, his party's position was beginning to weaken. Attorney General Pipes, who died in October 1909, had sometimes offended others by his abruptness, but his intellectual and oratorical talents were of a high order and he probably deserved much of the credit for the independent audit and public utilities legislation. In the choice of a successor it became evident that the Liberals were suffering from the same malady that formerly affected the Conservatives. Because of the plentiful federal and provincial patronage at their disposal, they were finding it increasingly difficult to find MLAs to fill the ministries with portfolio. To succeed Pipes, they had to go to the House of Commons and recruit forty-year-old A.K. Maclean, whom some considered a possible successor to Murray because of his legal attainments, intellectual qualities, and attractive personality.

To bolster the party, Fielding and Murray adopted the unprecedented course of a joint political tour in September, holding meetings from Yarmouth to Cumberland County. At Yarmouth Fielding declared — and he would often repeat it — that his greatest service to Nova Scotia had been to recommend Murray as premier. At a convention in June the Conservatives refused, despite the pleas of the Temperance Alliance, to commit themselves to prohibition and instead let each candidate make his own decision. Wilcox nominated Tanner as provincial leader but, perhaps remembering his previous failure to be recognized, Tanner asked for time to consider.

In the session of 1910 the Conservatives were in a weakened state. Wilcox had died and Tanner was still without a seat. However, Albert Parsons had taken Wilcox's seat in Hants and W.L. Hall had wrested Queens from the Liberals, each attributing his victory to a prohibitionist stance. Both would be prominent in Conservative circles for over two decades. Likely because of Attorney General Maclean, the government was strikingly more positive in 1910. His first major bill demonstrated a complete awareness of the growing strength of the temperance movement. By providing that the single tavern licence in Richmond County and the five or six in Halifax County outside of the city would not be renewed on their expiry, he, in effect, was ensuring province-wide prohibition except for Halifax city. There licences would be reduced from ninety to seventy as they expired, and to not more than one for each one thousand of population after the next census. Further, on the petition of one quarter of the city's ratepayers, a favourable plebiscite would lead to the abolition of the licences. Hall and J.M. Baillie of Pictou, who was leading the Conservatives, were pleased that the government had at last bowed to public opinion, but they regretted that it had not gone the whole way. A not unhappy *Herald* scoffed at "the agility of the Liberals in boldly appropriating the policy of the opposition."

Maclean's second bill, a surprising one for the Murray government, proposed the full male suffrage of the four western provinces. To him any benefits resulting from the restrictions on voting hardly compensated for the difficulties and uncertainties of applying the existing provisions. In the end, however, the act remained as it was because of the need to consult the municipal governments, which prepared the voters' lists both for themselves and the province. Hence it took another decade, additional pressure from the Conservatives' and the example of the Dominion Parliament before universal suffrage became a reality in 1920. In another bill the philosophy of Murray was clearly evident. Undoing the work of Fielding, it removed the responsibility for the management of the Victoria General Hospital from the executive council to an appointed board.

To opposition jeers the government sought again in 1910 to get the province's last major railway undertaking begun. The government accepted the Halifax and Eastern Railway Company's proposal to build a line from Dartmouth to Guysborough with branches to Country Harbour and to the ICR near New Glasgow, and agreed to provide a mileage subsidy of $6,400 up to a total of $2,560,000. Both government and opposition hailed the announcement in June that the Canadian Pacific Railway had acquired the 270-mile Dominion Atlantic Railway which, after coming into being in 1895, had consolidated all the lines from Windsor Junction to Yarmouth. Fearful that the province would lose additional seats in the Commons after the next census, Liberal backbencher E.H. Armstrong called for an amendment to the BNA Act which guaranteed each province no fewer members than it had in 1867. Although none disagreed, most members probably felt the same as Hall, who did not expect to get "so much as that," but hoped to "hold what we have."

In 1910 the assembly concerned itself particularly with the coal and associated industries, and with accompanying regulatory bills. The previous year's surplus had been only $15,422 because of strikes in Cape Breton and Springhill that had cut coal production and hence royalties. The strikes had resulted from a collision between the Provincial Workingmen's Association (PWA), long operative in the province, and the newly arrived United Mine Workers of America (UMW), which sought to supplant it. The Conservatives demanded that the government use its authority, "if it has any authority," to effect a reconciliation, but Murray insisted that no government was "big enough or strong enough to . . . tell [the miners] that they must go to work. . . . The company said no [to recognition of the UMW], and the men said unless you recognize us we will not work."[20] Although the *Herald* declared that the government had demonstrated its unfitness to act as trustees of the public domain, the *Chronicle* charged that its "salacious" rival had joined a conspiracy to destroy the province's principal industry.

The issue let Dr. Kendall outline his philosophy on corporate responsibility and take special aim at the Dominion Coal Company for its behaviour *vis-à-vis* the Nova Scotia Steel and Coal Company (Scotia). The latter had almost exhausted its coal holdings at Sydney Mines, and wanted to use the contiguous holdings of Dominion Coal but had been frustrated even though its rival had no immediate use for the coal. More generally, Kendall argued that both companies, without loss, could raise the wages of their workers and reduce the cost of coal to consumers. He also continued to call for the compulsory recognition of trade unions: "Let it be propounded by an Act of the Legislature that henceforth citizens of Nova Scotia shall be free men and not serfs, . . . that our industries to be developed here are for all the people and not for the few people who happen to have a lot of money."[21]

In this matter Dr. Kendall had the support of Conservative house leader Baillie but not of Premier Murray, who refused to have it referred to a royal commission. Instead, the premier praised the Dominion Coal Company for having doubled wages since its establishment, contended that any reduction in the price of coal would force some mines to close, and pointed out that neither the PWA nor the UMW had requested compulsory recognition. Clearly Murray had no wish to disturb the status quo in an industry upon which the province depended for its financial health. The sympathies of the *Chronicle* were with the PWA, whose career had been "long and creditable." The *Herald*, which pictured a government "wedded to the inglorious policy of drift," demanded action to keep the mines operating continuously.

Though Murray stated that a royal commission report on the hours of labour might be "one of the most valuable . . . ever submitted on this subject to any Legislature in any part of the world," his bill, partly based on its recommendations, was hardly earth-shattering. Accepting its conclusions that a compulsory eight-hour day would be fatal to industries, he proposed among other things that workers not be employed more than sixty hours a week and never more than six hours without an interval for meals. To ensure full discussion he took the highly unusual course of introducing the bill as a private member and then letting it die when it provoked opposition. Again resorting to superlatives, he also sponsored a workmen's compensation bill which he called the most important ever introduced in the province relating to the liability of workers. Though it belatedly adopted the basic principle of the British statute of 1897, Liberal E.H. Armstrong complained that, if excluded workers were taken into account, "you have practically nothing left."[22]

The most contentious bill of all was one relating to Scotia, which sought to intervene in a struggle for control of the company. Opponents of the bill, such as C.P. Chisholm, argued that it equipped Scotia's directors with "a legislative bludgeon to perpetuate their continuance in office." Left-leaning Liberals like Dr. Kendall and R.E. Finn hoped that it would prevent a takeover by the Forget interests of Montreal, which might transfer the company's steel-making operations elsewhere. As Finn put it, "We have lost all our banking institutions to the Upper Provinces with the exception of the Union Bank of Halifax . . . and certain financial interests are now after this industry." His opponents replied that the Forget interests were unlikely to "sandbag" an industry in which they had invested $5 million and that their property should be protected even if they were thieves.[23] This point of view prevailed and the bill ended up with a single operative clause that the company's head office was to remain in New Glasgow and that its shareholders' meetings were to be held in Nova Scotia. Clearly the growing industrialization was adding to the premier's difficulties with some of his backbenchers who did not regard vested rights as being as sacrosanct as he did.

For a time it was doubtful whether Murray would attend the 1911 session. Only with difficulty was he persuaded to remain in politics after a circulatory problem caused him to lose a leg above the knee. It grieved his friends to see a six-foot man of previously splendid physique hobbling about with the aid of a cane and an artificial limb. However, the premier refused to let his infirmity prevent his regular visits to his Victoria County constituents, even though he never learned to drive a car himself. At a banquet in February to celebrate his recovery he became more philosophical than usual. "True liberalism," he said, should always rest upon the one foundation, "that of caring for the interests of the democracy, of safeguarding the rights of the masses as against the classes and of preventing the encroachment of selfish greed and special privilege. . . . I have tried to live up to this principle." It delighted him especially that the "trapper boy" in the mines, through the night schools which his government had established, could gradually acquire the background needed for an engineering course. However, though Murray always espoused the interests of the masses in the abstract, "in practice he pursued a middle-of-the-road course which was more acceptable in the final analysis to capital than to labour," not, however, to the extent of alienating labour's support until 1920. "By venturing no further into the field of social and labour legislation than was unavoidable and by tacitly accepting the principle of protective tariffs," he often had the support of corporate interests, which generally favoured the federal Conservatives.[24]

For most of 1911 Nova Scotian politicians and newspapers concentrated on reciprocity, sometimes almost to the exclusion of everything else. In January Fielding concluded an agreement with the United States which in its essence removed or substantially reduced the duties on natural products and a few others. At first the federal Conservatives feared serious political harm to themselves, but in February they concluded that they could safely force an election on the question. Although the loyalty cries of the *Herald* did not reach the crescendo of two decades earlier, the newspaper did say that "the spirit that saved Canada in 1891 [was] urgently needed again today." Enthusiastic about reciprocity, the *Chronicle* lamented the "recrudescence of the old cry of disloyalty. . . . For the honor of the national backbone, let us hear no more of the cry of absorption or annexation." Left to himself, Murray might have avoided the question, but pressed by the federal Liberals he used his well-known "gymnastic ability" and had a backbencher introduce a resolution supporting the agreement. Thus his government avoided taking a stand.

In its legislative programme the government offered little of substance, and the session was over in five weeks. Of considerable interest, however, were the populist stances adopted by the Liberal Kendall and Conservatives Baillie and Hall. Baillie was outraged that the mines at Springhill still remained strikebound because the company refused to accept the miners' choice of the UMW as their union. When would the government finally tell the operators that they were not to keep the mines closed for insufficient reasons? He was no less perturbed by the high rates and low wages of the Nova Scotia Telephone Company. "If [the situation] is continued much longer we will be at the mercy of corporations and forced to cry out Lord help us, for we have failed to help ourselves."[25] For him the public ownership of utilities was the only answer.

Kendall vented his anger against industrialists in Montreal, Hamilton, and Toronto who seemed determined to prevent further development of steel-making in Nova Scotia in order to protect their own enterprises. It was their pressure, he said, that a few years ago had led the Bank of Commerce to withdraw its offer to lend money for a rolling mill in Sydney. "I say that the province of Nova Scotia with all its aspirations to become a great manufacturing centre is being reduced to the position of a hewer of wood and a drawer of water" for central Canada. The duty of government, and especially of liberalism, was to "regulate the forces of society so that the greatest good may be enjoyed by the greatest numbers." Though the head of Dominion Coal recognized the PWA, it was only because of a contract that had existed when he took over the mines. Unless he changed his tune, the miners would be forced to make him "dance to 20th century music." Was it not equally ridiculous that the directors of Dominion Iron and Steel refused to recognize Nova Scotia trade unions, while the same men as directors of the CPR recognized the strongest trade unions on the continent? "Bourbon-like, the lessons of history are lost on despots who in the second decade of the 20th century aim to set back the hands of the clock."[26]

As remedies, Kendall wanted abolition of a legislative council that was unsympathetic to the demands of labour, and a redistribution of the assembly that would take members away from thinly populated counties adverse to labour and increase the number of members from industrial counties more attuned to the substance of liberalism. In typical fashion, Murray refused to reject the upper house as such and objected only to its life appointments. Following the safest of political courses, he opposed taking away seats from any county but instead favoured additional seats for counties increasing in population. By this time even the newspapers were advocating representation for labour in the assembly. A year earlier, when trade unionist John Joy had been nominated to run, the *Herald* called on a party to adopt him. Belatedly the *Chronicle* and the *Acadian Recorder* said the same thing, and the *Herald* wondered why the Conservatives had not heeded the advice.

On another matter the usually conservative W.L. Hall also adopted a radical position. Following a resolution of the Conservative convention, he proposed to let non-owners fish along rivers and streams flowing through lands vested in others. Informed that a millionaires' lobby in Halifax was protesting his bill, he denied any attempt to "confiscate . . . rights to which these people are equitably entitled . . . to hear them talk, you would have inferred that . . . they would lose their bread and butter and become a charge upon the city."[27] However, the premier objected to taking away rights without compensation and helped to defeat the proposal.

Anxious to have an election during a lull in the struggle over reciprocity, Murray arranged for one on June 14th. This time the Liberals campaigned largely on the premier and his accomplishments, their slogan being: "Let Murray continue his good work." Typical of its campaigning, the *Chronicle* ran a front-page picture of him on May 16th with the caption: "all Nova Scotians . . . are proud of him." Fielding, realizing his presence was unnecessary, went on holiday in northern Europe but, as usual, made a generous contribution towards the "legitimate" expenditures of the Liberal candidates in Queens and Shelburne. Murray issued no manifesto and his party simply paraded a list of his governments's accomplishments since 1897.

The Conservatives having no recognized leader, the *Chronicle* asked "Where are the leaders?" It upheld the claims of Baillie because he constituted a lesser challenge to the Liberals, and it lambasted Tanner for his usual trick of "trying to fool the people with reckless statements." In turn, the *Herald* pointed out that the Liberals had been even more leaderless in 1882 and yet had been triumphant. In the absence of a Conservative manifesto, it published the resolutions of the party convention of 1909, an all-encompassing indictment of the Liberal record. Although the Liberals did not rapturously support reciprocity, the Conservatives alleged that they did and argued that its adoption would result in the fishermen losing their federal bounties and the miners their duty on coal.

Most of all, the *Herald* argued that continued one-party rule for nearly thirty years had produced a government lacking in imagination and innovativeness. However, this view did not prevent the newspaper from using something even older as a basic plank by calling the National Policy "the foundation of all progress" in Nova Scotia for more than three decades. An extraordinary event occurred in Halifax when both major newspapers supported longshoreman John Joy, running as the People's Independent candidate. The *Herald* asked all the "Sons of Toil" to vote for him, a Catholic, instead of the Conservative Catholic nominee. Likewise the *Chronicle* favoured him rather than R.E. Finn, the Liberal Catholic candidate.

The *Chronicle* brought out its rooster again on June 15th, but with much less exultation than usual. Not only had the Conservatives won eleven seats compared with five in 1906, but they had also polled strongly in every county except Kings and Victoria, polled 45.4 per cent of the votes to the Liberals 51.1 per cent, and defeated three cabinet ministers, including C.P. Chisholm, the commissioner of public works and mines. Fearful that these results might be interpreted as a reaction against reciprocity, the *Chronicle* sought to show that any Conservative who had strongly opposed the concept had been beaten. However, the *Herald* had much the better of the argument, pointing out that the Conservatives had gained one seat in each of the fishing counties of Lunenburg, Queens, and Yarmouth, and two in the mining county of Cape Breton, where Kendall, who had caused Murray as much worry as any Conservative member, had been beaten. Both papers regretted the defeat of Joy, but were pleased that he had polled 2,575 votes, only 1,400 fewer than the lowest of the three Conservatives running in the county.

Meanwhile Canada was moving inexorably towards a federal election. The reciprocity agreement passed quickly through Congress even as it was being filibustered in the Canadian Parliament. By mid-July Fielding had returned to Ottawa and, as he put it, started to pick up the pieces. Many Liberals, he later pointed out, thought at first that their opponents were bluffing and that eventually they would let the bill pass. However, because their leaders were now finding it difficult to recede from their position, an election might be inevitable. "Elections are at all times troublesome things, as you well know. . . . But if the opposition continue their course . . . the Government [may] take the view that election is the only possible solution."[28]

It proved to be so and early in August Fielding was enmeshed in preparations for the contest. This time he persuaded Laurier to spend three days in Nova Scotia, and he, in turn, promised to campaign in other provinces. In 1891 he had had to face charges of "veiled treason"; this time he faced the repeated contention that the reciprocity pact meant annexation or coercion and war. Day after day the *Herald* appealed to the "Sons of the Blood." How many of them wanted to travel the straight road to Washington? Though the newspaper also tried to show how the province's fishermen, farmers, and miners would suffer under the agreement and that the Laurier government was scandal-ridden, it relied basically on an emotional appeal. Shortly before the election it printed a picture of Rudyard Kipling accompanied by his letter stating that "it is her own soul that Canada risks today" and warning Canadians that they were deciding on a choice of flag, the Union Jack or Old Glory.

To counteract the *Herald*, the *Chronicle* castigated the "Unholy Alliance" of Borden and Bourassa and prophesied that the latter would dominate. It contended that, on balance, reciprocity would prove "an incalculable boon" to Nova Scotia and complained that the *Herald* would not enter into genuine debate on the subject. It pointed out that many of the province's industrial leaders, most of them Conservatives, were calling it "Nova Scotia's Great Chance," but in the end it found "the bogey or bugaboo" of annexation impossible to counter because its opponent refused to discuss the question rationally. It used, without much success, a cartoon picturing the shadow of Sir John A. Macdonald addressing Borden: "Say, Robert, I preached reciprocity for fifteen years and never saw any annexation danger in it. What kind of glasses do you wear?" Finally it labelled the Conservatives "lying 'Loyalists'" and quoted approvingly Samuel Johnson's statement that "patriotism is the last refuge of a scoundrel."[29]

Hailing Robert Borden's victory with the headline: "Laurier has finished his work," the *Herald* boasted that his "attempt to switch Canada out of the Empire" had failed. To the *Chronicle* it was a calamity that the Liberals' "noble battle for the common people" had been beaten by the money kings and an irrational appeal to loyalty. In Nova Scotia the vote could hardly have been closer. Each party won nine seats, and the Liberals took 50.8 per cent of the vote, the Conservatives 48.8. Both seats of which Cape Breton County was a part went Liberal, but in the fishing counties it was generally a different story. Though the Liberals routed their opponents in Yarmouth, they lost Shelburne and Queens, Lunenburg, and Digby. As the *Chronicle* put it, "a dead set was made against [Fielding], and . . . nothing was left undone which could be done" to beat him. Certainly a flood of money helped to elect his opponent, F.B. McCurdy. A future Conservative premier of the province, E.N. Rhodes, won in Cumberland, while the province's second cabinet minister, Sir Frederick Borden, lost in Kings, which he had represented for thirty-two years.

As early as 1891 Fielding had prophesied that some day "the blanks" would come to him, and he was actually more surprised by his party's national loss than by his own defeat. Because his seat had behaved so differently from neighbouring Yarmouth despite similar interests, he concluded that its voters had been denied the "free exercise of the franchise."[30] For a time he thought of contesting the election in the courts, but apparently he could not secure sufficient evidence to proceed. To a host of correspondents, however, he kept reiterating that his "policy was right." His greatest disappointment was that the Maritimes, which had stood to gain most, had accepted the agreement by only the smallest of margins. Although New Brunswick had given the Liberals a majority of three seats, the others had divided theirs evenly. His only consolation was that he had gone out on a great public issue.

For George Murray, too, the year's elections had unhappy results. In the first election he had lost his commissioner of public works and mines, in the second his attorney general, A.K. Maclean, who had returned to the federal arena. The inferiority of their replacements again indicated that he was being handicapped by the continuing departure of able provincial politicians for federal politics or office. The new commissioner of public works and mines, Ernest H. Armstrong, though known for his lengthy and highly researched speeches, was something of a "cold fish," lacking in charisma and unable to inspire confidence. In contrast, the new attorney general, Orlando T. Daniels, though highly congenial, had dubious legal attainments.

Perhaps worse, Murray would more and more have to confront the pressing problems of a society changed markedly by industrialism. The resolution of these problems would require governmental intervention that he would often find uncongenial, but which a stronger opposition would insist was necessary. Worst of all, provincial revenues would lose the buoyancy of the past decade just as demands for increased services were rising markedly. For Murray the easy road which had marked his premiership to date would soon be a distant memory.

CHAPTER 3

Murray: The Later years

Murray faced a different kind of house when the Thirty-Fourth General Assembly first met in February 1912. Confronting him was a formidable opposition, increased from eleven to thirteen as a result of by-elections. Once more he had to cope with Charles Tanner and his "hardy annual" of faultfinding. Tanner's return, after a three-year absence, meant that Rev. H.R. Grant would have a strong ally in promoting temperance.

As usual Grant assailed the lack of enforcement of the Nova Scotia Temperance Act in the larger centres and its non-applicability to the city of Halifax. "Nice Temperate Mr. Grant," said the *Chronicle*, "knows so much more about what is good for Halifax than do its own people." That did not stop Tanner from asking why its 50,000 people were singled out from 450,000 other Nova Scotians and why the city was "erected into a Kingdom . . . treated differently from the remainder of the Province."[1]

Though coal production had reached 6,208,444 tons in the previous year, exceeded only in 1908, the government acknowledged two serious problems. Competition from American coal in the Quebec market continued to increase, and strikes had cut down output, reduced royalties to $647,601 instead of the expected $750,000, and helped to produce a deficit of $179,710. Murray pointed out that, when royalties were increasing an average of 12.5 per cent yearly, Nova Scotia had not needed additional sources of revenue. However, that day had passed and he had no choice but to introduce taxes on financial institutions, express companies, and the like. Typical levies were

$1,000 on banks, $100 on each branch, and 1 per cent on the gross premiums of insurance companies.

Generally government bills met little opposition in 1912. One strengthened the Board of Public Utilities by granting it the powers of inquiry needed to fix rates; a second made use of the new federal conditional grants to encourage settlement on farm lands, especially by immigrants from Britain; a third, designed to deal with the Nova Scotia phenomenon of small streams that roads crossed and recrossed, received harsh treatment. When Armstrong proposed that culverts he constructed of permanent materials, Tanner questioned whether it was wise to entrust half a million dollars to a government which had gone on "blindly spending money for political purposes [and] . . . squandered thousands upon thousands, yes, millions of dollars."[2]

This year the *Herald* was outspokenly hostile to the Halifax Electric Tramway Company, something perhaps to be expected from the paper's second proprietor, William Dennis, who had taken it over in 1911 and whose Toryism did not prevent the frequent adoption of populist stances. Unceasingly his papers demanded limitations on the "everlasting monopoly" the company possessed over light and power, and transportation. To remove the "danger of allowing one group of men to control all the public utilities," the city ought to take over the company; at the very least its earnings should be limited to 16 per cent. The three Liberal members from Halifax supported the *Herald*, and although the legislature extended the company's exclusive franchise twenty-one years beyond 1916, it limited its bond issues to $600,000, its dividends to 8 per cent, and denied it the right to enter into second mortgages or issue additional shares.

Perhaps to forestall Hall, Murray as a private member took action to confer the right to fish in rivers and streams on citizens generally, but with one exception. Always a protector of vested rights, he refused to take away the privileges of some forty to sixty persons who had purchased and exercised under licence the exclusive right to fish in particular areas. Using provisions dating back to 1786 by which the local authorities determined where citizens might fish, he let the municipal councils issue licences to the holders of exclusive rights and determine the fee. Hall wanted the rights extinguished, but Murray refused to assume costs which might exceed $500,000.

To remove from the legislature the burden of having to handle a host of bills for the bonusing of industries by towns, the government accepted a private member's bill that authorized future bonusing by order in council if the proposal had the approval of a town's voters and would not injure an industry established elsewhere in the province.

Towards the session's close the newspapers were completely distracted by the *Titanic* disaster not far off the coast. "God gives the Land to Man," said the *Herald*, but "the Sea is His. He made it."

The year 1913 saw a return to optimism in the mining industry. Almost uninterrupted peace between labour and management permitted royalties to reach $791,000 and helped to produce a surplus of almost $38,000. The Murray government continued to provide useful, if not spectacular, legislation. A rural telephone bill let as few as three rural residents incorporate as a company with the right to connect with other lines, and provided a subsidy of $20 for each mile of construction. Another bill allowed women to sit on the Halifax school board; a third authorized the borrowing of $180,000 for the betterment of particular sections of roads under strict conditions.

It was not, however, a session of good feeling. Untypically emotional, the premier accused Tanner of being his usual unreasonable self and scorned his adulation of the Borden government. Did Tanner approve of Borden's refusal of a federal grant for the Guysborough section of the Eastern Shore railway, while the Musquodoboit section in the prime minister's own seat had been allowed to continue? Did he support conditional grants for highways, which would destroy provincial autonomy? Nova Scotia might be poor, but it would preserve the integrity of its legislature. As it was, the province had the most progressive highway legislation in Canada. "I want to leave no greater legacy than that from Cape North to Cape Sable every large bridge, every small bridge and culvert has been built of permanent material and the money expended honestly."[3]

The most vigorous debate occurred on the opposition's call for an "advanced policy" to keep people at home and encourage desirable immigration from abroad. Liberal spokesmen, especially J.C.Tory, defended their record on provincial development. Tory had won prestige for himself in his maiden speech a year earlier and had led observers to wonder if he would become more active in politics even at the cost of giving up his lucrative position with the Sun Life Assurance Company in Montreal. An aroused Murray lambasted the *Herald* for its attacks on A.S. Barnstead, the secretary of industries and immigration, and John Howard, the province's unsalaried agent general in London. The *Chronicle* vehemently denounced the *Herald* and William Dennis who, it said, ran "perhaps the most disreputable journal" in Canada now that the *Calgary Eye Opener* had lost the use of the mails. It had hoped, after Borden had made him a senator, that his "blackguardism" would cease, but his paper remained "the same old sheet," only more so.[4] Perhaps it should have ascribed some of the blame to William Henry Dennis, nephew of the proprietor, who had been appointed vice-president and general manager of the *Herald* in 1911 and had assumed increasing control over its direction.[5]

Conservative Howard W. Corning of Yarmouth took aim at the Nova Scotia Agricultural College for allegedly selling tubercular cattle. A Hereford cow, "Stella," purchased by Rupert C.S. Kaulback of Lunenburg and slaughtered because of disease, stole the spotlight and led H.H. Wickwire to "invoke the muse in a poem," embalmed in the records of the house. It began:

What's become of Stella? She is gone!
Vanished as the summer dew at morn.
Gone beyond the call of ken
Of Rupert and his faithful men.[6]

Other Conservatives launched out on more familiar topics. Tanner tried again to bring Halifax under the general prohibition law, Hall sought to make rod fishing completely open to the public, and J.C. Douglas found gross favouritism in the granting of Crown lands in Cape Breton and Victoria counties to the North River Lumber Company. On the other side, J.C. Tory blamed the cancellation of the Guysborough section of the railway on Halifax interests who feared that Country Harbour might become a rival. But the most bitter controversy surrounded the Halifax Electric Tramway Company, recently taken over by the E.A. Robert interests of Montreal. It pitted Conservative city officials, politicians, newspapers, and financial interests against their Liberal counterparts. A bill from the Halifax city council authorized the city, on the vote of ratepayers, to acquire the company with the alternative right of expropriation, while the company's own bill sought its reincorporation as the Halifax Tramway and Power Company with the removal of the limitations imposed on it a year earlier and the right to bring hydro-electric power into the city.

Behind Robert were G. Fred Pearson and the *Chronicle* interests, and Frederick Borden, who owned power rights on the Gaspereau River. Against them was a Conservative financier from Montreal, D. Lorne McGibbon, who controlled considerable Halifax property and was strongly supported by the *Herald* and its proprietor. Supposedly the battle was for financial supremacy in the city. Arguing that the company's bill would create a dangerous monopoly, the *Herald* demanded that "Halifax's vital utility . . . not be used as a monster sponge to soak up the back-wash of a tidal wave of watered stock." After the assembly rejected the Halifax city bill, supposedly because it repudiated a contract, the *Herald* accused Murray of siding against 50,000 Halifax citizens and helping unscrupulous promoters like E.A. Robert and Frederick Borden to become masters of Nova Scotia. However, the company bill had also failed because of the opposition of the three Liberal members from Halifax and a strong public agitation.

A second bill enabling the company to acquire the Gaspereau power interests suffered a similar fate. The *Herald* rejoiced that its defeat was due to an "historic" mass meeting of protest called by the Conservative mayor of Halifax. A bitter *Chronicle* condemned the legislative assembly for its surrender to a fictitious agitation fomented by self-seeking individuals who sought simply their own aggrandizement and the defeat of the Liberals. After the legislature eventually agreed to a bill permitting the existing tramway company to increase its capitalization, Tanner said that he would reject it if he took office, and the *Herald* accused the premier of giving "pirates permission to exploit the tramways" of Halifax.

At prorogation, the *Chronicle* vented its outrage on the "scandal-hunting" Conservatives through the comments of "a guy in the gallery." He took aim at Tanner, "the living example of the truth of the proverb that 'Language was given us to conceal our thoughts'"; at R.H. Butts, none "so reckless in his public statements as he"; at Frank Stanfield, "a very crafty man with a long purse, who has no special aptitude for politics, [and whose] forte is muckraking"; at W.L. Hall, who entered the assembly with a halter put around his neck by the Temperance Alliance; at Albert Parsons, who wore "a number 19 collar and a smile that would stop an eight day clock . . . [he] belongs to the harmless class"; and at Howard Corning, the "self-appointed agricultural leader," who "in his idle moments emulated the ruminants on his farm by chewing his cud."[7]

That year Nova Scotians showed great interest in the filibuster on the Naval Bill in Ottawa. Why, wondered the *Herald*, was "the great Grit Gabfest" not halted forthwith? When the Conservatives introduced closure rules, the *Chronicle* called them "Canada's shame" and "a blow at freedom." About this time Laurier expressed serious concern about the health of the province's leading Liberals. He especially regretted that "at Murray's time of life and with his infirmity it [was] impossible to expect from him the splendid work which he put up some fifteen years ago." As for Fielding, though much improved in health, he was "not the same Fielding of former days."[8] Attesting to the Liberals' growing weakness was Philip McLeod's success in Victoria County shortly before the session of 1913. It was the Conservatives' fourth successive by-election victory and the third in formerly Liberal seats. Although McLeod would be unseated because of his agents' corrupt practices, the *Herald* was elation itself as it displayed a dead rooster, with the caption, "the effect of zero weather on the Chronic-ill's pet bird." The *Chronicle* replied that "the Victoria game is not workable on a large scale."

The government was clearly suffering because the great boom period was over, financial stringency had become the order of the day, and it had little new to offer. The *Chronicle* used a defence that might have been Murray's own. Provincial administration, it argued, was a matter of personality and involved no broad questions of policy. The premier was mainly an executive who supervised expenditures largely fixed by statute. Party differences were not meaningful — everyone had agreed with the technical education programme, the railway question had come to fruition, and even on highways the

Conservatives proposed little that was different. The superintendent of education was a Conservative; so were the principal of the Agricultural College and the head of the Public Charities Branch. Would it not be wise, therefore, to leave the work of administration to Murray, whom experience and achievements kept adding to his stature?[9]

The "unfavoring tide" was not stemmed in 1914. Murray had to announce a deficit of $29,000 for the previous year and he forecast one of $212,000 for the next. As was common in these circumstances, he blamed the Conservatives at Ottawa for using "every means in their power to prevent the [provincial] revenues from being supplemented." The one substantive measure of 1914 increased the size of the assembly from 38 to 43, the first change since 1867. It produced no controversy, as a special committee of four Liberals and three Conservatives had agreed that Halifax County should have two additional members, Cape Breton two, and Cumberland one. This measure also satisfied the wishes of the politically astute George Murray that no county should lose seats. Tanner failed again to have the Temperance Act apply to Halifax city, but four counties abandoned the Scott Act and came under the more easily enforceable provincial act.

After 1914 the Murray government could no longer boast that it had never incurred even a breath of scandal. When the Halifax and South Western took over the Nova Scotia Central Railway from Middleton to Lunenburg it acquired its lands, although they later came under provincial control as security for a mortgage. Tanner charged that the government had improperly permitted the release of the lands and that Attorney General Daniels had received a note for $75,000 as a consideration in their sale. For three weeks the government took a battering from its opponents in the assembly and the press. Even after Murray promised an investigation by a royal commission, the *Herald* called for Daniel's resignation or dismissal. Although the commission found no wrongful act on his part, it declared him gravely imprudent in putting himself "in a position which might have involved . . . a possible complication between his private interest and his public duty."[10] He would remain attorney general for another eight years, but with diminished respect.

That year the level of vituperation was even higher than
before on the bill to incorporate the Nova Scotia Tramways and
Power Company with the right to purchase the Halifax Electric
Tramway Company and acquire water power interests on the
Gaspereau. Once again Senator Dennis and the *Herald* were up
in arms against "watered stock" manipulators; once again they
demanded that the province's water power be developed by the
government for public use. Mayor F.P. Bligh led a mass protest,
outraged that a private company with outside interests could
manipulate the stock of a Halifax company that the city was not
permitted to buy. Trade unions, the Sydney and Truro town
councils, and even the Liberal *Acadian Recorder* supported
him, but the *Chronicle* insisted, nonetheless, that the bill would
promote the growth of Halifax by ensuring cheap hydro-electric
power.

On April 16th, even before serious debate began, the *Evening
Mail* (the *Herald's* afternoon counterpart) published a letter
signed "Ian McLean" which declared that "some of the
gentlemen sent to the Assembly to protect our interests were
unable to resist the temptation and were bought body and
breeches." An investigating committee of the assembly reported
that W.R. McCurdy, the *Herald's* news editor, had refused to
name the letter-writer, contending that it would "violate the
ethics and traditions of the press and . . . injure his personal
reputation." Declaring his intention to maintain the assembly's
dignity, Attorney General Daniels moved that McCurdy be
jailed for forty-eight hours. Tanner read telegrams from
publishers across Canada, mostly Conservatives, stating that he
had simply exercised an editor's journalistic right. When a party
vote upheld Daniels' motion, the *Herald* sought to make
McCurdy a hero and a martyr. Some, it said, were born to fame,
but others had it thrust upon them. A band serenaded McCurdy
in jail, from which he wrote letters describing the "burlesque
bungling of the brute majority."

Over the opposition of Halifax's three Liberal members the
bill incorporating the power company became law. The Halifax
city council then asked the federal minister of justice to disallow
it. However, he refused, stating that disallowance "cannot
conveniently be invoked as a general means for the re-
consideration of Legislative measures." Later, Tanner requested

a full investigation of water-power resources with special attention to the public interest. Murray was sympathetic but pointed out that most of these resources were already in private hands. He agreed, however, that the legislature could exercise considerable control without doing an injustice to the incumbent holders.

With a world war raging the Conservatives lost some of their momentum in 1915. By that time the Allies were taking part in heavy fighting on the western front and in Asia Minor, and both political parties sought to avoid the impression of resorting to petty partisanship. The *Herald* was engaged in an orgy of patriotism that would last throughout the war. At this time it was up in arms over the charges of shabby treatment of the Nova Scotia Regiment on the Salisbury Plain made by Lieutenant Colonel Struan Robertson and strongly supported by Horatio C. Crowell, the correspondent for the *Chronicle* in Britain. Relying on Kitchener's condemnation of the reports as a "malicious falsehood," the *Herald* joined the *Sydney Daily Post* in charging that these reports would give comfort to the enemy. However, the *Chronicle* stuck to its guns and the premier agreed that the facts, if true, should be published.

The provincial deficit of $213,000 confirmed Murray's earlier prophecy that coal revenues would no longer increase sufficiently to meet rising costs. Transportation difficulties added to the financial problem — they prevented the sending of a gift of coal worth $100,000 to Britain and forced the substitution of cash. To share the cost equitably, the government decided to levy a tax of one mill per dollar on the total provincial property assessment of $124,258,000. When Murray intimated that the tax might be continued if the war led to smaller provincial revenues, a phalanx of Conservatives demanded retrenchment instead of direct taxation. Frank Stanfield, in particular, detailed various ways of saving money, including the abolition of the legislative council, an $80,000 saving by his calculations.

"Now the lean years are with us," lamented the *Herald*. Though Murray cut expenditures to the bone, he still had to forecast a deficit of $138,000. His greatest regret was that Nova Scotia, once in the forefront of technical education, had fallen behind because of a lack of money.[11]

This session saw the further liberalization of the Workmen's Compensation Act. Though the changes followed the Ontario act of 1914 and similar legislation in the State of Washington, its sponsor, E.H. Armstrong, emphasized that "we are not mere copyists." Henceforth, not only would the industry "bear the hazard of protection," but the injured would receive the largest award possible with the least amount of litigation. As usual, Murray argued that prohibition in Halifax should be approached gradually. Tanner, who wanted immediate action, lost in a tie vote on a non-party division, but it seemed likely that his wishes would soon be met. This year the Halifax papers gave less and less attention to the provincial legislature as the *Herald* revelled in the "glorious" conduct of Canadian and Empire troops, and the *Chronicle* bemoaned the activities of the boodlers and grafters at Ottawa.

George Murray approached neither the session of 1916 nor the subsequent election with enthusiasm. The session turned out to be all that he had feared. He offered little that was new, and his opponents started their campaign on the day the session opened with an unprecedented attack on him in person, and they continued their assaults without let up. At issue was his payment, in his capacity as provincial treasurer, of $48,500 in eleven separate transactions to R.G. Hervey in connection with the building of the Halifax and South Western. Allegedly the payments were illegal because they were not for work or supplies, as his contract required, and because an injunction had forbidden them. Although the Supreme Courts of Nova Scotia and Canada differed in opinion, the Judicial Committee concluded that "if it were the case of a private individual, [Murray] would be clearly liable to make good the wrongful payment, and purge his contempt." The premier contended that an injunction could not legally be served upon someone like himself who personally had no connection with the matter and whose duties as provincial treasurer were purely nominal as he had neither paid out nor handled money personally. However, the Conservatives charged that only technically was he not a lawbreaker and not liable to imprisonment for contempt of court.[12]

An election being imminent, finance became the opposition's second target. For 1915 the deficit had been $120,400, and for

1916 the forecast was much the same. Conservative J.C. Douglas showed that the provincial debt, only $3,443,000 when Murray became premier, had reached $13,410,000. Frank Stanfield prophesied that unless the government retrenched as he suggested it could not avoid massive direct taxation. J.C. Tory replied that none of Stanfield's proposals made sense, and Murray promised to carry on with "as little burden . . . and with as much generosity to the people at large, as in any country of a similar population on the face of the earth."[13]

In one significant way Murray recognized that an election was coming. The Protestant churches and the Woman's Christian Temperance Union (WCTU) had used the war situation to strengthen public opinion in favour of temperance. So when Howard Corning moved to bring Halifax city under the Temperance Act, the premier let the bill pass second reading after first indicating that he did not necessarily support it. However, when it emerged from committee without amendments, only the three Halifax members opposed it. Attributing his new position to a change in public opinion, Murray stated that in the interest of temperance he had wanted the bill to be introduced by a private member. Otherwise, "this great moral question [might be made] a matter of political difference in this legislature, or between the respective political parties of this Province."[14] Scornfully the *Herald* suggested that his delays had made him the laughingstock of the province, while the *Chronicle* lambasted the "self-appointed . . . guardians of other men's consciences." Charles Tanner and H.R. Grant finally got what they wanted.

When the session dragged on almost interminably, the *Chronicle* could not restrain its impatience. Why should the fiddlers "fiddle" and "the 'trenchant critics' trenchantly criticize" while "the fields of Flanders are being dyed red with British blood"? Could not the speeches be printed in Hansard without being delivered and with insertions like "cheers" or "vigorous handclapping"? Could not Hansard, as Mr. Dooley had suggested, become a "regular Bicyclopedia of useful information," and yet not prevent the assembly from conducting its business expeditiously? The *Herald* admitted that it was almost brutal to assail a government sitting in its old armchair. Would it last "long enough to meet the people at the polls"?

Had it not lost every by-election since 1911, while its dead hand stifled progress and prevented reform?[15] Forgetting its former lukewarmness, the *Herald* carried a large picture of Tanner with the caption: "The Next Premier of Nova Scotia."

Much of the election had been fought before dissolution on May 22nd. Condemning the government for a litany of sins, Tanner's manifesto promised to get rid of the carelessness, corruption, lethargy, and indifference deeply rooted in the thirty-four-year-old administration. In turn the *Herald* carried a profusion of cartoons and advertisements unprecedented in provincial history. It engaged McConnell, a Toronto cartoonist, to produce front-page cartoons which "featured an old, swaybacked horse representing the 34-year-old Liberal regime." One of the cartoons showed Murray, Armstrong, and Daniels slumbering while Nova Scotia said, "Sh-h-h, don't wake them, we'll just put them to bed." Almost daily the *Herald* alluded to the Murray-Daniels government, hoping to discredit it in that way. A cartoon entitled "Murray and his merry Manikin" pictured the premier carrying Daniels in his pack with a $75,000 note fastened to the attorney general and the caption: "A chain is only as strong as its weakest link." The *Herald* also expressed horror over the "crazy policy" of spending public money to bring in "a few Holland and Hun immigrants." How could the government dare show its "solicitude for its 'Hun' progeny" by wringing $50,000 out of the sweat and toil of patriotic Nova Scotians?[16]

The Liberal campaign was much more restrained. Murray argued that, in contrast with the Conservatives, the Liberals had taken the enlightened position on every major issue since 1882. His manifesto pointed out that only war conditions had interrupted a long series of surpluses. Although the province's debt had reached almost $7 million, its assets were far in excess of $26 million. No government in North America had enacted more advanced legislation in the interests of labour than his, especially in technical education, where "we have developed a system which will enable every Nova Scotian, boy and girl, to be trained efficiently to perform his or her work in the best possible manner."[17]

To counter charges of an aging government, the *Chronicle* pointed out that Murray was "not by many years as old as

Tanner" and that none of his ministers had served as long as ten years. It condemned the corruption practised by many prominent Conservatives in the Victoria by-election and hoped that they would not repeat these tactics at a time when the fierce fighting around Verdun should serve to purify hearts and minds. On finance it boasted of the government's success a year ago in floating a loan in New York City for 3.9 per cent, the lowest rate of borrowing by any province. It also found a new issue in the alleged distribution by the Conservatives of an "underground circular" which had lit the fires of sectarian strife. That publication accused Murray and the superintendent of education of gross favouritism to Catholics in school matters; unless they were checked the educational system would be handed over "body and soul to the Romans, and our Protestant children will be compelled to attend convent schools." Angrily, the *Herald* charged that "the incendiary bogus 'secret document' bears all the earmarks of being printed in the Chronic-Kill Office" and that only Liberals were passing around "the fire-brand circular."[18]

If ever the *Herald* and the Conservatives expected to win an election, it was this one. Great was their disappointment when they won only thirteen seats to the Liberals' thirty. Although their popular vote rose from 45.4 to 48.8 per cent, the electoral system worked strongly against them. Their only consolation was that they were highly competitive in every county and generally lost by small majorities.

For Tanner, who ran fifth in Pictou, this was to be his last election. In that county, said the *Herald*, it was a triumph of the liquor interests over the prohibitionists. Temperance Liberals had worked "cheek by jowl with the liquor dealers" to defeat men pledged to enforce the law. More generally, as William March points out, the *Herald* believed that the war had so absorbed public attention that "the people did not seem to realize the minor evils of a bad provincial administration as they would otherwise have done."[19] To the *Chronicle* the result was a natural reaction against a party which had left "nothing undone that desperate political adventures and mendicant politicians could do to beat Murray." A less partisan analysis might suggest that the negative politics of Tanner and his party simply could not prevail in a province with strong Liberal leanings against a premier whom the voters had learned to trust. Throughout his career Tanner had been unfortunate in having to run against Liberals of exceptional strength in Pictou. If long, vigorous political service was the criterion, he deserved the senatorship the Borden government conferred upon him in 1917.

The war overshadowed everything else when the Thirty-Fifth General Assembly began sitting in February 1917. Because of the spring offensive, the Halifax newspapers called for the prompt conduct of public business and the *Chronicle* had no complaints about wasted time until the closing days. Heading the government's programme was a bill that authorized borrowing up to $2 million for the promotion of shipbuilding and established a commission to acquire the necessary facilities. As Murray indicated, the change from sail to steam had been a highly disturbing one for Nova Scotia and for years it had made no attempt to adapt to different circumstances. Now the war made a new policy possible. Delightedly the *Chronicle* wrote that "Nova Scotia's situation and traditions warrant the assumption that in the future, as in the past, we should be the shipbuilders for and carriers of Canada's commerce."[20]

In the previous year the province had had a surplus of $33,000 because of unexpectedly large returns from royalties and succession duties. Nevertheless, Murray and Hall, who was leading the opposition, agreed that steps should be taken to avoid future deficits. The outcome was higher levies under the Costs and Fees Act, and taxes on long-distance telephone calls, the gross incomes of large corporations, and the excess profits of public utility companies.

That session the *Herald* ran a campaign along ultra-loyal lines, perhaps influenced all the more by the death in France of Captain Eric Dennis, the publisher's son. While criticizing the government for not economizing as the conditions of war demanded, it insisted most of all that Nova Scotia adopt an Ontario programme advocating "a vegetable garden for every home." Day after day, almost *ad nauseam,* it besought the legislature to stimulate agricultural production. To its indignation the government appeared "paralyzed" on the subject, while the opposition maintained a "mysterious" silence. "With all the horrors of a world famine staring us in the face Nova Scotia is still sound asleep." Did the members not realize that the heroism of the troops would be in vain if Nova Scotians failed in their duty? In the end it found little good to say about the members' conduct in 1917. They had done nothing for returned soldiers, they had paved the way for direct taxation, they had given the cabinet power to set aside any decision of the shipbuilding commission, and they had defeated two meritorious private member's bills.

Liberal R.M. McGregor sought to limit the legislative council to the suspensive veto imposed upon the House of Lords in 1911. The cabinet favoured it and Murray stated that he would regard the proposal's defeat as "an open defiance of popular government." He also declared that his exacting of pledges from all council appointees would "have an effect more or less some day or other in the bringing about of constitutional change."[21] However, the bill did not even reach the council after the assembly's law amendments committee recommended the three months' hoist. The *Herald* protested loudly that its action followed council threats not to pass any bills unless this one was rejected.

It also objected to the treatment accorded Liberal R.H. Graham's bill which granted women the right to vote. After the assembly readily agreed to remove any doubts about the admissibility of women to the bar, it seemed prepared to go further. The gallery was filled with women when it unanimously approved the principle of women's suffrage and sent the bill to committee. Graham exulted that "old ideas, old customs and old dynasties were crumbling in the flame of war." Attorney General Daniels declared that the women, led by the WCTU, had made the best presentation before a committee that he had ever witnessed. In the end, however, the drafting of the bill and the attitude of Murray apparently caused its demise. The premier wondered if Nova Scotia's women should have the franchise before those of Britain and suggested that public opinion, even among the women, seemed to be muted. Would it not be best to wait until women generally showed that they wanted it? "It will come in time," he concluded.[22]

As the session ended, debate had begun on the need for conscription to reinforce Canadian troops in Europe. In May Murray expressed the opinion privately that it would be dangerous for a party government to introduce it.[23] When it became official policy the next month, he told Laurier that the Liberal party faced one of the most serious situations in its history. He felt that the Borden government could not have handled things in a worse way and that the best course now was to set up a coalition government, notwithstanding the fact that party feeling was "as strong in me as any man in Canada." Conscription under existing conditions, he feared, might be divisive at a time "when we should be absolutely united." Could not Laurier state in Parliament his willingness to share in developing a policy under which Canadians could discharge their duty fully? That course could only "enlarge the strong personal affection" that Canadians had for him. At the same time Murray told Fielding that coalition would best meet the wishes of most Nova Scotians.[24]

Clearly Nova Scotia's Liberals faced a serious dilemma. Late in September R.M. McGregor called on them to declare their position openly; for him, conscription was a settled course not to be altered in any circumstance. Some of his colleagues wanted a county-wide conference of leading Liberals to decide on a coalition and Laurier's leadership, but it was not to be. On October 12th Liberals Sifton, Calder, Crerar, Rowell, and Mewburn entered the federal cabinet, and Murray, in Ottawa at the time, was still making up his mind. When he asked for Laurier's opinion, the latter replied that he could not presume to give him advice. However, to another Nova Scotian Laurier wrote that Murray's joining the Union government would be "the worst blow of all," and he hoped that the Lord would preserve him from "having to sit face to face and not side by side with my old friend Murray."[25]

Following consultations in Nova Scotia, Murray decided to stay out of the federal cabinet while agreeing to give it general support. Nova Scotian A.K. Maclean entered it with the blessing of Fielding. The latter, in a public statement,[26] took the position that although the coalition proposal came much too late, public opinion favoured it; moreover, since party members in other provinces, Quebec excepted, supported it, Nova Scotia's Liberals should not isolate themselves. He hoped, however, that all Liberals would co-operate with Laurier on non-military matters. It was an unhappy, reluctant Fielding who broke with

Laurier. Invited to address a conscriptionist Liberal convention in Ontario, he declined, saying that his public statement had been made simply to deal with a difficult situation in Nova Scotia.

The *Chronicle* was no less troubled. During much of October it continued to lambaste the Borden government for its inaction, scandals, and blunders, and for the iniquities of the War-time Elections Act. It continued its out-and-out support of Laurier and gloated over the early failures to secure a coalition. However, when the first Liberals entered the cabinet, it admitted that the new government was somewhat better than the old, and later, after Maclean's entrance, it agreed that a genuine Union government was in place. At dissolution on November 1st it urged Liberals who had doubts about the government to cease engaging in useless, fratricidal strife "while the Hun is at the gate."

Four days later it published Laurier's manifesto without detailed comment. Though agreeing with him that the war was a contest for the very existence of civilization, it knew of "none but partisan reasons for opposition to the Union government." When the Liberals refused to nominate A.K. Maclean in Halifax, it declared that he was as much a Liberal as anyone. A vote for Laurier, it said, would mean lack of support for Canadian soldiers at a time of crisis. Looking to the future, it almost begged the Laurier Liberals to give the Unionist Liberals the same freedom of opinion as they demanded for themselves. After all, it expected to "co-operate with [them] as fully and sympathetically as ever when the war is over."[27]

The *Herald* displayed none of the *Chronicle's* moderation. The Union Jack flew high over its editorial page as it hailed the formation of the Union government. For the province's chief Laurier Liberal, Pictonian E.M. Macdonald, it had nothing but contempt, calling him "Lose-the-War Macdonald." When Murray stayed out of the cabinet, it accused him of pandering to "Lose-the-War Liberals." It expressed outrage that the Laurier Liberals insisted on bitter, partisan fights in every Nova Scotian seat but Shelburne and Queens, where Borden persuaded his own party to let Fielding win by acclamation. Was it not a "damnable crime" to force partisan fights while "men of our flesh and blood are lying stark and cold in no man's land"? Did "the Laurier Liberals want Bourassa and his solid Quebec entrenched at Ottawa"? Shortly before election day it printed a little girl's note to Santa Claus: "My Mamma says that if you will bring the Union Government victory for Christmas that it will bring my daddy home sooner from the war, so *please, please do.* Daddy's little girl."[28]

The election put Murray and Fielding in the most uncomfortable position of their careers. Neither participated publicly in the campaign. When Senator Charles Tanner, a major director of the Union organization in Nova Scotia, put pressure on Fielding to assist him, the latter flatly refused. Tanner could play an active role without speaking against Conservative candidates, while Fielding himself would have to oppose Liberals with whom he had long been associated.[29] Like Murray, he was doing everything possible to avoid an irreconcilable break with old political friends.

None was more shocked than the *Herald* by the election results in Nova Scotia on December 17th. After the calamitous explosion of December 6th, voting had been delayed in the dual riding of Halifax, and Fielding, a Unionist of sorts, had been unopposed in Shelburne and Queens. In the civilian voting, Unionists were ahead in only three of the remaining twelve seats, and Laurier Liberals in nine — five by relatively small majorities. To the *Herald* it was a "Shameful Christmas Message to . . . Hero Sons Overseas." How could Nova Scotia stay-at-homes link themselves to a solid Quebec, something that no other part of British Canada had done? How could "this 'New Scotland' so largely settled by Scots and Celts, and English, and by United Empire Loyalists" behave so despicably?[30]

To Laurier the results in Nova Scotia were enormously satisfying. Why did Murray, "whose judgment is so clear and whose sagacity never was at fault . . . not understand better the temper of his province"? Later he called Nova Scotia "the bright spot . . . the sheet anchor upon which we must build our future hopes."[31] In the end he was much less satisfied. The *Herald* had pointed out that the civilian vote was not the voice of loyal Nova Scotians, and that when 25,000 of the "Brain, and Brawn, and Courage and Heroism, and Faith and Vision" had their say, the

Liberals would win only Antigonish and Guysborough, Cape Breton North and Victoria, Inverness, and Lunenburg. The newspaper was right, for eventually the Unionists took the five seats that had been close in the civilian vote, and the two Halifax seats. Not much manipulation of the soldiers' vote, if any, would have been needed to produce this result. Though the Laurier Liberals ended up with only four seats, it was remarkable that the normal Liberal vote remained so solid despite the absence of newspaper support and the backing of Fielding and Murray.

Interest in the 1918 session was slight. Even more than before, the *Herald* denounced the poltroons who saved their skins by staying at home; it delighted in the rounding up of the Blue Rocks men who had dodged the selective draft, believing that William Duff, the MP for Lunenburg, "could get them clear"; it railed against "treachery and anarchy" in Quebec City, and wanted the city placed under martial law and "every young Funker put in khaki." An optimistic speech from the throne hailed the construction of the province's first large steel ship. Somewhat disturbing was the decrease in coal output, partly because of mining disasters at New Waterford and Springhill, and partly because of shortages of shipping and labour. To remedy the situation, the government had the Coal Mines Act amended, conferring upon itself much the same power over the coal industry that the federal government possessed generally under the War Measures Act. To deal with the effects of the Halifax explosion, it set up the Halifax Relief Commission. Smaller revenues than expected from royalties, amusement taxes, and succession duties had led to a deficit of $200,000, but Murray still contended that the province's financial position was second to none.

Despite his lukewarmness the previous year Murray's government sponsored the adoption of equal suffrage for women. In contrast with 1917 only ten spectators occupied the public gallery during second reading. However, Legislative Councillor Robert Drummond, "a worshipper of the god of things as they are," was there and a late arrival was Mr. Justice Longley, who years earlier had given the quietus to women's suffrage. Conservative leader Hall even wanted to remove all property and income requirements for voting and introduce universal suffrage for men and women, but the government would have none of that.

Attracting interest in 1918 was D.A. Cameron's bill which required an employer to enter into discussion with a committee of employees within twenty-four hours after a labour dispute had begun. The premier used the opportunity to say that his record on labour legislation was "written in the statutes of the Province," which contained "as advanced legislation as . . . anywhere else." He had always stood by the workmen and would do so to the end of his public life. When he contended that Cameron's bill could not attain its objective, this remark doomed it to defeat. During a generally uneventful session the *Herald* ran a news story headed: "Will convention oust Premier Murray?" Successful and defeated Laurier candidates, it said, were to gather to affirm their opposition to the Union Government and to read out any who would "not eat crow." However, no convention met early in the year and, when one was assembled in December, Murray and Fielding were elected honorary presidents of the provincial Liberals.

An apparent departure from the old style of government was the appointment of H.H. Wickwire as minister of highways in June 1918. Since 1877 the number of ministers with portfolio had remained at three, while outside the Maritimes it had increased to seven or eight, and in New Brunswick to six. The Nova Scotia phenomenon was due primarily to George Murray, the architect of provincial government over a lengthy period.[32] More than once he had extolled the practice of setting up minor departments headed by experts subject only to the most general control by the three ministers with portfolio. Was it not better, he asked, to "let the people instead of having the judgment of a partisan . . . have men clothed with a fair measure of responsibility who . . . could not be accused of being in political sympathy with the administration"?

The result was that his department became something of a sump into which flowed most of the new and expanding functions of government. As provincial secretary, he was not only *ex officio* provincial treasurer and king's printer, but also supervised a wide variety of functions ranging from the incorporation of companies to the collection of municipal statistics, and exercised a general surveillance over three minor departments headed by the secretary of agriculture, the secretary of industries and immigration, and the provincial health officer, and, in varying degrees, over a large number of other officials and boards, such as the inspector of rural telephones, the Public Utilities Board, and the Workmen's Compensation Board.

When pressed, Murray expanded on the merits of this administrative set-up. Because broad questions of policy did not exist in the limited provincial field he saw little ground for partisanship in the management of local affairs. To the Conservatives this was a subterfuge enabling an astute politician to divest himself of his responsibilities. The premier, they alleged, had "put a 'buffer' between himself and every department of the public service. Let a member of the opposition . . . point to anything wrong in any of the departments, and the premier is on his feet ready to place the blame on some departmental head — or tail — who, he points out, is 'of tory antecedents,' and therefore can do no wrong, or if he had happened to do something wrong, the premier and his government are absolved from all blame!" By 1918 Murray himself conceded that the expanding functions of government required more than three ministers with portfolio: "He had not been able to leave the province but three times in ten years, and he thought the burden was too great to impose upon one man." However, Wickwire's appointment was no more than a half-hearted gesture. For the year before, ostensibly to remove the road system from politics, the government had appointed a bipartisan Provincial Highway Board with full responsibility for maintaining and constructing highways. Thus the new minister did not head a genuine department and was little more than a link between the cabinet and the board.

Talk of progress prevailed in the legislature in 1919 and the speech from the throne promised "the most revolutionary programme . . . within recent years." The *Herald* sought to provide a stimulus without engaging in partisanship. To avoid the dangers of Bolshevism, it asked the legislators to meet the moderate and just demands of labour and not merely "monkey" with bills. It described the labour delegates who had just created a new Federation of Labour at a convention in Halifax, as men interested in "a solid building of the fabric of society," not "fire-eating Bolshevistic Labour leaders" who would lead it to the edge of the precipice. "The real leaders in reform are not the Murrays, the Halls, or any such conventionalized band of political thinkers, but the MacLaughlins [sic], Danes and Baxters." In its view the provincial labour parliament had done more in four days than the provincial legislature was likely to do in four weeks. It was now up to the latter to produce "live legislation" and not act as a "a vaudeville show" or a place to catch up on correspondence.[33]

In quantity at least the assembly did produce a wealth of legislation in 1919. One bill provided for fair rents in towns and cities, and for restrictions on the eviction of tenants. Another took advantage of a federal act and granted loans to returned soldiers, working men and women, and persons of small means for the building of houses. A third broadened and liberalized the Workmen's Compensation Act but drew criticism for placing too heavy a burden on industry.

The first of two far-reaching bills, following an Ontario act, set up the Nova Scotia Power Commission of three members, one an executive councillor, to decide on all matters relating to the development of water power. Its sponsor, E.H. Armstrong, stated that the bill simply followed the general trend of trying to secure the cheapest power possible through greater government intervention. The more controversial companion bill went much further than an earlier act and allowed the new commission to appropriate any water course and vest it in the province. Conservatives W.L. Hall and Hector McInnes called it "legalized robbery" for disregarding grants made 150 years earlier for valuable consideration. Armstrong replied that private rights were amply protected by letting the commission provide compensation at its discretion. As he saw it, "the spirit of the times tended towards surrounding the public utilities with legislation so that they might be used for the benefit of the people at large."[34]

Under pressure the government also sponsored legislation to settle disputes on coal leases between Dominion and Scotia. Earlier it had forced agreement on a lease covering one-fifth of a square mile, but the *Chronicle*, indignant because the companies spent more time lobbying than trying to resolve their difficulties, demanded an overall solution. The outcome was a bill empowering the governor in council to ensure that existing leases of submarine coal-mining areas were employed in the province's best interests. Hector McInnes, a director of Dominion and a major defender of vested interests, declared that proceedings of this kind had occurred nowhere in the world except during Carranza's reign of lawlessness in Mexico. "It was despotic for the government to take property from one individual and transfer it to another." When Armstrong replied that the bill would be invoked only as a last resort, the *Chronicle* cautioned the government not to shirk its responsibilities through "a narrow conception of its duty."[35]

Especially troublesome for the government were the abuses under prohibition of the distribution of liquor for industrial and medical purposes. As it continued to do later, the government proposed tinkering legislation which would prove to be quite ineffective. Of greater importance was Wickwire's borrowing bill, which let the province take advantage of Ottawa's shared-cost programme for highways. Either a precursor or, in the opinion of some, the very beginning of a Maritime Rights agitation was J.C. Tory's resolution calling on Nova Scotia to demand compensation for the lands involved in the northward extension of Quebec and Ontario, for the transfer of lands to the western provinces if and when it took place, and for the unfair treatment accorded Nova Scotia in public expenditures since 1867. Central Canadian politicians, he declared, cared nothing for Nova Scotia and constantly used their influence against it. A department that knew anything about fish had never existed at Ottawa. "They couldn't tell a sculpin from a haddock." Supporting J.C. Tory with vigour, the *Chronicle* charged that the western provinces, with no larger populations, got revenues three to five times those of Nova Scotia from federal sources and could therefore provide immensely better services. In its view the Maritimes "had been plundered right and left. They have been heartlessly sacrificed and stripped . . . and [yet scorned] for . . . lack of progressiveness." Might not Nova Scotia be as well off under Bolshevism as under supposedly British institutions?[36]

With the accounts showing a deficit of $219,965, the government thought it high time to bring them into balance. Some additional revenue was to come from motor vehicle fees, but most from increased taxation on banks, trust and insurance companies, and the provincial railways. Even more serious was the outlook for coal. Output was down by 538,000 tons and only 134,500 tons had been shipped up the St. Lawrence, the smallest amount since 1878.

The session of 1920 opened without the "accustomed ballyhoo" and the spectators were few. George Murray was absent, suffering from illness caused by exposure after his car had broken down. He later appeared for a few days before departing for a holiday in the south. However, the *Herald* enthusiastically welcomed returned soldier J.L. Ralston and called his speech in moving the address "a refreshing breeze, sweeping the cobwebs of a dusty past from the nooks and crannies of the old building." After comparing him with the "Ghosts of the Old Order," it hoped for the day "when the last of these ghosts will be laid."

The speech from the throne expressed satisfaction with the increase of 14 per cent in coal production, which had resulted mainly from improvement in the steel industry. Armstrong was even more enthused when he introduced a bill — perhaps the most important in provincial history he said — that would let the province's two largest corporations, Dominion and Scotia, arrange to have their shares acquired by the newly formed British Empire Steel Corporation (Besco). Because steel could supposedly be produced more cheaply in Nova Scotia than anywhere else and because Besco would introduce new capital, he even hoped to see the province become an industrial centre of the Empire.[37] To the *Herald* it was "what Nova Scotia had been waiting for," especially after Besco had paid an incorporation fee of $75,215 into provincial coffers. However, Liberal R.H. Graham was worried that almost all the province's coal would be held by one corporation whose directors had greater interests outside Nova Scotia. Shortly few would have anything good to say about Besco.

Two government bills proposed the most ambitious highway programme in the province's history. The brainchildren of the Provincial Highway Board, they proposed to supplement a federal conditional grant by borrowing $2,250,000 to build 900 miles of high quality roads, and a further $8,775,000 to build another 300 miles of the same standard and to prepare 2,800 miles for surfacing, all to be completed in five years. By that time, said Wickwire, the province would have a greater proportion of its roads in good shape than the Americans. Unimpressed, Conservative leader Hall declared that the government, after sleeping on its road policy for thirty-eight years, had "awakened in a panic and was like a drowning man grasping at straws." He warned that it would have to accept full responsibility for a massive increase in the public debt, which after reaching only $8.5 million in 150 years would mount to $20 million almost overnight. Acting Provincial Treasurer Daniels replied that the government was simply signalling a new day in public financing: "an era had been entered upon in which the money would come in freely and without doubt, as easily as day followed after night. It was merely in the ordinary evolution of affairs."[38] In seeming confirmation he reported that revenues had exceeded $3 million for the first time in 1919 and would reach $4 million in 1920, none from increased taxation.

In 1920 universal suffrage for men and women over twenty-one finally became a reality. When Hall complained that the bill was almost identical to his own of the previous year, he was told that the government had waited until the federal authorities had decided that their voters' lists would be compiled from the provincial ones. That explanation led to legitimate Conservative demands for a change in the preparation of lists because of the government's ability to manipulate municipal officials who shared in the process. Difficulties had continued to rise in the sale of liquor for medicinal purposes under prohibition because, as one member put it, the law appeared to be ahead of public sentiment. Once more the government tinkered with existing legislation by setting up a Board of Vendor Commissioners to supervise the legal sale of alcohol. A basic problem was the huge quantity of liquor coming in from the British Isles, St. Pierre, the West Indies, and Quebec. As a result the province asked the federal government to hold a referendum on the importation of alcohol, and on October 25th all areas except Halifax, Dartmouth, and Woodside voted against it. Continuing his efforts of the previous year, J.C. Tory proposed a

Maritime Provinces conference to consider the problems associated with the federal government's transfer of land and resources to the other provinces. By his calculation Nova Scotia was entitled to credits of $8,917,000 for previous transfers and $65 million for contemplated ones. Naturally there were no dissenters.

Not highly antagonistic to the government during this session, the *Herald* pursued a minor crusade of its own by calling for a reform in education, especially in the German examination system, which it called as "little suited to us educationally as would be the Kaiser politically." It was delighted when A.H. MacKay, the superintendent of education, replied in a series of letters. "It is something to have induced our educational authorities to break silence." The *Herald*'s proprietor died early in July and was succeeded by his nephew, William Henry Dennis, a man lacking some of the populist strain of his predecessor.

Murray returned shortly before the session had ended and quickly sized up the political situation. An election had not been expected in 1920, especially because he had let the three previous general assemblies last their full five years. However, before long he had the assembly dissolved for an election late in July. Ostensibly he had four reasons: filling the six vacant seats would require a miniature general election to choose members who would serve for only one year, changes in the franchise had resulted in a largely increased electorate which should be consulted, the returned soldiers should have a chance to express an opinion on their government, and so should all the voters on the massive highway programme. Actually these reasons cloaked the real one, Murray's hope to nip in the bud a potential danger that no other premier before or since has had to face to the same degree.

It began on January 29th when, following the annual meeting of the Nova Scotia Farmers' Association in Kentville, many delegates stayed behind to form a new political party along the lines of the United Farmers of Ontario (UFO) and its counterparts in the west, and agreed to hold an organizational meeting in April. Until then Nova Scotia had seen little agrarian radicalism, even though provincial farmers' organizations had 269 locals with over 10,000 members. Several factors led to this more active behaviour: like other segments of society many of them had become disillusioned with the old-line politicians, inflation had hurt them badly, and for two years bad weather had caused them serious setbacks. The UFO's taking over the government of Ontario in 1919 seemed an auspicious omen.

As for Nova Scotian labour, it had been running candidates sporadically since 1886, almost always with dismal results. For some time it had felt that Murray's contributions to its well-being were mere sops. Recently it had been badly hurt by price increases in basic commodities and the closing of wartime industries, and it was appalled by the iniquities of the Union government, especially by the tactics that had been used in the 1917 election. Later that year it had brought the Independent Labour Party of Cape Breton into being, with J.B. McLachlan as its president.

In April 1920 a convention of the UMW in Truro was followed by the establishment of the Independent Labour Party (ILP) of Nova Scotia. Hoping to join the farmers for political action, it sent representatives to their convention, which was also meeting in Truro to organize the United Farmers of Nova Scotia. J.J. Morrison, secretary of the UFO, told the delegates that a farmers' government in Ontario would have been impossible without labour support; nevertheless, the farmers were hostile after learning that the labour convention had agreed to the eight-hour day. Arguing that their vocation made it impracticable, they rejected it with only seven or eight opposed. The Labourites were indignant: "You have killed your chances. . . . [We] came with a proposal for co-operation and joint action and before [we] had a chance to talk we were told to work longer hours."[39] The economic downturn had not been such as to attract much attention during the 1920 legislative session, but it may not be attributing too much to Murray's prescience that he foresaw rapid economic deterioration that would make an election in 1921 inauspicious for his party. Knowing the fate of old party governments in Ontario and Manitoba, he at least realized the need to move before labour and the farmers became fully organized for political action.

Murray's manifesto stressed, above all, his concern for the disaffected groups: the farmers "never made any request . . .

which has not received a generous support"; workers were enjoying the benefits of a generous compensation act, a complete system of technical education, and a great variety of social legislation. From the outset the Liberals used the premier as their chief weapon to win one last election. Because he would be travelling little, the *Chronicle* sent Horatio C. Crowell to Cape Breton to interview "the most widely and highly respected man" in the province, who "delights never so much as in talking Nova Scotia to Nova Scotians."[40] When Murray said once again that "on all the great Provincial questions in the last thirty years the Liberal Party has been right," his followers had a theme which they emphasized unceasingly.

At first the *Chronicle* thought that the Conservatives were the chief enemy, but it quickly changed its mind. For that party, so optimistic before the election of 1916, was in a pitiful state. Its principal cross to bear was a discredited Union government at Ottawa, whose sins the electorate placed largely on the Conservatives' shoulders. Surprised by the sudden dissolution, Hall was late in getting out his manifesto. A document in the Tanner mould, one of criticism and not of positive proposals, it condemned government for impeding the province's progress for thirty-eight years and putting its "own safety before the interests of the people to get a favourable snap verdict." Hall especially scorned the Liberals' watchword: "Don't drop the old Pilot." Should the public not be told that Murray had seldom been in the legislature for two years, that he continued only because his party did not wish to serve under his lieutenants, something quite understandable now that the Longleys, the Pipes, and the Drysdales had given way to the Daniels, the Armstrongs, and the Wickwires? As the campaign progressed, the Conservative position worsened. In some counties they could get no candidates; in others the candidates first nominated withdrew; in one county their convention had to leave nominations to the executive; in Pictou only Dr. John Bell, son of former leader A.C. Bell, would run and his party had no choice but to support a Farmer and a Labourite. It ended up by contesting only thirty-one of the forty-three seats.

The United Farmers had no provincial organization as such and left it to the county farm organizations to decide if candidates were to be run. Having no manifesto of their own, their candidates advocated the programme of the Canadian Council of Agriculture. The ILP manifesto outlined a leftist policy, especially on prices and housing; supported the initiative and referendum; and advocated fairer taxation, including much heavier levies on the affluent and taxes on land values rather than land. Despite earlier differences the parties did not oppose each other except in Hants where two Farmers and a Labourite ran against a Liberal and a Conservative. In four counties with fifteen seats — Halifax, Cape Breton, Cumberland, and Pictou — they presented joint slates. If J.A. Dillon in Guysborough is regarded as a Farmer, they numbered twelve Labourites and sixteen Farmers. Of the latter the majority had been Conservatives.

Seeing that the new parties were the chief enemy, the *Chronicle* devoted much of its editorial space to a condemnation of class politics. Neither the workmen nor the farmers, it said, had "any conceivable legitimate interest apart from those of the whole community." For them to set up separate political organizations was to "declare open political war on their fellow citizens." If they were successful, the assembly would contain small groups "not responsible to the people at large but only to those of their own narrow constituencies."[41]

From the outset the *Herald* conceded that the Conservatives could not win, but held out bright prospects for a government composed of Conservatives, Labour, Farmers, and Veterans of the World War.[42] Although it did not support the Conservatives as such, it delighted in singling out individual Conservatives like Grace McLeod Rogers as evidence that "we are at last breaking away from the Old Order."[43] It also cautioned the ILP to drop its impractical proposals and its resort to prejudice, passion, and class and to appeal to the great body of independent, reasonable voters "who are no longer enamored with old party shibboleths."[44] The *Herald's* first full-time cartoonist, Donald McRitchie, reinforced his party's general theme with cartoons depicting a contest between the "Government" and the "Opposition." One portrayed a "new Swimming Hole" entitled "Farmer-Labour government" from which Ontario and Manitoba extended an invitation to Nova Scotia: "Come in Bluenose: The Water's Fine."[45] This was anathema to the *Chronicle*, which accused the Conservatives of selling their birthright for a mess of pottage. It was confident, however, that the voters would reject Hall who, if victorious, would have to perform the circus role of a "bare-back rider of four, mutually hostile, unbroken and untried group steeds" labelled "Farmer", "Labour", "Veteran" and "Conservative."[46] Although it did not go to extremes in condemning the ILP, some county newspapers and especially their letter-writers went altogether beyond reason. In the *Pictou Advocate,* one writer alleged that the Farmer-Labour candidates "consciously or unconsciously preach the same doctrines as Lenin and Trotsky in Russia," and another referred to "this Bolshevist scheme to wreck our institutions under the guise of Farmers or Labour candidates."[47]

For the Conservatives the election was an utter disaster. Their popular vote fell from 48.8 to 23.3 per cent and they won only three seats, two in Richmond and one in Yarmouth, where Howard Corning defeated Armstrong. But Corning, though regarded as a Conservative, actually ran as a people's candidate. Hall, who lost his own seat, declared that "the reason is difficult to seek" why the people were satisfied with Murray. The Liberals, surprised by the "evident annihilation" of the Conservatives, depicted them as "not merely sleeping, but absolutely moribund."

Seven Farmers and four Labourites were successful — four in Cape Breton County, three in Cumberland, two in Colchester, and one each in Antigonish and Hants. They won ten of the twenty-two seats in eastern Nova Scotia, but only one of twenty-one in the western part. It was by far the greatest success that a third party grouping has ever had in Nova Scotia. Disillusionment with the old parties, the utter collapse of the Conservatives, and economic difficulties of varying kinds worked together as they have on no other occasion to produce the result.

The Liberals were fortunate to escape with only a minor setback. Their popular vote fell by 6 per cent to 44.4, and Armstrong and Ralston suffered defeat, but the party won twenty-nine seats, a loss of only one. George Murray had analyzed the situation correctly and struck at the right time. McRitchie summed it up neatly in a cartoon entitled "My Boy, My Boy!" It showed "Ma" Murray continuing to hold Nova Scotia comfortably in her lap.[48]

CHAPTER 4

Armstrong and the Liberal Débacle

The 1920 election was Murray's last triumph. His final twenty-nine months as premier would bring little but annoyance and frustration. Murray's troubles began in September 1920 when his earlier attempt to take highways out of politics through a bipartisan Provincial Highway Board backfired. A Conservative member of the board, Percy C. Black, alleged that contracts were being let without its approval; that the Department of Highways and its minister, H.H. Wickwire, were trying to make the board a rubber stamp; and that the cost of constructing eighteen miles on the St. Margaret's Bay road, estimated at $211,000, would reach $650,000. Eventually a royal commission found neither the minister nor the board as a whole at fault and attributed the delinquencies to the board's former chairman and its assistant chief engineer. The upshot was that A.S. MacMillan became chairman of a smaller, no longer bipartisan board.

In the assembly Wickwire put on a show for Liberal assemblymen by deriding former Conservatives on the board. However, this was too much even for Liberals like James A. Fraser, the veteran editor of the *Eastern Chronicle*. "The somewhat truculent tongued Minister of Highways," he said, had served Black and his friends "up hot on toast with tobasco [sic] sauce," but the fact remained that "money was wasted like water" on the roads and the government made no effort to punish the swindlers.[1]

In 1921 the ailing Murray appeared in the house only to be sworn in, and then left for a sanitorium in Battle Creek,

Michigan. His substitute, Armstrong, faced an assembly unlike any other in provincial history. Interestingly, it included three members with nearly the same name from three different parties: Dr. John Alexander Macdonald, Conservative from Richmond; John Alexander MacDonald, Farmer from Hants; and John Alexander McDonald, Liberal from Kings. What was altogether astounding, however, was that a non-traditional party had become the official opposition. Even the Conservatives seemed anxious to disguise themselves — Corning and his two colleagues called themselves the People's Party. Though six members of the official opposition regarded themselves as Farmers, four regarded themselves as Labourites, and A.R. Richardson saw himself as Farmer-Labour, all acted harmoniously this year under the leadership of Farmer D.G. McKenzie, and Corning's group usually supported them.

However, when the Farmer-Labourites contended that the group system would replace the two-party system, the *Echo* declared it incompatible with the "traditions of British responsible government," and Armstrong talked of the destabilizing influence of class groups whose assemblymen were mere delegates but not true representatives. When their whip, Forman Waye, "likened himself and the Labour party to the dying Nazarene," Liberal William Chisholm accused him of blasphemy.[2] The *Chronicle* became increasingly irritated by the Labourites' failure to realize that "the Provincial Assembly is not a meeting of Union delegates, which can proceed by resolution without regard to antecedents or consequences, but a highly important law-making body."[3]

The frustration of the *Chronicle* was small compared with that of the Labourites themselves. Waye was bitter about the lack of response to his demands for the relief of the unemployed and Steele was outraged at the government's refusal of an inquiry into old age pensions, and health and unemployment insurance, on the ground that the principles at issue were for federal consideration. The entire opposition rejected the opinion of insurance executive J.C. Tory that further impositions like the eight-hour day in specific occupations and increased workmen's compensation benefits would endanger industry. Steele was so frustrated that he came close to defying the speaker. However, the *Echo* deplored the "time-worn"

George H. Murray   1896-1923

Courtesy of Public Archives of Nova Scotia

references to the "poor laborer" and the "underdog working-men," and Armstrong called the new opposition "reckless and unreliable" and "far more troublesome in the columns of the Halifax Herald than . . . on the floors of the House."[4]

This year the bill to complete the Besco organization drew strong opposition despite Armstrong's pleas not to alarm capital. With Besco particularly in mind, R.E. Finn castigated the representatives of large corporate interests who lobbied legislators "on the streets, in hotels and even in the province building itself," while a front-page cartoon in the *Herald* showed two cooks representing "big interests" plucking a turkey and saying, "It's a Cinch" and "This is the Easiest Bird to Pluck I ever saw."[5] More explicitly, the persistent Finn, worried about stock manipulation and watered stock, feared that the directors of Besco, who held shares in unsuccessful companies, might manipulate them in a manner that would harm the Nova Scotia coal industry. In the end he got only limited ameliorative action for the ills of which he complained.

In several ways the session of 1921 provided a foretaste of what might happen under Armstrong's leadership. He first demonstrated his weakness when he failed to stop the passage of the Jane E. McNeil bill, which vested in one person property which, according to the Supreme Court of Canada, belonged to another. Eventually the governor general in council disallowed the bill. Armstrong's leadership was also suspect on the question of assemblymen's indemnities. No opposition arose on a proposal to increase the salaries of ministers with portfolio from $5,000 to $6,000. But the *Herald* denounced a resolution raising members' indemnities from $700 to $1,500 as a "grab" and continued its opposition so vociferously that one assemblyman called it a "dirty, rotten . . . press with red headlines." Although the resolution passed, the government did not proceed with a bill, allegedly because of a threat from the legislative council to go on strike unless its members got a similar increase, a charge which its president, Jason Mack, denied. Nevertheless, the assemblymen got the larger indemnities.

The manner of running the ICR, soon to be a basic part of the Maritime Rights agitation, emerged as an issue in 1921. For some time non-Maritimers, unaware of the regional considerations implicit in its construction, had been criticizing its allegedly privileged position. When, in 1919, railway integration meant that the ICR would no longer be a separate unit, Maritimers began to have fears, and in 1921, after large increases in rates on the line, some charged that they were being denied access to the rest of Canada. The Nova Scotia assembly resolved unanimously that "faithful observance of the terms and conditions of the compact of confederation and a generous

National spirit'' demanded that the primary purpose in building the ICR should be fully recognized.[6]

Late 1921 brought a federal general election under new leadership. Ailing Sir Robert Borden had given way to Arthur Meighen in July 1920 and his party contested the election as the National Liberal and Conservative party, a name he disliked. Following a national convention in August 1919, William Lyon Mackenzie King had succeeded Laurier as Liberal leader, but he probably would not have beaten Fielding had the latter remained a Laurier Liberal in 1917. King was also lucky that Murray and Fielding had handled the conscription issue as they did because practically all the old Nova Scotia Liberals were back within the party camp. Like the other provinces, Nova Scotia would have a three-party contest. After resigning from the Union government largely on the tariff issue in 1920, Thomas A. Crerar had joined ten other Farmer MPs to establish the National Progressive Party, which contested ten of Nova Scotia's sixteen seats.

In Meighen's tour of the province in October he spoke on twenty-seven occasions in eleven constituencies in six days. However, it was at a time when interest in politics took second place to the schooner races off Halifax, in which the newly launched *Bluenose* first defeated its Nova Scotia rivals and later Gloucester's *Elsie* in an international contest.

Meighen put his objective simply: "If I can but get the people in this country to see that the issue is Protection or no Protection, the battle will be won." In contrast, King emphasized the government's faults by the score, especially its responsibility for depression and unemployment. Avoiding a specific commitment, he advocated a "tariff for revenue only," causing Meighen to say that it was "just the circular pomposity of a man who didn't say what he means." The *Chronicle* lacked the vigour of the *Herald*, which called Crerar "the new Menace confronting Canada," and King a wriggling, twisting, dodging man, prone to give nauseating Sunday-school addresses. McRitchie's cartoons took special aim at King's imprecision on the tariff — one displayed a ketchup bottle labelled "57 Varieties: King's Policy Pickles: Made to Suit all Tastes.''[7]

Maritime and Nova Scotia issues as such played only a minor part in the campaign. In King's presence, at Amherst, Liberal candidate Hance J. Logan advocated a national coal policy and regional management of the ICR. "Maritime Rights," he continued, "must be our motto. . . . I pledge myself to . . . stand by Maritime Rights first, last and all the time." Later he revealed that he had planned to run as a Maritime Rights candidate, but that King's assurances relating to the ICR had made him change his mind. In his diary, however, King recorded indignantly that he had "made no promise to anyone to induce him to run."[8] Under pressure from Dennis and the *Herald*, Meighen promised a regional division of the CNR at Moncton.

Maritime issues likewise played no meaningful part in the outcome. Like Canadians generally, Nova Scotians voted to rid themselves of a thoroughly discredited government, and it was 1904 all over again — "a solid Liberal sixteen." The Conservatives polled only 32.3 per cent of the vote, failed to contest two Cape Breton seats and, except in Hants and Colchester, lost by abnormally large majorities. The Progressives were limited to 12.3 per cent of the vote, and only three of their candidates ran strongly. The youthful Isaac D. MacDougall, later a Conservative, lost by only 522 votes in Inverness, and two other candidates, one of them J.B. McLachlan, outpolled the Conservatives in the dual riding of Cape Breton South and Richmond. In the provincial election many voters had seen the third party as an attractive alternative to the old parties, but in the federal they sought the party most likely to defeat the Conservatives. Although the *Herald* was right that the "powerful organization of the Provincial Government," built up over many years, had extended its influence into every nook and cranny of the province, it was wrong in giving it the primary credit for the massive victory.[9]

By 1922 economic conditions had deteriorated badly. Because of a reduced demand and lower price for coal, Besco sought to reduce miners' wages from $3.80 to $2.44 a day, less, said J.B. McLachlan, than what a convict would get. Late in January miners overwhelmed the police and looted the company's stores. A few days later they rejected out of hand the report of the Gillen conciliation board which recommended a cut in wages by about one-third. In mid-March McLachlan issued a sabotage manifesto beginning: "Brothers: The war is on, a class

war . . . and it is up to the workers in the mines . . . to carry
that war into the country of the enemy."[10] Despite objections
from the UMW executive, he advocated a form of strike on the
job. In effect, he had made himself the leader of the province's
miners.

That was the situation the assembly faced in 1922. The
previous year, anticipating Murray's retirement, the legislature
had unanimously expressed its appreciation of his "lengthy,
untiring and unselfish public service" and had agreed upon an
annuity of $5,000 when he returned to private life. That had led
the *Herald* to conjecture about his successor. Armstrong, it
thought, had forfeited his chances. In itself the failure of two
government bills in committee indicated that his party had little
confidence in him. Hence, if Murray's successor were to be
found among the sitting members, it would have to be J.C. Tory
or R.M. McGregor; outside the house A.K. Maclean was a
possibility; but he had the disability of having been a Unionist
Liberal.[11]

Murray was still premier in 1922, only to face the most
uncongenial circumstances of his political life. Early in the
session, hundreds without employment "literally invaded
[Province House], packed the galleries, and carried out
tumultuous demonstrations. . . . [They] cheered and clapped
and stamped on their feet, at will, greeting every reference to
unemployment with demonstrative outbreaks."[12] For the first
time Murray was booed and treated with derision. Armstrong
continued his vendetta against the Labourites by alleging
communist stances in their advocacy of the cancellation of coal
leases and the eradication of capital. The Farmer-Labour group
responded with an attack on a basic practice of parliamentary
government by proposing that the defeat of a cabinet proposal
would not require its resignation unless it was followed by a
successful vote of non-confidence. Their leader, McKenzie, who
regarded "many ancient parliamentary usages as a museum
where one saw all the old style dresses worn years ago," wanted
a situation where "party could not be used as a club as it is
today."[13] He lost only by 14 to 13.

Taggart of the Farmers pressed for abolition of the legislative
council through payment of members' indemnities on a
diminishing basis over four years. The premier pointed out that

he had pledged all the councillors to abolition except the aging Conservative W.H. Owen, but that he had let "sleeping dogs" lie in the absence of public pressure on the question. That led Farmer Robert Smith to interject that Murray had also turned his coat in 1917, and led to one of the few circumstances in which the premier publicly showed personal pique. If it was "turning his coat" to abandon partisanship in time of war, "he had no apologies to offer," but he thought it unfitting that "such references . . . should continue to be made."[14] It was another instance of the disrespect now being shown for one who seldom before had been its victim. Though an assembly committee conferred with one from the council on abolition, no agreement was forthcoming.

Much more than the Farmers, the Labour members were interested in practical matters, rather than in parliamentary and constitutional practice. Waye wanted pressure put on Besco to give the miners a decent standard of living; Terris advocated a system of unemployment insurance; Morrison sought an eight-hour day for miners only to be told by Murray that it would require federal legislation. If it had been within provincial purview, "you will find here just as sympathetic minds and hearts as you will find on the American continent."[15] A bitter Morrison replied that the miners had expected bread and got a stone.

The government's programme in 1922 was slight, but it did change the rules of the road. Since most North American jurisdictions were enacting "drive to the right" legislation, Wickwire thought it desirable to make the change before traffic became heavier, but Liberal J.J. Kinley of Lunenburg called it a "cheap beef bill." He feared that the oxen used widely in his county could not be taught to observe the new rules and would have to be slaughtered. His position caused merriment in the assembly and the press. "India may no longer boast exclusively of the Sacred Ox. Lunenburg County evidently holds that bovine beast of burden in as holy regard as the pagan priests of the Orient."[16]

In his budget minister without portfolio J.C. Tory forecast that revenues would exceed $5 million for the first time. Agreeing with Roger Babson that a world staggering under a load of debt was trying to "start off in high gear," he urged

Nova Scotians to "get back in low gear" and urged assembly-men who made demands to remember that "we must measure our power to do things by the wealth of our people." Perhaps this was the reason for the lowering of members' indemnities to $1,000 after the inordinate increase to $1,500 the previous year. Such a reduction, boasted the *Echo*, had never before been made by any parliament. It was the first time too that indemnities in Nova Scotia were put on a fixed, statutory basis.

As the session closed, the Farmer-Labourite and Conservative members met in secret conclave, hoping to effect a combination to beat the Murray government. All were present except Richardson and MacGillivray, who were regarded as "Cinderel-las" altogether tainted with Liberalism. Forman Waye went to see what it was all about but concluded, "I am not prepared to die yet, and I know d — well what will happen if I tie up with the Tory party."[17] Nothing came of the meeting, but the Conservatives, bent on a complete reorganization, met at Truro late in June, assumed their old name, and chose Hall as their leader over Corning. Hall went out of his way to declare that the "carrying out of the party's principles" in the assembly was "absolutely safe . . . in the hands of Mr. Corning" and the latter conveniently forgot all about the People's Party. The *Herald* exulted in these events as it did in the appointment of MacCallum Grant to a second term as lieutenant-governor even though his politics were not those of the government at Ottawa. Grant, in fact, rivalled Sir James Kempt of a century earlier in being the most popular occupant of Government House, "a born governor" who had not "hedged himself about by cold formalities" or "forgotten to be human."

Against the advice of its leaders, including John L. Lewis, UMW District 26 went on strike in mid-August. When the government sent troops to Sydney to prevent the mines from being allowed to fill with water, the miners showed their deep resentment against the use of a military force by stoning the troop train at Sydney. A short time later they accepted a six-month agreement somewhat better for them than the Gillen award. During these proceedings Armstrong adopted a hard line, especially against anything that might give moral assistance to McLachlan. "If it were possible to dethrone him and his lieutenants . . . it would be a good day's work."[18] He could hardly have been pleased when the UMW appointed McLachlan as a delegate to the Red Internationale in Moscow.

Meanwhile rumblings beneath the surface of the Liberal party centred on a reconstruction of the government. In June 1921 G. Fred Pearson, associated with the *Chronicle* and long a mastermind of the Liberal party, pointed out to Fielding that Murray had experienced two serious illnesses resulting from blood clotting and might suffer a third unless he had rest and quiet. Since he could not run another election, would it not be well to have his successor quickly in place to give him time to win the party's confidence, mold his policy, and prepare for an appeal to the public?[19] Speaker Robert Irwin, Armstrong's fellow member for Shelburne, was much less solicitous. Starting early in 1922, he kept repeating that no meaningful activity could take place in Halifax "as long as the middle name of the Premier is Procrastination." In November he wondered if Murray could be "precipitated by any course of events" and urged his friend Armstrong to press his claim either for the premiership or the vacancy on the Supreme Court. Totally frustrated, he wrote on December 11th that the government could not "go on drifting towards a leeshore without making an effort" to turn about.[20] That same day someone, possibly Pearson or Irwin and more likely the latter, confided his fears to J.C. Tory in Montreal after first pointing out that the Conservatives, in girding their loins for battle, had appointed Joseph Hayes as organizer and that ambitious young Tories were "striving to snatch a bubble reputation at the cannon's mouth." Nonetheless, the government might still recover. He had been urging Murray's resignation for two years and the premier was now anxious and entitled to retire.

Although he believed that Armstrong deserved well of the party, some assemblymen thought that he lacked the essential qualities of a leader. Hence the best course would be to have Fielding arrange his appointment to the Supreme Court. Then Tory as premier, with an "all star cast of ministers," could make Nova Scotia "safe for democracy, meaning the grits."

Forsake the service of Mammon and come over and help us. Give up making the Sun [i.e., Sun Life] shine in Montreal and help to make the sun shine brighter in Nova Scotia where the rays first touch <u>God's</u> country. You can do it. You must do it and you will do it, won't you?[21]

Writing to Prime Minister King on December 22nd, Armstrong made it clear that if the choice was between the premiership and a judgeship he would be "obliged to choose the latter."[22] Meanwhile, procrastinator or not, Murray had no choice but to repair a riddled ministry. To replace Wickwire, who had died in November, William Chisholm of Antigonish became minister of highways, and to replace Daniels, who had retired, W.J. O'Hearn of Halifax took over as attorney general. However, as the premier intimated to Tory on January 4, 1923, the big moves were still to come and Tory might be one of the actors. Personally Murray wanted Armstrong to have the judgeship after the session if the federal government would wait that long. He soon discovered that it would not.

Beginning on Thursday, January 18th, the events constitute high drama. In Halifax Fielding and Murray made plans based on the supposition that Tory would accept the premiership but, on his way back to Ottawa, Fielding discovered that "our Montreal friend cannot make any move at present." Writing to Murray, Tory hoped that some way might be found to let Armstrong get the judgeship, although he remained "still as perplexed as ever about the matter." In three separate communications Fielding told Murray that Minister of Justice Sir Lomer Gouin wanted an early recommendation for the judgeship, the deadline for which was eventually set for early Tuesday, January 23rd.[23] Meanwhile Armstrong had gone to Montreal and again drawn a refusal from Tory. Instructed to see Murray when he returned on the Ocean Limited on January 22nd, Armstrong discovered that he himself was to be premier. Obviously Murray did not relish facing another session of the assembly, and he was fortunate that Armstrong would forgo the judgeship out of loyalty to him and the party. Later that day Murray received a telegram from Tory agreeing to be his successor.[24] Only by a few hours had Tory missed having his name added to the list of Nova Scotia's premiers. However, the near-term sequel would be much more favourable to him than to Armstrong.

George Murray served twenty-six years, six months, and four days as premier, a time still unequalled in the annals of British parliamentary government. Professor Ernest Forbes has stated that the present author's book, *Government of Nova Scotia*, is "tinged with a barely suppressed indignation" at the conservatism of the province's leaders, especially in the "omnipresent caution" I have attached to the Murray régime. He also suspects an "element of social criticism" in my "ringing indictments" of these alleged failings.[25] No one else has ever accused me of "barely suppressed indignation" or "ringing indictments" in my writing and, whatever my other faults, I plead not guilty in this instance. Opinion in Murray's own time was much the same as mine, and after a detailed review I would not alter my conclusions one whit.

From Fielding, Murray had inherited a party and a government that were essentially sound. He had also inherited a burgeoning coal industry that in turn had made possible a substantial steel industry. Together they had ensured the financial returns that for a dozen years had permitted him to provide more than adequate returns without resort to direct taxation. In this limited period even the National Policy had proved to be highly advantageous. The development of an advanced system of technical education might suggest that Murray was less conservative than he has been made out to be. However, at a time when the expanding coal and steel industries required highly trained personnel, this was the natural thing to do and reveals little about his ideological bent. The history contained in the preceding chapters confirms his conservative approach in everything from workmen's compensation to women's suffrage. "To bills of a radical character, he invariably put his unfailing test. Has it been tried elsewhere and with what success?"[26] His conservative approach to government is also seen in the host of boards, commissions, and the like set up to remove responsibility from the political executive.

Because Murray's conservatism fitted in well with the political culture of the time, he had enormous political success until the end of the First World War. The postwar period was uncongenial to him, but the tendency of Nova Scotians to support a politician whom they have learned to trust helped him win in 1920. Also assisting him were his personal attributes. Even those who disagreed with him, wrote the *Eastern Chronicle*, "came from his presence with the utmost respect for the man. There was nothing petty about [him]." The *Herald* declared him the embodiment of affability; under him "the rancors of partizanship . . . always somehow seemed foreign to the official quarters of the Premier and the Province building." In contrast, his successor seemed unlikely to "catch flies with vinegar."[27]

Armstrong retained his responsibilities as minister of public works and mines, and Chisholm and O'Hearn kept their portfolios. Legislative Councillor D.A. Cameron became provincial secretary and would seek election for Murray's old seat in Victoria. Too late, Pictonian R.M. McGregor, who probably could have become premier had he wished, advised Armstrong to make the able A.S. MacMillan the minister of highways. However, the latter remained as chairman of the Provincial Highway Board, somewhat reluctantly, because his personal interests were suffering.

Though Armstrong wanted his government at all costs to present a good face to the public, he began with problems which lasted throughout his premiership. At the outset he found the intemperate Chisholm absent, drowning his sorrows over the loss of Murray and celebrating the advent of a new premier. He had hoped to have Tory present when the session opened, but it was not to be. Irwin feared that he might be "peeved . . . through his failure to overcome that well known principle of Natural Philosophy which forbids any one body to occupy two different places at the same time." Rightly or not, Tory insisted that he needed to discuss company matters with men from London, but he did provide advice which seemed sound, to get through the session with "as little new matter as possible" and reserve "the best things until the year before you go to the country."[28]

To the assembly Armstrong presented an optimistic face, pointing to peace in the coal industry and prophesying the end of the depression; in contrast, McKenzie found "Change and Decay in all around I see." As usual, Armstrong had collected a mass of statistics to make his points, but his humourless and unconciliatory presentation did nothing to satisfy the opposition. In their turn, Liberal members attacked Forman Waye for having said that the only way to bring the Dominion Iron and Steel Company (part of Besco) to its knees was to "make them see that you don't give a damn for the property, that you intend to destroy it."[29]

In some respects the government looked good. It showed a surplus of $23,535 for 1922 and forecast one of $7,453 for 1923. However, as Corning pointed out, this surplus was made possible only by a profit of $350,000 of the Board of Vendor Commissioners in a time of prohibition — "Pretty good business that." Noteworthy were the initiatives of Attorney General O'Hearn. He was personally conducting the prosecutions in major criminal cases and, because the province appeared to have an excessive number of judges compared with Britain and Massachusetts, he proposed to reorganize the superior and county courts. Nothing, however, would come of it.

In other areas the government looked bad. Chisholm and D.A. Cameron attacked O'Hearn's bill to amend the Costs and Fees Act and drew the stern comment from the *Herald* that "'one for all, and all for one' is the very fundamental for government in all British countries." Chisholm suffered a similar rebuke when, to Corning's charges that the province had been "bled white" by contractors' wrongdoings on the St. Margaret's Bay and Port Joli roads, he made a frivolous reply. Armstrong had to admit the failure of his efforts to have the legislative council abolished, after that body declared its existence necessary in the circumstances of the day. Sheepishly the government confessed that it had asked to have its "drive to the right" bills disallowed after discovering that the effective date of implementation differed in the two bills. Although it righted the fault in 1923, the council, as the body supposed to detect errors of this kind, was made to look thoroughly incompetent.

The most memorable event of the session was Corning's "secession" resolution. After complaining of Nova Scotia's ill treatment in freight rates and the administration of the ICR, the indifference of Quebec and Ontario towards Nova Scotia's ports, the inequity of the tariff, and the failure of the province to develop under Confederation, he called for a referendum on the question of leaving Canada. Pressed to state his own opinion, he finally admitted that he was "for repeal." That led the Liberals to ask: Who inaugurated National Policy? How could this resolution come from a member of a "highly patriotic flag-waving party"?[30] In the assembly only the two other Conservatives supported Corning. Outside the house his party was markedly silent.

Labour provided the government's major opposition. Meeting with the cabinet, the UMW executive asked for minimum wage and eight-hour-day legislation. In Sydney the steelworkers pressed for similar measures and for a closed shop, all of which Besco summarily rejected. Decrying the presence of a "Red" element that "believed in revolution and [was] opposed to the British system of government," A.R. Richardson defected from the Farmer-Labour group. A bitter miners' meeting told him to resign his seat or take his place "among the rest of the flunkeys of Besco."[31] Liberal assemblymen professed horror at the "Red documents" being circulated in Cape Breton, and on April 11th the *Herald* devoted a page to publicizing them, indicating that their genesis lay in deplorable economic conditions: "This is not Soviet Russia. It is Nova Scotia. . . . The bayonet makes a poor coal-pick. . . . Lenine is not premier of Nova Scotia — yet. . . . Premier Armstrong, don't you think it time to clean up this impossible situation?"

Assemblyman D.W. Morrison likewise attributed the extremism to the evils generated by Besco, a corporation which had not introduced new capital and had made it necessary for the coal industry to support the steel industry. Although the miners had finally got the eight-hour day written into their contract, Waye wanted it fixed by statute. When the government refused, he accused it of bowing to Besco. After the session Armstrong's labour problems multiplied. Late in June 2,700 steelworkers struck for a wage increase and a closed shop, and within days rioters broke into the steel plant and did considerable damage. When 600 soldiers were sent to Sydney the disorder worsened. Early in July 8,000 miners struck in sympathy. Three days later J.B. McLachlan and "Red" Dan Livingstone were sent to Halifax to be tried for seditious libel. Not until John L. Lewis revoked the charter of UMW District 26 did the force go out of the strike.

Both Armstrong and Prime Minister King worried about the repercussions, political and otherwise. King feared that, without a thorough investigation, a like situation might occur at any time. Armstrong agreed to make it a joint undertaking but, quite out of touch with reality, perceived no fundamental grievance to account for the violence. A defender of Besco, he found highly perturbing the propaganda against the company and his government. Fearing that the premier would want to treat McLachlan too harshly, R.M. McGregor told him to pursue a middle course and not make the man a martyr. Two years would be right and would constitute a "salutary lesson to the Reds,"[32] and that turned out to be the sentence. However, civil libertarians, then and since, have excoriated the trial for its alleged unfairness.

Worried about the state of the party, Armstrong proposed to Fielding, since 1921 Minister of Finance again, a series of joint political meetings. The aged and ailing Fielding was not enthusiastic: "It is too much like work," and "if these meetings are held at the early stage of [the] game [i.e., too far ahead of an election] they are forgotten." Fielding had also refused to acknowledge any basis for Maritime complaints, and the King government had shown little sympathy for Maritime demands, whether related to compensation for western lands, the directing of ocean trade through Maritime ports, genuine decentralization of the ICR, or freight rates. An "imbalance of regional forces at the federal level," the more so because of King's determination to win back the seats taken by the Progressives in 1921, tended to nullify the Maritimes' bargaining power at Ottawa.

This was a vital factor in 1923 in the blossoming of Maritime demands for recognition and ameliorative treatment of the region's problems. Boards of trade, regional clubs, community associations, municipal councils, and like organizations acted strongly to promote these ends. Foremost as a publicist was a former teacher and journalist from Dartmouth, H.S. Congdon. Whether the activities of many disparate groups, united neither in strategy nor specific goals, could be called a "movement" is a matter of definition, but certainly these groups agitated for Maritime Rights with a vigour unequalled before or since. Professor Ernest Forbes, an authority on the subject, suggests that although "the postwar recession did not cause the Maritime Rights movement . . . it did profoundly affect its development."[33] Certainly, if the postwar depression had not been so deep and so prolonged the agitations of Nova Scotians would not have assumed the proportions they did. Indeed the recovery was more than slow, and the province would never regain its former position. The National Policy, which had facilitated the rise of the coal and steel industry, would be much less beneficial to the region under conditions in which those industries had lost their competitive position.

The attitude of the Liberal government at Ottawa prevented the provincial party from putting on the mantle of Maritime Rights. That enabled the Conservatives to take over the agitation, lock, stock and barrel, and during the next three or four years the *Herald* pressed its salient points with almost tunnel vision. It was the newspaper's barrage of propaganda in a Halifax by-election in December 1923 that helped to break the "solid sixteen" Liberals at Ottawa and elect seventy-six-year-old W.A. Black. An even more surprising Conservative victory in Kent, New Brunswick, three weeks later reflected the new mood in the Maritimes.

The coal industry, not Maritime Rights *per se*, overshadowed everything else in the 1924 legislative session. J.C. Tory was too busy taking over the New York Life business in Cuba to be at the opening, but he wrote consolingly: "I do not anticipate any difficulty." He was partly right, for after a coal strike of less than a month, Besco capitulated by not insisting on a massive wage reduction. However, though the speech from the throne was almost flamboyant in its optimism and promised an eight-hour day for miners by statute, Besco continued to raise its ugly head. McKenzie wondered what force was delaying the coal investigation. "Is the British Empire Steel Corporation the real government of Nova Scotia and this [assembly] only an auxiliary?" Wisely Armstrong sought to distance himself from Besco. The government, he declared, had not created it but had simply asked the legislature to deal with the transfer of shares. He also warned McKenzie not to dig too deeply lest he "hurt some individuals closer to his own party than he thinks."[34]

Forman Waye drew applause from workingmen in the gallery when he moved to revoke Besco's charter and revest ownership in its constituent companies. He evoked a similar response when he condemned O'Hearn for his "unjust vindictiveness" towards McLachlan. The attorney general replied that, because of McLachlan, Sydney had been "in the hands of a mob" and that not even McLachlan's lawyers had denied that he was guilty of seditious libel. Much as the government wanted it, Besco simply would not leave the scene. Though the assembly passed Richardson's resolution calling for an increase in the duty on American slack coal, it was not before the government had been accused of being too "close" to the corporation, charges that McGregor and Cameron angrily denied. In March, after most miners had rejected a proposed wage pact, McLachlan — recently released from Dorchester penitentiary on ticket of leave and greeted as a hero in Cape Breton — denounced the UMW executive for conspiring with Besco to have the pact accepted. Besco made its final appearance of the session when the miners' hours of work bill was returned from committee with an amendment which required eight hours of work from "coal face to coal face" rather than from "bank to bank." Apparently Besco's representatives had argued that the original provision would so increase costs as to prevent coal mining in Nova Scotia. A bitter Waye called the bill a "gigantic bluff," which left the miners no better off than before.

After the *Herald* learned that revenues had exceeded $5 million in 1923 and would rise by $400,000 in 1924, it wondered if "professions of 'retrenchment' and 'economy' [were] worth the paper they were written on." However, in this instance at least the government had ready answers. The expenditures were rising because federal conditional grants for highways and agriculture were coming to an end; taxation was light and Nova Scotia had neither income taxes as in Ontario and Manitoba nor land taxes as in other provinces; and the funded debt, except for Prince Edward Island, was the lowest in Canada. Was it not absurd in any case for the opposition to call for retrenchment when it was demanding new and separate departments of agriculture, health, labour, and education?

Once again the cabinet displayed serious splits within itself. J.J. Kinley saw nothing wrong in introducing a resolution on finance seemingly critical of a government in which he was a minister without portfolio. This led a thoroughly annoyed McGregor to tell the premier that no minister should present resolutions that "have not been properly before the government." Not taken aback, Kinley went even further by proposing the three months' hoist to O'Hearn's bill to abolish grand juries on the ground that it might increase the power of the Crown and work injustice. This time the *Herald* wondered if the government understood the principle of "collective cabinet responsibility." If Kinley wished to oppose the cabinet's measures, he should resign from the ministry forthwith.[35] As general secretary of the Social Service Council, H.R. Grant complained that the Temperance Act lacked the machinery to deal with an increasing sale of liquor by bootleggers and dive keepers, and even more vigorously that the Board of Vendor Commissioners was permitting sales by druggists and others not in accord with the spirit of the act. Though the assembly appeared to satisfy him with its amendments, he was highly displeased when the legislative council rejected a proposal to put the temperance inspector in chief in the attorney general's department.

Drama abounded and the assembly resounded with high-flown oratory on a bill relating to the establishment of the United Church of Canada. The major protagonists in the non-partisan proceedings were highly articulate Presbyterians in the assembly and Presbyterian lawyers, many of great distinction, who appeared at committee hearings. To some the bill was an "act of God," to others it was coercive and tyrannical, violated trusts, contained no provision to protect minorities, and constituted a gross breach of faith with the Presbyterian Church. Catholic members, not relishing massive legislative interference in the affairs of a religious body, voted solidly against the bill. It passed nonetheless, even though R.H. Graham lamented that continuing Presbyterians were being "left like sheep wandering in the wilderness." He felt better when the legislative council made changes providing that, although all the Presbyterian congregations would become part of the union, any one of them might vote itself out within six months and not be deemed to have been in the union. An indignant *Sydney Daily Post* declared that the council's action on this bill and the Temperance Act meant that it had signed its own death warrant.

In September Armstrong suffered a serious loss when R.M. McGregor, the minister most sympathetic to him, died after a heart attack at age forty-eight. Three weeks later the Conservatives were also hurt when Howard Corning, whom Armstrong considered the "strongest and best posted Conservative in provincial politics," succumbed to typhoid fever at age forty-five. Meanwhile the premier was making it clear to Nova Scotia's second federal minister, E.M. (Ned) Macdonald of Pictou, that his major concern was the coal and steel industry. Although he could not forecast Besco's attitude, he would insist that it not be allowed to sacrifice the province's one big industry; "neither can we afford to let them sacrifice us."[36]

As 1924 advanced, the agitation for Maritime Rights continued unabated. After H.S. Congdon reproduced speeches of the Fathers of Confederation contending that the union would promote the welfare of Maritimers, the clamour seemed to grow. Even the one federal concession to the agitation, the setting up of a regional district office of the CNR at Moncton, struck "a blow at the *amour propre*" of the region by excluding the section from Rivière du Loup to Montreal.[37] Armstrong's correspondence shows little sympathy for the agitation, and late in the year the *Herald* quoted him as being opposed to the appointment of an "indiscriminate, irresponsible commission" to investigate the affairs of the Maritimes. As Armstrong saw it, he had strongly supported Maritime claims that had "distinct merit" and he would relieve neither the federal government nor the CNR of their responsibilities in these matters. However, he had "no use for the dog-in-the-manger slogan of 'Nova Scotia First'" and, to those who wanted party lines to be submerged at Ottawa to press for the province's rights, he replied indignantly that "those who talk most glibly about 'rights' evidently do not understand the meaning of the term. The Liberal Party, and no other Party, . . . [cannot] afford to be teaching that which creates discontent."[38]

Armstrong prepared himself as best he could for the 1925 session. By having George Murray intervene, he got J.C. Tory to arrive earlier than usual. To allay criticism of his attitude towards the legislative council, he had lawyer Vincent C. MacDonald prepare a bill to alter its constitution and discussed the proposal with R.G. Beazley, a veteran councillor. However, one thing he could do little about — his unsatisfactory relations with the King government, which seemed to have no concern about his survival in a general election. To serve its purposes, the provincial government wanted J.C. Tory to have the lieutenant-governorship, but James Robson Douglas got it instead. One of Armstrong's ministers wrote that "evidently E.M. [Macdonald] wanted to show that he was 'czar'." More than ever, said John A. McDonald, "our Federal Gov. is not being a help but rather a hindrance to our political welfare. . . . It would seem as though we had to fight for our rights at Ottawa as much as though an unfriendly government were in office."[39]

The lack of co-operation in labour matters proved even more serious. Besco had wanted to put a lower wage rate into effect when the old one expired on January 15th, but the UMW executive refused. When it then requested a conciliation board under the federal Industrial Disputes Investigation Act (IDIA), the miners refused to name their representative and the Minister of Labour had to name one for them. This occurred at the very time when the Judicial Committee of the Privy Council declared much of the IDIA to be *ultra vires* in the *Snider* case, and thus the board did not get down to work. As the situation developed, Armstrong continued to complain to E.M. Macdonald. He was especially indignant because King would not co-operate in appointing a commission of "an outstanding and national character" to investigate the coal industry. If he had a slapdash inquiry of his own, it would be "extremely doubtful if Capital could ever be encouraged to invest another dollar in this Province."

In mid-February Armstrong vented his anger against both King and Minister of Labour James Murdoch who, because of the *Snider* decision, seemed to be washing their hands of the situation in Cape Breton. "I have had nothing but embarrassment since I had the honour of becoming Premier. . . . I do not want to see things go crash in this Province but they will unless somebody is a little careful." By month's end he feared that "the thing is now beautifully staged to influence the coming elections."[40]

When, early in March, King and Murdoch both used the constitutional argument in the Commons to avoid responsibility, Armstrong's lamentations swelled. Murdoch, he thought, was riding his BNA horse to destruction. It was all very well to "take the high and authorative [sic] attitude 'that the mines are owned by the Province and therefore we wash our hands of the whole business,'" but that had never been the view before the recent decision. He was outraged too that Murdoch dared to suggest that the large revenues which Nova Scotia received from coal royalties made the province entirely responsible for the industry's health. Finally he castigated Ottawa's new-found tendency to blame all the ills on Besco. Certainly the company's management left much to be desired, but the basic problem was "politics and Communism." Self-pityingly he concluded that "everybody seems to have run away from the real situation, and seem very anxious to place the 'baby' upon my doorstep." Towards the end of March, when the miners struck and again demanded an inquiry, he was certain that their actions were "engineered for political purposes."[41]

Armstrong was also keeping an eye on the Maritime Rights agitation, which received a boost on February 17th when James A. Fraser's *Eastern Chronicle* outlined the effect of the tariff on the Maritimes' foreign trade. By diminishing imports, the tariff had robbed the area's ships of the return cargoes needed for profitable operations. "It arrested our natural growth, destroyed the commerce on which we had thrived," and in a few years it would produce "primeval solitude" through the exodus of people. Alienating himself from the federal Conservatives, another Maritime Righter, F.B. McCurdy, wanted a dismantlement of the National Policy through a drastic reduction of tariff barriers. Even at this late date, however, Armstrong gave little stock to the agitation. "We have some problems and some difficulties, but these so-called Maritime Rights are so vague and so ill defined that I have no patience with them. . . . Why should we humiliate ourselves . . . by attempting . . . to 'steal a thunder of the Halifax Herald' and a few so-called secessionists?" Nevertheless, even he conceded that much of "our troubles" resulted from transportation and tariff policies, and he proposed to demand remedies for specific ills. As if he had not enough difficulties, the new lieutenant-governor was making exorbitant demands for renovations at Government House.[42]

Despite his inward feelings Armstrong dressed up the 1925 speech from the throne in optimistic garb. In a paragraph indicating his recent conversion to a limited version of Maritime Rights he gave notice of a resolution which would state the province's position on the tariff and the regulation of trade and the fisheries. However, things had already gone wrong for the government. A month earlier D.A. Cameron had resigned as provincial secretary as a result of irregularities (but not shortages) in the accounts of Cape Breton County, of which he was treasurer. Armstrong took over his portfolio and assigned public works and mines to Chisholm, who relinquished highways to A.S. MacMillan, the government leader in the upper house. Then, not long after the session began, shortages were revealed in the King's Printer office and the vendors' liquor stores. When opposition members demanded an independent audit of all the departments, Armstrong denounced them as "calamity howlers" and "whisperers of death."

Hoping to win favour, he initiated a bill providing that new legislative councillors would hold office for ten years, subject to reappointment, and would retire at age seventy-five. In addition, any public bill the council rejected two years in a row would become law if the assembly passed it a third time. Moved to ridicule, the *Herald* wondered why the "confirmed abolitionist" had suddenly come to regard the council as "a necessary and useful body." Once again the upper house could look after itself. By insisting on amendments that prevented the suspensive veto from being applied to money bills or bills affecting the council's constitution it removed any danger of abolition by the unilateral action of the assembly.

Altogether indefensible was an act which, in effect, recognized that the government had lost the miners' vote. The act divided Richmond and Cape Breton counties into three seats: Richmond-Cape Breton West, Cape Breton Centre, and Cape Breton East, and "hived" most of the miners into the last seat, thus limiting their influence to the election of two members. For the first and only time a county, Richmond, was deprived of electing an assemblyman on its own. Apparently the premier followed the advice of a Cape Breton Liberal MP that "in making your plans make them to win and be guided by expediency alone."[43] Conservative B.A. LeBlanc of Richmond bitterly declared that "the expulsion of the Acadians took place in 1755, and it seems to be the [government's] determination . . . to obliterate the last trace of Acadian influence . . . in the year 1925." When Forman Waye pointed out that it was "a long distance to go" to include Little Bras d'Or and Sydney Mines in Cape Breton East, Armstrong could only reply: "Not as far [as] from Quebec to Cape Sable." The *Herald* trumpeted "Brazen Gerrymander in Cape Breton," and Conservative leader Hall declared that of all unprincipled bills he had ever seen "this one surpasses them all."[44]

The government's financial management appeared creditable, budgeting as it did for a surplus of $26,000. However, the debate on labour matters submerged everything else. The Labourites failed in their last attempt to get an eight-hour day for steel and construction workers in the towns and cities. Armstrong devoted his energies to the Industrial Peace Act, his version of the IDIA in thirty-one printed pages and 121 sections. But it differed markedly from the federal act in providing that, if a conciliation board failed to resolve an industrial dispute, the conflict was to be dealt with finally through compulsory arbitration. The intention was to use the act to settle the miners' strike which had begun on March 6th, but it would remain a dead letter on the statute book.

As the session progressed it must have disconcerted Armstrong to read day after day of large Conservative nominating conventions. When Frank Stanfield, the president of the province's Conservative association, sought to cast a non-partisan aura over the nominees, Armstrong found it simply too much to bear: "Scratch a Russian and there you find a Tartar; scratch one of these so-called non-partisans and you will find the true brand of Toryism." In a short time the *Echo* reported that rank-and-file Conservatives were dissatisfied with Hall; that Meighen's emissary, E.N. Rhodes, a former MP for Cumberland, had arrived from Ottawa; and that much spilling of blood and shedding of tears would occur before the leadership question was settled. To that Hall replied that he was "not concerned who will be called leader," and Rhodes stated that he had returned to Nova Scotia to make it his home and help put it under a competent government.[45]

Actually Armstrong was more worried about the situation in the mining areas than about the Conservative rejuvenation. The president of Besco, R.M. Wolvin, warned that part of the trouble resulted from the avowed purpose of some miners to "wreck the industries." He ensured that the trouble worsened by denying the miners, already in receipt of $185,000 in credit, any additional advances at the company's stores. Day after day the

Herald used the situation to bolster its case against the government. For example, a front-page picture showed a starving family with the caption, "These are the real sufferers," and a McRitchie cartoon of a mother with babe in arms was entitled, "they can't stand the gaff." Meanwhile the *Chronicle* and the *Echo* expressed horror that McLachlan had received $5,000 from the All-Russian Miners' Union for destitute Cape Breton miners, and the two newspapers did their best to identify the miners' leaders with the "Reds." When Wolvin repeated that Nova Scotia coal could not compete with the cheaper American product in the St. Lawrence market unless the miners accepted a reduction in wages, the *Herald* told him that he had failed and that the government should take over the industry.

Nothing that Armstrong did satisfied his opponents. They were outraged when he insisted on careful consideration before spending public money to relieve destitution. They were indignant when he refused to have all the members go to Sydney to examine the situation at first hand, and even more so when the prime minister declined to get involved, largely on constitutional grounds. In turn Armstrong complained that unfair publicity had damaged his government and that an editorial conspiracy all over Canada had misrepresented the Cape Breton situation. In his difficulties he had little help from Fielding. The old anti-Confederate and repealer simply told him that the provincial discontent was the natural result of the protective tariff and that an increase in subsidy was impossible unless it was granted proportionately to the other provinces. Armstrong replied that, above all, he would like the same *ad valorem* duty on semi-finished steel as on the finished product. Although he still had no clear conception of Maritime Rights, he admitted to a general disquietude in the province and attributed it to the widely held belief that Nova Scotia had been the "favourite milch cow of Canada ever since 1867." He also recognized a pronounced feeling that he show some independence from Ottawa and stand for Nova Scotia first.[46]

His response, almost at the session's end, was a lengthy resolution which damned the protective tariff as the primary cause for the province's failure to progress, called for the preparation of a case showing how federal policies had injured Nova Scotia, and demanded the modification of federal fisheries

and tariff policies to promote the province's interests. Fielding
was not impressed. Armstrong might say that he was not
advocating secession, but in wanting Nova Scotia to determine
its own tariffs, was he not, in effect, doing so? Armstrong should
remember that "Government and Parliament . . . represent all
the Provinces and . . . any special effort to serve one will
probably encounter opposition."[47] Clearly Fielding lacked the
energy to play a vigorous role in allaying provincial discontent.

Some Nova Scotians urged Armstrong to take stronger action.
William Rand of Canning told him to "leave the kid gloves and
put on brass knuckles." He himself was "a good pot shot" and
"I will sling a rifle tomorrow if you will call." Why did the
premier not proclaim Dominion Day a day of mourning?
"Every flag should be half masted . . . believe me, ninety per
cent of the people . . . are secessionists. Give them the chance
and see." H. Percy Blanchard told him that his resolution,
though "interesting as constitutional history," would accom-
plish nothing by itself. The best course was an appeal to the
king based on the 1869 letter of the colonial secretary, the Duke
of Buckingham, which had instructed the government and
Parliament of Canada to modify their trade and other policies to
meet Nova Scotia's complaints, and which had never been
honoured. If a committee which included a Conservative like
McCurdy and a Liberal like himself were sent to London, it
might do some good.[48]

Dissolution quickly followed prorogation, and the election
was to be held on June 25th. Apparently Armstrong hoped to
capitalize on the Conservatives' problems after Hall's resignation as leader on May 12th, which had followed a *Chronicle*
story of Hall being assaulted, knocked unconscious, and robbed
of his automobile and $40 on the St. Margaret's Bay road. The
party's provincial president, Frank Stanfield, announced that,
because of insufficient time to hold a convention, the provincial
executive and nominated candidates would select a new leader
on May 21st. When these men chose E.N. Rhodes, the *Chronicle*
and the *Echo* denounced an alleged conspiracy which enabled
"an inner circle" to supplant a popularly elected leader and
replace him with Meighen's nominee, an apostle of high tariffs.
They pictured the "Gold Dust Twins," Stanfield and Dennis,
wrenching a resignation from an unwilling Hall and a board of

strategy inducing him not to publish a "dramatic statement" calling his dismissal "a political hold-up." One of his friends reportedly said that "Ellis [the executioner] never made a quicker job."[49]

By admitting that he alone had effected the resignation, Stanfield assumed sole responsibility for the change in leadership. Both within and without the party doubts had existed about Hall. H.S. Congdon, for one, had "little use" for him: "He gets boozed up at times. He was the party that ran into the silent police man some time since. There was a rather gay party on. Then again he is plain lazy. No snap. Nothing inspiring at all. The easy way is the best way for him."[50] Rumours that the recent escapade on the St. Margaret's Bay road was something more than met the eye added to the doubts. Stanfield, Dennis, and others, sensing victory within their grasp after years of defeat, did not want it snatched away by having to run under a leader whom the public might think unsuited to be premier.

Four days after dissolution Rhodes was ready with his manifesto. Some of it condemned the government's past failings — the "Big Lease" in Victoria County, the "stern and unworking legislation" for settling strikes, and the doubling of the provincial debt in five years. Some of it made specific promises: searching investigations into the coal industry and the ICR, an independent audit of the public accounts, and the creation of a Department of Labour. The most significant part was that which sought to live up to its name: "A New Era for Nova Scotia." Like Conservative speeches and publications generally, it emphasized the need to get rid of "the machine." A fifty-two-page booklet had the title: "Responsible Government or Machine Rule?" A McRitchie cartoon pictured a woe-begone character named "old fashioned partisanship" with a bag marked "plunder" on his back leading a dog labelled "The Old Machine" along the road to "Obscurity." Naturally the Conservatives made much of their candidate Frank J.D. Barnjum who, when nominated in Queens, promised a 200-ton-per-day paper mill on the Mersey River. Highly telling, too, were the advertisements dealing with "bringing the boys back home." At the bottom were sentences such as: "Vote against the government that drove him into exile." At the upper part might be the picture of a sorrowing mother asking, "Where's my boy?," or of a child imploring, "When is daddy coming home?"

Amazingly, Armstrong became a Maritime Righter with a vengeance. His manifesto promised, above all, to "press the legitimate claims of Nova Scotia upon the Dominion Government and Parliament to a conclusion." A week before election day he announced a royal commission which included F.B. McCurdy to investigate how the economic system of the Dominion had damaged Nova Scotia industry. To revive a flagging campaign, the Liberals launched a savage attack on the tariff in the closing days of the race. Had not the boys been driven away in the first place by the Conservatives' policy of protection? Were Nova Scotians not paying an annual subsidy of $25 million to the Canadian Manufacturers Association? Had not Tory plotters sent Rhodes, Meighen's friend and emissary, to ensure that Nova Scotians would be held in leash to Upper Canadian manufacturers? The Liberals also denounced Barnjum, whom they described as the "self-acclaimed millionaire of Boston and Montreal." To get pulpwood for his own mill, they charged, he would demand an embargo on its export to the United States. His scheme would therefore ruin the woodlot owners of Nova Scotia and "make the rich richer and the poor poorer."

None of this could take the voters' minds off Cape Breton. The Liberals declared the strike to be of political origin and found the villains in the *Sydney Daily Post* and more especially the *Halifax Herald*, "a veritable firebrand, obsessed with the diabolical design of keeping the strike going until the elections came on." Whether or not these newspapers were partly to blame, violence occurred between June 11th and 15th, the worst possible time for Armstrong. The powerhouse at New Waterford was wrecked, looting and destruction occurred in Glace Bay, and several buildings were burned down in Reserve Mines. But by far the most serious incident occurred at New Waterford on June 11th when Besco police fired into the crowd and killed William Davis, a father of nine.[51] Circumstances like these made it hard for the Liberals to convince the voters that "the Armstrong government is a GOOD Government" and that "it has done well for Nova Scotia."

In other ways, too, Armstrong found the going difficult. He could not get the candidates he wanted. Although he finally induced highly respected Dr. J.L. McIsaac to contest Antigonish by telling him that he would not have to take part in "what you might call 'public speaking'," he failed to convince J.L. Ilsley to run in Kings. George Murray would not come early as he requested, saying that he could exercise as much influence from Montreal as by "hanging around the Bras d'Or House" in Victoria County. When he finally arrived, the *Herald* told him that "things are not what they used to be in Nova Scotia." The youthful Harold Connolly agreed. The Liberal party, he thought, had fallen into the hands of "a well-meaning, but unknowledgeable clique," and Armstrong was "the antithesis of everything that Murray was. . . . Nobody except on rare occasions could ever get to see him." All the prestige built up by his predecessor had "withered on the vine."[52]

The landslide bore out the Conservative prophecies with a vengeance. William Chisholm and Dr. McIsaac won the two seats in Antigonish and D.B. McLeod one of the two in Victoria, but they were the only successful Liberals. The Conservatives took the other forty seats and an almost incredible 60.9 per cent of the vote to the Liberals' 36.3. This time no candidates had run as Farmers. In Cumberland, D.G. McKenzie had called himself a Farmer-Conservative and Archie Terris had presented himself as a Labour-Conservative, but in fact both were Conservatives. The third-party renegades in the last assembly, MacGillivray and Richardson, had not contested the election. Ten Labourites had, but they polled a meagre 2.8 per cent of the vote and only Morrison and Waye in the gerrymandered riding of Cape Breton East did at all well.

The *Herald* boasted that the victors had overcome two serious obstacles: "the heart-breaking handicap of a horde of office-holders on the Machine payroll" and election lists heavily weighted against them. However, it was outraged at three death-bed appointments to the legislative council, an attempt, it alleged, to embarrass the incoming government through the non-elective chamber. Conservative rank-and-file workers, winless for forty-three years and having "not the slightest idea of the landslide" in the absence of pre-election polls, did nothing

Ernest H. Armstrong   1923-25

Courtesy of Public Archives of Nova Scotia

until the result was absolutely certain and then enacted "scenes beyond description . . . at Tory headquarters throughout the province."

Armstrong's post-election letters revealed all sorts of reactions to the outcome.[53] William Rand blamed the province's ills on Ontario. "Why do you not recognize its actions as a declaration of war and accept the challenge?" A defeated candidate in a western county where the majorities were relatively small could not understand why "there were few indications . . . of what was in store for us." Others suspected weaknesses in the party's local organizations: "perhaps the long tenure of office . . . had tended to make some . . . members a little too arrogant in their dealings with the public generally." More than one suggested that "another hoax had been put on the people" and that shortly the Liberals who had strayed would "cheerfully come back to their first and old love."

A.S. MacMillan knew what had been happening. Having spoken every night for three weeks, he would later "smile to himself when I think how to little avail all the speeches were." On election day he canvassed up to the last minute in a torrential rainstorm and returned to tell his wife that "we were going to be wiped out — beaten to a frazzle." Against his better judgment he went to the *Chronicle* office to await the returns. "I have attended a few wakes in my time but I must say that the wake I attended that night was more dismal than any I had ever experienced."[54]

Some have made Maritime Rights the basic issue in the election and attributed the Conservative success to that party's taking it over and using it for its own purposes. Actually the factors giving rise to the agitation without the benefit of the agitation itself would have resulted in a Conservative victory, although not of the same magnitude. Deep-seated, almost catastrophic ills in the province's two basic industries were preventing a quick recovery from the postwar recession. Likely Murray would not have won in 1925; under a leader who lacked personal appeal and showed an incapacity to deal firmly or adeptly with the economic problems, the Liberals' political situation deteriorated beyond hope of recovery.

Wanting to be "out in the world as short a time as possible," Armstrong relied on E.M. Macdonald for a quick appointment, hopefully to the Supreme Court. It was a long time in coming and then it was only a county court judgeship. It was cold comfort to Armstrong to have Mackenzie King tell him, in his usually ponderous style, that "the quiet haven, whatever its limitations may be, is in some regards, the greatest of rewards to one who has shared the storm and stress of political life, particularly in times like our own."[55] More and more, he suspected that he was being penalized for his political reversal. When Stuart Jenks and V.J. Paton, whose contributions to the party were slight compared with his, became Supreme Court judges, he complained bitterly, only to be told that the Minister of Justice, Ernest Lapointe, refused to deviate from a rule, followed for twenty years, of not promoting county court judges to a superior court. Armstrong declared the practice to be unsound, judicially and politically, but finally accepted the fact that he was without bargaining power. Although none could deny that he was a man of integrity and industry, skilful in marshalling facts to present a case, nonetheless the name "Hapless Politician," which A. Jeffrey Wright attached to him, seems painfully appropriate.[56]

CHAPTER 5

Rhodes and Harrington: A Conservative Interlude

The transition to Conservative government was uneventful. In the absence of Armstrong and O'Hearn MacMillan arranged the old government's obsequies. Rhodes reiterated his intention to "break up the political machine which has had such a hold on the Province."[1] Keeping the provincial secretaryship for himself, he gave public works and mines to Gordon Harrington, counsel for UMW District 26; highways to Percy C. Black; and the attorney generalship to John Douglas, not to Hall. A fourth portfolio went to a political newcomer, John A. Walker, who headed the new department of natural resources, the first of many to be separated from the provincial secretary's office.

Years later Walker would express regret that the new government had not forgotten about deficits and been more "forward-looking."[2] No less troublesome than finances was the clamour for office of the party workers, largely deprived of provincial patronage for forty-three years; for the government it became nothing less than a nightmare. However, the government could boast of one quick success. By August 10th Rhodes and Harrington had secured an agreement under which the miners returned to work, at least until a commission of inquiry had reported. However, the settlement would cost the government one-fifth of its coal royalties over the next year.

The travails of Nova Scotia's Liberals would continue as they fought a federal election set for October 29th. Maritime Rights dominated the front pages of the *Herald* as it accused the province's Liberal MPs of being so busy "helping the Prime Minister to make friends in the West" that they forgot Maritime interests. However, in supporting Meighen to the hilt, the newspaper came into conflict with Norman McLeod Rogers of Acadia University's history department, who opposed anything which threatened national unity. To the Liberals of Kings County he declared that, though brought up in an "ultra Conservative family" (his mother had run as a Conservative in 1920), he had "in the broad clear light of day" become a Liberal because Meighen's policy on the tariff would disrupt Confederation. Later in the *Chronicle* and *Echo* he argued that for survival federations required both economic and patriotic bonds, and that Meighen's position seriously threatened the economic foundation. He feared too that the patriotic foundation was being undermined by the Conservative appeals to provincial prejudice. The province ought not to accept the motto of "Nova Scotia first," but that of the Three Musketeers, "All for Each and Each for all."[3]

In reply, the *Herald* simply asked, how could the motto of the Three Musketeers be followed in a federation which practised the principle of "Everybody for Himself — and the Devil take the Hindmost"?[4] Late in the campaign it overflowed with delight when the three Maritime premiers, "The Three Musketeers," Rhodes, J.B.M. Baxter, and J.D. Stewart, spoke at Amherst with one voice on Maritime claims. It was no less pleased when, early in October, Rhodes announced the appointment of a royal commission headed by Sir Andrew Rae Duncan to inquire into the coal industry, something which Armstrong had wanted but never got.

Although the Conservatives continued to treat King's comments on Maritimes Rights with derision, he continued to say that the greatest of these rights were tariff relief, free trade, and wider markets. More and more the Liberals contended that Maritime Rights and Meighen's tariff policies were irreconcilable. Starting in mid-October their Halifax newspapers ran nine front-page articles comparing high tariffs to the tribute exacted by the brigands of old. Allegedly, through these tariffs, manufacturers were levying tribute on all the citizenry and putting it in their own pockets. However, these arguments were

Edgar N. Rhodes   1925-30

Courtesy of Public Archives of Nova Scotia

of no avail and it was a massive Conservative victory in Nova Scotia.

Of fourteen seats, reduced by two as a result of redistribution, the Conservatives won eleven to the Liberals' three and increased their popular vote from 32.3 to 56.4 per cent. Fielding had retired and E.M. Macdonald retained a seat only by moving from Pictou to Antigonish-Guysborough. Maritime Rights played a bigger part in the federal contest than the provincial, not unexpectedly in a province that continued to suffer from serious economic malaise. Also contributing to the result was the unfavourable impression that Nova Scotia, like much of English Canada, held of the King government's first term. Though Meighen was seven seats short of an overall majority, Nova Scotia was generally content with matters political. However, it would have been appalled had it known of the King government's decision, made in light of Nova Scotia's dwindling proportion of the national population, to take away what the province had possessed since 1867 — an entitlement to two members in the federal cabinet.

No ministry was ever better prepared than the Rhodes government when the legislature opened in February 1926. In numbers at least it had little to fear from the opposition. Respected surgeon J.L. McIsaac came mainly to get a rest; Harold Connolly stated that McIsaac always gave the same speech and it amounted to "those damn Tories." D.B. McLeod, who thought in Gaelic, spoke once a year, urging better roads for Victoria County, and became principally known for his proficiency with Gaelic songs at the end of sessions. With William Chisholm it was altogether different. Often incapacitated by asthma, and forced to walk with a crutch and a cane because of an accidental gunshot wound which never fully healed, he could be forgiven for sometimes taking to the bottle. For three years he almost single-handedly confronted the government, and Harold Connolly has credited him with starting the Liberal rejuvenation. Chisholm had help from newspaperman George Farquhar, who often drew up the resolutions that the MLA moved. "Our minds met," said Farquhar, "and we worked together like a pair of twins."[5]

The attack on the "machine" began on the session's opening day when the government presented a report of P.S. Ross and Sons showing that the deficit for 1924 had been $1,741,139, not $7,364 as stated, and that the shortfall for 1925 had also been grossly underestimated. Although the shortages were small, the keeping of the accounts was obviously out-of-date and the provincial auditor, W.H. Studd, though honest, was "hopelessly incompetent." Accordingly the government moved to replace the existing audit act with one declared to provide a genuinely independent audit. Though its effect was to deprive Studd of tenure during good behaviour, the legislative council thought it wise not to intervene. The lieutenant-governor assented to the bill on one day, and the next day Studd and his staff were out of work.

It took the government only a few days to introduce virtually its entire legislative programme. One bill would repeal Armstrong's compulsory arbitration act, which Harrington said did more harm than good. Several other bills sought to bring an antiquated administrative machine up to date. That was especially true of one bill which was to abolish the Provincial Highway Board and put the roads directly and fully under the department of highways and its minister. Another was to amend the Workmen's Compensation Act to permit more expeditious treatment of its clientele and provide greater protection based on legislation elsewhere. With the departure of A.H. MacKay after thirty-six years as superintendent of education, the government announced its intention to revamp the entire educational system. One measure outraged the government's most prominent backbencher. It proposed to abolish the office of purchasing agent and confer its functions on three departmental officials nominated by the minister of public works and mines. In committee Frank Stanfield moved the three months' hoist and, to the Liberals' delight, expressed fears that the change might "open the door wide for graft."

Sometimes the legislative council intervened to stymie the government's plans. It did not oppose in essence the bill to lay the foundations of a modern forestry policy, but it did force a change in a provision to come into effect at a later date that taxed all pulpwood cut but not manufactured within the province. It found even more objectionable the tenure of office bill which allegedly made officers holding tenure during good behaviour amenable to the people through their elective representatives. Unable to resist the swarm of Tory applicants for office, the government had already dismissed many officials holding office during pleasure, and Chisholm contended that it now wanted to apply the spoils system to major office-holders. Rhodes replied that he sought to deal only with the few officials who, "sheltered by an artificial wall," felt that they could defy him and thereby let the "dead hand of a defeated and discredited government" prevent the "effective administration of public affairs."[6] In the end the council refused to make the bill applicable to incumbent office-holders or judicial and quasi-judicial officials and thus defeated Rhodes' intentions.

Finances were the government's greatest immediate problem, the result mainly of previous massive expenditures on highways. Roads had in fact taken 68 per cent of the total revenues in 1925. In announcing a deficit of $1.1 million, Rhodes promised to put the financial house in order, to which Chisholm replied that "professions are one thing and accomplishment is another." To secure abolition of the upper house, the premier offered $1,000 a year for ten years or a lifetime annuity of $500 to its life members and a smaller amount to its ten-year appointees. Liberal councillors called it "insulting to high-minded, honourable men" and Councillor Neil Gillis introduced a resolution extolling the second chamber's usefulness. When F.P. Bligh, the newly appointed government leader in the council, called that body the "servile follower and slave" of Liberal governments, he received a rowdy reception. Rhodes himself charged that the only bills the upper house had not accepted in the past were ones which "the government passed, with its tongue in cheek," knowing that the upper house would reject them and assume the blame.[7]

The premier realized that an abolition bill must fail, as the only other Conservative councillor was W.H. Owen, who had survived forty-three years of Liberal rule and had previously favoured retention. Nevertheless, he forced the council to reject the assembly's bill to prevent its abolition. He also asked the lieutenant-governor to appoint councillors in excess of the normal membership of twenty-one. Properly the governor sought an opinion from Ottawa on the constitutionality of the request; improperly Prime Minister King made known these proceedings to Chisholm and drew from Rhodes a sharp reprimand for being so lacking in a knowledge of constitutional procedure as to divulge a governor's confidential communications. Though the federal law officers declared the council's legal maximum to be twenty-one, Rhodes insisted that he would secure abolition even if he had to go to Westminster.

As the session closed, Chisholm thanked Rhodes and the *Herald* for their considerate treatment of a small opposition; D.B. McLeod sang solos such as "Horo Nighinn Donn Bhoigheach" ("My Brown Haired Maiden") and "Mo Shoir-ridh" ("Good Night"); and the *Chronicle* lambasted the "barren record" of a "Kindergarten Government," declaring that the honours of the session went to Chisholm, whose performance, "as a matter of physical endurance," was "remarkable."

The federal election of 1925, in which the Liberals took only six of twenty-nine Maritimes seats, had made the prime minister acutely aware of the existence of these provinces and apparently led, in January 1926, to his announcement of a royal commission to inquire into Maritime claims. Three months later, Sir Andrew Rae Duncan, who had just completed an investigation of the Nova Scotia coal industry, became its chairman. The commission had only begun its work when late in June a violent eruption occurred in Ottawa: the customs scandal, the King-Byng affair, the assumption of office by Arthur Meighen, his parliamentary defeat, and an election to be held on September 14th.

Nova Scotia's Liberals did not stress the constitutional issue and avoided criticism of Lord Byng, apparently realizing that no votes could be won in that way. However, they castigated the province's Conservative MPs for voting against the Robb budget's reduction in taxation, and they criticized the Conservative-dominated Senate for rejecting the Liberals' old age pension bill. More positively, they promised sympathetic consideration of the Duncan Commission's recommendations and looked forward to a full-time minister of fisheries. Their closing advertisements proclaimed that "Meighen can't win" and "If you want stable government give King a working majority." A noteworthy feature of the campaign in Nova Scotia was that eighty-five-year-old James A Fraser, the proprietor of the *Eastern Chronicle*, who had led the repeal movement in the 1880s and last ran in 1890, was induced to become the Liberal candidate in Pictou. At his nominating convention he described himself "a Liberal, but a secessionist first" and declared that if Meighen agreed to Nova Scotia's secession, he would support him. Nationally the Liberals secured a comfortable majority, but Nova Scotia and British Columbia became the only provinces in which the Conservatives did better than they had in 1925. Though their Nova Scotia popular vote was down somewhat, they won twelve of the fourteen seats, a gain of one. James A. Fraser lost badly, but J.L. Ilsley won Kings for the Liberals. To the *Herald* the "finest feature" of the election was the province's continued firm stand for its rights in Confederation.

When the 1927 session opened, Rhodes boasted of the "new feeling abroad in the province." Nova Scotians, not as strongly Liberal and Conservative as they once were, would no longer fall for the beating of the party tomtom but would judge parties by measures and results, and if that was so, "I do not fear the issue when it is in front of the people."[8] However, the premier continued to be severely limited by financial constraints. The deficit had been $800,000 and would have been much higher but for the payment, at long last, of $172,000 in succession duties on the Enos Collins estate and the receipt of $182,000 from the Canadian National Railways (CNR), a grant in lieu of taxation for two years. In forecasting a deficit of $1 million for 1927, Rhodes blamed the declining proportion of federal subsidies to overall expenditures. In 1900 it had been 66 per cent, by 1920 it was only 11 per cent, and it was still falling. When told to "cut his coat according to his cloth," he replied that any increase in expenditure "only seemed bigger, because the people . . . for the first time were told the whole truth about the public accounts."[9]

The possibility of increased revenue through the legalized sale of liquor loomed on the horizon. The *Chronicle* and the *Daily Star*, the successor to the *Echo*, continued to rail against the securing of liquor from the Board of Vendor Commissioners through physicians' prescriptions. "Drop the [doctors] scripts," urged the *Star*, and let the present hypocrisy, mockery and fraud occasioned by their use and misuse be stopped." John F. Mahoney, an articulate Conservative from Halifax, asked the government to replace the so-called prohibition with government sale and control, but was told that the change would have to be dependent upon a favourable vote of the people. Mahoney's vehemence dissuaded the new attorney general, W.L. Hall, from proceeding with an amendment that would allegedly deprive persons convicted under the Temperance Act of the right of appeal to a higher court.

The state of the finances prevented the government from offering new, eye-catching legislation. The Conservatives did sponsor amendments to the Education Act to provide more adequately for the teaching of mentally defective children, and to the Mines Act to stimulate greater activity. However, they focussed their attention on matters they had begun in 1926. More explicitly than before, Harrington explained the reasons for proceeding again with the tenure of office bill. Forty-three years of one-party government, he contended, had produced a civil service which acted as an integral part of "the old Grit machine," and had even led to leakages of confidential matters with which "we are powerless [to deal] at the present time."[10] Not unexpectedly the council amended the bill as in 1926 and it failed to become law.

Meanwhile the premier continued his fight against the upper house. The Supreme Court of Nova Scotia had considered the basic questions (Did councillors appointed before the statute of 1925 hold office during pleasure and was the lieutenant-governor in council limited to appointing a maximum of twenty-one?) and had divided evenly on the tenure and maximum number of councillors. Rhodes held the view that he could take action to remove all the life councillors and could appoint an unlimited number of new ones. He threatened, if unable to have his way through legislative or court action, to conduct a referendum on the question. For the moment the council stymied him, and "not a sound was heard, not a funeral note, as the corpse of the [abolition] bill was hurried to the graveyard of forgotten measures."[11]

As often happens to governments with overwhelming majorities, party discipline became a problem in 1927. Seeking to protect the users of gasoline, Conservative W.B. Armstrong objected to an increase in the sales tax from three to four cents a gallon and joined four other Conservatives, including Stanfield, in voting for the three months' hoist. More serious was the opposition to raising from $6,000 to $7,000 the salary of Deputy Provincial Secretary A.S. Barnstead, who was steadily moving towards becoming the province's leading public servant and had won the premier's favour in preparing the province's case for the Duncan Commission. Populist John Mahoney refused to accept Rhodes' contention that a lawyer of Barnstead's calibre could earn upwards of $10,000 a year and argued that in a time of financial stringency the money might be put to better use. Even after an hour's recess and the use of the whips, ten Conservatives voted against the increase in salary. For a time, wrote Horatio Crowell of the *Chronicle*, the government itself was endangered.[12] That paper called it "an inglorious ending" to a session which lasted only thirty-nine days — one of the shortest in modern history — and produced little substantive legislation.

Sir Andrew Rae Duncan was a fast worker and by December 1926 his commission had finished its report. Professor Forbes is right that, since it sought to alleviate Maritime difficulties without arousing opposition elsewhere, its proposals were really exercises in "the fine art of the possible." He is equally correct that the King government, never enthusiastic about the Maritime Rights agitation, wanted "pacification . . . with the fewest possible concessions."[13] In March 1927 it announced the adoption of the commission's proposals to divide the Department of Marine and Fisheries into two separate departments; to set up harbour boards in Halifax and Saint John on the same lines as those in Montreal, Quebec, and Vancouver; and to subsidize new coking plants using at least 70 per cent of Canadian coal. Accepting the commission's contention that normal commercial rates ought not to apply to a railway like the ICR which was 250 miles longer than it needed to be, it legislated a 20 per cent reduction over the ICR portion of the line on traffic originating in the Atlantic Division destined for outside points, as well as on traffic originating and terminating in the division. The commission, finding that the cost of government was "surprisingly low" in the Maritimes and the rate of taxation 16 per cent above the national average, had concluded that the three provinces were in a state of fiscal need and recommended interim annual subsidy increases of $875,000 to Nova Scotia, $600,000 to New Brunswick, and $125,000 to Prince Edward Island until the amounts could be definitively determined. Again the federal government agreed.

The commission had made no attempt to investigate the effect of the tariff on the Maritimes, although it did refer the claims of Nova Scotia steel and coal interests to the Tariff Advisory Board. Later the Liberals would contend that the short-lived Meighen government had instructed Duncan not to deal with the tariff, but that seems unlikely. Professor Forbes suggests that for the commission to "have entered the tariff controversies directly would have accomplished little and possibly prejudiced the report as a whole."[14] But the failure to recognize a primary complaint was a serious gap in the commission's findings. Although the King government had dealt favourably with many of the report's recommendations, the prime minister exaggerated in saying that they were implemented "virtually in their entirety." Yet, in attempting to undermine the Maritime Rights agitation, his basic objective, he had had considerable success.

A revitalized government faced the Nova Scotia legislature in 1928, partly the result of the Judicial Committee's decision of the previous October which accepted in full Rhodes' view of the council's constitution. Accordingly he requested the resignations of all the life councillors except for Conservative W.H. Owen, who had never been pledged to abolition, and Liberal A.W. Redden, who favoured it. The others offered to support the council's extinction, but the premier refused the promises of men who, he said, had previously violated sacred pledges. Instead, he had the six who failed to resign removed by order in council, leaving only Redden, Owen, and six ten-year appointees. Next he had fourteen Conservative councillors appointed, thus demonstrating that the council's membership was not limited to twenty-one and making sure at the same time that each county would share in the impending constitutional change.

None, wrote Horatio Crowell, ever described Rhodes better than William Chisholm when he referred to Rhodes' "distinguished urbanity." All of it was in evidence in 1928, sometimes in pointing out the real progress being made by the province, sometimes in extolling the items of his legislative programme, sometimes in categorizing the Liberal demand for old age pensions as "political window dressing." In the assembly the abolition bill passed without ado. In the council the new government leader, R.H. Butts, castigated the upper house's record as never before and over the opposition of only two ten-year Liberal members, President F.P. Bligh declared the bill carried with the words: "Sic transit gloria mundi." Horatio Crowell characterized the age as "so irreverent" that some spectators smiled and some impressionable females actually giggled. To the *Star* "a touch of pathos and bathos too" surrounded the councillors: "They had basked in the light of political greatness. And now all this was over. . . . The Legislative Council is dead. "Morituri Te Salutamus."'[15] Former councillor A.S. MacMillan declared that the men given a sessional indemnity to act as undertakers were "not the type . . . who could have been elected to any elective body." The result was "nothing more or less than a drunken spree. One room in [Province House] was used for the purpose of a bar room . . . the Feast of Belchazzar was a Sunday School picnic in comparison to the closing days of the Legislative Council."[16]

Some Conservatives called Rhodes the Howe of "our day" for the restoration of "real responsible government." Certainly his success lifted his optimism. He boasted of reducing the deficit to $275,000 and forecast a still lower shortfall of $227,000 for 1928. "We could very easily have produced a budget surplus," but thought it unwise to cut education and highway expenditures when the province was on the upgrade. In the assembly he talked of "a new vision today" and at a complimentary dinner he foresaw "the dawn of a new day for the Province."[17]

In addition to providing a contributory pension scheme for teachers, the government kept an election pledge by contributing to the cost of maintaining the streets in towns and cities, announced proposed capital expenditures of $3.6 million on trunk and secondary roads, and promised grants towards the cost of insurance premiums in the fishing industry. However, despite Liberal pressure it refused to enter the federal conditional grant scheme of old age pensions and instead appointed a royal commissioner to determine the number of likely beneficiaries and ways of meeting the cost. That year it did not introduce a tenure of office bill but sought more limited ends through amendments to the acts relating to the Public Utilities Board, the Workmen's Compensation Board, and the registrars of deeds. This outraged the *Chronicle*, which charged that the evil of partisan influence would intrude into decisions affecting private and property rights where independent judgment was imperative. Not realizing the possible adverse political effect, Natural Resources Minister Walker responded favourably to petitions by requesting the federal government to undertake the tuberculin testing of cattle.

After years of complaints against Besco and its president R.M. Wolvin, new interests headed by Holt, Gundy and Company took over the steel corporation with promises to put industries in Cape Breton that would win approval not only in Nova Scotia but in all of Canada. When the legislature considered a bill to incorporate an operating company, the Dominion Steel and Coal Corporation (Dosco), in place of the holding company Besco and its fourteen subsidiary companies, the premier declared that it would not only cut overhead and operating expenses but also "squeeze out the water" as recommended by the Duncan Commission report on coal. Frank Barnjum had not built a paper mill and therefore had resigned his seat, but in March the government announced an agreement with a group headed by Izaak Walton Killam of Royal Securities to build a mill at Brooklyn, Queens County. Although the *Chronicle* called the Rhodes government's performance at its third session as "much the worst," the government actually emerged in better shape than in 1926 or 1927.

The *Chronicle* kept prophesying an election, but to most Nova Scotians the dissolution on September 5th came like a bolt from the blue. Basically Rhodes contended that, because of the change wrought by the abolition of the legislative council, sound constitutional practice required new assemblymen "clothed with all the authority of this enlarged mandate."[18] Chisholm and the *Chronicle* would have none of that. To them the premier was simply in a "mad rush" to secure a "snap verdict" because the ground was "fast slipping from under [his] feet."

Rhodes' manifesto reminded the voters that he had inherited "years of maladministration" which had demoralized every branch of the civil service and resulted in faulty handling of the province's revenues often by incapable and dishonest officials. It expressed confidence that the policies he had adopted in education, agriculture, mining, and forestry would "result in multiplying our wealth, increasing our provincial revenue and make for prosperous and contented citizens." Chisholm's manifesto, necessarily prepared in haste, emphasized that he himself was leader only because he had survived the 1925 election and that the party would be free to elect a new one after the election. It declared that Rhodes had called the election not on constitutional principles but out of panic, that the total shortages in forty-three years of Liberal rule amounted to only $42,000, and that despite promises of economy the Conservatives were "spending more prodigally than any previous government."

Finances dominated the campaign. The Liberals kept repeating that the province's credit rating had slipped badly. One of their cartoons showed Rhodes strutting in peacock feathers saying, "The Sun Keeps Shining!," his elation caused by federal grants totalling $11,340,000 inscribed on five of the feathers, including one of $1,750,000 for two years of Duncan award payments.[19] For Chisholm's financial statements Rhodes had nothing but contempt: "Millions mean nothing to him and he can knock down his financial houses as quickly as he can construct them."[20] Eventually he became so exasperated with some financial charges that he threatened to give anyone who made them a chance to prove them in court.

Once again the Conservatives warned of the danger in bringing back the "old gang." The *Herald* published pictures of Chisholm, MacMillan, Cameron, Kinley, and Comeau and asked: "They want to get back — Do the people of Nova Scotia want them?" A McRitchie cartoon pictured two roads, one leading to the return of "the old machine," the other to prosperity and opportunity. In a full-page advertisement the Liberals heaped scorn on earlier Conservative promises to "bring the boys back home," and declared that Rhodes would "never play again on the heart strings of the aged mothers of Nova Scotia." Another pictured the premier ignoring two elderly people and saying: "Yes we have no pensions today." Sometimes the Liberals went too far, as in suggesting that the Mersey Paper Company did not intend to build a plant at Brooklyn. As a result, its president, Colonel C.H.L. Jones, ran an advertisement condemning these "reckless statements" as completely false. The Liberals were on better ground in criticizing the premier for not divulging months earlier the resignation of Conservative Alexander O'Handley of Cape

Breton East who, contending that he had not been consulted on constituency matters, campaigned this time for the Liberals.

The Liberals received an unexpected boon from the tuber-culin testing of cattle. The *Chronicle* held that the requests for testing had come not from farmers generally but only from stockbreeders, that milk from infected cows did not constitute a hazard, and that their owners should be fully compensated. Nowhere did the Conservatives suffer greater harm from the issue than in Lunenburg County, where the county warden and Liberal candidate, Gordon Romkey, helped stage a carnival-like gathering on the grounds of the municipal home at Dayspring. There, in the presence of scores of farmers, some condemned animals were slaughtered and, by the luck of the draw, found to be free of disease. Rhodes, somewhat thin-skinned in the face of strong and sometimes unfair attacks, took it out on the Liberal press: "Of all the servile party hacks, masquerading under the name of a newspaper . . . anywhere in Canada," the worst, "with the possible exception of the Sydney Record," was the Halifax *Chronicle*.[21]

That of 1970 excepted, the election of October 1, 1928 produced the closest results in provincial history. Not until about ten o'clock, when three Conservatives were declared elected in Cumberland, was the return of the government assured, by twenty-three seats to twenty. In an exceptionally large swing the Conservative popular vote fell from 60.9 to 50.6 per cent, while the Liberal vote rose from 36.3 to 48.3 per cent. To the *Herald* it was largely a case of a government paying too much attention to providing good administration and too little to politics. It attributed the defeat of Walker and Bligh in Halifax to the extraordinary condition of the voters' lists, "the sensation of the campaign." More generally, it blamed the Conservative losses partly on the retention in office of some members of the old régime who, while professing friendship, did incalculable harm to the administration by "boring from within." Elatedly the *Chronicle* pointed to the election of the five Liberals alleged to have been part of the "old machine" and to the defeat of five cabinet ministers. In its view the government had suffered a moral defeat which was "tantamount to 'the handwriting on the wall.'" According to the *Star*, the premier had made himself a "truly pathetic figure" by his invective against the Liberal newspapers.[22] George Farquhar was right that the attempt to make the council's abolition a major issue failed because "the Council had no defenders. It was a dead issue."[23]

In his letters Rhodes had all sorts of explanations and justifications. He told a defeated candidate that ninety-five of a hundred Conservatives favoured the timing of the election and that the government's position would have been worse a year later. He expressed indignation to Dennis of the *Herald* that, after being assured that the lists in Halifax were in good shape, he had found them "shocking." For example, Deputy Attorney General Mathers had appeared in the lists as a "law student," proof that they had not been revised for thirty years. He complained to others that the government suffered from an archaic system of representation which gave inordinate power to counties with small populations. "We will remedy this by a fair distribution of seats."[24]

Running through the letters was disappointment in the character and ingratitude of Nova Scotians. To him they were "more concerned with the interests of their Party than . . . of their Province." Party politics seemed to "take the place of religion. . . . There is little idea of service. The general viewpoint is an expectation to receive some benefit." He felt especially "the lack of appreciation . . . of our endeavour to give progressive business Government . . . to give a real lead to our people in matters worth while." He had likewise been "very much mistaken" in his impression that "a new era [was] afoot in the Province." Yet he would carry on hoping for "some slight change of attitude." Perhaps he might even "remain in office sufficiently long to . . . do some lasting good."[25] He was especially chagrined about two cases of ingratitude. Despite the time, money, and effort to help Inverness County, including $100,000 to keep its mine in operation, it had voted Liberal. Even more he regretted the defeat in Yarmouth of double-amputee John F. Cahan, who had served his constituency well. How, he asked the loser's father, C.H. Cahan, could J.L. Ralston have gone out of his way to fight against a man "with a war record such as Jack's? . . . [His] attack was barbaric and gives the real measure of the man."[26] Naturally Rhodes left out two other factors which accounted in part for the Conservatives' poor showing: dissatisfaction within the ranks because of his inability to meet his members' inordinate demands for patronage and the return of many Liberals to their traditional party.

Within a fortnight, however, Rhodes took comfort that the party's losses had led to a splendid reaction. Hitherto, he said, the majority had been too big and too much was expected of the government. "Today our ranks are closed."[27] Subsequent events proved him right. Over the next five sessions only one sign of divisiveness appeared in Conservative ranks. That occurred before the house opened in 1929 when, according to Liberal newspapers, the premier bowed to D.G. McKenzie's threats to act as an independent unless he was made speaker. Relegated to the backbenches was ex-speaker Albert Parsons, "the Tory war horse" of Hants County and Rhodes' running mate.

Although the Liberals called it "nothing but dishwater," the speech from the throne in 1929 did call for the complete implementation of the Duncan Report recommendations, demanded a readjustment of subsidies if the western provinces received their natural resources, forecast legislation to redistribute the assembly's seats and to amend the franchise and election acts, and announced a plebiscite on the liquor question and a gift to construct a public archives building.[28] The opposition focussed its attack on the "unreasonable delay" in adopting old age pensions, a criticism that would continue throughout the Thirty-Eighth General Assembly. Keeping in mind the report of royal commissioner H.E. Mahon that the annual provincial outlay would be $2 million not including administrative costs, the premier replied that it was "one thing to pay the pensions with resolutions that mean nothing, and it is another thing to dip into the pockets of the people . . . to pay [for] them."[29]

The government indicated a deficit of $860,773 for 1928, forecast one of a similar size for 1929, and voiced its hope to balance the budget in 1930. With supply running out, the opposition introduced a host of non-confidence motions. Rhodes warned against creating a situation in which the civil service would not be paid, highway work would cease, and a default would occur in the payment of interest on the provincial debt. "They can introduce . . . as many amendments as they please, but they are not going to stampede the government into taking any other course than that which [it] believes is sound and constitutional."[30] The opposition heeded the warning.

However, it reacted almost in fury to a dismissal and a non-dismissal. Provincial Health Officer Dr. A.C. Jost found himself unemployed when, without consulting his minister, he laid down a policy for his department in a letter not marked private. "I say he was stupid," declared the premier, "and that his action constituted insubordination of the rankest kind."[31] The Liberals were on better ground in the case of Robert Gordon, the deputy provincial treasurer, who, a few days before the election, allegedly made remarks of "an offensively partisan character" which were "uncalled for" and "untrue." Although agreeing that it was generally undesirable for public servants to engage in public debate, the government took the view that Gordon considered it his duty to reply to opposition comments on finances which were not only false but reflected on the credit of the province. When defeated by 21 to 19 in their attempt to remove him, the Liberals cancelled the use of pairs, which they had agreed upon earlier.

The government's redistribution bill reduced the assembly's size from 43 to 38 by giving the six counties with the smallest populations one member instead of two and by adding one to Cape Breton's four. Though Attorney General Hall declared that it equalized representation to the greatest extent possible, Chisholm called it "inexcusable, unjustifiable, untimely, inconsistent, illogical and unprincipled." Since five of the six counties to lose seats had voted Liberal in 1928, he labelled it a "measure of retaliation and revenge."[32]

The Liberals had institutional proposals of their own. Because of their precarious position in the assembly, the Conservatives rejected outright J.J. Kinley's bill requiring by-elections to be held within three months of a vacancy. Chisholm fared no better with an independence of the assembly bill designed to prevent a member from holding any office but that of prosecuting attorney. The premier told him that "we are living in a practical age" and reminded the Liberals that they had always turned down bills of this kind before 1925.

John F. Mahoney, who had succeeded Walker as Minister of Natural Resources, acted to increase the maximum compensation for injured workmen. Rhodes won praise even from the *Chronicle* for the composition of the board which was to administer the new public archives building. The opposition showed keen interest in a bill providing for a liquor plebiscite. Originally the voters were to be asked only if they wished to retain the Nova Scotia Temperance Act, but a second question was added in committee requesting an opinion on the government sale of liquor. Worried about the political implications of the plebiscite, the Liberals feared that Rhodes, while professing neutrality, was telling the people that if they wanted old age pensions they should vote for government sale.

Prolonged debate occurred on a hardy annual issue, the dentistry bill. For years attempts had been made to prevent unqualified persons from practising under the supervision of qualified dentists. This time Mahoney and Chisholm led an unsuccessful fight to retain cheap dentistry for poorer patients. Both the cabinet and the parties split badly on the question. Finally, R.H. Butts moved closure at 5 a.m., the first time it had been used since 1914, when he had also been the one to invoke it.

Before the house met in 1930, two significant events occurred. Although late in October nine counties had voted to retain the Nova Scotia Temperance Act, an overall majority of 15,929 opposed it, of which 15,669 came from Halifax County. An even larger majority of 34,565 favoured the government sale of liquor. Earlier Rhodes had announced that if the vote went as it did, he would introduce the best features of acts elsewhere and provide an independent commission to administer the legislation and an efficient constabulary to enforce it. Of unusual political significance was the death in an automobile accident on September 2nd of the partying John Mahoney, a proven vote-getter with a seemingly bright political future. This tragedy necessitated one of the most important by-elections in provincial history — indeed the premier called it "a miniature general election" since the fate of his government hinged upon it. To Sir Robert Borden he expressed indignation that the

Liberals contested it since the vacancy had resulted from an act of God and Mahoney had led the poll in Halifax County only a year earlier. Clearly worried, he pointed out that for the Conservatives Halifax was never "easy fighting ground" and that this time they would have "the whole force of the Federal machine through the Harbour Commission and the waterfront vote" brought to bear against them.[33]

He was fortunate in getting the highly respected Halifax physician Dr. George H. Murphy to become the Conservative candidate and a minister without portfolio. Against him was the old Liberal war horse R.E. Finn whom even some Liberals agreed had gone "too often to the well." However, it could at least be said of Finn that his name permitted the obvious if unimaginative slogan: "Vote Finn and Win."

Almost unceasingly the Conservatives echoed the refrain, "Continue the March of Progress." The premier was also profuse in new promises: a deficit $750,000 less than estimated, appointment of a board to make the women's minimum wage act effective, mothers' allowances, completion of the road from Dartmouth to the Strait of Canso within the year, and old age pensions as soon as expected new financing became available. Basically the Liberals campaigned on the government's failure to keep its promises. One advertisement dealt with bringing the boys back home. "He never came back. Neither will Rhodes." An Olaf cartoon pictured one taxpayer telling Rhodes: "More money taken . . . than ever before and deeper in the hole." An editorial declared that if the premier got four cents he would spend five.

Although it was midwinter, Halifax County was canvassed as it had never been before. Conservative cabinet ministers, former ministers, assemblymen, and Crown prosecutors flooded every hamlet of the county and the Liberals responded similarly. January 21st brought Murphy a massive majority of 5,128; in the city itself Finn carried only six of the eighty-five polling districts. All the *Chronicle* could do was to call on the Liberal members to see that the premier "performs as well as he promises." To correspondents across the country, who included Meighen and R.B. Bennett, Rhodes expressed elation on three counts. He had at last overcome "the prejudices of many who had regarded him as an outsider." His effort to give strong, constructive leadership had finally been recognized and had made the effort "worthwhile." Most important of all, the victory had had "a galvanic effect upon the Party" and "we are in the best position we have ever been." As far as he knew, "there was not . . . a single recalcitrant," and the women's work was "beyond all praise." Even though a "glare of ice" and a snowstorm at midday made it almost impossible for sleighs and automobiles to move, the workers had brought out the largest percentage of voters ever polled in the county.[34]

The opening of the house in 1930 saw the use of a mace for the first time in the assembly's history. The gift of Chief Justice Robert Harris and his wife, at the time anonymously, it evoked for the *Daily Star* the memory of "dim and ancient things, the ghosts of a vanished past." Rhodes had already announced the setting up of a women's minimum wage board, but when it became evident that some of his by-election promises would not be implemented at once, the *Star* asked angrily: "If the statements of public men do not mean what they say, then what are the people expected to make of them?"

Among the government bills was one to change the name of the Department of Natural Resources to the Department of Agriculture. Much more significant were those which provided for the government control and sale of liquor and which established a Nova Scotia police force. Of the former Chisholm said: "The spirit of temperance is absent. It breathes forth a desire on the part of government to sell as much liquor as possible for the profit to be got." He was even more critical of the "arbitrary and tyrannical power" to be exercised by the Liquor Commission established under the act; it might even set up liquor stores in the convocation halls of St. Francis Xavier and Acadia universities.[35] Because this was an issue specially suited to the talents of George Farquhar, trained in law and now the editor of the *Chronicle*, his paper abounded with editorials headed: "Arrogating Responsible Government," "the New Despotism," and "Is Responsible Government to Die?" To him the commission was "as autocratic as the Czar of Russia. It can . . . snap its fingers in the face of the legislature, the Government of the day, public opinion, and natural justice." Since 1848, he concluded, "the principle of responsible government has never been seriously challenged until the present winter.

The Rhodes Liquor Bill strikes at its foundations." Eventually the premier had no choice but to give way: "whole pages [were] torn from the bill, section after section . . . changed, other sections . . . mutilated."[36] No longer, for example, could the commission put stores wherever it saw fit and certainly not in dry counties. In the end even the opposition gave grudging assent.

If anything, the opposition raised an even greater furor against Bill 151, which let the governor in council ban the export of pulpwood from holdings of more than 1,000 acres. The government contended that, while in no way affecting small-woodlot owners, it would permit the retention of natural resources so as to benefit the province, not foreign countries. Some opponents declared that its intent was to force Nova Scotians to sell their pulpwood to the Mersey Paper Company at depressed prices, a charge which Colonel Jones described as a "canard" against his institution. Others contended that it would be disastrous to small woodlot owners, who often sold their wood to large proprietors for export. Generally the opponents labelled the bill "legal theft." After applying Lord Chief Justice Hewart's *The New Despotism* to the situation, the *Chronicle* and the *Star* charged that the bill took away "property without compensation. It is the revival of the Star Chamber, the death knell of Responsible Government, and the overturning of every principle imbedded in the British system of liberty and fair play."[37]

Before the law amendments committee the *Star* reported that the "staid old portraits in the [Legislative] Council chamber nearly left their frames" as speaker after speaker, including Conservative lawyer Hector McInnes and Conservative MP Thomas Cantley of Pictou denounced the bill. The *Herald* shrugged off the proceedings. It had expected a host of smallwoodlot owners before the committee; instead it saw only prosperous-looking capitalists, high-priced lawyers representing American interests, and a few large local owners arguing vested rights. Why should Nova Scotia not do what Ontario and other provinces were doing in the interest of forest conservation?[38] After the government promised not to proclaim the bill if the operators behaved responsibly, it carried the bill by the two-vote majority which was typical in 1930. The government also rejected the pleas of Liberal Gordon Isnor for free textbooks in the public schools. Rhodes declared that he would oppose the measure even if the treasury were full. "The instinct of property in the child would best be safeguarded by each using his own books."

Although Rhodes had reduced the previous year's deficit to $108,000, he forecast one of $400,000 for 1930 and evoked the usual charges of extravagance. However, the main financial and economic debates centred about Maritime Rights. MacMillan charged the Conservatives with preventing the Duncan Commission from investigating the effect of the tariff, while Harrington argued that the Liberals had assailed the Maritime Rights agitation from the start, and boasted that the Rhodes government had been instrumental in having the Duncan Commission established. Both parties hailed the coming into effect of the bill for the elimination of Besco and the setting up of the Dominion Steel and Coal Company. McRitchie's cartoon, "The Big Squeeze," suggested that $150 million of watered stock was being "squeezed out."

By June 1930 a national general election was under way as Mackenzie King sought a victory before economic conditions worsened. Reversing the usual stands of the two parties, the Liberals used the Dunning budget to increase the British preferential tariff on 270 items. To counter the highly protectionist Conservative leader R.B. Bennett, they also raised the general tariff on iron and steel products, fruits, and vegetables; and, anticipating the higher Hawley-Smoot tariff later in the year, they proposed a system of countervailing duties on sixteen articles if the United States increased its tariff. Through professing his "love for our Empire," Bennett became the most ardent of Canadian nationalists and promised to use tariffs to "blast a way into the markets that have been closed."

The Liberals stressed that higher tariffs would have their usual deleterious effect on Nova Scotia, while increased British preference would lead to greater trade and its concomitant benefits, especially for Halifax. They also pointed out that of the millions paid out by the federal government in old age pensions, Nova Scotians had received not a penny; instead Rhodes had "exploited the heartaches" of old people during elections and then failed to keep his promises. Lastly the

Liberals boasted that they had implemented every major recommendation of the Duncan Commission Report and benefited Nova Scotians to the extent of about $40 million. They might have said too that Bennett had no coherent policy for Nova Scotia and relied on a host of promises on every conceivable subject. Naturally he made full use of King's "surprising slip," that he "would not give . . . a five cent piece" to any Tory provincial government. Throughout the campaign the *Herald* emphasized that Bennett, a native Maritimer, would be highly receptive to the province's demands for fair treatment.

Nova Scotia contributed towards Bennett's victory on July 28th by electing ten Conservatives to four Liberals. However, like British Columbia, the province did not support the Conservatives as strongly as it had in 1926: their popular vote in Nova Scotia fell by 1.2 per cent and they lost two seats. Perhaps that was to be expected, since in 1926 they had had their biggest federal success to date and two years later they had almost lost the provincial election.[39]

The election significantly altered Nova Scotia's provincial politics. Four Liberal assemblymen — D.A. Cameron, E.J. Cragg, E.C. Doyle, and J.J. Kinley — had run and lost. By refusing to fill the vacancies, the provincial government made certain that it could not be beaten in the assembly. Indeed it was safe for Premier Rhodes to resign on August 11th to become federal minister of fisheries. Patrician in appearance and attitude, he had been more respected than popular. An excellent though somewhat cold platform speaker, he had to win audiences by arguments rather than by charisma. However, he did have superior ability and the knack, throughout his career, of being able to win elections. His successor was Gordon Harrington; although the choice was that of the cabinet, it was an obvious one and none objected. John Doull became provincial secretary and in December Dr. Murphy took over a new portfolio as minister of health.

At Chisholm's request the Liberals met to choose a leader on October 1st. In the previous weeks only two candidates, both Lunenburgers, had presented themselves — J.J. Kinley, one of the provincial party's old guard, and William Duff, a veteran federal politician. A.S. MacMillan refused nomination but said later that "if my name had gone before [the delegates], undoubtedly I would have been selected." This is dubious for, as Harold Connolly indicated, the delegates "wanted none of the old clique . . . associated with Armstrong." Chisholm urged able George Farquhar to run, but he refused, saying that he had no money and could "exert more influence through the columns of his paper."[40] F.B. McCurdy was dismissed as a possible candidate for not being "a genuine Liberal," even though, as proprietor of the *Chronicle*, he let Farquhar run a highly partisan paper.

Kinley and Duff were nominated with little enthusiasm; then, after some delay, the largely unknown Prescott Blanchard of Truro put forward the name of Angus L. Macdonald, who had had a distinguished war record, studied and taught law, received the degree of Doctor of the Science of Jurisprudence at Harvard in 1929, and opened a practice in Halifax. Earlier, because of massive Liberal defeats federally and provincially in Canada, Macdonald had conceded that the party might go the way of its namesake in Britain, but he was confident that it would survive "if it gets back to fundamentals and gets rid of a few men who have led it into the bog."[41] In 1930 he had lost the only election that he would ever lose when he was defeated federally in Inverness by the popular I.D. (Ike) MacDougall. Only a month before the convention he had been a prime mover in drawing up the party platform. His nomination by Blanchard, whom he did not know even by name, came as a complete surprise to him.[42] Although he did not think that the crowd reacted strongly to his nomination, he realized that the situation was quite different when L.D. Currie, in seconding the nomination, eloquently insisted that anyone associated with the Armstrong government should not be selected.

According to Harold Connolly, Macdonald "touched the heart strings of the crowd and so without any analysis, without any logic, with nothing but sheer emotion they decided that Angus L. was to be their leader." Macdonald told the delegates that "being a poor man and having just opened a law office, I could not possibly accept." J.L. Ilsley and others pressed him to change his mind and MacMillan, holding him by the coat tails, said: "We'll find the money, you take the job."[43] Macdonald declared, however, that the words of Senator Hance Logan influenced him most: "Don't be a fool. This is a thing that only

comes once in a lifetime." So he let his name stand and easily
carried the convention: 314 votes to Duff's 110 and Kinley's 64.
Macdonald's correspondents reflected the general feeling. J.A.
Hanway wrote from Amherst that "the spectre which has
haunted the local party for a number of years disappeared
yesterday"; R.A. MacKay told him that he possessed the "new
blood, new ideals and freedom from corporate interests,"
required to "lead [the party] out of the wilderness."[44] A Cape
Breton priest declared that a Highland Scotch Liberal premier
was now certain: "that means that many of [my] worldly desires
shall be fulfilled."

As premier, Gordon Harrington contrasted sharply with
Rhodes. Not as good a debater as his predecessor, he possessed
more of the common touch and the warmth that was somewhat
lacking in Rhodes. However, their greatest differences were
ideological. Whereas Rhodes was orthodox in his conservatism,
Harrington would probably be described in modern parlance as
a "red Tory." For Harrington, it was unfortunate that financial
constraints prevented him from moving towards the social ends
which he favoured. For Angus Macdonald he professed the
greatest respect; for his followers nothing but scorn for their
masquerading under false colours in calling themselves
Liberals. Although many Liberals thought highly of Harrington, not so Macdonald. In public he never forgave Harrington
for not letting him enter the assembly through a by-election. But
in private Macdonald confessed that "if the truth were to be told,
I was some times afraid that they would open a seat and deprive
me" of the chance to argue that they were "very mean" and were
exhibiting a sign of weakness.[45]

With Chisholm suffering from health problems, MacMillan
succeeded him as Liberal house leader in 1931. Though the
Conservatives lost another member when Frank Stanfield
became lieutenant-governor, the government was in no danger
of defeat. Yet MacMillan's aggressiveness almost seemed to
indicate that he thought he could bring it down. Harrington's
advent was heralded in a speech from the throne which the
Herald called a "human document contrasting warmly with
those cold, stereotyped and sterile speeches of bygone years." In
contrast, the newspaper denounced MacMillan as "the apostle

of gloom and doom" and a McRitchie cartoon pictured him as introducing a retinue of "despair" and "whisper of death."

As usual, finances were at the heart of almost every opposition attack. To keep his promise of action on old age pensions, Harrington sponsored a bill which would permit their payment whenever the act was proclaimed; MacMillan demanded that it become effective immediately. For the next year Provincial Treasurer Doull forecast a deficit of $320,000. Though the Liquor Commission would provide a profit of $1 million, this would be more than swallowed up by the loss of $300,000 from the vendor commissioners and payments of $300,000 for the provincial police, $360,000 for mothers' allowances, and $850,000 for unemployment relief at a time of mounting depression. To MacMillan it was simply the case of a government whose revenues had gone up 94 per cent from $4.8 million to $9.3 million reiterating "the same old story we have heard for five other Sessions, that they cannot make the two ends meet." The Liberals continued their two-year attack on allegedly wasteful expenditures by the Nova Scotia Power Commission in building a hydro-electric system for the Mersey Paper Company, but eventually the house agreed, by the four-vote margin which was common in 1931, that the money had been spent economically.

By necessity Harrington could do little but present resolutions which involved no expenditures: to admit the Canadian Pacific Railway (CPR) into Nova Scotia and especially the port of Halifax; to invite co-operation with Ottawa in dealing with the fishing industry, but avoiding reference to the steam trawler, whose use was becoming a burning question; and to secure expert advice on the adoption of a national fuel policy. The last resolution provoked an angry outburst from MacMillan: "What do we want of expert advice? We object to this procrastination, this side-stepping. We say to act now." Not as adamantly opposed to free school books as Rhodes, Harrington promised Gordon Isnor to reimburse half the cost to school boards that provided free texts to needy students.

Generally the session was unedifying. This was especially true of the debate on the bill to allow the town of Berwick to provide a fixed assessment on an apple-brandy distillery to be built in the town by Richard Steppanski. The Liberals described him as a Russian emigré plumber engaged in bootlegging operations in the United States and a "persistent violator of the law." During the debate R.H. Butts, provoked by MacMillan, asked: "What about the member of the opposition who went over to France last summer with Bill Miller, the most notorious rumrunner in Nova Scotia?" When he refused to give the member's name, MacMillan declared that he should be in the gutter, not the house. Later Butts, who some years earlier had tweaked a member's nose, slapped MacMillan across the face; a few blows were struck and names like "liar" and "coward" bandied about. Butts again held centre stage when he accused Angus L. Macdonald of shaking his fist at them from the gallery. Contemptuous of him, the *Chronicle* belaboured him for sitting "slumped in his seat . . . with his hat slouched over his eyes."

The *Chronicle* also lambasted Dr. T. Ives Byrne, the deputy minister of health, who, while assisting Dr. Murphy with his estimates, crossed the floor and told a Liberal who was annoying him: "I'll get square with you." It was equally outraged when a Conservative member "won bursts of applause" from the gallery without the speaker's rebuke. "Could that happen in any British Legislature outside of Nova Scotia? . . . ancient traditions are being broken to pieces and the whole temper of our public life threatens to fall to wretched levels."[46] Actually the failure to observe the amenities was symptomatic of a situation in which a large, vocal opposition was chomping at the bit to take office and a slightly larger government force was doing all it could to prevent it.

Late in the session the government unveiled its long-awaited Electoral Franchise Bill. Previously, electoral lists had been kept up to date annually through the municipal machinery and whenever they were compiled in a manner which the Liberals found displeasing, they did not "hesitate to take advantage of their continual control of the Legislature to enact special legislation in their own interests."[47] Allegedly these factors had cost the Conservatives two seats in Halifax in 1928. The act of 1931, at least excellent in its conception, provided that voters' lists be prepared immediately before each election by provincially appointed registrars and revisers. Because of the lateness of the session, debate in the house was relatively short, but in the *Chronicle* George Farquhar forecast difficulties in the cities because only three days were allowed for registration. To him the bill "inevitably throws into the hands of the party in power the making up of the lists in populous centres and militates against its opponents. Is this the object?"[48] He prophesied better than he knew.

Before the house met in 1932, Attorney General Hall had gone to the Supreme Court to be succeeded by John Doull, who handed over the office of provincial secretary (and treasurer) to J. Fred Fraser. The economic situation was, if anything, worse. Because of serious losses, the Dominion Steel and Coal Corporation was insisting on a wage cut of 12.3 per cent, which the UMW leadership summarily rejected. The government then appointed a royal commission, the third to be headed by Sir Andrew Rae Duncan, which reported a few days before the session opened that a reduction in wages and the closure of some mines were needed. Following the completion of the debate on the address in reply, Harrington went to Ottawa where he was promised an increased subvention sufficient to permit the sale of an additional million tons of Nova Scotia coal in Quebec and eastern Ontario. Though the miners rejected the wage cut, they decided to remain at work until District 26 of the UMW met in convention in mid-April. That gathering passed without dissent a motion censuring Harrington, something which a *Chronicle* editorial declared was deserved. Frustrated and hurt by the humiliation inflicted on him by miners whom he had long served, Harrington launched an attack on *Chronicle* editor George Farquhar, a former United Church clergyman, whom he described as "a person of warped judgment, perverted vision . . . a renegade clerk in Holy Orders, who has tried his hand at many occupations . . . unsuccessfully."[49] In late May, after holding out for months, the miners finally accepted a wage cut.

After seven deficits the Conservatives at last forecast the smallest of surpluses. In a few cases J. Fred Fraser met obvious needs by increasing the grants to hospitals and the pensions of teachers who had retired before 1928. Mostly it was a case of savings and increased revenues. The savings, relatively small, were to be effected by a reduction of 5 to 10 per cent in the salaries of ministers and officials earning more than $2,000 a year. The additional revenues were to be procured by raising the gasoline tax from five to six cents a gallon and by increasing corporation taxes, succession duties, and amusement taxes. How, asked MacMillan, did the government balance its budget? "By spending less? No, by spending more." However, Fraser pointed out that, except for Prince Edward Island, Nova Scotia had the lowest per capita expenditure of any province.

Once again the government's legislative programme related to matters that would cost little or nothing. One bill set up a department of labour to be headed by a minister in charge of another department. Another, which proposed a department of municipal affairs, contained drastic provisions relating to regulation and control, particularly of municipal sinking funds. Municipality after municipality protested being forced to hand over these funds and pay for their management by the new department. In the end Harrington fled before the storm and withdrew the bill.

Criticized most of all was a redistribution bill to replace the still unused one of 1929. Allegedly intended to save money through the reduction of members, the government wanted to entrust the matter to a two-party committee, but the Liberals, opposed to the principle of reduction, refused to sit on it. A committee composed of Conservatives at least used a set of principles in determining the size of the house. The unit of representation was to be 20,000, one-fifth the population of Halifax County. A county would get a member for each 20,000 of population and an additional member if the excess was greater than 25 per cent of that number. No county would be without representation of its own. The application of these principles meant that the assembly would be reduced in size from 38 to 30, Cumberland and Pictou each losing one of their three members, six other counties one of their two.

Since five of the eight seats lost were in counties held by Conservatives, the Liberals found it difficult to allege unfairness. Nevertheless, they presented a host of amendments. MacMillan declared that he would be against the bill if for no other reason that it had the same number — Bill 151 — as the objectionable forest bill two years earlier. Basically he argued that the savings would be miniscule and that a population drop of 10,000 in ten years hardly justified a reduction in representation from 43 to 30. Perhaps the most significant effect of the bill would be a change in the type of politicking in Halifax and Cape Breton counties, both of which had been divided into five single-member ridings.

During 1932 the depression continued to deepen in Nova Scotia, and in 1933 the speech from the throne was anything but optimistic. Not unexpectedly MacMillan called it "blank and barren" and denounced the entire administration. That led Harrington, convalescing from a serious operation, to decry his opponent's tactics: "I do not usually ask for quarter . . . [but] we have seen things that none of us ever expected to do. We have seen democracy dethroned" in Germany, Russia, and Poland. Hence Harrington deplored any criticism which tended to "destroy public confidence in our institutions, in our public men and thus break down the very structure by which our public is benefited."[50]

Within a week the government had encouraging news: the promise of a $2.50 per ton federal subvention on coal which might permit the sale of the province's coal as far west as Toronto. However, it all went for naught when Fraser announced a deficit of $163,000 for the preceding year and forecast one of $384,000 for the next. Worse still, he intimated that the old age pension act could not be proclaimed until the interim Duncan Commission award was increased substantially. The ensuring onslaught was the beginning of the Liberals' election campaign, and they had an able ally in the *Chronicle's* new cartoonist, Robert Chambers, who delighted in picturing Pied Piper Harrington leading the province down a road of government waste, debt payments, and growing unemployment. In the house the Liberals added supporting details such as the Power Commission's overexpenditure of 50 per cent on the Tusket power development. They also wondered about the five-sided Pentagon Building near the waterfront which housed the Liquor Commission's headquarters on the bottom floor and above it the Conservative provincial headquarters with its three paid organizers, an organization "such as no political party in Nova Scotia throughout its history" had ever before possessed. "Who pays for it?" asked the Liberal critics. When Harrington complained of unfair treatment, the *Star* told him that he wanted "anything like politics" banned from political discussion: "what nonsense these crocodile tears and all this blether about criticism."[51]

To save money MacMillan told the premier to reduce the number of RCMP officers, who had recently replaced the provincial police force. What was the need for 300 "booted and spurred and heavily armed men . . . marching up and down this law-abiding Province?" The *Chronicle* added that "we need disarmament right here in Nova Scotia." That led Harrington to warn the Liberals against any course calculated to disturb the "reign of law and order."[52] To allay conditions created by the depression, the government sponsored a bill for the relief of mortgagees which provided a moratorium on principal and interest payments. It also became an offence for employers of more than twenty-five men to hire outside labour in preference to provincial workers.

Even before the session ended, the government faced another crisis, the going into receivership of the Nova Scotia Steel and Coal Company, again operating on its own. This threw into jeopardy the livelihood of 1,900 miners in two collieries at Sydney Mines and more than 1,300 in four collieries in Pictou County. On the order paper was MacMillan's resolution calling for amendments to the Electoral Franchise Act which, he argued, would give equal advantages to both parties. When lack of time prevented discussion, he asked to have the changes made by order in council. Certainly he had warned the government of the dangers fraught in the act.

Harrington waited almost a month after prorogation before having an election set for August 22nd. He started out by trying to show that the tide had turned with the revival of gold mining, the prospects of a large apple crop, and an improvement in lumbering. He promised, in his manifesto, to implement old age pensions no later than July 1, 1934; to keep the per capita cost of government the lowest in Canada, Prince Edward Island excepted; to provide free school books for needy students; to continue the efforts to save the coal industry; and to keep on asserting forcefully the province's rights within Confederation.

The Liberal campaign was one of supreme confidence. Typical was a Chambers cartoon showing Don Quixote Harrington on a steed named "the government's eight year record" tilting futilely against windmills marked "public sentiment at the polls." Macdonald's manifesto, labelled "Restoration of Responsible Government," promised to eliminate waste and balance the budget; to pay old age pensions immediately; to provide free school books up to Grade 9; to embark on a programme of hard surfacing the main highways; to appoint an independent commission to inquire into the conditions which had crippled the province's economic life; and to enact "fair and just" franchise laws.

The last promise reflected the fact that the working of the franchise act had dwarfed manifestoes and normal election proceedings as the main focus of attention. In each of the three Halifax City ridings — North, Centre, and South — the returning officers had appointed only one registrar of voters. One account, that of Liberal newspaperman H.B. Jefferson, says that the premier called Macdonald to his office to "fix things" when the "first squawk" was raised about the number of registrars, but that on his way the Liberal leader met George Farquhar who persuaded him not to go and instead take advantage of the "greatest bonanza" that ever befell a Nova Scotia party. A second and more likely version, that of Farquhar himself, is that he persuaded a reluctant Macdonald to see the premier before he started legal proceedings and that Harrington "brushed" him off by intimating that it was not his function to tell returning officers their duties.[53]

So on July 19th the Liberals applied for a writ of mandamus requiring the returning officers in Halifax to appoint additional registrars. For an entire evening leading lawyers of both parties argued the question before Mr. Justice Carroll of the Supreme Court. For the Conservatives, C.B. Smith told him that he ought not to assume the functions of the legislature; but Carroll replied that the aim of the statute was to give the vote to all qualified citizens and "if it is not clear, like this one, then I may decide what course should be taken." Accordingly he interpreted "polling district" in the act to mean "polling division" as defined in the previous act and ordered registrars to be appointed for each of the divisions described in that act: 16 in Halifax North, 10 in Halifax Centre, and 14 in Halifax South.

Why the premier let the situation develop as he did is incomprehensible. Legally he may have been right in not giving instructions to the returning officers, but an astute politician would have realized the dangers in letting the impression be created that citizens were to be deprived of the right to vote. Even covert hints to the returning officers might have avoided the events of July 19th. As it was, following what the *Chronicle* called "the most sensational and unprecedented political hearing since the days of Joe Howe," Macdonald read aloud Carroll's decision in the court house at midnight to the tumultuous cheers of his followers. No newcomer to the provincial political scene has ever become so quickly, widely, and favourably known in such a dramatic fashion.

This was only the beginning. In the days that followed complaints were numerous that the registrars' lists were hopelessly incomplete, or had been posted in inaccessible places, or had not been made available to the public or to Liberal workers. Mr. Justice Graham promised a writ of mandamus to Liberal lawyers if the registrars did not rectify the last two ills in Halifax West. By far the most critical situation occurred in the three city ridings, where the names of thousands of citizens, including that of MacMillan, were left off the preliminary lists. Hundreds lined up to be registered, the process sometimes slowed by registrars asking aged people if they were twenty-one, or youths if they were judges of the Supreme Court. Photographs in the *Chronicle* showed "indignant crowds" massing at the registration centres. Beneath a picture of Joseph Howe it ran a front-page editorial declaring that "Nova Scotia is once again in the throes of a fight for Responsible Government" and quoted an eminent Halifax Conservative as saying, "As I walked past the Province Building, I would not have been surprised had Joseph Howe stepped off his pedestal." Life-long Conservative Dr. W.D. Forrest declared that the "raw franchise deal [was] too much to swallow" and left the party. Retired Supreme Court Judge Benjamin Russell said that "Tammany Hall was never guilty of so vile a conspiracy to destroy the constitutional rights of a political community."[54]

Too late the Conservatives attempted a defence. The *Herald* of July 27th carried a front-page statement by Harrington that the condition of the lists had been greatly exaggerated for partisan purposes and that the final lists would be "the fairest and most

Gordon S. Harrington   1930-33

Courtesy of NSIS Photo

complete and accurate ever used in an election in the Province.''
The next day, under the heading, ''So the People May Know:
Here is the Evidence: You are the Judge,'' the *Herald* displayed
fifteen pictures of registration booths with few registrants. In
the end, when the total provincial registration turned out to be
294,538 compared with 253,047 in 1928, the *Herald* boasted of

almost complete lists, but, try as they might, the Conservatives never recovered from being discredited early in the campaign.

The last days were largely anticlimax as both parties turned to the issues raised in their manifestoes. However, more and more, as the Liberals realized their leader's attractiveness, they emphasized Macdonald the man in every way possible. Similarly the Conservatives stressed Harrington as the friend of labour who had promoted thirty legislative enactments which it had advocated, as the man of influence at Ottawa whose forceful presentations had made valuable gains for the province, and as the man of experience who contrasted sharply in that respect with his opponent.

August 22nd brought defeat for the man of experience, his party winning only eight of the thirty seats, its popular vote falling from 50.6 to 45.9 per cent, and five cabinet ministers losing their seats. Three Co-operative Commonwealth Federation (CCF) candidates, the province's first, polled 2,336 votes, and three Unity Front candidates, who included J.B. McLachlan, received 2,469 votes. The *Star* was elated that the honour of Nova Scotia was vindicated and that "the traditions of Joseph Howe are not dead." Conservatives like John A. Walker told Macdonald that, since the people wanted a Liberal government, "there is no one I would prefer to see at the head of it than yourself," and H.P. MacKeen hoped that his new high office would not preclude "the more social amenities of life to which your company is always an acquisition."[55]

Later Harold Connolly would say that the dramatic court appearance before Mr. Justice Carroll was "more effective than any other single thing in turning out the Government."[56] However, that is going too far. Between 1931 and 1935 all the five Conservative provincial governments went down to defeat and, as the *Herald* put it, "there is a psychology which always operates [against an] administration" in times of economic difficulty. Nothing that Harrington might have done could have saved him, but the election would certainly have been closer had it not been for the franchise affair. Macdonald himself might have had difficulty in Halifax South, where the respected Dr. Murphy lost by only 620 votes. The franchise scandal had other victims as well. One observer suggests that it was the reason for "the poor salaried Conservative who planned the monstrous scheme . . . [ending] his days in the Nova Scotia Hospital for the Insane."[57] Macdonald was correct in predicting that anyone connected with it would never sit in the legislature again. With it in mind, he would say to the end of his career that the Conservatives were "condemned to an eternity of hopeless effort for misdeeds and errors of judgment in the past."[58]

CHAPTER 6

Angus L. Macdonald: the Development of a Mystique

The cabinet that took office on September 5, 1933 was probably Nova Scotia's strongest. In contrast with others, all its ministers with portfolio would perform outstandingly well. Macdonald himself became provincial secretary and hence provincial treasurer; MacMillan took on highways; J.H. MacQuarrie the attorney generalship; Dr. F.R. Davis, health and welfare; John A. McDonald, agriculture and marketing; and Michael Dwyer, mines, public works, and labour. Determined to show that he meant to keep his promises, the premier had the Old Age Pensions Act of 1931 proclaimed on the day he took office. Anxious to move towards a balanced budget, he appointed a cabinet committee of three to effect economies in expenditure. Also high on his agenda was the appointment of a royal commissioner to inquire into the operation of the Electoral Franchise Act.

The part of governing he liked least was dealing with patronage. He had no trouble in dismissing Conservative office-holders who had been active campaign workers but, as he told his brother, he did not want to be "brutal" about it. "In the case of a widowed mother who is the sole support of a small family or any similar case I have always believed that it is wiser, and certainly more Christian, not to dismiss them."[1] Never able to avoid details, he had so overtaxed himself by the end of the year that he had to seek medical advice. From Antigonish William Chisholm told him not to wear himself out accommodating friends who were promoting their own interest, and to go on a trip to the West Indies.

The speech from the throne in March 1934 forecast the keeping of another pledge through the appointment of a royal commission to determine how national policies had affected the provincial economy. At the outset Harrington declared that "the buttons are off the foils from now on." During the election Macdonald had said that he wanted to get him on the floor of the house to settle "three years of old scores." "Here I am," said the Conservative leader, who called the inquiry into the working of the franchise act "the most inquisitorial one can imagine," denounced the wholesale dismissals with which "the headman's axe has been winning blood every day," and called the premier's resort to principles of liberalism "a veil to cover the pork-barrel and the trough." Macdonald's reply, his maiden speech, demonstrated that he would become one of the great orators of the Nova Scotia assembly, so effective that only a few years later the opposition would be sometimes reluctant to launch criticism for fear of devastating replies. Had the Conservatives forgotten that they had dismissed four times as many civil servants between 1925 and 1928? Why could they not find enough money to pay for old age pensions when his government would be sending out cheques to 6,000 recipients by the end of March? Why had they prevented the Duncan Commission from investigating the effect of the tariff? In contrast with them, Macdonald would not begin his fight "for justice for this land, this Nova Scotia."[2]

One dismissal continued to cause trouble. Because several organizations protested the removal of war veteran Ann Allan as superintendent of nurses at the Nova Scotia Sanitorium, the cabinet appointed lawyer J. Welsford Macdonald to investigate the case. He found that Nurse Allan had repeatedly urged the workers under her supervision to vote for a government "who are giving us our bread and butter." The premier invited editor George Farquhar to attend a cabinet meeting and gave him a copy of the report, saying, "With this you will be able to write many editorials." Farquhar replied, "I will have to read it over first," but in the end he did nothing. He felt that Macdonald "must be made to understand that I was as free and independant [sic] in my field as he was in his." The premier never again tried

Angus L. Macdonald   1933-40
1945-54

Courtesy of Public Archives of Nova Scotia

to tell him what to do, "but from then on there crept in a slight sense of strain in our relations."[3]

For the previous year Macdonald indicated a deficit of $1.6 million and despite an increase in the gasoline tax from six to eight cents a gallon and additional taxes on business, he forecast one of $1.3 million for the next year. None could have done more than he to cut expenditures. He studied to the last detail every departmental budget, often sending them back for further paring. After approval, however, "each minister was master in his own domain."[4] Pointing out that federal grants to the provinces had been revised at least twenty-six times since 1867, he called for a new approach to federal-provincial relations by which "the Dominion would assume the entire cost of certain services which are national in their incidence." When Harrington accused him of betraying a trust for not presenting a balanced budget, he cut him short. If the previous government had not exceeded the estimated deficit by $1.2 million, he would have come close to a balance, but when faced with a deficit equal to 20 per cent of the gross revenue, he found it "impossible in one year to turn that deficit into a surplus."[5]

The session's most significant and certainly most controversial bill was the Gasoline Licensing bill. Primarily MacMillan's work, he later called its passage "one of the outstanding events of my public career."[6] He had become concerned that the retail price of gasoline was 29.5 cents a gallon in Halifax compared with 22.5 cents in Toronto even though a refinery at Woodside processed crude oil brought in by tanker. Accordingly he asked G. Fred Pearson to investigate the distribution system and the latter's proposals became the basis of the bill which placed the entire gasoline trade, wholesale and retail, under the regulatory control of the Public Utilities Board. By ending the contracts that required retailers to buy from specific wholesalers, it helped to remove monopolistic conditions in the trade. Because Pearson considered that only 1,100 of the 4,000 pump outlets in existence were needed, retailers would have to prove "public convenience and necessity" to the Public Utilities Board before being allowed to operate. In prolonged committee hearings this became the single most controversial provision. What right had the government to take away the livelihood of a person who, in good faith, had invested his money in a gasoline retail outlet? "He's paying for his folly of going into business," replied MacMillan.[7] Later it was said that any Liberal who had previously sold gasoline was able to secure a licence through pressure on the board.

The bill to increase the gasoline tax provoked angry debate on an ancillary issue. When Percy Black and Macdonald disagreed on the mileage of paved roads the Liberals had promised, the premier wished that he "could see the honourable member outside for five minutes." That did not prevent Harrington from saying that his opponents were pledged to pave all the roads. "The people had it dinned into their ears from a hundred platforms; they heard it from a thousand canvassers; they read it every day in the press." The premier's response was a fearsome attack on the Conservative leader and his party. Harrington's criticism, he said, demonstrated "colossal effrontery, inconceivable conceit and absolute disregard for the intelligence of the public." The Tory virus had infected his blood with the Tory instinct of unfairness. Typical Tories believed that the Lord had ordained them to rule. They might have to "make promises [they could] never keep . . . to turn government offices into election booths . . . to waste money on political roadwork, but what of it?" Of his own government Macdonald hoped eventually to say, "We found [Nova Scotia] brick and we have left it marble."[8]

To MacMillan's satisfaction, his licensing act resulted in the tank wagon price of gasoline falling by 1.5 cents a gallon on the very day the new tax became effective. Thus the consumer paid only half a cent of the increase. The situation improved further and by August the province had received $964,000 from the tax increase, of which the public had paid only $22,000. Indirectly MacMillan had made possible a very substantial contribution towards the road-paving programme.

When the government sought to keep another promise by repealing the much reviled Bill 151, the opposition denounced the absence of a substitute measure to ensure forest conservation. Lands and Forests Minister MacQuarrie intimated that a complete forest survey would take place before the government ventured on a full-scale conservation plan. The grievous thing about Bill 151, he said, was that the government could exercise arbitrary power without knowing how much damage was being done to the forests or property rights. To no avail the Conservatives protested that an act which had never been proclaimed could have done little harm.

In tabling the report of Mr. Justice Ross on the franchise act, Macdonald declared that it contained "a record of incompetence, and of planned corruption . . . of which there never was a parallel in the history of the province." Registrars, especially in Halifax, had prepared or presented as their own work lists which sometimes omitted the names of more than half the eligible voters. Employees in five departments had compiled faulty lists, which the registrars were sworn to prepare themselves. The premier blamed not only the Conservative organization but also cabinet ministers who should have seen that election officials carried out their duties. The *Chronicle* went so far as to ask, "Does anybody . . . believe that Premier Harrington, or Mr. Black, or any of the rest of them were so blind that they did not know what was going on in their offices under their very noses?"[9] Harrington replied that the act was a good one since it registered more voters than ever before. Though admitting that some election officials had not done their duty, he called the inquiry a political inquisition that had convicted suspected offenders out of their own mouths. The public, he declared, did not want its representatives to "continue political campaigns on the floors of the Assembly" but to conduct the public business. Though in a difficult position, Harrington could at least take comfort in the fact that many prominent Liberals refused to believe that he had knowledge of electoral fraud.

The mining industry continued to cause concern. After the receiver-liquidators of the Nova Scotia Steel and Coal Company cut the wages in the Pictou collieries, the miners walked out. When the liquidators asked the courts for permission to close the Allan and Thorburn mines, the decision was inconclusive. Although the wage deadlock was broken, the end of coal mining on a major scale in Pictou County appeared to be not far off. Mines Minister Dwyer took strong action to remedy the difficulties occasioned by the existence of two unions, the UMW and the Amalgamated Mine Workers (AMW). By requiring a coal company to deduct dues for only one union, he hoped to facilitate negotiations for a new wage contract in November.

In July Macdonald kept another promise by appointing a Royal Commission of Economic Inquiry headed by Professor Harry Jones of the University of Leeds to investigate the effect of

Canadian fiscal and trade policies on the province's economic life and to make recommendations for the removal of any economic, financial, or other disability from which the province suffered. The premier had already authorized his friend Professor Norman McLeod Rogers of Queen's to prepare the province's case, and the latter's submission to the commission, based partly on developments in Australian federalism, became a new *modus vivendi*, elements of which Nova Scotia's governments have continued to use.

According to Rogers, any attempt to neutralize the taxing capacity of the provinces through higher subsidies to the weaker ones would produce friction rather than harmony. However, allowing the provinces the sole right to levy income taxes would accentuate the differences between them. His solution was to give the full use of this power to the Dominion government on the understanding that it would act as "a conduit through which a portion of the income . . . transferred from the other provinces to Quebec and Ontario as a result of the protective tariff [would] be returned to the provinces [adversely] affected." To ensure stability of payments for fixed periods and remove the danger of political manipulation, an independent commission would determine the amounts every ten years using an appropriate test of fiscal need.[10] Rogers himself estimated the province's net loss from the tariff in 1931 to be about $4.5 million and, although economists did not generally accept his assumptions, some agreed that his conclusions might be regarded as "descriptive probabilities."

Working rapidly, the Jones Commission reported in December 1934 that the tariff had damaged Nova Scotia's economic development and suggested that the province's industries should apply to the Tariff Commission for either a reduction in duties or an extension of the drawbacks on the materials they bought. It also recommended that the federal government consult the provinces before making changes in tariff policy. Its basic financial finding was that Nova Scotia's subsidy was grossly inadequate and that provincial subsidies should be periodically adjusted according to "fiscal need carefully defined." It suggested too that the federal government assume *in toto* the burden of old age pensions, unemployment insurance, and other social services. Other proposals included the establishment of a permanent civil service, an economic council, and a municipal affairs branch in an existing department.

By 1935 circumstances had begun to favour the government. Early in the year the White Commission recommended an annual increase of $425,000 in the Duncan Commission's interim award of $875,000, and economic conditions finally showed some improvement. Macdonald accepted Harrington's proposals to have only the two of them speak during the throne speech debate, and then proceeded with the main part of his agenda, bills to implement the Jones Commission's proposals. One established the Nova Scotia Economic Council, an advisory body authorized to explore the possibility of expanding industry and utilizing the province's natural resources. Another went further than the Jones Commission recommendation and set up a full-fledged department of municipal affairs to be administered by the attorney general. The new department lacked the powers that had caused the previous government's bill to founder. This time even Harrington wanted to be assured that the municipalities did not lose the "rights of home rule."

On the bill to create a permanent civil service under a one-man commission, Harrington found himself accused of having "an amazing acrobatic turn of mind" when he approved its principle but doubted its practicality. He made much of the feeling in Nova Scotia that if a party did not confer personal advantage it would not be supported. "If that feeling is general it is useless to . . . consider the bill." He also doubted if the period following an orgy of head-slashing was the right time to set up a civil service commission. The premier argued that the numbers of Liberal and Conservative appointees were about the same. "When was the service to be established," he asked, "if not when the two were fairly even balanced?"[11]

Liberal newspaperman H.B. Jefferson, who had "inside information," later said that Macdonald did not want to be bothered with a civil service commission, "but the *Herald* was belly-aching about it and he knew that . . . if they belly-ached long enough, they would work up a public demand." Accordingly he established the commission and then "relegated it to the corner . . . they called for applications but . . . they knew before they ever put the ad in the paper, who they were going to appoint."[12] He may have exaggerated, but years later when R. MacGregor Dawson investigated conditions in the public service he found that the commission possessed little prestige under its first commissioner, seemingly because the act was not rigorously enforced. The lack of an adequate system of classification and the omission of many public servants simply magnified the defect.[13]

To meet the Jones Commission's advocacy of a shortened working day in industry, Labour Minister Dwyer sponsored a bill setting up a board of adjustment headed by his deputy minister which would determine limitations on the hours of labour in industries such as mining, manufacturing, and construction. Harrington called it a "vacuity," "nebulous," the same as no bill; worst of all, it abrogated the powers of the house because it let a board arbitrarily determine the industry to which it applied and the maximum hours of work in that industry. Speaking in a brogue that kept the house in stitches, Dwyer likened Harrington to a chameleon that changed its spots. How, he wondered, could the legislature possibly determine the industries in which a limitation of hours of work was practicable, or the appropriate length of the working day in those industries? In its determination to follow the Jones Commission's proposals the government declared its intention to press the federal authorities for tariff modification and to negotiate with them for a national park in Cape Breton.

In keeping with its election pledges it also forecast a major program to pave the trunk roads. Farquhar rightly calls MacMillan the "real father of the paving program." He visited a number of American states, studied their methods and, to cope with Nova Scotia's severe frost conditions, devised "a mixture which, when the frost was coming out, would heave . . . without cracking and when the frost was gone would sink back into place as before." He underdrained the roadbed thoroughly, covered it with coarse gravel, then finer gravel, and finally his own mixture, which was more flexible than any used in the United States. Initially he tried it on experimental stretches of the Truro and Annapolis Valley roads. "That first winter, he spent many a sleepless hour wondering if he was right, would the paving stand up under our frost conditions. It did, and the province was away."[14] During 1934 the government had 200 miles prepared for paving, forecast an additional 300 miles during 1935, and hoped to have 500 miles actually paved by the end of 1936.[15] All this was "done in the long depression of the thirties when the province was operating on a shoe-string."

Unrelated to the Jones Commission's proposals was legislation to provide free school books for the first eight grades and a new franchise act based on the federal act of 1930, which provided that enumerators prepare the lists in communities of more than 5,000, and registrars in other areas. Gone, boasted the *Star*, would be padded lists, fictitious names, and the other iniquities of 1933.

In announcing a deficit of $1,129,167 for the previous year, Macdonald used the occasion to make a lengthy examination of federal-provincial relations since 1867. From the beginning, he contended, the financial arrangements had been unfavourable to Nova Scotia. In those years it had not been thought that the provinces would have to resort to direct taxation. Now, in light of growing demands, Nova Scotia could not carry on under the constitutions's financial provisions. The speech marked another stage in the development of the premier's oratorical powers. Chief Justice Sir Joseph Chisholm told him that not "since the days of Joseph Howe in the meridian of his power" had it been surpassed "in elegance of diction and emotional appeal; it is chaste, patriotic and eloquent." Macdonald himself feared that because of "a mass of routine matters," he did "not enjoy the elasticity of mind and physical fitness which are prerequisite to the preparation and delivery of a worthwhile speech."[16] Nevertheless, he almost always prepared his speeches by himself with great care and, as a later premier pointed out, he had the happy knack of making them sound extemporaneous. Whatever the quality of his speech on this occasion, Harrington again chided him for failing to keep his promises. "I can almost see the stains of tears on the carpets over here which were shed over the deficits of the past, but such is the change that a slight change of position makes."

Harrington made the same sort of charge when Macdonald forecast a deficit of $1,040,232 in his budget which, because of a change in the fiscal year, covered fourteen months instead of twelve. The premier felt encouraged, however, since, but for the outlay of $734,000 on old age pensions and $136,000 on free school books, he would have come within $21,000 of a balance in the next twelve months. It was a nasty debate in which the sins of the past, accusations of jugglery and robbery, and even the Dionne quintuplets intruded. To Harrington's charge that the government was driving the province into debt at the rate of over $100 an hour, Macdonald simply replied: "I said that we would balance the budget, and we will balance the budget" before the next election.

By mid-August Canada was in the throes of a general election. Before dissolution E.N. Rhodes went to the Senate to be succeeded as minister of fisheries by W.G. Ernst of Queens-Lunenburg. Harrington was made chairman of the newly established Employment and Social Insurance Commission, part of Prime Minister Bennett's "New Deal." In a *Chronicle* cartoon, "Bob" Chambers pictured five provincial Conservatives recently appointed to high office joining in "close harmony" to sing: "I got mine, boys; Oh — I got mine."

In Nova Scotia the Liberals and Conservatives generally used their parties' national arguments, adapting them slightly to the provincial situation. Mackenzie King strongly denounced Bennett's high tariff policies. "There are those who think that 'trade is in the nature of war' . . . This view is the typical Conservative one." The Conservatives hailed the prime minister as "the Statesman of Empire," pointed out that the first preference written into the Canada-United Kingdom agreement of 1932 related to fruit, and hoped that fish would soon be added.

Both the Liberals and Conservatives indicated their distaste of the new parties, the Co-operative Commonwealth Federation and Social Credit. Warning against their panaceas and radical policies, Ernst asked: "Are we going to destroy society as we know it and disregard where we will drift?" He had nothing to fear from them, however, since the only candidates to challenge the old parties in Nova Scotia were the independent J.B. McLachlan and eleven nominated by the Reconstruction Party of H.H. Stevens. The latter applied his usual arguments to Nova Scotia's industries. The inordinate concentration of control in the fishing industry, he contended, meant few buyers of fish and little competition in purchasing. No firm or corporation had the right to exploit the man who risked his life at sea by giving him only half a cent a pound for his fish. The Reconstruction candidates included labour spokesmen, co-operative leaders, and a United Church minister, all of whom in other circumstances might well have run for the CCF.

When the campaign started, Angus L. Macdonald was in Scotland receiving plaudits both as the great-grandson of a man who went to Nova Scotia from Moidart in Inverness and as the only Gaelic-speaking premier in the world. On his return he became an active participant. In Halifax he found that Mackenzie King's speech had aroused little enthusiasm and his friend Alexander (Alex) Johnston wondered if King had "lost the art of pumping force and vigor into his speeches." Macdonald himself won praise for helping Liberal candidates. "Every time you make a speech," a grateful J.L. Ilsley told him, "whether it be political or nonpolitical, you raise the stock of yourself and your government." Norman McLeod Rogers, running in Kingston, Ontario, was delighted to have an old friend as "one of the sponsors at my political christening." Because Macdonald had made some enemies during two years in office and because some Liberals who still sought jobs were prophesying that the party would fare badly in Nova Scotia, he wanted it to do particularly well. The victory of Liberals in all twelve seats was, to him, "a complete answer to [the] croakers."[17]

Although only one Reconstruction candidate in Nova Scotia saved his deposit, the party's showing was the best in all of Canada, — 13.9 per cent of the popular vote, somewhat more than the 11.5 per cent that it polled in Ontario. Undoubtedly this party drained away many more Conservative votes than Liberal and helped to account for the Conservatives' abysmal showing. Though the Conservatives lost Colchester by only 206 votes, Cumberland by 315, and Queens-Lunenburg by 738, their defeats were generally overwhelming by Nova Scotian standards, and they took only 32.1 per cent of the vote. Nova Scotians may not have accepted the Liberal slogan, "King or Chaos," but they had at least concluded that the certain way to get rid of a discredited government was to vote Liberal.

Improved economic conditions began in 1935 and continued throughout 1936. The coal mines were more active that they had been for years, the Sydney steel plant was operating almost at capacity, agriculture and lumbering were relatively healthy, and the need for direct relief had fallen off sharply. Accordingly,

Macdonald objected to a *Chronicle* editorial which predicted that any government going to the polls would be beaten, and he told Farquhar that he should have pointed out that Taschereau in Quebec and Bracken in Manitoba had won elections. Undoubtedly he much preferred the paper's earlier comment that he possessed "more of the characteristics of [Joseph] Howe — the ethos of his thinking and speaking — than any Premier who succeeded him."[18]

The speech from the throne in 1936 concentrated on the government's success in implementing the previous session's measures. Harrington, who had resigned the Conservative leadership but not his assembly seat, was back leading the opposition unofficially after giving up his federal appointment when the King government referred Bennett's New Deal legislation to the courts without attempting to implement it. The Liberals thought about denying him his seat but decided that the Nova Scotia laws did not prevent a federal servant, retired or not, from being a provincial MLA at the same time. Besides, Macdonald considered him the best opposition leader the Liberals could have since someone else was likely to be more dangerous. Not only had his progressive outlook "always been displeasing to a certain number of Tories," but some Halifax Conservatives blamed him for the franchise scandal.[19] Not surprisingly, Harrington urged an amendment to the BNA Act that would allow the federal Parliament to embark upon a broad programme of social legislation, including unemployment insurance, health and accident insurance, and maternity benefits, but the government opposed him on the ground that the question of jurisdiction on these matters was before the courts.

For the previous fourteen months the premier indicated a deficit of $898,000, estimated one of about $360,000 for the next year, and hoped to present a balanced budget in 1937. As usual, the opposition heaped scorn on a government that could boast only about keeping within its estimates. Why should it be elated with an increased expenditure of $1.5 million and an addition of $18 million to the funded debt?

Indicating that he favoured an increase in membership, Macdonald got the house to set up a redistribution committee. When Harrington wondered if thirty members were "in any way unable properly to represent the people," the premier told him that it had always been recognized that Digby should have two members to ensure representation from both racial groups and that a similar case might be made for Yarmouth and Inverness. Though the committee tentatively proposed an additional five members, it asked for more time to reach a definitive conclusion. The session was uneventful and harmonious. At the end the members sang "Let Me Call You Sweetheart" and "Pack Up Your Troubles," and finished by joining hands in a boisterous rendition of "Auld Lang Syne." "I'll bet we could stump any legislature in the whole Dominion as singers," said MacMillan.

Before Macdonald the one Catholic premier of the province had been John S.D. Thompson, who had served only fifty-four days. During Macdonald's long period of office-holding not even a whisper was raised in public that his religion had affected his political behaviour. Behind the scenes, however, his relations with Catholic leaders in the diocese of Antigonish were sometimes unpleasant. Older Antigonish Liberals, almost all Catholic, were to his knowledge still embittered by the memories of Bishop John Cameron, who had actively inter-vened more than once to secure the election of John Thompson in Antigonish. Macdonald himself found it curious that the bishops almost always sided with the Tories. The situation was not helped when, not long after he became premier, he did not call on Bishop James Morrison while on a short visit to Antigonish. Later, he said, the bishop received him with "a coldness which amounted almost to rudeness"; it would be a long time "before I call upon him again."

About this time his brother and confidant, Father Stanley Macdonald, told him of one priest who complained that the premier was showing signs of anticlericalism. Premier Macdonald in turn heaped scorn on the type of cleric who disliked Catholic laymen who become prominent in public life "for the reason that any division of prestige or glory will show these narrow-minded and often ignorant people in a very poor light." As for himself, "I am as good a Catholic as ever I was and if I do not answer them when some tu' penny ha' penny cracks the whip it is because I realize that I am not the Catholic Premier but the Premier of all the people and I have to do what I think is in the general interest." He could never forget that his "warmest supporters are to be found among the Protestant people." Besides, he would likely perform "a much greater service to the Church . . . by attempting to discharge the duties of this office honestly and efficiently than I will by listening to every little local politician who has neither the brains nor the desire to see things in a broad light."[20]

Things political continued to develop much as Macdonald wanted in 1936. When Harold Connolly won a by-election in Halifax North, he prophesied that the new member would be "a valuable man to us in future." He was no less pleased that the Conservatives again chose Harrington as their leader in July. At the convention Harold Bissett had provided a jarring note by declaring that anyone "who either primarily or secondarily was connected with the franchise scandal of 1933" should not be leader. When someone shouted, "He's a Liberal spy," Bissett sat down. To suit its own ends, the Liberal *Star* declared that the choice of anyone but Harrington would have been a "miscarriage of justice."[21]

In 1937 the speech from the throne again reflected the optimism growing out of the improved economic climate, tempered in part by difficulties in the fishing and coal mining industries. The provincially run Inverness mine continued to suffer heavy losses and the bankruptcy of the coal companies made the future of mining in Pictou County look bleak. Harrington was concerned chiefly with the failure to provide "a social programme to secure people who are now insecure." He wanted an extension of the Workmen's Compensation Act to cover fully any accident that prevented a workman from providing for his family, and he also advocated increases in old age pensions and mothers' allowances. As he saw it, a national social security programme might have been on its way if, a year earlier, the government had not refused to express itself in favour of a constitutional amendment making it possible. In a front-page editorial, "The Only Way to Do It," the *Herald* supported his demand for "social legislation, centralized in Ottawa."[22]

In an elaborately prepared, highly political reply, Macdonald pointed out that every party had a characteristic social outlook. The philosophy of liberalism had developed through the centuries as men of liberal mind rebelled against authority and adopted equalitarian measures. After extolling the accomplishments of British Liberals since the 1820s, he showed that in Canada, too, Liberals had battled entrenched Toryism for years before overthrowing arbitrary government. In Nova Scotia almost all the humanitarian and social measures had been "the products of Liberal minds and Liberal hearts," whether it was the Victoria General Hospital, the Nova Scotia Technical College, the Workmen's Compensation Act, or old age pensions.[23] By inference, Macdonald seemed to say that Liberal governments alone could be counted upon to provide whatever social legislation the circumstances required and permitted.

Dissatisfied because the premier's history lesson had little direct relevance to the existing situation, Harrington sought to outline his position by resolution, only to have it hopelessly emasculated. Liberal members such as MacQuarrie and L.D. Currie sympathized with him, and the latter told him that "his temperament and his reading long ago bent his mind in the direction of social security legislation," but he should realize that no Tory leader in Britain or elsewhere had been able to carry his party with him for long in the policy he was advocating. Besides, he could not expect Liberals to support Tory efforts to use the working class as "a political rumble-seat to ride into power."[24] This incident says something about the meaninglessness of party ideology in Nova Scotia.

In a likely pre-election session the government took obvious pleasure in a rural electrification bill which provided that, wherever the cost of providing electricity went beyond a specific amount, the excess would be paid out of the consolidated revenue fund. It also boasted of amendments to the Workmen's Compensation Act which raised payments to two-thirds of an injured worker's wages and let the board deal with individual cases without undue consideration of precedent. Hitherto opposition members had always been the ones to introduce independence of Parliament bills, but this session the government itself sponsored one which forbade business transactions between an MLA and the government. When Harrington objected to an exception being made to dealings of "a casual nature," MacQuarrie replied that he was giving too broad a meaning to the phrase and that it was intended to cover only such things as the sale by a member's employee of a few gallons of gasoline or a few feet of lumber. "However eager we may be to have this act as strong as can be, we should be equally careful against causing some person to be unseated through some inadvertent act through no fault of their own."[25]

Harrington was a step ahead of the government with a vital piece of labour legislation that required companies to bargain collectively with unions that constituted a majority of their workers, and to make compulsory checkoffs of dues if a union favoured it. Actually it was almost a replica of the bill which the Trades and Labour Congress of Canada had sent to every legislature. Angry Liberals charged that Harrington had proceeded with a bill that they were considering but had not introduced because of the absence of the minister of labour; once again they accused him of currying the support of labour in the general election to come. Nevertheless, the bill passed with minor amendments.

It was on its financial record that the government expected major electoral support. When, instead of an anticipated deficit, Macdonald announced a surplus of $151,718 for 1936-37, the reaction was not surprising; "the House sat for a moment, as if not comprehending the good news, then rocked with acclaim, at least the Government side of the House did, though the opposition, stilled and stunned-like, sat like figures carved in stone. A great effort of will, for 'Even the ranks of Tuscany could scarce forbear to cheer'."[26] In throwing cold water on the accomplishment, Harrington declared that it resulted partly from improved economic conditions, partly from an increase in the provincial debt of $20 million, and partly from exacting an additional $3 million from the public. MacMillan's rejoinder was that Harrington fulfilled one definition of a conservative: "a person who would not look at the new moon because of his respect for the old one."

The favourable news continued when Macdonald forecast a surplus of $104,285 for 1937-38 and promised the abolition of the highway poll tax for persons between eighteen and twenty-one, a reduction in charges to patients at the Kentville Sanitorium, and an increase in civil service salaries. He also announced a capital expenditure of $7.5 million on highways, reminding rural Nova Scotians at the same time that, as the paving programme moved towards completion, less money would be required for the trunk highways and more would be available for the county and local roads. As the session closed, C.W. Anderson, a minister without portfolio, resigned when it was revealed that the Nova Scotia Lumber Company, of which he was president, had been fined $42,513 for cutting on Crown lands and violating the size-limit regulations. The matter would enter dramatically into the forthcoming election.

The preliminaries to that election were in some ways more exciting than the election itself. Macdonald wanted it over by the end of June, but he was going to the coronation of King George VI and he did not want politicking during that period. So he had newspaperman H.B. Jefferson installed secretly in the Halifax Hotel to get the Liberals prepared for the next election. Returning to New York on May 19th, he was joined by MacMillan the next day as his train passed through Truro and told that everything was in order. A night session of the cabinet preceded a drive by a circuitous route to Government House where, shortly before midnight, and fewer than two hours after his return to Halifax, he had secured a dissolution and had an election set for June 29th. The *Herald* called it "Dark Lantern Tactics," but this was simply a case of the pot calling the kettle black, for three days before the dissolution W.H. Dennis, a senator since 1932, had lured Robert Chambers away from the *Chronicle* by the offer of a two-thirds increase in salary. The premier never spoke to Chambers again.[27]

From the outset Macdonald decided to make no specific promises and to run on his record. Declaring that he had fulfilled every pledge, he hoped now to play a part in securing constitutional amendments designed to establish a national social welfare system and put into place a new system of federal-provincial relations that might be recommended by the recently appointed Rowell-Sirois Commission. Liberal advertisements had a major refrain: Did Nova Scotians want to continue the steady progress of 1933-37 or to go back to the dismal Rhodes-Harrington years? An especially effective advertisement contained a map showing the 378 miles of trunk roads already paved, the 324 miles to be paved in 1937, and the 300 miles set for 1938. Early in the campaign the *Chronicle* used effectively some of Chambers' 1933 cartoons which stood in sharp contrast to the ones he was now producing. Actually, in changed circumstances, Chambers was much less effective than in the earlier election. E.M. Sellen of Toronto, whom the *Chronicle* engaged for the campaign, lacked his subtlety, but he kept reminding the Conservatives of something they would rather have forgotten: one example was his picturing of Harrington in a tub, a towel marked "Pentagon Hotel" near by, and his back, labelled "franchise scandal," being scrubbed by a lady called the "Conservative party" lamenting: "It Won't Come Off."

For his part, Harrington condemned the government's failure to keep its promises, the rise in the provincial debt, and the sacrifice of the public good by ministers with a conflict of interest. More positively, he advocated an expansion of electric power, new facilities for advanced education, the improvement of secondary roads, and an expansion in social legislation. Assisting him with an incredibly active campaign were the *Herald* and its proprietor who, apparently convinced of a Liberal defeat, became more and more the "victim of his own propaganda."

This was too much for Macdonald. Speaking in Halifax West, he declared that the "Napoleon" of the *Herald* was attempting through his bullying and threatening tactics to dictate the political, social, and economic life of the province. Later in Yarmouth, when the premier, not for the first time, called the *Herald* "Public Enemy No. 1 in Nova Scotia," its president, Agnes Dennis, addressed a letter to the people of the province expressing surprise and indignation, and declaring that the paper always spoke in "clarion calls when the rights of the people were likely to be invaded by selfish interests."[28]

Undoubtedly Macdonald had become particularly indignant over the constant condemnation of Anderson's illegal cutting of pulpwood. Day after day one corner of Chambers' cartoons showed a woodpecker pecking away at Anderson's chair which was marked "vacant" and which steadily diminished as the election progressed. By the last cartoon on June 26th nothing was left of the chair and the woodpecker was flying away with the "vacant" sign. That same day the Conservatives ran a full-page advertisement containing nothing but a large woodpecker and the words: "What has the Woodpecker Government done for you?" However, as George Farquhar pointed out, much of the steam went out of the issue after it was revealed that former

Conservative Executive Councillor Albert Parsons had been guilty of the same offence as Anderson. Still, it goes down in history as the "Woodpecker Election." In the end the victorious Liberals had the last laugh. On the day after the election Farquhar drew on his poetic abilities to write an "in memoriam":

The woodpecker pecked on the Senator's door;
He pecked and pecked till his bill got sore;
At last worn out he could peck no more,
And fell stone dead on the Herald floor.

The Liberal victor in Shelburne told Macdonald that "the Woodpecker can now stay in the Herald office and work on the wooden head of Dennis and his gang."

For the Conservatives it came as a shock to win only five seats and to have their leader defeated. Harrington had drawn large crowds everywhere, George Nowlan had had a much better reception than Agriculture Minister McDonald in Kentville on nomination day, and the Conservatives had thought in terms of victory to the very end. Though they won seats only in Cumberland, Colchester, and Queens, they polled 46.0 per cent of the vote, up 0.1 per cent from 1933. Confident from the outset, the premier had forecast the election of twenty-four Liberals and got twenty-five. Through his post-election correspondence ran two major themes. One was that, although his meetings were not as enthusiastic as in 1933, "there was a deep note of seriousness," which indicated that the people realized how important it was to "have the right sort of Government in office." The other was that the democratic process must be working properly when a party could win an election without making promises and the public could "discriminate so completely between the true and the false."[29]

His followers might have said instead that Macdonald himself was the major factor in their victory. "A regal looking figure, monastic in appearance," he had already created the impression, according to Harold Connolly, that "he would say nothing unless he was absolutely sure it was correct so that his honesty and integrity were never in doubt." Both his background and his speaking talents were adding to his appeal. A Gaelic-speaking father and a French mother had made him thoroughly conversant in both Gaelic and French, and he had "a native eloquence that gripped an audience." The result, said George Farquhar, was "a wide personal following not seen . . . since the days of Howe. At times, his words were winged with an almost mystic quality; in striking contrast to the cold matter-of-fact Anglo-Saxon."[30] The Angus L. mystique was well on its way to full development.

Harrington resigned as Conservative leader in September, saying that "the situation now indicates that I cannot be useful . . . in [the leadership] capacity." Before the legislature met in 1938, Macdonald and MacQuarrie placed Nova Scotia's case before the Rowell-Sirois Commission in a 114-page brief. They expressed a willingness to transfer to the Dominion government the full responsibility for old age pensions and mothers' allowances, and to give up the right to collect income and inheritance taxes and to regulate marketing. They also proposed an Australian-style federal grants commission that would determine the payments to the provinces according to fiscal need and before which the provinces would appear as of right, not as supplicants or as raiders on the federal treasury.

Percy Black, the new Conservative house leader in 1938, was a puzzle to the premier who thought, despite Black's occasional signs of skill, that he generally indulged in "stump speeches, where one might say almost anything and expect, perhaps, to get by." Macdonald found especially disconcerting Black's "unvarying habit" of misrepresenting things. When the premier promised to consider an opposition suggestion, Black would say "now that the government has agreed to give favourable consideration to the matter" or something to that effect.[31] Early in the session Black accused the government of being tied up with the liquor interests, using news stories purportedly based on a statement of Assistant Commissioner M.H. Vernon of the RCMP. However, as Attorney General MacQuarrie pointed out, Vernon himself had complained that the Dennis papers had turned remarks given in a confidential interview into a "sensational, exaggerated" article. Were the *Herald* and *Mail* not guilty of "newspaper ventriloquism," MacQuarrie wondered, by becoming Edgar Bergen and attempting to make Charlie McCarthys out of members of the public? Should they not remember that McCarthy occasionally said: "Don't nudge me, Bergen."[32] Black also came under fire for a resolution that condemned putting the port of Halifax under the "remote control" of the National Harbours Board. Never, said Macdonald, had a resolution been "supported by so little evidence, so little argument, so meagre a display of figures." He blamed it on the *Herald*, likening it to the Nazi-controlled press in Germany. The paper's aim, he contended, was not to give "honest views," but to subordinate news to "the fantastic ideas and the selfish policies of those who control [the] paper."[33]

A final encounter with Black and the *Herald* occurred on the use of the steam trawler in the fishing industry, a hotly disputed question since the early 1930s. After 1935 the *Herald* had joined the fight against the trawler and in 1938 Black pressed the premier to take a stand. Macdonald refused, saying that it was the federal government's decision to make and that Black simply wanted publicity in the "columns of Public Enemy No. One." He again charged the Conservative members with being Charlie McCarthys who did little but follow their Bergen-like dictator, the *Herald*. That led each of the five to assert his independence and the *Herald* to state that, whenever someone mentioned the trawler question, the premier lost his poise and indulged in name-calling like "Ignoramus" and "Public Enemy No. One."[34] From Ilsley, since 1935 the minister of national revenue at Ottawa, came word that the federal authorities would agree to license trawlers only if the companies owning them would be willing to buy all the inshore fishermen's catches.

It did not worry Macdonald that Lunenburgers J.J. Kinley, MP and Senator William Duff were crusading against the steam trawler. Ever since he had defeated Duff for the provincial leadership, he had suffered from "his ridicule, his opposition, and his disapproval." However, it did concern Macdonald that more than half his own members opposed licensing. So he allowed Dr. Davis, his minister of health, to express his views openly and to go to Ottawa to lobby on the question. Though his critics condemned his "strange understanding of collective responsibility," he saw nothing wrong in cabinet ministers differing on matters beyond their jurisdiction. Shortly Ottawa would license two steam trawlers owned by the Maritime National Company.

To the plaudits of the *Herald* the attorney general sponsored a bill — not proclaimed — that let the courts adjust any outstanding account considered oppressive in its terms. A second bill forced dealers using instalment plans to go to the courts to repossess goods on which 75 per cent of the purchase price had been paid. This bill passed even though a battery of lawyers called it "unfair, unreasonable, and almost unheard of." However, the two most important measures in 1938 were a natural products marketing act that let the province establish and enforce grading regulations for all agricultural products, and an act that sought to improve the justice system by authorizing the appointment of full-time magistrates with considerable legal experience.

The public accounts showed a surplus of $285,000, made possible by liquor profits of $1,285,000. Both H.R. Grant and the *Herald* pointed to an "alarming increase" in sales of hard liquor. For the next year Macdonald budgeted for a surplus of only $7,900 after agreeing to pay municipal taxes on liquor stores and to grant the municipalities one-third of the CNR payment in lieu of taxes. MacMillan took action to increase the gasoline tax from eight to ten cents, most of it to be absorbed by the wholesale dealers.

By this time Macdonald's position on the use of facts had become manifestly clear and it was to remain a basic part of his approach to politics. His principal charge against the *Herald* and the *Mail* was that they did not possess the factual knowledge to justify their conclusions. He pointed out particularly that they did not tell their readers that trawlers caught only 10 per cent of the fish, but let them believe that it was 90. Rather than follow Howe's dictum to "apply the keenest intelligence to all our problems if we are to survive in the economic race," they almost always took the opposite course. "Instead of getting all the facts, reasoning upon them, and coming to a solution, they take a few facts which will prove a suitable source for flaming headlines, and then they endeavour to stir up the people." Hence, though the *Herald* and *Mail* supported a few philanthropic enterprises like Rainbow Haven, "they constitute the greatest menace that we have in this Province."[35]

This indictment of the Dennis press was made to Donald F. Fraser, who had succeeded his father, James A. Fraser, as editor and publisher of the New Glasgow *Eastern Chronicle*. To him Macdonald confided that the best newspaper work in the province was being done by the weekly and semi-weekly papers, while the daily newspapers borrowed "their style and their ideas from the cheap American tabloids and the sensational press." Macdonald did not say whether this criticism applied to the *Chronicle*, which Farquhar was leaving following his appointment to the Public Utilities Board.

During the autumn of 1938 both Macdonald and Fraser expressed outrage at articles written by Howard Dingman of the Toronto *Globe and Mail* and "Rideau Banks" of the Toronto *Saturday Night* that presented Nova Scotia in a bad light and had allegedly been inspired by Evelyn Tufts and others on the *Herald* staff. From a visit to about twenty-five fishermen's homes around highly depressed Terence Bay, Dingman had reached conclusions that he then applied to the whole province. In an interview Macdonald found Dingman the most pig-headed man he had ever met and hurt the newspaperman's professional pride by telling him that he had "fallen into the Herald trap and . . . been duped."[36] Likewise Macdonald and Fraser condemned the *Herald* for its treatment of Pictou County's mining problems. The Dominion Steel and Coal Corporation had taken over the mines and intended to close the Vale colliery in Thorburn, generally regarded as a drag on the entire industry. When the *Herald* sought to rouse public opinion against this closure, Macdonald stated that Dennis was using the same tactics that he had employed to defeat the Armstrong government — the newspaper's views did no more than create "a feeling of hostility to the governments here and at Ottawa, and thus incline people not to vote for any particular thing but against governments."[37]

At this time the premier was also taking exception to what he considered the exaggerated claims of the "Antigonish Movement" centred in the Extension Department at St. Francis Xavier University. The previous year he had told Professor A.B. MacDonald to be "moderate in descriptions of the work done by the movement," that "in the long run it pays to understate rather than overstate a case." Clearly he was indignant that some supporters had referred to Liberal members, including himself, as "enemies to the cause of social justice." By October 1938 he had become thoroughly exasperated, especially with A.B. MacDonald who, despite his advice, had continued to describe politicians and businessmen as racketeers and exploiters. After interviews with him, Father Coady, and others, who were clearly looking for money, Macdonald gave nothing but advice. Pointing out that the co-operative movement would not have progressed as it had without government assistance, he told them that it should now be "standing on its own feet and appealing to people on its own merits . . . to make good some of its pledges made three, four and five years ago."[38]

Before the house met in 1939, Macdonald again found the conduct of the *Herald* distasteful. Serious storms a few months earlier had caused fishermen, especially in the Terence Bay area, to lose many of their lobster pots. Macdonald contended that if his government compensated them for their losses, it would commit itself to a general policy with no limits. Perhaps, he told Alex Johnston, the time was coming when governments would have to pursue "this fairy godmother policy, but it seems to me that we should endeavour to postpone that time."[39] Hence he would go no further than provide additional road work for the fishermen. There the matter might have ended if the *Herald* and Evelyn Tufts had not exercised influence on R.E. Finn, the Liberal MP for Halifax, whom the premier had long considered a discredit to his party. Finn used a Commons speech to attack Macdonald for being unsympathetic to the fishermen.

That was bad enough, but when federal Fisheries Minister Michaud joined the others in creating an unfavourable impression of the province's behaviour, Macdonald became completely exasperated. "I have gone out of my way several times . . . to defend publicly certain policies of the Federal administration even at the risk of some local unpopularity. . . . However, in this game I suppose everybody feels that he must look out for himself."[40] He contented himself with a simple statement, which both he and his friends felt received too little attention from the *Chronicle*. That paper, he feared, was slipping backwards and would not maintain its circulation or even its existence unless it followed a more consistent policy. For a time it "gets very sensational, and reports scandals and all sorts of curious stories, and then it will take another tack and become very reserved and correct in its tone. It may have one or two good men around it, but, on the whole . . . the staff is a good deal weaker than it has ever been in my memory."[41] The overall picture was that of a premier confident in his opinions and not reluctant to express them privately or even publicly as the occasion warranted it.

The speech from the throne in 1939 was mainly a review of the government's successes and the session proved to be shortlived and relatively uneventful. Percy Black tried to criticize but found it difficult, said the *Chronicle*, because the government was doing a good job and he knew it. Sometimes he faced a bombardment of questions from the Liberal members and had to "hurry along to his next topic."[42] Because the previous year's surplus of $146,000 had been based on liquor profits of $1.3 million, the *Herald* carried a news story headed "Budget is Balanced by Booze" and an editorial entitled "A Liquor Economy." With expenditures expected to rise faster than revenues, Macdonald forecast a deficit of $186,000 for 1939-40 but still hoped for a surplus. "I have always been on the safe side, and in every instance the financial position of the province at the end of the year had been better than I estimated it to be."[43]

In legislative measures the most novel provision appeared in a bill to consolidate the Municipal Affairs (Supervision) Act. The bill permitted the governor in council to replace a municipality's elected council with officials appointed by itself if the municipal council failed or appeared likely to fail to pay its sinking fund instalments and other obligations, or to levy and collect sufficient moneys to meet its expenditures. Though a few municipalities were critical of these drastic, ill-defined powers, the bill passed with little ado.

The major controversies occurred on matters other than bills. Again steam trawlers came to the fore when Black proposed a resolution asking the federal government to ban their use and received support from Dr. Davis and two Liberal backbenchers. Eventually MacMillan moved an amendment requesting that no trawler licences be issued in 1939 if hook-and-line fishermen could catch an adequate supply. When the *Herald* called it "political shadow-boxing," both MacMillan and Macdonald accused the newspaper of faulty reporting. That led Black to charge Macdonald with being under MacMillan's domination. When the latter told him not to say it again or "he'll answer for it outside the House," Black replied, "I'll have to ask for protection by the sergeant at arms as I go back and forth in this building."[44] MacMillan carried his resolution by a straight party vote.

More and more Macdonald was coming to the conclusion that the fight was not between the fisherman and the trawler but between the Lunenburg vessel and the trawler. Personally he would have liked complete provincial management of the fisheries but, though Ilsley had no objection, some of his own ministers shrank from the task.

Once again the premier indicated his distaste for inaccurate statements, especially when coupled with impracticable resolutions. After examining the material purporting to support a demand of the Florence miners, he declared that "more ridiculous resolutions [had been] passed in Nova Scotia than would fill a room" and that the persons passing them should be put in "padded cells." However, he reserved his greatest scorn for the "flying squadrons" from Ontario who had joined the "scandal corps" of the *Herald* in painting the blackest picture possible of Nova Scotia. "This aggregation of pseudo-economists, make-believe political scientists, fireside constitutional lawyers, social workers and medical experts, not one of whom [had] the faintest glimmer of knowledge" on these subjects, had been going around the province setting themselves up as experts. Staff correspondents of the *Herald* had posed as learned medical men, diagnosed diseases, determined the number of tubercular persons in particular localities, and advanced the most curious economic ideas, "all the while prating about freedom of the press, which they are very anxious to maintain for themselves, but often unwilling to concede to others."[45]

Editorially the *Herald* informed Macdonald that he should have been told years ago that "he has no 'corner' either in brains, ability or experience." It called him a politician who wanted the "advantages of office, but not the critical scrutiny to which public acts always must be subjected." Surely a premier would do better to address the province's serious problems "instead of indulging in such attacks upon a newspaper that has always treated him and his office with dignity and respect." In the view of the *Star*, however, Macdonald's speech thoroughly "debunked" the opposition and showed the premier's critics that they "DIDN'T KNOW WHAT THEY WERE TALKING ABOUT." It reported that even the assembly's gallery erupted in laughter and applause, and that the five Conservative members sat silent as the premier's attack turned into a massacre.[46]

Nonetheless, genuine conflict between the *Herald* and the Liberal party was about over. For some time clear signs of an attempt by Dennis to "disengage his party from the Conservative party" had been evident and were reinforced by the wishes of the paper's solicitor and editor-in-chief to dampen a "fire-and brimstone approach to politics." The results of the 1937 provincial election may have convinced them of the futility of contending against Macdonald. Much of Dennis's "remaining interest in politics" disappeared the next year with the retirement of his model, R.B. Bennett, as national Conservative leader. Other facts in his abandonment of partisan politics were the Conservatives' deplorable condition, federally and provincially and, now that the circulation of the *Herald* and the *Mail* was double that of the *Chronicle* and the *Star*, a business consideration, "the growing Dennis inclination to pay heed to the various political preferences of his expanding army of readers."[47]

The attitude Macdonald maintained throughout his political career manifested strongly in 1939: that Nova Scotians should rely on their own devices and not become unduly dependent on government. He demonstrated it especially in condemning the miners' conduct in Inverness. For years the province had operated their mine at a loss; yet the miners seemed not to appreciate how precarious the operation was. Though productivity had been falling steadily, they "just don't care whether they get out two tons of coal per man per day, or whether they get out one and one-quarter tons, or even less than a ton. . . . A mine cannot be run on a basis like this."[48]

The premier also noted that the CCF was slow in getting off the ground in Nova Scotia. In 1936 J.B. McLachlan and others had formed the Cape Breton Labour Party, apparently hoping to make it a smaller version of the national CCF. In the election of 1937 its candidate in Cape Breton East ran second to the Liberals. When mining prospects began to look bleak, the UMW's convention in 1938 called for the establishment of a provincial branch of the CCF. In due course UMW locals approved the affiliation, and the national party was delighted at the first official alliance of a union with the CCF in Canada. In Nova Scotia its first leader was Clarence (Clarie) Gillis, a miner and union executive. In a by-election in Cape Breton Centre in December 1939 Douglas MacDonald became the first CCF assemblyman, largely because of a splitting of votes between a Liberal and an independent Liberal.

The wartime session of 1940, interrupted for two weeks to let the assemblymen participate in the federal election, was one of the shortest and most uneventful in history. Black having given up his seat to run federally, Fred Blois led the Conservatives. Other than stating that the government had set up a department of industry by order in council and that the war had led to improved conditions in the coal and steel industry, the speech from the throne contained little. Only the premier, Blois, and Douglas MacDonald spoke on the address in reply and all three promised to avoid partisanship during the war. When the CCF member advocated the public ownership of the coal industry, the premier replied emphatically that it was "not the function of government to operate coal mines unless we want to socialize industry. We've had our experience with one coal mine [Inverness] and we will not go into another." Denouncing illegal strikes, he also declared that the new department of industry would be ineffective in the absence of industrial peace. "No one is going to risk his money if he is in constant fear of strikes and disturbances."[49]

With the poor economic conditions during part of the previous year, Macdonald had to announce a deficit of $193,000 and to forecast one of about the same amount for 1940-41. As usual, he was cautious and hoped that he might end up with a surplus. Except for the debates in its closing days, this might have been called the "speechless session." The galleries were almost always empty, and one humourist said that "the gate receipts have been way down." Behind the scenes, however, an issue arose which demonstrated that Macdonald could not be induced to take action that might be considered as favouritism to his own church. A priest pointed out to him that the town of Dartmouth required St. Peter's parochial school to pay property taxes even though other municipal governments exempted similar schools. All that was needed, he was told, was fifteen votes in the assembly and "a word from you might, indeed, would give a clear majority . . . you seem to underestimate your own influence." Macdonald replied that all his members and at least one on the other side agreed that the cause of the Dartmouth Catholics was just, but passing a bill in their interest would "lead to complications in other parts of the province that would be of a very serious nature." The absence of taxation on Catholic schools elsewhere resulted from municipal action and the legislature at no time proceeded with a bill affecting a single municipality except on its request and approval. Otherwise, "the question of local autonomy would at once be raised, and a cry of this kind has always proven very effective."[50]

No federal election in Nova Scotia has had more of a national character and less of a provincial one than that of 1940. After Liberal Premier Mitchell Hepburn and most of his supporters had condemned the federal government's war record in the Ontario legislature, Prime Minister King convened Parliament to keep a commitment to hold a pre-election session and then secured a dissolution before debate could begin. From the start Angus Macdonald stated that the only thing the opposition had going for it was the shutting off of debate, the calling of a quick election, and the shortage of boots, clothing, and other soldiers' necessities. Whom could the people turn to but King after looking at Conservative Manion, the CCF's Woodsworth, Social Credit's Aberhart, and New Democracy's Herridge? The public, he was convinced, took little stock of Manion's proposals for a National Government, and in wartime would not support Woodsworth and his party, "a pacifist, near-Communist group." He quickly noted a drift in favour of the Liberals as "the alternative of Manion for King grew less and less attractive." Did the Conservatives, he wondered, really believe in National Government since first they espoused it, then dropped it for a while, and finally took it up again? To his own knowledge, old-line Conservatives were thoroughly disgruntled by the dropping of the party name.

In Halifax Macdonald was delighted that Finn had realized that he could not win a Liberal nomination and had withdrawn his candidature. Macdonald confided to one Liberal MP that, after he became leader, one of his first objectives had been to get rid of disruptive elements like Redmond, Dickie, Russell, and Byrne, who got what they wanted by packing Liberal association meetings, and whose sole motive was personal advancement. This time the delegates had decided, even before the convention, that Finn's usefulness, if it ever existed, was gone. Macdonald wondered too if "we are seeing the last agonies of the Conservative party."[51] Though it had recruited several Liberals, including Pictonian James Cameron, as National Government candidates, it was clearly in trouble. The persons whom it wanted as candidates in Halifax would not run and in some seats it had difficulty in securing any candidates.

This time too the party was, for all practical purposes, without the support of the *Herald*. At the start that paper had applauded Manion's call for National Government, but later it had lapsed into silence. On his arrival in Halifax it had stated that "he came not as a party leader" and that: "Party Government is not good enough for Canada in wartime." However, thereafter it had given little direction to voters. Ilsley, Nova Scotia's representative in the federal cabinet, kept using the general Liberal argument that a Manion government would be less experienced, less united, more erratic, and less fair to citizens than the existing one. Would it not be tragi-comic to include CCF and Social Credit members in the cabinet?

In all but one instance Macdonald prophesied the Nova Scotia results accurately. He thought that Percy Black might win a personal victory in Cumberland and he did by a mere dozen votes. He was also right that Liberal Gordon Purdy would do well enough in Tory Truro to take Colchester-Hants. However, he was surprised by the victory in Cape Breton South of Clarie Gillis, the first CCF member to be elected federally in Nova Scotia. Apparently the miners, especially in Glace Bay, were the Liberals' Waterloo. Altogether shocking to Macdonald was Finn's ability to poll more than 9,000 votes in Halifax as an independent Liberal. In all, the Liberals took ten of the twelve seats and 50.6 per cent of the vote.

In July an unexpected event, the death of National Defence Minister Norman McLeod Rogers in a plane crash, altered dramatically the Nova Scotian and Canadian political scenes.

Ralston gave up finance for defence; Ilsley replaced him in finance; and Angus L. Macdonald became minister of national defence for naval affairs, more from a sense of duty than a desire to enter a wider political sphere. In Ralston, Ilsley, and Macdonald, Nova Scotia had the strongest representation it has ever had in the federal cabinet, even though only Ilsley held a Nova Scotia seat. To succeed himself, Macdonald recommended A.S. MacMillan who, in the circumstances, became premier and party leader without the benefit of a leadership convention, much as Harrington had done in 1930. Only two months earlier, when the prime minister had asked Macdonald to suggest possible choices for the provincial lieutenant-governorship, Macdonald had listed MacMillan as a possibility: "No one now living here has fought more sturdily and for so long a time the battle of Liberalism." But although MacMillan was sixty-nine and not likely to run again, "he would be perhaps more pleased to be left where he is," and so Macdonald's first choice had been Deputy Attorney General Fred Mathers, probably the dean of Canadian civil servants, with "a charming, gracious wife."[52]

By the time Macdonald left for Ottawa he was, like Fielding and Murray before him, political master of the province, one who could win elections on image alone. Background, appearance, oratory, talent, and a general appreciation of what he stood for blended to envelop him in a mystique which Howe, but neither Fielding nor Murray, had possessed. In the earlier stages of his premiership he may have been checked somewhat by older and more experienced colleagues who would not have tolerated undue interference, but even they did not object to his subjecting their departmental budgets to the minutest detail in order to work towards an overall balance. Before long Macdonald's replies to opposition assemblymen had become so devastating that they hesitated to challenge him except on the safest of grounds. Almost invariably he wrote his speeches himself and, because of his magic with words, that was understandable. Some of his stances stood out unmistakably. He did not want Nova Scotians to depend unduly on government but to be self-reliant. To all appearances, he was a liberal of the right. As a lawyer and former professor of law, he disliked intensely inaccuracy of facts and illogic in reasoning. No premier has ever taken greater care to ensure that his election promises were realizable, none greater pains to see that they were realized. Two questions remained unanswered: would he return to Nova Scotia, and how long would his physical resources stand up to the acute attention he gave unceasingly to the business of government?

CHAPTER 7

MacMillan: The Gap Filler

None had doubts about A.S. MacMillan succeeding Macdonald as premier. He had, at George Murray's request in the 1920s, remained as chairman of the Provincial Highway Board at great personal cost; he had played a prominent part in resuscitating the Liberal party after 1925; he had been the father of the highway-paving programme and had devised the Gasoline Licensing Act to help pay for it. Liberals without exception agreed that the premiership was a fitting reward, but likely to be short because of his age.

To choose a leader the Conservatives met in convention, although not harmoniously, in October 1940. Harold Bissett, a disturbing influence at the last convention in 1937, charged that the proceedings had been "cooked up," but was quickly silenced. Leonard W. Fraser, the only known candidate, stated that he would not be deterred by a small group whose intention was a "political blitzkrieg." His nominator, George Nowlan, declared that "we didn't come here to participate in any frame-up," and his seconder, R.A. Donahoe, insisted that "a full and fair opportunity [existed] for any man to be nominated." So, without further ado, Fraser, aged thirty-eight, once secretary to E.N. Rhodes, president of the party's provincial association, excellent in appearance, and vigorous and articulate, took over the leadership.[1] He did not have to wait long for a seat. Late in October the parties agreed to avoid contests in five by-elections being held to fill vacancies, and Fraser took over Black's seat in Cumberland.

None could ever accuse MacMillan of lack of hard work. Until the day before the house opened in 1941, he held no fewer than nine administrative positions, including premier, minister of highways and public works, provincial secretary (and treasurer), minister of industry and publicity, and chairman of the Power Commission. Fraser, though declaring his intention to avoid partisanship, proceeded under the guise of "constructive criticism" to attack MacMillan for having vested in himself the "greatest concentration of administrative power . . . that this province has ever seen," for not changing with the times, for being "no longer suitable to meet the problems of today," and for not doing enough to promote the war effort. CCF Douglas MacDonald accused the government of protecting "the ruling and possessing class against loss . . . Social improvement is not the concern of this Government. . . . Labour can't be exploited like a sucked orange and then thrown away."[2]

MacMillan, who considered anything that savoured of socialism as absurd if not dangerous, dismissed MacDonald summarily but answered Fraser with a personal testament outlining his career and attitudes. He regretted that the Conservative leader, who as a boy lived only a few doors from him, had deserted the straight and narrow way of Liberalism. Modestly, he admitted to being "just an ordinary business man — my attitude towards affairs is to carry into government the experience gained in private business and to deal with matters on business principles. . . . No politics are talked in my office." Perhaps he might be forgiven for waiting until very recently to give up the highways department in order to concentrate on the offices of provincial secretary and treasurer. "I helped to build it up — it was my life's work to a large extent." Refuting the most serious of Fraser's charges, he contended that one-third of his time was devoted to dealing with war measures. "Suggest what you want and it will be done if it is in our power, we told the Dominion Government."[3]

The little debate that occurred in 1941 centred on the public accounts and the budget. The previous year's surplus of $946,000, the largest in history, resulted primarily from liquor profits of $2.25 million, magnified by sales to servicemen's canteens and ships' stores in a Halifax bustling with war activity. A somewhat apologetic MacMillan promised a genuine

A. Sterling MacMillan   1940-45

attempt to decrease these sales. He took the offensive, however, when Fraser accused him of juggling the public accounts, inviting the young Conservative leader to "make the statement outside of the House if you dare." To help the war effort, he asked the opposition members to take a turn at farming. When Conservative George Dickey asked him when he last milked a cow, he replied: "I can milk a cow as fast as you can, but it's a different kind of cow." Boastingly, he told of his own farm, which had forty to fifty cattle, grew all its own feed, and the previous year had a profit of $900.

For 1941-42 MacMillan estimated a small surplus but admitted to great uncertainty because he could not divine the financial policies of the federal government. He outlined his major objectives as "the winning of the war" and "giving the very best possible service with the money placed at our disposal," along with the hope that he would never have to impose a personal income tax. When Fraser blamed him for not encouraging shipbuilding in time of war, he replied that he "could not take the shipbuilders by the neck and command them to build ships." Pleased with the short businesslike session, he boasted that "like the Italian navy the Opposition fired some heavy guns but didn't score any hits," only to have Fraser reply that "like the Italian navy . . . the Government has been fleeing for cover on every occasion."[4]

To Fraser's contention that an election should not be held while the Empire was being severely tested, the premier indicated that one was unlikely in 1941. Nevertheless, in mid-September he had one set for October 28th. To an extent true of no other Nova Scotia election, its timing became a major issue in the campaign. MacMillan argued, since the life of the assembly would, in any case, expire by the efflux of time in June 1942, that polling could take place with less disturbance during a lull in the war than in the spring or early summer when an invasion of Britain might occur. He pointed out too that neither he nor Fraser had a mandate from the people and that only twenty of the thirty assemblymen had been returned in a general election. The *Chronicle* and the *Star* supported him vigorously, although the argument that their party traditionally favoured elections every four years was clearly wrong; since the passage of the Quinquennial Act Liberal governments had actually waited five years on four of six occasions.

The *Herald* took practically no part in the contest except to protest its timing and to disagree strongly with those who argued that any extension of the life of the assembly would be "undemocratic." How could it be undemocratic to "adopt the course the people of this Province want to see adopted"?

Deploring the expense, distraction, and disunity of an election in time of war, Fraser extolled the action of Britain, which had extended the life of Parliament. "What is good enough for Westminster and the Mother of Parliaments" ought to be good enough for Nova Scotia. "Between the example set by Winston Churchill and the present Premier of Nova Scotia, I prefer the former."[5]

The difference in positions resulted largely from differences in electoral prospects. From the beginning the *Chronicle* declared that "the verdict of the electors is easy enough to foresee." The premier's manifesto made only one specific promise, to proceed with "a comprehensive plan to provide our people, young and old, with educational facilities equal or superior to anything on the continent."[6] Otherwise he campaigned on the Liberal record, on its domestic accomplishments and its war effort. In preparing the party's advertisements, relatively few in wartime, it appears a literary person had a hand. One, quoting Lord Tennyson, described MacMillan as "Foremost captain of his time, Rich in saving common sense"; another went to Samuel Johnson for advice to the electorate — "He is no wise man who will quit a certainty for an uncertainty."[7]

No politician ever faced more impossible odds than Leonard Fraser. His twenty-three-point manifesto promised "vigorous action now to prepare for the future," but it was neither striking nor innovative, and his opponents simply dismissed it as costly and impossible to fulfil. Actually its content mattered little since interest in domestic issues was almost non-existent and Nova Scotians were largely satisfied with the provincial government's war effort, facts attested to by the low turnout of 63.1 per cent.

The Liberals' popular vote of 52.7 per cent was much the same as in 1937 although they elected only twenty-three members instead of twenty-five. The Conservatives elected four members rather than five and their vote fell from 46.0 to 40.3 per cent. In its first serious entry into a Nova Scotia general election the CCF ran six candidates, five in Cape Breton County, where they outpolled the Liberals and took three seats. In addition to Douglas MacDonald, they elected Douglas Brodie and Donald MacDonald, who became their house leader and later the president of the Canadian Labour Congress. The major parties each suffered a serious casualty, Fraser in Cumberland and Mines Minister L.D. Currie in Cape Breton East. A bitter MacMillan told Angus Macdonald of an arrangement by which the CCF had agreed not to run in Cumberland and the Conservatives not in Currie's seat. Though it had not saved Fraser, it had brought about Currie's defeat. The premier blamed Percy Black, who was as "nasty as it was possible for a man to be. . . . If there is any man in Canada who deserves punishment at the hands of the Liberals, [he] is the man." Macdonald himself denounced Black for taking credit for the province's road-paving programme, even though in eight years he had done no more than pave twenty to twenty-five miles between Sydney and Glace Bay and put a light coat on the Waverley road, a rate which would not have seen all the roads paved until 2273.[8] Though annoyed by Black, MacMillan breathed a sigh of relief that he himself had not let the party down.

The war intensified in 1942 and dominated the session even though the speech from the throne promised a variety of domestic measures such as increasing the number of persons entitled to mothers' allowances and permitting counties to adopt the large school unit. Fred Blois led the Conservatives in the assembly, while Fraser continued as provincial leader. Somewhat dissatisfied with the province's contribution to the war effort, the premier declared that the government might soon have to tell people where they were to work and have to put women on the farms to increase production. "The Hun is at our gate. . . . There are submarines right around our coast. I for one would not be surprised if the enemy made an attack." When Donald MacDonald called for the immediate conscription of war industries, accumulated wealth, and financial resources, a Liberal called the CCF members agitators. MacDonald reminded him that years ago "a very great man, the Saviour," had been similarly described. This remark led the premier, to whom the CCF continued to be anathema, to accuse MacDonald of sacrilege: "He can't put himself or his friends in a class with our Saviour."[9]

Paradoxically the treasury was overflowing and yet the government continued to be worried about it. Liquor profits of $3.32 million had permitted a declared surplus of $894,000 but .

actually one of $1.96 million when the moneys placed in a general reserve fund and the capital expenditures paid out of current revenues were taken into account. Anticipating public disapproval of financing based on alcohol, MacQuarrie outlined measures for cutting down its consumption. For the next year MacMillan forecast a surplus of only $12,000, while admitting that "never was it more difficult to estimate revenue and expenditure than at present. In all honesty, the figures here are only a guide."[10] Part of his problem was to gauge the loss of revenue from gasoline rationing, but most resulted from his inability to estimate the effect on revenue of the wartime taxation agreement that he would be signing shortly with the federal government.

The previous year, at a federal-provincial conference to consider the Rowell-Sirois Report, MacMillan had indicated that, if asked to give a categorical approval of its recommendations, he would have to answer, "No." Yet he would accept its main principles if the details and methods of applying them could be worked out satisfactorily. Hence he was highly indignant at the three premiers who caused the conference to break down before meaningful discussion could occur. In 1942 he had little choice but to sign an agreement for the duration of the war that neither he nor MacQuarrie found advantageous. It followed the Rowell-Sirois Report in requiring the province to withdraw from the income tax and succession duty fields, but otherwise it differed markedly as a province's revenues would depend in part upon those it had received from the same sources in 1940. This meant, said MacMillan, that provinces which, like Nova Scotia, had practised thrift and not levied a personal income tax would suffer. With some truth Donald MacDonald suggested that Nova Scotians were being punished for their past short-sightedness in not imposing heavier taxes to provide improved services.

Looking to the future, the premier was far-sighted enough to see that the legislation confirming the agreement might be "the most important . . . that has come before [the Nova Scotia] House since Confederation." To him it appeared to herald radical changes in federal-provincial financial relations that would lead to Ottawa's dominance in this area.[11] So concerned was the assembly with the misgivings of MacMillan and

MacQuarrie that it indicated in an unprecedented way its opposition to the agreement being considered as a permanent arrangement, and it ordered the speeches of the two ministers to be published in the assembly's journals.

The legislative proceedings in 1942 set the style for the next three sessions. When, in 1943, the speech from the throne forecast little other than increases in old age pensions and mothers' allowances to those in extreme need, and a tightening of control over public utilities, Blois called it "more or less a waste of paper" and Donald MacDonald declared that it was "far more noteworthy for what it did not contain than for what it did contain." Despite MacMillan's earlier doubts the public accounts showed a surplus of $2.7 million, again resulting largely from the liquor profits of $4.8 million. This year the government did not seem to worry about the possibility of the province's residents drinking themselves into insensibility or, more likely, about a hostile public reaction to the swelling sale of alcohol. "The finances of the province are in excellent shape," said the premier, and "the credit of the province was never better." A decrease in the gross funded debt from $108 million to $101 million — one of the rare occasions when a reduction has occurred — amply confirmed his statement. For 1943-44 MacMillan forecast a surplus of only $250,000, expecting that drops in liquor profits, gasoline taxes, and motor vehicle returns would bring $2.5 million less in revenue. Once again, however, he admitted that "due to conditions not of our making we are unable to determine what our revenue will be." Yet he could boast that he would not have to impose tobacco, meal, and hospital taxes, from which other provinces derived millions of dollars.

The premier had no difficulty in gaining approval of a bill, dear to his own heart, that required power companies to sell electricity at cost for purposes of rural electrification. However, two other government bills met heavy going. Despite prophecies that every public utility would be reduced to bankruptcy in five years, the government persevered with a bill that permitted the Public Utilities Board to set a "just and reasonable" rate instead of allowing a utility company to earn 8 per cent on invested capital. MacQuarrie was not as fortunate with a bill that would have let him, as minister of municipal affairs, remove or suspend a municipal officer for any reason he deemed sufficient. Eventually he withdrew it when he was accused of giving himself "more power over the town and municipal officials than the elected body which placed them there and more control over them than over the officers of his own department."[12]

Following a mining engineer's report, the Inverness mine again came to the fore in 1943. When Halifax Liberal J.E. Rutledge discovered that its accumulated deficits had reached the "astonishing sum" of $1.3 million since 1925 and were gradually getting bigger, not smaller, he demanded that it be closed. The premier conceded that the townspeople "can't expect us to keep it going" indefinitely at a loss of $100,000 a year, or $2.00 on every ton of coal mined. After Inverness member A.H. McKinnon contended that closure would mean certain doom for the town of Inverness, the *Herald* hoped that it was "not beyond the ingenuity and resourcefulness of this Province . . . not only [to] maintain it as a community, but better it and strengthen it as the years go by."[13]

More than one department was considering steps to minimize postwar economic dislocation. For Harold Connolly and the department of industry it was proposals such as the production of foamed slag for industrial purposes and the development of the Irish moss industry. For Mines Minister Currie it was the building of the Strait of Canso causeway, and the improvement of the transportation link as part of a national fuel policy that would also include improved subventions and tariff protection for coal. For the premier it was a matter of providing work through the paving of every travelled highway and the widening of highway bridges. For him, too, it meant the rehabilitation of the province's fishing industry by employing "the best fishing expert to be found in North America" and it might even mean taking over the private power companies to avoid the payment of federal income taxes, reduce the cost of electricity, and release millions of private capital for other purposes. To offer guidance to the government in its postwar planning, the premier announced the appointment of a one-man royal commission on provincial development and rehabilitation with Professor R. MacGregor Dawson as the commissioner.

When, in 1944, the speech from the throne again promised a study of "all the possibilities for development in the reconstruction period, this had a hollow ring to the opposition because of recent announcements about the closing of the Acadia sugar refinery at Woodside and the rolling mills and the nut and bolt departments at Trenton. MacMillan himself admitted that at the recent conference on reconstruction in Ottawa he had warned that unless there was a policy of decentralization the Maritimes would be out of industry. This year he forecast a rapid expansion of rural electrification and warned the private utilities of their responsibilities: "they cannot expect to get all the cream and leave the skim milk." He also promised to double expenditures on education and to give the province the best educational system in Canada, including rural high schools with appropriate transportation facilities. As usual, the CCF's plans drew sharp rebukes. Blois likened their policy to a pill "which, in itself, contains many excellent vitamins, but which is poison in the centre, the poison being that of state socialism." Liberal J.R. Murphy referred to the actions of the Nazi leaders and then asked, "do the CCF members in the House know . . . how far [their leaders] intend to go?"[14]

Liquor profits had soared again, this time to $5.5 million, helping to produce another record surplus of $2.9 million. MacMillan made it known that he would use this extra revenue to obviate the need to go to the money markets in the near future. He found highly disconcerting the demands of delegations for millions in expenditures: "We cannot have everything that . . . larger, more thickly populated provinces are able to afford." Would Nova Scotians be willing, he wondered, to accept some new form of taxation like a sales tax for substantially improved social services?

The bill that stood out in 1944 was one to treat milk as a utility and let the entire industry, fluid milk producers and creameries, be regulated by the Public Utilities Board. "We felt the time had come," said MacMillan, "when the industries should be placed directly under a board with judicial standing. [Then] no man can complain as to the justice they get." Throughout the session Liberal ears were attuned to the speeches of Conservative leader Fraser outside the house, especially one in which he introduced his new federal leader,

John Bracken, to a Halifax audience. They were not amused when Fraser described the Nova Scotia cabinet as "the greatest combination of small time political office holders" in provincial history, sustained by enormously increased revenues made by selling poor liquor, and hoping that Nova Scotia's problems would be "solved, sometime, somehow, by somebody somewhere, before Gabriel blows his horn."[15]

Meanwhile the future of Angus L. Macdonald was coming to the fore. A year earlier, when his friend, Conservative H.P. (Harry) MacKeen, had expressed a wish to see him on the bench, Macdonald had replied that the idea was not "entirely without its attraction." The last ten or twelve years had been very strenuous and "it has not been easy."[16] In the autumn of 1944 he told his Kingston riding association that he would not be contesting the next federal election. The prime minister, he said, was unlikely to hold an election before the European war was over and by that time he would have substantially completed his own work in Ottawa. Though uncertain about his future, he had decided that it would be in Nova Scotia. Clearly a return to provincial politics was foremost in his mind. He knew of a few things which he could do for the place of his birth, "although there are, no doubt, many others who could do them as well, or better. In only one respect will I admit no superior, and that is in my affection for the Province."[17]

The session of 1945 was much like the previous two. Though the government continued to express great concern for postwar economic development, the speech from the throne was specific only in its promise of "the largest program ever undertaken in this Province for the extension of light and power in rural Nova Scotia." Both Blois and Donald MacDonald labelled it an utterly barren document. Seventy-four-year-old Premier MacMillan was even more vigorous than usual in a reply marked both by joviality and biting criticism. For MacDonald he had his usual anti-CCF logic: socialism led to regimentation and regimentation led directly to dictatorship. Tantalizingly, he asked Blois if he was a Progressive Conservative Brackenite or one of the old high tariff Tory guard. Bracken, after all, had been a low tariff man, while Blois worked for Stanfield's, which thrived on tariffs. He had the most fun of all in describing Fraser as "the looseleaf leader" in imitation of the accountant who, when he did not like his mistakes, simply removed a page from his ledger.[18] Despite his "good, sound age," the premier was "prepared to meet this young Lochinvar mentally or physically."

With no little prescience, Mines and Labour Minister Currie outlined two serious problems. The war had eliminated the sale of Annapolis Valley apples in Britain and the prospects of regaining that market were gloomy. These years had also seen the complete loss of the province's coal market in Ontario and to a large extent in Quebec with little likelihood of recapturing either. "What is needed," he said, "is that coal should be declared . . . to be a national public necessity, so that this country will be as independent as possible of the coal resources of another country."[19]

After many years the city of Halifax was making another attempt to operate its own power and transportation system by taking over the assets of the Nova Scotia Light and Power Company. However, the bill failed because the city did not provide the factual data needed to justify the proposal and because the Halifax citizenry was apathetic — only twenty people attended the committee hearings. The premier was much more interested in extending power into "the dark places" of the province. Though he had no desire to acquire power distribution systems anywhere, he was determined to proceed with rural electrification and "any body or company, big or small, which stands in our way, will have to be taken over." To that end his bill provided that the Nova Scotia Power Commission could extend power lines to areas with only three actual and four potential customers per mile; it also offered assistance to private companies to carry out extensions to areas with a similar number of possible customers.

Though smaller this year, the surplus was, nevertheless, $2.28 million, again resulting largely from liquor profits of $6.5 million. Ever pessimistic about financial prospects, MacMillan forecast a surplus of only $91,000 in 1945-46 and prophesied that provincial revenues would soon fall to the level of prewar days. Because "we cannot take a backward step so far as our services are concerned," some new form of taxation might soon be necessary. However, as most of the new outlay would be on education, the remedy for the moment was largely in the hands of the school boards through their right to levy property taxes.

During the session the government tabled the Dawson *Report on Provincial Development and Rehabilitation*, which, largely matter of fact in nature and lacking in innovative ideas, must have been a disappointment to MacMillan. As usual, it attributed much of the province's difficulties to national policies, especially the tariff, and declared that the province had lost its bargaining power because of the federal usurpation of its taxation fields. For even a "restrained and fairly frugal" reconstruction programme the province would have only about $12 million to meet estimated annual costs of $20 to $21 million. The report adjudged education to be the most hopeful field of endeavour for promoting Nova Scotia's well-being, and had two special recommendations on economic policy: the province should develop to the utmost "those special activities in which her advantages are definite and unmistakable" and, above all, should stand for excellence — "merit and conspicuous ability must characterize Nova Scotia industry."[20]

Because Prime Minister King was insistent that no action be taken to extend the life of Parliament, the federal election machinery had been set in motion before the European conflict had come to an end. As often with King, luck was with him. Germany collapsed before the campaign got well under way, and hence he could minimize the manpower question which late in 1944 had led to the resignation of Defence Minister Ralston and caused his government serious internal difficulties. This did not sit well with the *Herald*, even though the newspaper continued its generally non-partisan stance. To it "manpower had been, and still is, the paramount consideration," and the government should not be allowed to evade it or confuse it with postwar issues.[21]

At dissolution King had accepted the resignation of Angus L. Macdonald, who had not enjoyed political life at Ottawa, had experienced difficulties with the prime minister, and did not think that he had received the recognition he deserved from either King or the press. In contrast, Ilsley had won country-wide respect as wartime finance minister. Liberal advertisements pictured Captain Ilsley and his crew, the party's eleven other candidates in Nova Scotia, below the caption: "They'll bring you safely into port." National, rather than provincial, issues dominated the campaign. The Liberals boasted of their financial record, of the success of Ilsley's controls in keeping down the cost of living, and of everyone sharing in the economic well-being. Their basic slogan, "Vote Liberal and Keep Building a New Social Order for Canada," accorded well with a government advertisement, in effect a Liberal one that asked parents if they had registered their children for family allowances.

Meanwhile the Conservatives were employing Mckim Advertising — the first Canadian use of an advertising agency in this manner — to sell the virtues of relatively unknown leader John Bracken, who had caused his party to be renamed Progressive Conservative. The emphasis was on the "deep earnestness . . . all-embracing humanity and the most startling simplicity and sincerity of this Lincolnesque man." However, whatever his virtues, he lacked the dynamism and allied qualities to sell himself to the Canadian people.[22] Conservative Premier George Drew of Ontario had originally announced a provincial election for June 11th, but when a federal one was announced for the same day, he had it advanced to June 4th. His hope was to win a massive provincial victory that might carry over to the federal election a week later. However, though the Conservatives won twenty-three additional federal seats in Ontario, their gains elsewhere were few. In Nova Scotia Conservative Percy Black and CCFer Clarie Gillis easily won re-election, and the only seat to change hands was Colchester-Hants, which Conservative Frank Stanfield won by eight votes. By running a full slate of candidates in Nova Scotia, the CCF's popular vote went up by 10 per cent, while that of the Conservatives and Liberals went down by 3 and 5 per cent respectively.

Starting in mid-February the question of MacMillan's retirement and Angus L. Macdonald's future had again come under discussion. It began when the latter asked MacMillan if he would like his role to be "translated" to an easier life in the Senate. At the same time Macdonald indicated that he himself was still uncertain what he wanted to do, but that his case did not enter into the question. MacMillan replied that, for his own part, he had reached the time of life when he should have less to do, but that his colleagues in the legislature did not want him to retire. He realized full well that none of them could succeed him and carry on successfully without the backing of a convention. However, if Macdonald himself decided to re-enter provincial politics, he would give way immediately.[23] Clearly Macdonald did not want to have it appear that MacMillan gave up the premiership simply to accommodate him. MacMillan, on the other hand, realizing that his resignation would end the active life on which he thrived, wanted at least to have it understood that he had paved the way for Macdonald's return to provincial politics. The latter's attempt to keep the two events separate failed when the prime minister refused to allow MacMillan to be made a senator because of his age. An annoyed Macdonald contended that if age was a consideration then a retirement age should be introduced for all senators. "There are some old birds there who are ninety. At one time there was a fellow . . . who was one hundred and four." As for King, he was seventy-one, and if a prime minister could be that old, age should be no impediment to MacMillan's appointment.[24]

Meanwhile, leading Liberals were keeping Macdonald informed of the lay of the land in Nova Scotia. Cape Breton West MLA Malcolm Patterson told him that, although L.D. Currie might have an eye on the leadership, he knew of no private member who did not want Macdonald to take over before the next election. Nor did he think that a leadership convention was necessary since Macdonald had already been chosen by one, had won two elections overwhelmingly, and had left only for the duration of the war. Macdonald's reply indicated that since he was "not wholly clear as to the future," he was giving some consideration to a legal or business career which would provide security of tenure and the opportunity to make money, an important consideration for someone with four young children.[25]

At the same time MacMillan was wondering if Macdonald fully understood his position: "I am quite willing to make the necessary change here at any time that it is convenient." Why did Macdonald not speak his mind fully? "Do not give any consideration at all to my feelings, for you know quite well just how the matter stands with me." Still Macdonald hesitated.

From distant Ottawa, he said, it was hard to determine the two matters which were crucial — MacMillan's wishes and the party's wishes. No one wanted MacMillan to go if he wished to stay. As for himself, five years' absence had made a great difference in the political scene and if the party had ideas that did not include himself he would be satisfied.[26]

Some masterminds in the Liberal party, thinking only of the next election, wanted to get rid of MacMillan immediately. Their spokesman, Nova Scotia Senator Wishart Robertson, President of the National Liberal Federation of Canada, asked Harold Connolly to tell him that it was time to go. However, they went no further when Connolly warned them that if they attempted to force the old man out of office, "I would canvass my friends for enough money for as many radio hook-ups in the Province as I felt necessary and I would denounce them by name."[27]

In the end Macdonald and MacMillan apparently settled the matter by telephone on June 22nd. Even then Macdonald wrote the next day that only if MacMillan really wanted to be relieved of his burden and the party was agreeable, would he consent to succeed him.[28] According to Connolly, Macdonald believed that "the Leadership of the Liberal Party was his [own]" and that "the principle of the Divine Right of Kings, not the democratic principle that a Liberal is supposed to embrace" governed his thinking,[29] but nothing in his correspondence or public actions warrants that conclusion. Returning to Nova Scotia, Macdonald took up residence at Baddeck and from there invited Connolly to play golf. Connolly went without his golf clubs and after a long, circuitous discussion told Macdonald what he wanted to hear, that he would not be challenged for the leadership.[30]

Connolly was right. Macdonald carried the convention without opposition on August 31st. Of MacMillan he said, "The great Liberals of the past, Howe, Fielding and Murray, will sound their trumpets in honor of his name." In typical style MacMillan boasted of the Liberals' continuing record on highway paving and rural electrification. Recently 625 miles of utility poles had been ordered, and 95 applications would be acted on as soon as they were processed. Referring to innuendo about himself, he deplored statements that politicians amassed great fortunes by straying from the straight and narrow path.

"When my will is probated people will know how much I have made. . . . I haven't yet found the way."[31]

Not many Nova Scotians know much about A.S. MacMillan, but the literature on him, though meagre, attests to the high opinion of his colleagues. To retain his services George Murray was prepared to go well beyond the usual remuneration. Harold Connolly called him "the great idea man" in the Liberal governments of the day and "perhaps the most underrated administrator of my time in Nova Scotia provincial affairs." L.D. Currie though that he possessed "the most creative mind of those with whom he had been associated."[32] As one who had succeeded by unceasing, hard work, MacMillan felt, like many Nova Scotian politicians of his day, that democratic socialism would be an absolute menace to the social fabric. Basically he was the down-to-earth businessman who was largely responsible for the building of material things of great value to Nova Scotians. Though his greatest accomplishments occurred before 1940, he ran the province superbly during the war, helped by the swollen revenues resulting from the unrestrained drinking habits of Nova Scotia's residents in wartime. Even the difficulties of war had not prevented him from taking the first tentative steps towards modernization of the educational system. He deserves a high place among Nova Scotia's politicians.

CHAPTER 8

"Angus L. is Back"

On September 12, 1945, only thirteen days after Macdonald became leader, he had the legislature dissolved for an election on October 23rd. The *Ottawa Journal* wondered why a man with such "a civilized mind, character, and understanding of government policy" had been allowed to leave Ottawa. For the *Halifax Chronicle* he was the man needed to "hammer into the federal mind that we are against further centralization . . . that we want nothing to do with any proposal to exchange what remains of our birthright for a slightly increased mess of federal pottage."[1] From Ottawa his friend Thomas (Tom) Crearar wrote that the prime minister had "words of warm approval" for Macdonald's calling of the election and that "metaphysically he has taken you again to his bosom."[2] Macdonald's reaction can only be imagined.

Harold Connolly found that this man was not the same Macdonald. "He had always been slow to make a decision . . . [Now] he became a procrastinator, not because by nature he was a procrastinator, but because [he] was not well." His ability to act quickly and his health both suffered because he found it difficult to delegate. "He had a terrible deep-rooted suspicion of anybody's efforts except his own . . . he would put [a matter] on his desk and he'd mull it over, and he'd mull it over again, and again, and again, and the more often he looked at it the more doubtful he became."[3] Connolly conceded, however, that his thinking was always good and his eventual decisions almost always right; further, he had lost none of his appeal to the Nova

Scotian voter, who generally could not have cared less if he was slow making up his mind.

L.W. Fraser was left to fight the Conservative campaign much by himself. One party member declared that he should have sued the *Herald* for non-support, and even the *Eastern Chronicle* expressed sympathy for a "likeable" and "decent" fellow. His manifesto placed special emphasis on Dominion-provincial-municipal relations. It denounced centralization, rejected Ottawa's reconstruction proposals, demanded sufficient revenue to maintain first-class provincial services, and promised a new deal for the municipalities, including the sharing of liquor profits and a readjustment of the burden of social services.

Macdonald quickly showed that he had lost none of his ability to demolish his opponents. Fraser's manifesto, he declared, had "everything in it except an atomic bomb — and one of those will be needed by the Tory party in this election." To him Fraser's comments on centralization came ill from the leader of a party whose tariff policies had produced more of it than anything else. Highly critical of the Conservative record between 1925 and 1933, he singled out once again the "shameful and disgraceful" attempt to steal an election by manipulating the voters' lists. Despite his criticism of Fraser's manifold promises, his own eleven-point programme for the future seemed to be no less all-inclusive.[4]

When Fraser declared that the main issue was the province's representation at the forthcoming Dominion-provincial conference, Macdonald took off the gloves. In his view the Conservative leader's speeches indicated that he knew nothing about the problems of the federation; as for himself, though he had had differences with the prime minister, he was "still his friend." Actually, it turned out to be the quietest of elections and Macdonald knew the reason: "After people have gone through the agony and worry of war for six years, many other matters must seem unimportant." So in a province in which 85.9 per cent of the voters cast ballots in 1933 and 79.7 per cent in 1937, the turnout was just 64.7 per cent in 1945, only 1.6 per cent greater than in 1941.

For the first time since Confederation the Conservatives elected no one at all. Their popular vote fell to 33.5 per cent and their best showing was in Cumberland where A.B. Smith lost by

269 votes. Like the Conservatives, the CCF lost its leader, but though it polled only 13.6 per cent of the vote, it would constitute the legislative opposition in the persons of Russell Cunningham and Michael MacDonald, who had won the mining seats of Cape Breton East and Centre. The premier was especially elated that the Liberal provincial majorities were substantially higher than the federal ones. "After having been away five years, it was pleasing to know that one was not entirely forgotten."

The plaudit he liked best came from the principal of the Normal School who declared that his "being a true son of Nova Scotia" was his greatest asset. "Our hills, valleys, forests, streams and traditions appeared to be a part of you in that 'Nova Scotianess' Dr. MacMechan so aptly termed." During the campaign, although not part of it, Macdonald had been thoroughly annoyed by a monsignor of the Catholic University of Washington who, while travelling in Canada, complained that Macdonald had not seen to it that Catholics did better in the navy. "I have never asked for anything more than that my own religion should not hurt me in public life, and as a necessary sequel to that I did not ask to have it help me." Why did some priests expect every Catholic politician to "go around with a large placard on his back bearing the words, 'I am a Catholic.'"[5]

At the Conservatives' annual meeting in February 1946, Leonard Fraser declared that an effective leader had to lead both usefully and hopefully. Because of the results in two elections he was "forced to the conclusion that I can no longer lead this party hopefully and that leaves me only one course to follow . . . Ladies and gentlemen, I am through."[6] In different circumstances his not inconsiderable abilities might have produced more favourable results.

The speech from the throne in 1946 revealed the basic philosophy that would dominate the rest of Macdonald's premiership. Governments, he said, "cannot put pie in the sky," but they ought to create conditions under which their citizens should work out their own salvation. Accordingly his government had plans to aid the basic industries, build better highways, supply electricity to areas without it, improve the educational facilities, and stimulate research. Because Canada's annual spending on research was only 25 cents a head —

something that Macdonald deplored — he took action to set up the Nova Scotia Research Foundation, headed by a council constituted along the same lines as the National Research Council in Ottawa. For the moment finances remained buoyant, revenues exceeding $20 million for the first time and producing a surplus of $1.2 million. However, over one-third of the revenue, $7.2 million, came from liquor and this figure was certain to drop in the postwar period. Hence Macdonald forecast a surplus of only $51,000 for 1946-47 and warned that the province would soon have to depend on "peacetime standards of revenue."

A bill that caused much speculation was to provide a salary for the premier without his having to be head of a department. However, those who prophesied that Macdonald was about to give up his portfolio clearly did not know the man.

As an extension of the health care system, Minister of Health Davis announced the provision of free care for tubercular patients. Once again the government expressed doubts about continuing its coal operations in Inverness but hoped, by opening the McBean mine in Pictou County, to keep 350 men employed for twenty-five years. In their first session Russell Cunningham and Michael MacDonald found it difficult to deal with the whole gamut of provincial affairs, especially legal matters, but on the ills of the declining coal industry they were highly vocal. Cunningham could not say how much of the fault lay with the company, but "I have worked for Dosco since I was so high, and I know they are monopolists of the first degree."

Throughout 1946 and much of 1947, the premier's major concern was with federal-provincial financial relations. A conference in 1945 had broken up after Ontario and Quebec had summarily rejected Ottawa's somewhat grandiose "green book" proposals. Macdonald also did not like the federal government's approach. He wanted constitutional changes to come first, and taxation arrangements afterwards, and he deplored the abandonment of the principle of fiscal need. Why should a basic Rowell-Sirois conclusion, "framed by a Commission appointed by the Dominion government . . . now be disregarded and abandoned by that Government"?[7] For Nova Scotia he put forward his long-held views against centralization, and from them he would not budge. He conceded that the province would have to surrender personal and corporate income taxes and succession duties in return for per capita grants that would provide for greater returns than Nova Scotia could secure through its use of these fields, but he adamantly refused to give up minor fields such as amusement and pari-mutuel taxes, which the federal government had not entered until the Second World War. To him it seemed obvious that if a semblance of federalism was to survive, the provinces needed some fields which they could call their own, and he was nonplussed that his political ally, Finance Minister Ilsley, did not see things the same way.

The federal government's 1946 budget watered down its earlier proposals in making a monetary offer to the provinces for abandoning the major tax fields. It then sought agreement with the provinces one by one, a process which Macdonald described as undignified and likely to promote jealousy. In December 1946 he told the prime minister that Nova Scotia should not have to rely on newspapers for its knowledge of the other provinces' agreements, and he asked for the resumption of the adjourned federal-provincial conference and the calling of similar conferences at fixed dates. King rejected the first proposal because of the continued recalcitrance of some provinces and the second because it would be "importing a principle foreign to our constitutional practice, involving undesirable rigidity."

That same month Douglas Abbott became federal minister of finance and adopted a somewhat less rigid stance than Ilsley had. Within a month or two he had agreed to abandon gasoline taxes and to retain the existing provincial subsidies. Though pressed by the province's federal Liberal members to sign an agreement, Macdonald believed that he could gain "further concessions by holding out a little longer." He told his friend Alex Johnston that the basic difference was "on the question of principle versus money. . . . The Dominion people have the idea that by giving a little more money to this or that province they can hush it up. I feel that the essential problem is whether they want provinces . . . or not."[8]

Macdonald's backbenchers supported him to the hilt, as did his cabinet colleagues, although Currie and Connolly were not as firm as the other six. The premier knew that some of his former associates in Ottawa regarded him as a "very sinister fellow" who was holding out "for personal reasons and to satisfy personal grudges." He also found it annoying to have the *Globe and Mail* link him with Drew and Duplessis, and ask, what does Nova Scotia want? Drew, he thought, was a Christian who believed in God. "Was it therefore to be expected that I should renounce my belief in a Deity?"[9]

When the legislature opened in March 1947, Macdonald reminded the federal government that "the four old provinces . . . created the Dominion and Ottawa did not create the provinces." By that time Abbott had agreed to get out of amusement, pari-mutuel, and electricity taxes if the federal government received compensation. Though Macdonald found that unacceptable, negotiations continued. Clearly Ottawa badly wanted an accommodation with Nova Scotia and hence to reach agreements with all the provinces except Ontario and Quebec. Just as the session ended in May, success came. Ottawa recognized the principle of exclusive provincial tax fields and abandoned the taxes it had not used before the war. Though Macdonald could not get a promise of regular first ministers' conferences, he was assured of one for consultation at least a year before the termination of the five-year fiscal agreement. Clearly he had "not been laggardly in putting forward the just claims of the provinces."[10] His major regret was not to have the principle of fiscal need fully recognized.

Liquor profits had soared again to $8.9 million, and Macdonald had a surplus of $2.59 million which he used to provide substantial increases in teachers' salaries. He also reiterated an earlier announcement that the government would pay the entire cost of constructing rural high schools and 75 per cent of the operating costs. Russell Cunningham, more and more finding his feet as a critic, demanded that the federal government increase its subvention on coal so that miners might receive the $1.40 hourly wage increase they were demanding. However, Mines Minister Currie was more concerned about the Allan shaft in Stellarton filling with water if striking unions refused to operate the steam plant.

As Minister of Labour, Currie came under heavy attack from Cunningham for a provision in the new labour code that was to replace the wartime federal act. This provision required a majority of workers in an industry, not merely a majority of those voting, before a strike could be called. Cunningham became even angrier when the provincial branch of the Canadian Manufacturers Association requested the outlawing of the closed shop, and angriest of all when Liberals Purdy and Rutledge made statements which he described as "the ugly head of Fascism rising in this country." If hobble-straps were to be applied to labour, the government should ensure that "those who are money-mad and drunk with power from the exploitation of their fellow-men [should have] the straps put on them also." The outcome, said the *Star*, was "the institution of Nova Scotia's first labour lobby," when representatives of the Nova Scotia Federation of Labour, the UMW, the steel workers, and other unions demonstrated at Province House.[11]

Macdonald expressed his feelings further on federal-provincial relations after the session. C.G. (Chubby) Power told him that, despite the highly unfavourable publicity that his conduct had evoked, real Liberals like Tom Crerar and himself were with him. "No Liberal in the old days," replied Macdonald, "would dare to beat down the Provinces in the manner attempted by the present crowd at Ottawa." In his view the federal ministers were "too much under the influence of their civil service advisers." Nevertheless, to demonstrate that the provincial and federal Liberals were still one, he entered vigorously into a federal by-election in Halifax in which the Liberals did as well as in the general election. "I felt that by doing this I had satisfied any doubting Thomases."[12] In the autumn, after a good deal of reading, he concluded that philosophers and academics generally agreed with him that "the heart of liberalism is to be found in the emphasis on human personality and on the rights that attached to man as a being with a soul."[13] This conclusion reinforced his belief that socialism stood for a planned, controlled economy under which individual rights all but disappeared. To counter the CCF he told Dalhousie University students that the inevitable results of a socialist government would be dictatorship, and he later said the same thing at St. Francis Xavier.[14] David Lewis called him "either dishonest or illogical."

The debate on democratic socialism continued in 1948 when Cunningham condemned the government's programme as doing nothing to relieve unemployment or improve conditions in the coal and steel industry. "We are returning to the economy of the hungry thirties — to poverty, destruction, and want for thousands of our finest people." At a time when communism was spreading elsewhere, "here among our unemployed we foster the very breeding ground for this ideology." An angry Macdonald replied that the CCF, by trying to convince people that capitalism had failed, was laying the ground for communism. The inevitable result of the CCF's planned economy, he stated once again, would be totalitarianism without a parliament or elections.

Again the prophecies of falling revenues failed to materialize. Because liquor profits remained high at $8.15 million, and because the fiscal agreement provided at least $3 million more than the province could have raised through its own resources, the public accounts showed a record surplus of $9.5 million. Determined that it not be "frittered away" and that "long after we are gone from these halls, the effects will be evidenced throughout the province,"[15] Macdonald decided to use $4 million to reduce the provincial debt, put $1 million in a revolving fund to make loans to new industries, and set aside $4.5 million to make long-term, low-interest loans to municipalities for capital expenditures on schools and hospitals. Though he forecast a surplus of $1.35 million for 1948-49, he pointed out with his usual caution that the growing cost of services or a recession might quickly alter the state of the finances.

Since the liberalization of the liquor laws appeared fraught with political danger, it came as a surprise that the government sponsored a bill authorizing the sale of beer or wine by holders of dining room licences or tavern licences, but only in municipalities which had expressed their approval through plebiscites. The bill did not permit hard-liquor cocktail lounges. The CCF argued, without avail, that privately operated taverns would take Nova Scotia back to the era of "bar rooms and the beer barons."[16] Perhaps it was surprised that these changes produced relatively little in the way of controversy.

The previous year the premier had initiated steps to redistribute the assembly's seats, arguing that a small house minimized the role of the private member and exaggerated the importance of the eight-man cabinet; that the province's population, estimated at between 630,000 and 640,000, had increased by one-quarter in the last twenty-five years; and that a larger house would let the counties be better represented on the basis of population. In 1948 a committee headed by R.M. Fielding found additional reasons for a larger house: except for Prince Edward Island, the legislature was the smallest in Canada; it should be large enough to let committees sit while it was in session; and large, sparsely settled counties ought to have more members. Using a unit of 15,000 people with a controlling factor of 25 per cent, the committee concluded that Cumberland, Digby, Hants, Inverness, Kings, Pictou, and Yarmouth counties should each have an additional member. However, it declined to apply its formula to Halifax and Cape Breton counties on the ground that thickly populated counties were sufficiently represented. It also proposed to continue the move towards single-member constituencies by dividing all the counties which gained seats except Kings, Yarmouth, and Inverness. The house accepted all its recommendations even though Cunningham wanted to give Halifax and Cape Breton the number of members that their populations warranted. "Ten thousand voters in an urban constituency should have the same representation as ten thousand voters in a rural constituency."[17]

This year Macdonald expressed satisfaction with the general attitude of Nova Scotians. A spirit of despair had long prevailed because of the injustice of Confederation, but "I believe our people have begun to fight again as they did 100 years ago when we were a great country. They realize that some things Government can do, some things they must leave to individuals."[18] At the end of 1948 the *Chronicle* and the *Star* disappeared, amalgamating with their competitors under the names *Chronicle-Herald* and *Mail-Star*. In the case of the *Chronicle* it meant the demise of the paper which had been the province's chief Liberal organ since 1844. According to Macdonald, it could not have been saved since it had lost $1.5 million in the previous twenty years. Actually its failure put the two parties on an even basis in the Halifax press since the *Herald* had given little support to the Conservatives since the late 1930s.

In 1949 the *Chronicle-Herald* advised the members to cut the debate short instead of ranging "over every subject from aphids in orchards to zymurgy." The newspaper's critics immediately reminded it that Parliament was a talking place in which to exercise free speech on public matters, not a place for a meeting of a board of directors. The speech from the throne and the premier's accompanying address were, in effect, the preliminaries to the election campaign to follow shortly. The throne speech announced the completion of rural high schools at Digby and River Hebert, the planning of seven others, the commencement of regional vocational schools in Halifax and Yarmouth, and the completion of the new Victoria General Hospital. To counter Conservative charges outside the house that the government had "only one good man in it and he is overworked," the premier elaborated fully upon its record. Of the proposals to eliminate the highway poll tax in rural municipalities and to remove the tax on gasoline used in farming operations, he boasted that "we are able to do that . . . because the affairs of the Province are being wisely and soundly administered." Turning to a matter that he never forgot, he promised a fair election in which no attempt would be made to "debar thousands . . . from the right to vote."[19]

Two highly charged political issues emerged during the debate on the address in reply to the speech from the throne. Currie was indignant that 200 UMW delegates meeting in convention had forced 12,000 miners, without a vote or plebiscite, to contribute to the CCF. "You are stealing when you take money...from Liberals and Tories alike who . . . have no desire whatever to pay into the CCF party fund." Cunningham replied that deductions were possible only if a local had chosen to affiliate with the CCF, and some had not.[20] The second issue arose when the *Chronicle-Herald,* in an article neither polemical nor partisan, pointed out that the previous year's redistribution bill gave the same voting power to 4,000 voters in Victoria as to 18,898 in Halifax North and, even worse, separated Cumberland West into two distinct parts. Though R.M. Fielding insisted that "there are no corridors between any of the constituencies," the premier later admitted to a mistake in the printing of the redistribution act which would be rectified by statute."[21]

The long-prophesied financial squeeze finally appeared to be at hand. Though the previous year's surplus had been $4.88

million, the premier forecast one of only $492,000 for 1949-50 despite an additional $600,000 from Ottawa resulting from increases in population and gross national product. Liquor profits were declining as expenditures on health, education, and public works were rising. Nevertheless, the government was setting aside $1 million to assist cities and towns in building junior and senior high schools and to make larger contributions to a new teachers' pension scheme. However, when Michael MacDonald wanted an extension of the free school book programme to cover high school texts, the premier declared that the province had "gone as far as it can at the present time."

To meet labour demands the government agreed to change the conditions for recognizing unions as legal bargaining agents. Henceforth certification would require not a majority of workers in an industry, but only a majority of workers who voted in an election. Lawyers representing the Halifax Board of Trade, the Canadian Manufacturers Association, the Nova Scotia Automobile Dealers' Association, and Dosco strongly opposed the measure, and lawyer Frank Covert declared that it threatened the principles of democracy, but the government refused to budge. A second measure producing wide differences of opinion was the minister of agriculture's bill to regulate the sale of margarine. Representing an urban point of view, J.E. Rutledge wanted a completely unrestricted sale, but the resulting act let the governor in council regulate the quality and colour, and in deference to the agricultural interest Nova Scotians were reduced to buying an anaemic-looking product and to applying their own colouring material.

Shortly after prorogation Macdonald promised an election not on a "cold dreary December day, but rather when the sun is shining and the beautiful Annapolis Valley blossoms are in bloom." Before long he had it set for June 9th, a time he expected would not conflict with a federal election. When June 27th turned out to be national election day, it meant that Nova Scotia's politicians could concentrate on the provincial contest and still have more than two weeks to campaign federally.

This time the Conservatives would be the Liberals' chief opponents. After Fraser's resignation in 1946 they had decided to build up the riding associations before holding a leadership convention. Later that year, at their thinkers' conference at the

Hackmatack Inn in Chester, Frank Stanfield noted his brother Robert and said, "Well, I'm glad at least to find out that you're a Conservative." By Robert's own admission, however, "I hadn't thought of myself as a Conservative, not with a big *C* anyway." As newspaperman Geoffrey Stevens sees it, that meeting was "the beginning of the rebirth of the Conservative Party in the Province, if only because it was the start of Stanfield's political career."[22]

Over the next few months a group of young Conservatives gathered around Stanfield and discussed a revival of party activity. From the provincial executive they received permission to set up policy and organization committees. During 1947 they held a dozen meetings throughout the province and at the provincial association meeting in November Stanfield reported both on policy and leadership. On the former he stated that "the principal task of government in Nova Scotia is to foster [the] initiative and enterprise" of its people, a policy "just as positive as that of any socialists." On leadership he opposed the idea of an immediate choice: "A dynamic leader would be a great help. A poor choice here would, however, finish us. It is surely better to drive ahead without a leader until we see the man we want."[23] Perhaps, as a reward for his work, the association appointed him president and a year later a convention elected him leader over C.F. Fraser by 426 to 76. Not all Nova Scotians thought highly of the choice. Some who heard his first stammering radio speech as leader said, "The Conservatives have done it again," but at least he had the financial resources to make his leadership a prolonged one if he so desired.

In 1949 his party campaigned at first on "The Tide has Turned", later, on "Ride the Tide." His fifteen-point manifesto emphasized the government's failure in postwar development; once again "the exportation of brain and brawn" had become "our major industry." Though prosperity ultimately depended upon the people's resourcefulness, the government should give leadership "instead of using your money to wish you a Happy New Year in large advertisements." Stanfield also promised to restore responsible government to the municipalities by reallocating revenues and responsibilities; complained that Cumberland West was still split into two parts, joined by a corridor with no inhabitants and all forests; and asked for a chance to "scrape some of the barnacles that have accumulated in the course of sixteen years of continuous government."[24]

Russell Cunningham's manifesto contained the proposals that were to be expected from a democratic socialist party: nationalization of the steel and power industries, expansion of the steel secondary industry, and implementation of a low-cost hospital plan like that in Saskatchewan. Neither Macdonald nor Stanfield, however, paid much attention to the CCF and acted as if the contest was one between themselves.

In private, R.M. Fielding admitted to the premier that Stanfield was right about Cumberland West but rationalized his mistake: "to have no corridor is a good general rule . . . but it is more important to provide a fair and reasonable measure that is suited to the special circumstance of each particular county . . . it is the failure of the Tory Party to pay any attention to what people *think* and *feel* that has relegated that party in many cases to the political discard."[25] He was right that the Conservatives could make little out of the corridor question.

Against Stanfield the premier fought his usual type of campaign. His opponent, he said, had talked about the export of brain and brawn, yet had not disclosed "one new measure, one new policy or one new item to correct this situation." Perhaps it was as in 1925 when the Conservatives talked about bringing the boys back home and lost 11,000 people in a few years. Naturally Macdonald boasted of his government's financial record. "Is it to be a lapse back to the dark days of deficits . . . or a continuation of the amazing record of intelligent financing?" Not taking Stanfield lightly, he issued an unusually long manifesto detailing both past accomplishments and promises of what was to come, including a $100 million public works programme, the appointment of a minister of education, free medical care for recipients of old age pensions and mothers' allowances, and assistance for the Canso causeway and the Halifax-Dartmouth bridge.[26]

Actually the Liberals needed little more than the slogan, "All's Well with Angus L." Stanfield might counter with "All's Well with Robert L." and his party might conjure up catchy pronouncements like "Nova Scotia's a Place to Live — not Leave"; "It's the Doctor That's Hopeless: The Patient was Never Better," and "Let's Stop Bailing and Fix the Boat," but against Macdonald their successes were limited. Yet, much as Frank Stanfield, Sr. and W.H. Dennis had helped raise the Conservatives phoenix-like from the ashes in the 1920s, so Stanfield's son performed the same function in the 1940s. As a result his party increased its popular vote from 33.5 to 39.2 per cent and elected seven members, soon to be eight. Through Stanfield, G.I. Smith, and T.A. Giles it could articulate its case effectively in the legislature. The Liberals' popular vote dropped only marginally, the chief loser being the CCF, which, though it re-elected Russell Cunningham and Michael MacDonald, had its popular vote cut from 13.6 to 9.6 per cent. When, during the campaign, the premier found that road work was hurting his party in Digby and Hants, he complained that "the Highways . . . cause more criticism than all the other transactions of the Government combined." The local party committees, he said, "tend to feel that all patronage in the district should go to them personally"; similarly, road foremen took the position that their trucks, sons, brothers, and in-laws should all be employed on the roads.[27] Macdonald's worst fears were realized when the Liberals lost three of the four seats in the two counties and retained Hants West by a single vote. Generally, however, he was satisfied that his party had kept its twenty-eight seats in a house enlarged from 30 to 37 members.

The federal election turned out to be a dreary one. Prime Minister St. Laurent declared that no outstanding issues were at stake, and certainly Nova Scotian issues as such played little part in the campaign. The Liberals told the voters to "make your last years your most secure years with increased Liberal old age pensions"; the Conservatives stressed the hackneyed "It's time for a change"; the *Chronicle-Herald* said simply, "Let's get out and vote." Conservative leader George Drew swept through Nova Scotia with "a tremendous display of physical vigour and his notable gifts for invective." St. Laurent captivated Nova Scotians, as he did Canadians generally, by putting on the mantle of "Uncle Louis."

Little change occurred in the Nova Scotia seats. The Conservatives retained their two seats, the CCF their one, and the Liberals their nine as well as adding the seat gained through redistribution. Conservative George Nowlan lost Annapolis-

Kings by four votes, allegedly because of voting irregularities at RCAF Greenwood, but would win the seat later in a by-election. The Conservative popular vote was much the same as in 1945, but the CCF experienced about the same drop as in the provincial election, from 16.7 to 9.9 per cent, while the Liberal vote rose from 45.7 to 52.7 per cent. Premier Macdonald reported some Conservatives asking, "Is the wound mortal?" He himself wondered if their loss betokened the end of a party that had made a host of errors since 1897. He believed that St. Laurent had fought a good, though not a brilliant election, and he acknowledged him to be a man of ability and character who, in contrast with King, got "nearer to the people" and was "frank and straightforward instead of being obscure and devious." He also expressed shock, and obviously chagrin, that St. Laurent had done a little better in Nova Scotia than he a fortnight earlier. To him it showed "the uncertainty of elections. . . . There was some undercurrent at work. . . . I do not think that anybody could gauge it." Perhaps, he said, the provincial campaign had shown weaknesses in the Liberal organization that had been corrected, or perhaps much of the fight had gone out of the Conservatives after their provincial loss.[28]

In the previous, one-sided assembly, where Liberals occupied many seats to the left of the speaker, the premier had asked some of his members, including Henry Hicks, to question the government critically and appeared not to mind the occasional embarrassment of ministers. After 1949 Liberals no longer needed to act as devil's advocates. By this time too Macdonald was demonstrating more and more his preeminence within the party and cabinet. For one thing he wanted his decisions effected almost as he made them. When, in September 1949, he decided to make Hicks the province's first minister of education, the latter had barely time to consider the invitation or consult his law partner before he found himself installed in office. Anyone who held a gun to the premier's head received short shift. When a Liberal from eastern Nova Scotia, nominated by a convention, declared that he would not run unless assured that specific highways would be paved in his county, the premier refused to fall into line and had a second Liberal ready to file nomination papers. The first person ran without the assurances he wanted, but was never forgiven and had to wait for one of Macdonald's successors to appoint him to the cabinet.

Except for MacQuarrie, Macdonald was the youngest and least experienced member of his first cabinet and he made no attempt to interfere in departments not his own. But after MacQuarrie left in 1947 and Comeau in 1948, he alone remained of the original cabinet and cases of interference occurred, especially when he was not challenged. In exaggerated fashion, although with a considerable element of truth, H.B. Jefferson wrote that one minister of highways used to be sent around the province looking for potholes while the premier and the deputy minister ran the department, deciding which roads were to be paved and which not.

Macdonald did not always get away with interference. Though, like Hicks, a strong believer in rural high schools, he insisted that the rate of building them be related to the state of the province's finances. Accordingly a temporary halt was placed upon further construction and Hicks notified the school authorities in Hants of that decision. But in his absence the premier met a delegation from that county and agreed to build a rural high school at Kennetcook. To Macdonald's dismay Hicks offered his resignation on his return, and the government got out of this dilemma only by deciding to build three rural high schools, including the one at Kennetcook.[29] Hicks also intimates, and the evidence attests, that despite Macdonald's great sympathy for the disadvantaged of the society, his later years indicated more and more that he "would have to be classified as a Right-wing Liberal, as very much a small 'C' conservative."[30]

Stanfield's maiden speech in the legislature in 1950 was not a resounding success. It called on the premier, whom he described as a man of democrative views, to take action against the monster he was helping to create. That monster was an all-powerful cabinet which had made the legislature a rubber stamp and was using its spending power to build up a new privileged class based on government favour. "We have reached the stage when the Government doesn't even bother to get the approval of this House before making public announcements of important commitments." Clearly it had been more successful in undermining "the pillars of democracy" than in mining coal. Among other things, every effort should be made to preserve municipal independence as a bulwark against overweening cabinet power.[31]

Macdonald's response was to prophesy for Stanfield "a long, strenuous, and it may be distinguished, career as Leader of the Opposition." Nova Scotia's problems had begun, he continued, when Tupper forgot his responsibilities and settled for revenue sources which met little more than half the province's needs. "No wonder Nova Scotians raised the cry that they were sold for a sheepskin." That was only the first of a litany of crimes which condemned the Conservatives to "an eternity of hopeless effort." As for building up a privileged class of dependents, public servants did a government more harm than good; as for legislatures, none in Canada was more genuinely democratic than the Nova Scotian; as for the municipalities, his government, in contrast with the Conservative, had provided grants that enabled them to function effectively.[32]

Considering content only, it might have been hard to decide which had been the better speech, but from the point of view of oratory, there had been no contest. Just as Macdonald had demolished Conservative assemblymen in the past, so he appeared to do the same with his new opponents. Indeed, the latter were left wondering if they could compete with him on anything like equal terms. Fortunately for them the premier's speech on the address in reply was given on Friday, and G.I. (Ike) Smith, who, though normally the most considerate of men, would often assume the role of "hatchet man" for his party, had ample time to prepare a reply for Monday evening. Why, he wondered, did most of the premier's speech deal with the past? What contribution could such a speech make to solving the pressing problems of the day? Then he did something that few had attempted to do — he challenged Macdonald's statement of the facts. Had not Liberals such as Howe, Archibald, McCully, and McLelan all become Confederates and accepted the financial terms of Confederation? Reviewing a long list of dismissals in Colchester County, he showed, despite the premier, that patronage was rampant.[33] When he finished, the Conservatives breathed a sigh of relief. Macdonald was open to attack and, in some respects, highly vulnerable.

The long-expressed fears about finances had at last come true. Despite revenues of $35 million the surplus was only $113,000 and Macdonald forecast a deficit of $1.8 million for 1950-51. Like federal Finance Minister Abbott, he declared that any large increase in expenditure would have to be balanced .with increased taxes. He found it especially worrisome that, despite the earlier reduction in debt, 16 per cent of the revenue was needed to meet sinking fund and interest payments. To those who wanted money he gave a stern warning: "It is not enough to point out that something is desirable. It must also be shown that the service is within our means."[34]

Patronage in one form or another led to a host of Conservative attacks in 1950. However, when Stanfield criticized the large number of Liberals among the government suppliers, the premier noted that Conservatives like R.B. Colwell and T.P. Calkin were also included. When G.I. Smith requested that the Purchasing Bureau cease leaning towards Liberals, the responsible minister would only say, "I am prepared to issue instructions to my purchasing agent to purchase the supplies that are needed." When the premier sought to divert attention to the Conservative record on patronage, Stanfield was delighted to have him go into the past "because then I know he is not prepared to face the present."[35]

Though Henry Hicks contends that Macdonald had the "wonderful faculty" of being almost always right on general policy and gauging public attitudes accurately, he makes an exception in the case of liquor legislation. "Too conscious of being a Roman Catholic," he may have "tried too hard to make sure that he didn't antagonize Protestants."[36] That was perhaps true in 1950 when he gave no support to a bill that permitted a plebiscite in a single polling district on the sale of beer and wine with hotel meals. The Conservatives objected to abandoning the principle that a change in liquor laws required the consent of the whole municipality and, although cabinet ministers Connolly and Stevens supported the bill, it failed to pass.

Against the government's cabinet pension bill the Conservatives fought tooth and nail. The premier called it an act of "simple justice," similar to legislation in Great Britain, New Zealand, Australia, and five American states. Stanfield

contended that cabinet ministers were "taking care of themselves before looking after the people of Nova Scotia," that the
bill would greatly increase the power of the premier by giving
his ministers "pecuniary reasons to become 'yes-men'," and that
it would promote the idea of long service by a minister and
prolonged one-party rule, neither of which was necessarily
conducive to good government. On giving a minister security,
he argued that "if a man is interested in security, he shouldn't be
in politics." Cunningham called it "class legislation" because
ordinary persons received old age pensions only at age seventy.
In its one political editorial of the session, the *Chronicle-Herald*
expressed doubts about giving "a pension to every man who has
served ten years in government,"[37] but Liberal backbenchers
dutifully supported the bill. This year the government was still
considering what to do with the Inverness mine which had lost
$3 million in twenty years, but clearly the session's most notable
feature was the reappearance of an opposition that could keep
the government on its toes.

Because of the financial crunch the government's programme
in 1951 was a limited one. It did promise legislation to
implement the federal government's latest offer on old age
security — pensions for everyone over seventy without a means
test and pensions for persons between sixty-five and seventy
with a means test — and it did promise to help secure a
constitutional amendment that would permit a provincial retail
turnover tax. In private, however, Macdonald had already
expressed fears that the first changes would be inflationary.
"Why should I save, and find myself in my old age with a fixed
sum of dollars, which will buy only a fraction of what they will
buy today?" Not to his surprise, he had discovered that Clifford
Clark, the federal deputy minister of finance, had altered his
view on the "green book" proposals of 1945 with their blueprint
for a new world in which there would be "no unemployment,
no financial problems, neither . . . sickness nor death any
more." He concluded, as he had suspected in 1945, that they had
been produced in "the ivory towers" and had not been
considered by the appropriate cabinet committee and perhaps
not by Clark himself. "That, I fear," Macdonald told Tom
Crerar," is what is going on all the time. Nobody seems to be

gathering the loose ends together and weaving them into one consistent web."[38]

This year the Conservatives were even more confident in their attacks. Stanfield accused the government of "doing much in a hit-and-miss fashion which is costing the Province dearly" and promised to fight a provincial sales tax until the government put its house in order. As usual, the premier dwelt on the Tory past. Did anyone want to go back to the days "when we had no paved highways, no free school books, no old age pensions, no rural electrification, no vocational schools, no regional libraries"? The people would remember those evil days so long as the Conservatives "simply set a sail to catch any wind, no matter from where it comes." On this occasion Tom Giles told him that "it is time we forget about what either party did in the past, and turn our attention to the present."[39]

Though revenues had exceeded $40 million for the first time, the public accounts showed a deficit of $850,000 with little likelihood of an early improvement. In defence, Macdonald pointed out that Nova Scotia was spending more per capita on highways than any other province and that it was impossible to get out of other programmes even though the costs were escalating. Education Minister Hicks added that the provincial government was also paying the highest percentage of education costs in Canada and that education, which took 11.4 per cent of the revenues ten years earlier, now took 20 per cent. As a result, the premier made a proposal he did not relish, the imposition of a provincial sales tax of 3 per cent when the proposed constitutional amendment came into effect. "If the time ever comes when we can dispense with [it] . . . no one will move more quickly than I" to eliminate it. Stanfield commented tersely: "there is no budget control . . . and the estimates are not genuine."[40] When a constitutional amendment did not materialize, the legislature met in mid-June to remedy the fiscal deficiency. Savings in building rural high schools and increased amusement, liquor, gasoline, and other taxes improved the situation by $3.5 million. Cunningham would have preferred royalties on gypsum instead of the new taxes; Stanfield condemned the government for its expansive mode in years when it had enjoyed surpluses.

The speech from the throne in 1952 contained a veritable grab bag of proposals, but Stanfield focussed his criticism on an aspect of relations with the municipalities. Teachers being on strike in Antigonish and Cape Breton counties, he argued that higher salaries were needed to maintain proper standards in education and that the province had to participate in the solution. "The municipalities have only one major source of revenue," the taxation of real and personal property, and "this source is approaching exhaustion in many, if not in all municipalities." Macdonald rejected this argument outright. In the last ten years the provincial contribution to education had multiplied more than five times, while that of the municipalities had increased only from $851,000 to $1,186,000. Surely it was time that "somebody else do a little giving." How much further did Stanfield want to go — to take over 60, or 70, or even 100 per cent of the total cost? "Why not . . . leave the towns, cities and municipalities . . . with no contribution, whatever, with no control consequently over educational affairs in the local community."[41]

For the next year Macdonald forecast record high expenditures of $45 million and a surplus of $525,000 even after increasing municipal cash grants from $600,000 to $900,000. Stanfield charged that the government was defeating itself through its "lop-sided expenditures and extravagance." Its spending spree had included a rural high school programme which could cost tens of millions to complete, millions to operate, and millions to service the debt, but it had left the province with old, narrow, and dangerous bridges. "The Conservative party in Nova Scotia has many effective workers," but its "most effective workers are among the members" of the Liberal party.[42]

This year the opposition centred its financial criticism in the public accounts committee, hitherto a largely somnolent body. "It's just as important to investigate spending of public money as to vote further expenditures in the House," declared G.I. Smith. Because the Conservatives considered five hours of meetings a week to be insufficient, they demanded that the committee meet four days a week at specific times, only to have the premier call their proposal ill-timed, undesirable, and not in accord with the practice of the house. They then acted as if the committee inherently possessed the power to summon witnesses and call for documents. After the Liberal chairman refused to comply, they pressed the point until the house explicitly conferred those powers. When the *Chronicle-Herald* feared, from its own reading of Beauchesne, that the newspaper would violate the privileges of the house if it published the testimony given to the committee, G.I. Smith sought to erase any doubts but was turned down by the Liberal majority, who resented the suggestion that the newspaper's reluctance had resulted from threats on their part. The premier himself charged the opposition with seeking to create the impression that the government was concealing something wrong. "Let the newspapers . . . or their solicitors decide whether or not they should publish [the evidence]. Let not this House be a court of law, telling them what they should do."

In the end the speaker decided that it was proper to report the committee's proceedings except when its chairman ruled otherwise. Nevertheless, the Conservatives discovered little new or startling in 1952. Though they found four companies to be in default on industrial loans, the amounts, none more than $21,000, were insignificant. Their investigation of the accounting at the Inverness mine revealed deplorable practices, but its manager was already under arrest.[43]

Following CCF demands, Mines Minister A.H. McKinnon proposed a tax of 10 cents a ton on gypsum, estimated to yield $300,000 a year, but only after departmental studies indicated that, even with the tax, the Nova Scotia product could undersell the American in the United States. In committee the gypsum producers declared the tax to be discriminatory and injurious to the industry and, despite Cunningham, it was finally set at six cents.[44]

To give him flexibility in the timing of a general election, Macdonald had the legislature convened early in 1953. Though coal production was down by 6 per cent, the speech from the throne went out of its way to present a roseate picture. The Halifax-Dartmouth bridge was well under way; tenders had been called for constructing the lock and entrance piers at the Strait of Canso; the rehabilitation of Uniacke House was completed; the rural high school at Sutherland's River had been opened, and construction had started at Cambridge, Amherst, Oxford, and Sherbrooke; 100 miles of highway would be paved; a substantial grant would be made to the Bar Harbour ferry; and all the municipal units would receive larger grants.

This year Stanfield concentrated his attacks on the inadequacy of industrial development planning and the piling up of debt. The government, he charged, had not anticipated the change from coal to oil on the railroads and had failed to attract foreign capital. While other provinces had sent their premiers to Europe, Nova Scotia had sent a junior minister. "The man to have gone to England promptly, not once, but several times, was the premier of this province." The result, despite the boom elsewhere, was little expansion since the war. On debt Stanfield complained that the government had financed its construction programme by borrowing $100 million of it. "It was a grave mistake to double the debt of the province in seven years."

In a typical pre-election speech, Macdonald replied that the Conservative record could never lead any sensible person to conclude that they were capable of governing the province; they would therefore have to "reconcile themselves to . . . a very much longer stay in the cool shades of opposition." They relied on the "most feeble set of political arguments" and their criticism was "carping and petty." For about a year they had talked about "such a world shaking event as the paving of Province House square. [But then] they are allergic to paving." Again it was left to G.I. Smith to remind the premier of the fate that had befallen his Liberal friends in New Brunswick, and to tell him that "pride goeth before a fall," that his speech was designed on the premise that the best defence was a strong offence, always hoping that, by distracting the public through unjustified attacks on his opponents, it might forget the real issue, the incompetence and carelessness of the government.[45]

Because the fiscal year had been changed to end on March 31st rather than November 30th, the public accounts were applicable to a different period. For the year ending March 31, 1952 Macdonald showed a deficit of $186,000. However, fortune had taken a hand in the prospective financial accounts for the next year. With more bountiful returns from the new five-year tax agreement with Ottawa, the premier estimated a likely surplus of about $900,000 for 1952-53 and another of $532,000 for 1953-54, and exulted that he had left behind the atmosphere of deficits, to which he was not accustomed. In eighteen years the Liberals had had only five deficits and in the aggregate surpluses had exceeded deficits by more than $25 million.

Anticipating Stanfield's criticism, Macdonald noted that much of the public debt had resulted from road construction. Contrasted with other provinces, Nova Scotia's municipalities had not paid one cent on highways, except for an annual highway tax of $245,000 imposed many years ago and never increased. That did not satisfy Stanfield, who blamed the government for doubling the public debt at a time when revenues swelled beyond the wildest dream of any prewar government. It would have been difficult, he contended, to spend $300 million in seven years without having something to show for it.[46]

When the Conservatives condemned the shortage of $62,000 in the Inverness mine accounts, they drew an impassioned reply from Mines Minister McKinnon, himself a member for the county. "If the Opposition must depend on the distressing situation at Inverness to garner some voters for their cause, they . . . have not even a colour of right to appeal . . . for a mandate to govern." Had not the first aid given since 1925 enabled a community of 3,000 people and a marketing centre for 15,000 people to survive? Surely, replied G.I. Smith, it was the opposition's duty to investigate such things as the lack of records of the mine's operation. As it turned out, the mine's latest travails quickly led to the abandonment of the government's coal-mining operations in Inverness.

Once again the Conservatives used the public accounts committee to inquire into various facets of government. When George Morrison, the chief liquor commissioner, refused to reveal the name of the Nova Scotian representative of a liquor company because he was a personal friend, G.I. Smith told him that the committee "cannot take that answer from anyone, whether he be high or low in the land." Eventually Morrison gave the name, but when Smith wanted to summon four persons to testify about the activities of liquor agents and another to discuss the practicality of the commission itself handling the sale of empty beer bottles, the committee chairman ruled that the matter had no connection with the public accounts. T.A. Giles than walked out because, in his view, the Liberals had set up a veil of secrecy amounting to a virtual "iron curtain."

The Conservatives also questioned the administration of the Securities Act after the certificate holders of National Thrift Corporation seemed likely to lose $300,000. Though the responsible minister, R.M. Fielding, declared that no government could guarantee that securities offered for sale were without risk, he agreed to an investigation by a one-man royal commission with sweeping powers. Fraught with exceptional importance for the future was Education Minister Hicks's announcement of the appointment of Judge V.J. Pottier as the commissioner to conduct a sweeping inquiry into the financing of the school system and to determine particularly the amounts and proportions that should be paid by the various authorities for the support of schools.

During the session Stanfield took great pains to counter the premier's criticism of his opponents. A government, he said, ignored an opposition as long as it could do so safely. When it began to answer its critics, the public knew that they were bothering it, and when it started to abuse and belittle them, the public realized that it was "fighting for its life with every weapon at its disposal." With satisfaction Stanfield declared that no leader had ever had more loyal, co-operative, and industrious colleagues. "We have been able not only to man the House Committees and examine legislation, not only to conduct searching enquiries in the public accounts committee, and not only to criticize what the Government has been doing; we have also been able to tell the Government what it should be doing." Nor, despite the premier's comments, had their criticism been merely "carping." Certainly it had been constructive in showing that the government was no longer interested in industrial development. Because of his satisfaction with things as they were, Macdonald should step aside and let the Conservatives run affairs. "We have no magic wand. We don't pretend that the promotion of industry is easy in Nova Scotia. We do say that a far greater effort should be made."[47]

Macdonald would have none of that. To him the Conservatives had done so little that it was "unthinkable that the people

. . . should ever consign them to anything but their present role
— that of opposition." Stanfield might, in fact, have made his
farewell speech to the legislature.

After deliberating the pros and cons of having the provincial
election at the same time as the federal, Macdonald decided to go
first — on May 26th. Confident of the outcome, he told Senator
Crerar that the Conservatives had fallen down badly at the last
session. "They do not seem to be able to grasp at anything
substantial and are rather inclined to seize on small matters
which, in due course, peter out."[48] He gave Stanfield an
additional reason for respecting him: when asked by the
Conservative leader if it was wise to take his wife on a planned
trip, he replied, "If I were you, Bob, I don't think I'd do that, but
you and I are the only ones who know that."[49]

Some observers suggested that the Liberal organization was
creaking a little, the result of its workers beginning to think that
their party had a perpetual lease on power. However, to Dalton
Camp it "purred with familiar efficiency, employing the
acquired skills of two decades in power, combining public
works and private charity to fashion its massive victories."[50] The
Conservatives did receive help from an unexpected quarter. Dan
Lewis Macdonald, brother of Angus L., declared that many
Nova Scotians were suffering from "yellow-dog politics" and
would vote for a "yellow dog" if he was a Liberal. To him a
once-vigorous government had developed "hardening of the
arteries, stiffening of the joints and the thing . . . to do now is
. . . ask them to leave. It will do them no great disservice because
they've all been looked after."[51]

Vital to the Conservatives was the work of R. MacD. (Rod)
Black, son of Percy, who had been patiently building up an
organization to cope with the Liberals. Earlier Dalton Camp
had masterminded Hugh John Flemming's victory in New
Brunswick. Now Black installed him in the Lord Nelson Hotel
where, with the help of a publicity committee, he devised the
Conservatives' advertising campaign and at least some of the
party's strategy. He quickly recognized obstacles: the diffidence
of Stanfield, the problem of handling a party which believed
that it had lost before campaigning had begun, and the
difficulty of coping with an opponent so entrenched and so
invulnerable that it was dangerous to attack him. Later he

found another annoyance: the *Chronicle Herald's* insistence that he submit advertisements forty-eight hours in advance so that they could be given close scrutiny. For him this denied the immediacy that he wanted in an advertising campaign.

As usual, the Liberals put their record against that of the Conservatives between 1925 and 1933 and argued that "Wrong-way" Stanfield would take the province back to 1925. Once again they contrasted the franchise scandal and deficits with surpluses, old age pensions, free school books, and rural high schools. The Conservatives re-emphasized the ills they had raised in the legislature and, alluding to the length of the Liberal régime, used the slogan: "Twenty's Plenty." To that the Liberals replied: "Twenty's Brought Plenty" or "Twenty's Plenty Silly." Reflecting Camp's writing, a Conservative advertisement stated that their opponents were running on "an asphalt program . . . the paved road to power. The coat-of-arms of the Liberal party must be a bag of cement against a pile of gravel." Another made fun of the loss of industrial loan money by an angora ranch in Colchester County. To that the Liberals retorted angrily that someone else had taken over the farm and the public had lost nothing. The Conservatives had the most fun of all with the visit of Minister of Trade and Industry Wilfrid Dauphinee to Europe from which, they said, he had returned empty-handed except for having danced with Rita Hayworth. "That may have worried the Aly Khan," said Leonard Fraser, "but what good does it do a miner in Westville?" This jocularity did not amuse the premier, who called it "a fine commentary on the gallantry and courtesy of the men who write the advertisements for the Conservative party." To him it meant that his opponents were "not only bankrupt of constructive ideas" but had "lost all sense of proportion and balance as well."[52]

The liquor business entered prominently into the campaign. The Conservatives attacked the bottle exchange system, contending that it was an easy way for the Liberals to raise party funds. Managed by prominent Liberals, it was, in effect, a government-created monopoly. More serious was the matter of liquor agents, which the Conservatives had been prevented from exploring fully in the public accounts committee. Undoubtedly some Liberals were receiving commissions on the sales of specific companies to the Liquor Commission, and after repeated goading Macdonald himself made at least a slight admission: "There may be liquor agents in the province. However, if I were on oath I could not say there were. We do not recognize liquor agencies. We pay them no commission and they have no effect on the price of liquor."[53]

Most serious of all was an informant's revelation that Health Minister Connolly had received a number of shares from an Ontario distillery company as a gift. "The motives may well have been innocent," wrote Dalton Camp, "but the possibility of risk to the public interest should have been obvious."[54] Reluctantly, at the end of his last campaign speech, Stanfield dealt with the matter in a manner that both showed the nature of the man and rendered the effect nugatory. Prefacing his remarks with "Now they told me to say this," he commented briefly on Connolly "in a flat, unemotive, half audible voice." Camp could hardly believe his ears.[55]

Overall the results were not surprising. The CCF retained its two seats; the Conservatives won twelve, five more than in the general election of 1949; and the Liberals lost five to fall to twenty-three. For the only time in Macdonald's five elections, his party's popular vote fell below 50 per cent to 49.2. The Conservative vote rose to 43.4 per cent, while that of the CCF dropped again from 9.6 to 6.8 per cent. It was perhaps the best Stanfield could have done against Macdonald in 1953. Interest in the election had been sufficient to bring out 75.8 per cent of the voters.

The election had a few bizarre things about it. Every sitting member in the last house except Harold Connolly, Russell Cunningham, and Michael MacDonald was defeated or had his majority reduced. Stanfield's majority of 422 was much the lowest he would ever have. "There seemed to be a feeling," said the premier," that somehow went against all sitting members." The result also indicated a dichotomy between eastern and western Nova Scotia. Halifax with its large Irish Catholic population and the eastern counties with their heavily Scottish background remained almost solidly Liberal. Except for four seats in Cumberland and Colchester, the Conservatives' other eight victories were in western Nova Scotia, even though they lost their previous two seats in Digby. Macdonald attributed it mainly to the fishing counties being "a bit sour" for several reasons — the low price of fish, the loss of gear by lobster fishermen, and the bothering of other fishermen by income tax collectors. For him the biggest surprise was Lunenburg, where the Conservatives secured their largest majority — more than 1,300 — over Speaker Romkey and his colleague. For those results Macdonald never received an explanation that satisfied him.[56]

Prime Minister St. Laurent waited until after the coronation of Queen Elizabeth II before going to the polls on August 10th. Not surprisingly, interest in a midsummer election was low both in Nova Scotia and across Canada. Macdonald and Stanfield participated moderately in a campaign that was largely nationally oriented. The former spoke eloquently of the "glories of Liberalism" and the failures of Conservatism; the latter, as became his custom, emphasized federal inaction on matters of concern to Nova Scotia. What, he wondered, had happened to the Liberals' promise of cheap power and new markets for fish, lumber, and coal? Apparently they "threw their own resolutions into the garbage bag" and "instead of action we have a wretched economy." In Ottawa Dalton Camp found the Conservative national organization isolated from the country in knowledge and understanding. It did not appreciate that the party's main plank, a reduction of $500 million in taxes, would not be looked upon favourably in the Maritimes since "the less the government took in, the less it paid out in tax-sharing arrangements." In the end, however, the major determinant was the inability of George Drew to cope any more successfully with Uncle Louis than he had in 1949.

Nova Scotia played its part in the overwhelming Liberal victory. George Nowlan and Clarie Gillis retained their seats, but the Liberals took Cumberland and Colchester-Hants from the Conservatives on the retirement of Percy Black and Frank Stanfield. The Liberal popular vote remained much the same at 53.0 per cent, while the Conservative vote rose from 37.5 to 40.1 per cent, about the same that the CCF vote dropped.

Before the next session Macdonald paid his last visit to Scotland. Noting that it was 150 years since his great-grandfather had left the shores of Moidart, he exulted that Nova Scotia was "the greatest Scottish-Gaelic community in the

world outside Scotland itself . . . [that] more and more clansfolk
were wearing the tartan. They had the old songs, the stories, and
some 30,000 people spoke the Gaelic." When he unveiled the
Nova Scotia tablet in Edinburgh Castle, the *Sydney Post-Record*
declared that he entered "upon his own domain — a place
within the castle that is part of Nova Scotia and has been so
recognized in Scotland for many generations."

The 1954 session was typical of the Macdonald-Stanfield
years: a speech from the throne promising more highway
construction and paving, more rural high schools, and pensions
for the totally disabled, followed by Stanfield's non-confidence
motion lamenting the government's lack of effort to develop
new industries. The federal and provincial governments, he
feared, were going to let the steel industry at Sydney remain in
a "lame-duck" position and going to force Nova Scotians to
work in the highly protected industry of central Canada.
Macdonald called it a speech of gloom and wondered if the
house should have a short recess while pipers marched around
playing "The Flowers of the Forest." As usual, he paraded a
host of Liberal achievements over nearly twenty-one years, and
again it was left to a dissatisfied G.I. Smith to follow with a ten-
point programme for Nova Scotia's industrial development.

More than one observer has suggested that the quality of
material which Macdonald had available for the cabinet had
deteriorated, and the evidence seems to confirm it. Nevertheless,
in January he had eased his own burden by finally entrusting
finances to other hands. To the new provincial treasurer, R.M.
Fielding, he left a healthy inheritance.[57] For the last complete
year the surplus was $2.57 million, for the current year it was
likely to be $650,000, and for 1954-55 it was estimated at
$350,000. Like Macdonald, Fielding boasted of sixteen surpluses
in twenty-one years and the most favourable financial rating of
any province, but Stanfield replied that capital borrowings and
the failure to keep expenditures in line with revenues were
leading the province to the edge of a financial precipice. Because
an additional $5 million from Ottawa had saved the province
the previous year, Fielding seemed "blissfully satisfied that
"everything is great," an attitude that "reflects the most
antiquarian and indeed reactionary attitude towards government that I have heard for many a day."[58]

Members of both parties had become increasingly worried about the coal industry, in which production had dropped by over 100,000 tons and conditions seemed likely to get worse with growing oil consumption. Mines Minister Malcolm Patterson, supported by the *Chronicle-Herald*, demanded a federal policy that would make Nova Scotia coal competitive with American coal in the Ontario market, something that had been demanded off and on with mixed success for two decades.

The Conservatives roundly condemned the government in other areas. Though the Robertson report on the National Thrift Corporation was "very temperate in its language," Stanfield declared that it told "a story of gross negligence" by the provincial administration. Henry Hicks replied that it was ridiculous to blame the government for the hoax that one dishonest man had perpetrated. Stanfield insisted that it was his duty as opposition leader to "tell the people of Nova Scotia how lousy their government is." He did not oppose increases in members' indemnities but took strong objection to pensions for members based on Ottawa's Retiring Allowances Act. Those who had served at least ten years would, at age sixty, receive a maximum of $1,800 annually. The premier contended that, if the stature of MLAs was permitted to decline, "we shall come to a sorry state in Nova Scotia." However, Stanfield found the proposal even more objectionable than cabinet pensions since it might create a precedent. How could town and municipal councillors be expected to "devote a tremendous amount of time with little or no reward" if the legislature took this step?

In the last contribution of significance that he would make to the assembly's proceedings, Macdonald reacted in typical fashion to municipal councils that had complained about the provincial government's record on snow removal. If they continued, he promised to bring the appropriate sections of the Highways Act to their attention. "Let them assume their responsibility. Let them not criticize those who are trying to do the job."

Just as the session was ending, a shocked Nova Scotia woke up to discover that Angus L. had died, a legend in his own time. Like all great men, he had weaknesses. Some would suggest that for one who boasted of his liberalism he was too far to the right in economic matters, that the tendency increased with age, and that his obsession with balanced budgets took precedence over desirable social objectives. Some colleagues and confidants contended that he lacked a genuinely creative mind and that he was a procrastinator who took an intolerably long time to reach decisions. Others said that he wore himself out by concerning himself too much with detail, a tendency supposed to have become more pronounced in later years because of his lack of confidence in newer ministers. That may have been the reason for his apparent undue reliance on a civil service adviser such as Charles Beazley, the deputy provincial secretary, who, someone said, "got his nose into every nook and cranny of Provincial business." Supposedly, "Let Charlie do it" became a watchword at Province House.

However, even the critics conceded that Macdonald's decisions, when made, were the right ones, politically and otherwise, and invariably received the stamp of public approval. Though his sympathy for the disadvantaged was undoubted, he also believed that rank-and-file Nova Scotians should be allowed to work out their destinies using their own capabilities in their own way. Clearly he was highly skeptical of costly social legislation that might burden the whole society and reduce initiative. Perhaps that was natural for one who, born into a large and anything but affluent family, had successfully made his own way from an early age. Yet he believed strongly that government must provide the framework within which Nova Scotians could pursue their development. Hence, though the most careful of financiers, he doubled the provincial debt in a relatively short time to provide a modern highway system, rural high schools, and the like. Moreover, he did this late in life when some said that he was extraordinarily cautious and lacking in flexibility of mind.

Yet his philosophy of government had little to do with his hold over Nova Scotians which may have been even stronger than Joseph Howe's. His natural eloquence and his gifts of intellect and judgment had "led to a wide personal following not seen in the province since the days of Howe." Other things were equally important. By adhering scrupulously to his campaign promises, he established himself as "the man who kept his work"; by not resorting to empty rhetoric and insisting on factual accuracy, he added to the trust that Nova Scotians placed on him. Few of them understood that his insistence on retaining at least a degree of provincial autonomy in taxation was intended to preserve Canadian federalism, but if Macdonald wanted it, it was good for Nova Scotia. The first Roman Catholic to hold the premiership for any length of time, he made it abundantly clear that no particular denomination played a part in his political decisions. As H.B. Jefferson put it, no one ever considered if he was Protestant or Catholic or Hottentot. The only complaints came from behind the scenes from a few Catholics who expected special treatment.

None had greater confidence in Macdonald or supported him more strongly than the Nova Scotia Scots. Though only one-quarter Scottish — his mother was French and his father one-quarter Irish — he was, according to Harold Connolly, "a Scot first, last, and all the time." Jefferson pictures him at the Highland Games in Antigonish, sitting on an automobile bumper, in kilt and surrounded by children and others anxious to shake his hand or have their picture taken with him to "remember him by." Everywhere he went he was surrounded by people who wanted to talk to him, attracted by "the wittiness of his conversation" which, as Henry Hicks points out, was by no means limited to politics. Indeed, when he invited Hicks into his home after a night session of the assembly, they seldom talked about politics. Instead Macdonald dwelt on Burns and the Scottish tradition, and twitted Hicks about the latter's interest in Poe and Oscar Wilde. "He was a gentleman," says Hicks, "but a gentleman in the tradition . . . of the Scottish chieftain."[59] And in breadth of interest he could be compared to Howe, the man whom he admired most.

CHAPTER 9

The Problems of Transition: Connolly and Hicks

Nova Scotia governments have always been most vulnerable after a change in leadership and that was certainly true following the death of Angus L. Macdonald. Some wanted Geoffrey Stevens to take over the premiership in a caretaker capacity, but he would have none of it. The cabinet itself rejected a proposal that the person acting temporarily should not contest the convention, and instead chose senior minister Harold Connolly without restrictions even though Alistair Fraser, the lieutenant-governor, was reported to have considered the choice unwise.

Some party members were already suggesting that it was time to have a Protestant premier. At the time Connolly himself would have preferred a senatorship and might have accepted one with appropriate action from Ottawa. However, Nova Scotia's federal cabinet minister, Robert Winters, did nothing to facilitate it. For a time some thought that Winters might be a candidate himself, but he quickly disavowed it. Dalton Camp believes that Winters was "accountable for much of the damage" to be inflicted upon his party and notes the comment of Henry Hicks that Winters was "not much of a politician."[1] Hicks, clearly the ablest man in the cabinet, surveyed the situation and, concluding that he could not win, at first decided not to run. Later the worst possible situation developed for the Liberals. Connolly officially entered the contest on August 25th, Hicks about a week later. The former came close to proclaiming himself the "legitimate heir" to Macdonald suggesting that "Angus L., on his deathbed, had more or less ordained that . . . his leadership should fall on him." In the convention on September 9th six candidates were in the running, five cabinet ministers and veteran Liberal Hector Hill of Truro. On the first ballot Connolly was within fifty-eight votes of winning, Hicks third. In subsequent ballots it was clearly a case of stopping Connolly, and this was accomplished when Hicks won on the fifth ballot.

	1st Ballot	2nd Ballot	3rd Ballot	4th Ballot	5th Ballot
Harold Connolly	216	232	228	224	229
Henry Hicks	83	108	178	263	312
A.W. Mackenzie	89	106	98	54	
R.M. Fielding	69	56	33		
M.A. Patterson	54	42			
Hector Hill	36				

Unfortunately for the Liberals it appeared as if the delegates had ganged up to defeat the only Catholic among the contestants. A parish priest in Truro wrote in a church bulletin, "A Communist candidate would have had more chance than our esteemed friend . . . well it's nice to know where we stand as Catholics. As to the Liberal party, we can only say: 'Requiescat in Pace'." Though a substantial number of Antigonish and Cape Breton Catholics had voted for Hicks, and none knew the extent to which the vote was polarized along religious lines, the media and much of the public believed that the Liberals had suffered a serious split.[2]

In their new leader the Liberals had someone unexcelled as an extemporaneous speaker and in his ability to size up situations with rapidity and precision. However, fairly or not, he suffered from an image problem which he would never overcome. According to Dalton Camp, he had "the small man's suggestions of vanity and aggressive confidence. He rushed his fences as though they were not there."[3] At times he annoyed others because he was too clever for them and would not tolerate foolish statements lightly. As a result, the Conservatives delighted in contrasting him with their own leader who, they

Harold J. Connolly   1954

Courtesy of NSIS Photo

said, was "not a flashy introvert . . . not the scintillating wit that flashes like heat lightning on a summer evening and then leaves the night darker than before," but a man possessing "those qualities that Nova Scotians demand and trust."[4]

Hicks had other difficulties not of his own making. The Liberal organization had fallen somewhat into disrepair and the quality of the cabinet had declined, though neither factor would have prevented Macdonald from winning the next election. Thus the basic Liberal weakness resulted from the loss of one whose shoes none could be expected to fill. Hicks rearranged his cabinet minimally, unable for the moment to rid himself of an unhappy Connolly. To fill three assembly vacancies he had by-elections set for mid-November. It was uncertain whether his chief opponent would be Stanfield, whose wife had been killed in an automobile accident, leaving him with four small children. Apparently the highly respected Dr. George Murphy had much to do with Stanfield's continuing in politics. "Just take your time about these things," he said. "You may find you can do both, that you can look after your children and still carry on as leader."[5] He did, although for some time he insisted, wherever he was, on driving home at night to have breakfast with his children.

In the by-elections the Conservatives went all out to win Halifax South, the seat of Angus Macdonald. Rod Black personally managed the campaign; Dalton Camp, now the national party's public relations adviser, planned the party strategy, once again from the Lord Nelson Hotel; and Mayor Richard A. Donahoe of Halifax, always the faithful party servant, became the candidate and used his "rich, resonant voice, [and] robust Irish wit" to the full. Donahoe's easy victory was as much a morale builder for the Conservatives as it was an ominous sign for the Liberals. It also meant that Donahoe would join Stanfield and Smith in keeping the Hicks government on its toes.

Though the speech from the throne in 1955 seemed somewhat routine, it referred to two matters — educational reform and changes in representation — that would lead to significant legislation. Naturally the government exulted over the completion of the Canso causeway late in 1954 and the near-completion of the Halifax-Dartmouth bridge. As usual, Stanfield belaboured it for failing to cope with the crisis in coal or to bring in new industry to offset unemployment and finance education and social services. He also gave his first warning about going too fast in implementing the proposals of the recently released Pottier Report on school financing lest they burden seriously the primary producers and the municipalities.

The premier replied simply that his government would give the leadership needed to bring about desirable change.

The province's finances were in relatively good shape, a surplus of $2.16 million for the last complete year and one of $128,000 forecast for 1955-56. However, the latter would be possible only by raising the gasoline tax from 15 to 17 cents a gallon, the highest in North America. Provincial Treasurer Fielding pointed out that every dollar received in highway taxes was spent on the roads, together with $2.5 million from general revenue. Nonetheless, Stanfield was highly critical of a government without a mandate raising taxes within a few months of its taking office, and of a rapidly mounting debt which had become the second highest per capita in Canada. G.I. Smith accused the highways department of being riddled with patronage and waste, and of being run as "a political arm" of the government. When the premier asked for proof, Smith simply replied: "There are some things you don't have to prove. Such as that the sun rises. They're obvious."[6]

Stanfield also wondered if "the government [was] getting full value for all the money it is spending." In effect, that was the beginning of his party's attacks on Mercury Fisheries, which had obtained a government loan of $367,000 to develop a herring industry. When the company's plant at Cheticamp burned down before it went into operation, a Conservative member warned that it was "the people who are going to get caught, not the herring." Subsequently it was revealed that the loan had not received the approval of the appropriate board and that its planning arrangements left much to be desired. Though the government seized the company's ships, it never recouped its financial or political losses.

Hicks revealed himself as a man of action in the quick implementation of his two major proposals. When he called for an assembly committee to consider an enlarged house based on the 1951 census, Stanfield wanted an independent commission. Liberal J.E. Rutledge pointed out that neither the Dominion nor any province used this device, and Hicks doubted if democracy worked well through independent commissions. In his view, "the check of public opinion [was] more apt to guard the public weal more closely." Within fifteen days the committee had made its report, the Liberal caucus had approved it, although not unanimously, and a bill to implement it had been introduced. Angus Macdonald would have carried these proceedings over to the next session, but a new master was in charge. Basically the bill enlarged the house from thirty-seven to forty-three members by giving two additional seats to Halifax and one each to Cape Breton, Annapolis, Kings, and Lunenburg. Stanfield contended that no case had been made for a larger house and he objected particularly to the additional seats for Lunenburg and Kings. The committee's chairman, R.M. Fielding, pointed out that the Nova Scotia assembly would still be the third smallest in Canada and that the changes would permit the law amendments and the private and local bills committees to meet without interrupting the work of the other committees.[7]

The government may not have suffered from its representation bill, but it undoubtedly sustained considerable damage from its implementation of the Pottier Report. That a report so recent in origin and so sweeping in character could be adopted with such speed was unprecedented in Nova Scotia. It was possible because, even before the appointment of the commission, the same basic proposals had been under active consideration by the department of education and its minister, Henry Hicks. Hicks secured the approval of his caucus, one member excepted, and proceeded despite the absence of full discussion throughout the province. In essence, Bill 66 established a foundation programme providing a basic level of educational services, including the maintenance of schools, the transportation of pupils, and the remuneration of teachers on a scale calculated to relieve the shortage. The contribution of the sixty-six municipalities was to be determined by their ability to pay, which was based, rightly or wrongly, on the value of their real and personal property. After the commission had worked out, as best it could, an equalization of municipal assessment throughout the province, it concluded that 80 cents per $100 of equalized assessment would be a fair rate of municipal taxation. That would leave the province to pay one-half the cost of education, a proportion that the commissioner thought desirable. The outcome would be that each school child would receive no less that the foundation programme and the burden of providing it would, at least in theory, be evenly distributed.

In the premier's view the bill revolutionized the financial and administrative basis of the educational system and provided a foundation as soundly based as any on the continent. He was careful, too, to point out that the province was making a larger contribution than the report recommended. Neither Stanfield nor Cunningham opposed the bill, but both wanted greater time for consideration. To Stanfield that was especially necessary since fifty of the municipal units would incur heavier burdens, some much greater, amounting to $2 million in all. G.I. Smith argued strongly that taxation on property did not constitute a measure of ability to pay. However, the premier insisted that the bill did not reflect any sudden departure of the department of education. "It is the culmination of many years of thinking . . . If when it is applied to municipalities undesirable results follow, the legislature might be recalled. This Bill is the best I could do as Minister of Education."[8] It will always remain debatable if in this instance Hicks showed a lack of "two vital political qualities . . . judgment and patience," which newspaperman Geoffrey Stevens thought was to prove fatal. The latter wrote, over dramatically, that though as "a kamikaze pilot" Hicks would have been "a spectacular success; as an air marshall he proved a disaster."[9]

The speech from the throne in 1956 contained sufficient promises of health, welfare, and labour legislation to convince the opposition parties that an election was contemplated. High on the government's agenda was the promise of a health plan in line with recent federal proposals, which evoked from Stanfield only criticism for the government's failure to prepare the province much earlier for a health insurance scheme. As usual, however, he considered more serious the government's apparent unwillingness to initiate steps to develop the economy. Why did it not venture upon a bold course that would take the province out of the doldrums? One possibility was the development of Fundy tides, not a "project for timid souls," but one which "staggers the imagination if [it] could be carried through to a successful conclusion." Hicks, in reply, adamantly opposed any suggestion that the government operate business enterprises in fields rightfully belonging to the private sector or spend money to duplicate research on tidal power being done elsewhere. The government, he insisted, should work only to create an atmosphere that would allow Nova Scotians to solve their own problems.[10]

Despite record expenditures of $59.5 million the government estimated a surplus of $62,000 for 1956-57. Once again the Conservatives lamented the increased burden placed on the municipal units, particularly the rural ones, by the changes in the financing of education. When Agriculture Minister Colin Chisholm promised to join the department of municipal affairs in preventing any increase in taxes from becoming a serious burden on agriculture, he drew a stinging reply from Stanfield: "You may as well keep in close touch with the Aga Khan. Who in the Department of Municipal Affairs knows anything about agriculture?"[11]

Stanfield also condemned Ottawa's unwillingness to recognize the principle of fiscal need in the negotiations for the new five-year fiscal agreement to begin in 1957. However, when he proposed a resolution condemning the federal government, the premier replied that he himself had already presented Nova Scotia's case forcefully and that, though the resolution might be newsworthy, it could do no good. Later, after Hicks concluded the negotiation, he reported that the province would receive additional revenues of $5 million in 1957-58. Though not explicitly recognizing fiscal need, the new arrangements went a considerable way in that direction by providing equalization grants which tended to produce a parity in provincial returns. Hicks also drew Stanfield's fire when he failed to use the fiscal need argument in the province's submission to the Gordon Commission on Canada's Economic Prospects. When the premier replied that he had confined himself to factual information the commission could use to produce suitable recommendations, Stanfield called that a lame excuse and told the government to get busy. Hicks replied sharply that it was Stanfield's right and duty to make his own submission if he felt so inclined.

In seeking to ward off further criticism of the Mercury Fisheries venture, Trade and Industry Minister Dauphinee argued that the government was doing all it could to recover its outlay and that the project had demonstrated the feasibility of catching herring in the Gulf of St. Lawrence on a commercial basis. G.I. Smith still alleged "hopeless incompetence. . . . If they approve of such a hopeless muddle in dealing with public funds, they must accept responsibility . . . for removing themselves from office.''

Outside the assembly a more serious situation was developing for the government in the matter of hospital administration. The government had appointed a royal commission to investigate charges of inadequate medical services, maltreatment of patients, and general inefficiency against the Cape Breton Hospital, a mental institution in Sydney. Though the government had nothing to do with the hospital's day-to-day administration, the public was led to believe that it was responsible, in part, perhaps, because the board administering the hospital consisted largely of Liberal municipal officials. The Sydney press reports of the deplorable situation brought to light by the royal commission boded no good for the provincial government.

Throughout the latter part of 1956 an election appeared imminent. Like others in his position Premier Hicks did not like to be reminded that he was serving someone else's mandate. Besides, he wanted to constitute a cabinet that he could genuinely call his own. He also had to consider his narrow majority in the assembly. Excluding the speaker, the standing was nineteen to fifteen following some deaths and the departure of Connolly to the Senate. The sometime absence of two Liberals further reduced the majority to two, a margin too close for comfort. To the premier a general election may have seemed more attractive than a possible endangering of his government through three by-elections, particularly as his caucus gave him estimates ranging from an optimistic thirty-six seats to, at worst, a small majority.

As early as September 6th the *Chronicle-Herald* picked October 30th or November 6th as the date of polling. Almost at once the Conservatives announced that "Exercise Victory" would be held in the Halifax Forum on September 15th. Five thousand attended a day of entertainment and speech-making and heard Stanfield declare that victory was in sight with Angus L. Macdonald's death and Hicks's mistakes in implementing the Pottier Report. They also listened to G.I. Smith complain that the government's development program was "a promise here, a begging trip there, somewhere else a loan, maybe good, maybe bad, "but nothing sound;[12] and they applauded Richard Donahoe as he compared the two leaders none too subtly in his introduction of Stanfield: "You will find neither intolerance nor cynicism, no flippancy in his approach to public matters, no slightest hint of insincerity." Two days later the premier announced an election for October 30th. Exuding confidence, Hicks declared that, since the Conservatives would not win a seat on Cape Breton Island, they could not possibly eke out a victory.

Throughout the campaign the Conservatives sought to damage the premier's credibility. They were helped because his quick mind sometimes created the impression that he resorted to glib answers. When Stanfield promised to pave all the roads that were "ready or near ready" for paving, Highways Minister A.W. Mackenzie stated that the cost would be $222 million. Stanfield having declared that he could do it for about one-tenth of that amount, the premier insisted that it would require at least $200 million. The Conservative leader, undoubtedly advised by Dalton Camp — again masterminding strategy from the Lord Nelson — did not miss a golden opportunity and succeeded, after an exchange of letters and telegrams, in getting Hicks to concede that the phrase "ready or near ready for paving" might mean different things to different people and that the premier's calculations were based upon all 7,786 miles of graded and gravelled roads.

Despite the statement of newspaperman Geoffrey Stevens that "the people of Nova Scotia never did figure out where the facts lay in the paving dispute," the question was not nearly so complicated as he made it out to be, and not a few Nova Scotians concluded that the Liberal leader was trying to "play fancy games with the facts." It ended up as Stanfield (or Camp) had hoped: a province-wide radio speech in which the Conservative leader declared that he did not propose to campaign by "being cute with the truth. We are going to talk sense and talk straight, and if we can't then we shouldn't say anything at all." Strangely Stanfield's indifferent speech-making turned out to be a positive asset, especially on television, which was being used for the first time, at least in a limited way. "His stumblings heightened the impression that here was an honest man trying to be as sincere and frank as possible."[13] It must have been particularly galling for the premier to read Stanfield's statement that "we must make allowances for [Hicks's] inexperience. But having contested two elections against that redoubtable warrior, Angus L. Macdonald, I must say that I hardly recognize that I am in a fight against the same Liberal party."[14]

An examination of the advertisements of the campaign indicates that, for interest and eye-catching appeal, Dalton Camp easily outbested the firm of Cockfield Brown, which worked for the Liberals from the Nova Scotian Hotel. As Camp expected, their material bore "the mark of professional skills; but it [was also] bloodless, even somewhat alien." He thought, however, that some of their advertisements had "a desperate cleverness," especially their picture of Henry Hicks "looking like a sombre general turned junta politician, wearing conspicuously in a lapel buttonhole his Second World War veteran's pin" to emphasize that he had been in the armed services and Stanfield had not.[15] In contrast, Camp's advertisements were far less staid. One showed pictures of some of Hicks's 7,000 miles of roads that were quagmires and asked: "Would you say these roads are 'Ready for Paving'?" Another that duplicated scores of advertisements of land for sale taken from the *Chronicle-Herald* asked, "Who never had it so good?" and declared that "a Stanfield government will face the facts of farm life." A third, just before election day, asserted that "after 8.395 days of *one-party* rule Nova Scotia has only 5 days more to go." Almost all the advertisements said: "Elect a Stanfield Government," an indication of the importance of their leader to the Conservatives.

The specifics of the parties' programmes as contained in the leaders' manifestoes had little effect upon the outcome. The Liberals began their statement with the promise of a $100 million highway programme, the priority to be given to secondary roads, and then they continued with more of the same. The Conservative counterpart emphasized the failure to provide a climate for industrial development and, though silent on Bill 66, insisted that taxation should not become a crushing burden when determining the proportion of education costs to be borne by the municipalities. In reply, the premier promised $1 million of the additional moneys coming from Ottawa to meet the rising municipal expenditures on education.

The election produced the closest popular vote in provincial history: 48.6 per cent for the Conservatives; 48.2 per cent for the Liberals. For the third time in a row the CCF vote fell seriously; that party had dropped from 13.6 per cent in 1945 to 3.0 per cent in 1956. Russell Cunningham lost, but Michael MacDonald retained Cape Breton Centre. With an exceptionally high voter turnout of 79.8 per cent, the Conservatives took twenty-four seats, the Liberals eighteen, and the CCF one. The results are not easy to analyze and opinions still differ. Though a swing of varying proportions to the Conservatives occurred generally throughout the province, the Liberals regained the two seats in Yarmouth where they had experienced internal difficulties in 1953, and they actually did better in several other counties.

In Halifax Centre and South the Liberal candidates reported no strong reaction against the government but found some sentiment that it was "time for a change," that "the Liberals had been in too long," and that the other side should be given a chance.[16] Because of the previous large Liberal majorities in Halifax, this feeling led to no changes in that county, but it may well have produced Conservative gains elsewhere. Indeed, in the post-mortem conducted by the cabinet and Liberal officialdom, this reason was prominent among those given for the Liberal defeat; so was the opinion that barnacles had developed in the Liberal organization after twenty-three years of power.

However, something more is needed to account for the Conservative victories in five of the six Cape Breton County seats, an impossibility according to the Liberals, yet the principal reason for their defeat. Earlier some, including myself, attributed it to the loss of Catholic votes in a heavily Catholic county, but this was certainly not the major factor. The Cockfield Brown representative said simply that the miners were "unhappy with everyone," a fact apparently not realized by Liberals in Halifax. In Sydney, however, newspaperman H.B. Jefferson had received a reasonably accurate forecast prior to the election, and on voting day UMW executive officer Freeman Jenkins had told him that the miners were going to their natural enemy, the Tories. Partly it was because the Liberals' interest in them had been perfunctory since the latter days of the Macdonald government and partly because they had decided not to waste their time on the CCF when it was not genuinely trying

Henry D. Hicks   1954-6

to become the government. Jefferson also discovered many steelworkers switching to the Tories because of the hospital question,[17] which accounted in part for the Conservative victories in Cape Breton South and Nova, the seats with the largest steelworker vote.

Another issue probably tipped the balance. Earlier I wrote that the Hicks government might "still have weathered the storm if it had not . . . lost some predominantly rural constituencies in western Nova Scotia where increased property taxes were a key issue."[18] Hence I described the passage of Bill 66 as "an act of unprecedented political courage." However, Henry Hicks has indicated that he had not considered it a danger to his government and doubts whether it had adverse effects of consequence. Yet the testimony of Liberal candidates, the editorials of weekly newspapers, and other post-mortems confirm my original opinion and even extend the area of the issue's import. Liberal Senator Charles Hawkins declared that it almost cost the Liberals the Guysborough seat and accounted for the greatly increased majorities for Stanfield and Smith in Colchester. The president of the Cumberland East Liberal Association attributed the Liberal reversal in part to the "tremendous increase in taxes" for education. In Lunenburg Centre Liberal Harold Uhlman unequivocally blamed his loss on Bill 66, and the Lunenburg *Progress Enterprise* agreed that it had led to Uhlman's rejection in the rural districts. In Digby, Victor Cardoza also put it foremost among the reasons for his loss: it "hit the voters in a vital spot — the pocketbook, and they reacted like the farmer with the sickle when stung by a bee." Finally, in Shelburne, where the Conservatives argued that it was not cowardly to avoid "jumping before you can see where you are going to land," cabinet minister Wilfrid Dauphinee listed Bill 66 among the causes of his defeat.[19]

For once, image politics favoured the Conservatives. Stanfield came from a family almost universally known by name and widely respected throughout the province. A decade in politics had let him demonstrate the qualities Nova Scotians like in their public men. The Cockfield Brown representative pointed out ruefully the electorate's admiration for him and its desire to give him a chance. Unfortunately for Hicks he had characteristics that the media could exaggerate with almost malicious delight. One inaccurate, unfair, almost brutal example was Austin Cross's description of his leadership: "he began . . . in cocky style, even though he was originally sixth on the convention ballot. Then he came to Ottawa and talked in a show-off style. All down through the piece Henry has let his brains run to his head. Any Rhodes scholar has to watch this. The road to nowhere is strewn with cerebral cells of Rhodes scholars."[20]

In hindsight something else appears to have made the Conservative victory possible. The 1956 election turned out to be a watershed and is to date the most significant in this century. If the 1928 results are treated as a carry-over from 1925, as they ought to be, the 1956 election was the first since Confederation that the Conservatives had won under non-crisis conditions. It seems obvious now that during the immediate postwar period a slow erosion of the province's traditional hereditary voting had begun — partly because of the movement of population and growing urbanization, factors that tend to produce more volatile voting habits. So long as Angus L. Macdonald continued to win elections on personal appeal, the change was not observable, but the situation altered under a successor who was not, and could hardly be expected to be, another Macdonald. The process of erosion would continue during the Stanfield and Diefenbaker régimes until it could be said that Nova Scotia was no longer a Liberal but a genuinely two-party province.

CHAPTER 10

Stanfield: A Conservative Establishes Himself

The Stanfield cabinet started with seven ministers with portfolio, of whom only Edward Manson, the minister of trade and industry, was without legislative experience. Though this situation gave Stanfield time to assess his new members before appointment, it meant that all his ministers but one had two portfolios, he himself becoming both provincial treasurer and minister of education. From the beginning, he warned his party that the government must be moderate and not bitterly partisan. As there were not enough Conservatives to keep the party in power, it must "increase the respect of people who are non-Conservative."

During the 1957 session the premier took action to implement two major promises: to pave all roads ready or near ready for paving and to establish an industrial development corporation. On other matters he adopted a policy that would become a hallmark of his government: to secure all the relevant facts before making decisions. Accordingly, a royal commission would report on the much-criticized Workmen's Compensation Act; a full-time planning body would investigate the proposed national hospital plan; and surveys would be made of provincial-municipal relations and the deteriorating coal industry. Despite increasing costs the premier also promised to work Bill 66 as best he could, but he almost begged the municipalities not to proceed with new school construction unless increased enrolments made it necessary.

For the Hicks government's last year, Stanfield announced a deficit of $4.5 million and, although he forecast a surplus of $88,000 for the next, he warned that the escalating costs of social services would soon require him to seek additional revenues. "Jeers, sneers and laughter" greeted Hicks's contention that he had left an overflowing treasury. When Hicks complained, G.I. Smith recalled that he himself had suffered similar treatment during his seven years in opposition. For the first time following a party change in government little debate occurred on dismissals, and in the one instance of substance the government had no difficulty justifying the removal of the director of industrial and tourist information on the grounds of unsuitability and gross insubordination. It kept another pledge by repealing the cabinet ministers' pension bill. Hicks warned of the possibility of a cabinet composed only of persons with acquired or inherited wealth, but Attorney General Donahoe insisted that the greater danger was to keep someone in office simply to allow him to fulfil the ten-year requirement for a pension. Generally the Stanfield government's first session was not a dramatic one and, according to the *Chronicle-Herald*, it lacked "knock-them-down, drag-them-out" debates.

By session's end the province's politicians were fighting a federal general election. This time the Conservatives were led by John Diefenbaker, whose "thunder-and-lightning oratory" made him a "sort of Billy Graham of Canadian politics."[1] Early in the campaign Stanfield left the province briefly following his marriage to Mary Hall, the daughter of a former Conservative leader, but on his return he campaigned vigorously and persuaded candidates to run in some seats where the Conservative prospects looked poor. For the first time since the twenties, Maritime Rights dominated the Nova Scotia campaign. Scornfully George Nowlan declared that the Liberals, who for years had acted as if those rights were "birth, death and a free ride on the ICR," had finally discovered them after their defeats in Nova Scotia and New Brunswick. "Did you ever in your life see . . . so much last-minute repentance?" asked Diefenbaker. Where were the province's Liberal MPs between 1949 and 1957? "They say they don't speak in Parliament, they speak in caucus," but apparently they spoke in neither place "because

Robert L. Stanfield   1956-67

Courtesy of NSIS Photo

not till Robert L. Stanfield won in Nova Scotia did we start to get some federal action down here."[2]

Coal and power dominated the headlines in Nova Scotia. Diefenbaker, at Stanfield's request, pledged himself to a subvention on coal for power development. St. Laurent declined to increase the production of coal "because I don't think that would be fair to future generations." That led Stanfield to say that "a Liberal vote in this election is a vote against the coal miner of today."[3] When, on election eve, the federal government proposed to spend $200 million on power development in the

Maritimes, Robert Winters tried to create the impression that the Nova Scotia premier was "looking a gift horse in the mouth." Stanfield replied that he would sign an agreement at once if cheaper power and the use of Nova Scotia coal were guaranteed. He had no intention, however, of "letting the power proposals become a political football."[4]

The Conservatives expected gains in Nova Scotia, but few would have believed that they would defeat Robert Winters and take all the province's seats except Inverness-Richmond and Shelburne-Yarmouth-Clare. In Nova Scotia, as in much of English Canada, the image of Uncle Louis collapsed before Diefenbaker's evangelical oratory. However, the Conservative popular vote in the province was much less impressive than the number of seats since the Liberals took 45.1 per cent and none of the Conservative majorities was exceptionally large compared with those in later elections.

The provincial speech from the throne in 1958 announced an agreement with Nova Scotia Pulp Ltd., a subsidiary of the Swedish firm Stora Kopparbergs, to build a mill at Port Hawkesbury; expressed approval of Diefenbaker's Atlantic Province adjustment grants, which meant an additional $7.5 million for Nova Scotia during each of the next four years; and announced that the hospital insurance plan would come into effect on January 1, 1959. This year Hicks was unrestrained in criticizing what he called a "do nothing . . . passer of the buck" government, blaming it for growing unemployment, a bad bargain with Nova Scotia Pulp Ltd., and failure to give the municipalities any of the new moneys from Ottawa. An annoyed premier warned him not to stir up distrust of the new company or to undermine public confidence in Industrial Estates Ltd. (IEL), which the legislature was establishing with a borrowing capacity of $12 million for "the promotion, diversification and development of industrial activity in Nova Scotia." The government was abandoning Nova Scotia Development Ltd., a creation on paper of the previous year, after Stanfield had been persuaded that industrial estates offered a more effective way to attract new industry: "Many prosperous companies today have a policy against investing any money in a site or factory."[5] For the next dozen years IEL would seldom be far from the top of the political agenda.

Responding to the opposition, the premier expressed regret that Attorney General Donahoe had substituted a warning instead of allowing a traffic charge to be proceeded with against a cabinet colleague. "I believe that a Minister of the Crown . . . must conform to a more rigid standard than a private citizen."[6] Never again did he have to deal with a similar case.

In forecasting a surplus for 1958-59, Stanfield made it clear that his estimates had nothing to do with hospital insurance, which would be financed through other legislation. Health Minister Donahoe's bill, following closely the report of the planning body set up earlier, provided for a hospital commission to administer the plan. Also in accord with the planning board's proposals, Stanfield sponsored bills imposing additional taxes on liquor and cigarettes, and a general sales tax of 3 per cent, food and children's clothing to be exempted. Hicks wanted to have some of the cost, estimated at $12.5 million for the first year, financed out of the new moneys from Ottawa, but did not oppose the taxes for fear that his action might be "construed as voting against the hospital plan." Because of its careful approach the government would emerge unscathed politically from its adoption of the sales tax. Despite the phobia of Nova Scotians against direct taxation, they accepted the so-called "health tax" without complaint, treating it as their contribution towards a highly approved service.

Because the indemnities of assemblymen and the salaries of cabinet ministers were almost the lowest in Canada, a house committee recommended substantial increases in both. Stanfield agreed to raise members' indemnities and expense allowances by one-third, to $3,200 and $1,600, but he took no action on ministers' salaries, always reluctant to do anything that might be regarded as self-serving. He did, however, fulfil another of his election promises by establishing a provincial counterpart to the auditor general of Canada.

Insisting that the legislature not be distracted, the premier had it adjourned for about a month during the federal campaign of 1958. The specifics of the Liberals' *New Charter for Nova Scotia* and of the Conservatives' Atlantic Provinces manifesto could not have mattered less. The message of the prime minister at Sydney became a clarion call for the Conservatives: "for the first time in history there is a realization by government of your problems. . . . John Sebastian Cabot discovered this part of Canada in 1497 but the Liberal party not until 1957's election." Backing this up with specific accomplishments, he listed special assistance to the Springhill collieries, legislation to promote power development, an annual increase in fiscal payments of $2,784,000, and annual adjustment grants of $7.5 million for four years. More would come, he promised, when he launched a development plan that would catch the vision of John A. Macdonald and the other creators of the country.[7]

Against campaigning of this kind, Lester Pearson was ineffectual, and for the first and only time the Conservatives won all of the province's federal seats, even defeating Allan MacEachen by sixteen votes. Their popular vote rose from 50.4 to 57.0 per cent as the Liberals' fell from 45.1 to 38.4 per cent. The CCF continued to do badly, nominating only four candidates, who polled a meagre 4.5 per cent of the vote. The Conservatives' upswing continued in municipal elections in October, especially on Cape Breton Island, where they broke a strong Liberal hold on two counties and challenged strongly in the other two. Their activity annoyed Henry Hicks: "If [they] intend to make the municipal elections a battle-ground for party politics . . . the Liberals will be ready with the time and the money to oppose them properly."[8] Since 1958, however, partisan politics in municipal elections has steadily waned.

In 1959 Hicks focussed his criticism on the coal industry, which continued to decline because of the hydro surplus in Quebec, the dieselization of railways, and competition from natural gas and cheap American coal. He pointed out with relish that, although he had kept all the mines open, Stanfield had permitted closures in Pictou, Inverness, and Cape Breton counties, and more were likely to follow in Springhill. Stanfield replied that federal subventions of a year ago had permitted Nova Scotia to market 500,000 tons in Ontario. Later, when he was able to arrange a $4.3 million subvention of which Nova Scotia would pay $500,000, both Hicks and Michael MacDonald objected to the province having to contribute, but Stanfield did not think it "unreasonable in view of the large commitment by Ottawa and of claims by other parts of Canada." The *Chronicle-Herald* approved the joint action, but it warned that the assistance was "only first aid" and did "nothing to solve the basic problem."[9]

Hicks also attacked IEL which, he charged, was costing more than $100,000 annually in overhead with little to show for it. That led Stanfield to tell him that he should know better than to destroy it for purely political purposes. The Liberal leader also took aim at the American management consulting firm of Jerome Barnum Associates, which the government had been employing for fifteen months. Was the government not tacitly admitting that it could not conduct the province's business? This time Stanfield took the offensive. Had Jerome Barnum not permitted substantial savings by showing that a building costing $2.5 to 3.0 million was unnecessary? Was Hicks not fouling his own nest by ridiculing the firm he himself had hired to act as a consultant to the Power Commission? Had he not spoken for two hours without making one useful suggestion? Did he picture himself as a de Gaulle by not disclosing his policies and "asking to be accepted on faith as the Saviour of the Province"?

After reciting a list of government accomplishments, including changing the old system of poor relief to social assistance at acceptable standards, the greatest road-building programme in provincial history, and the establishment of an aggressive organization for the promotion of industry, the premier boasted that "all this has been done in two years without an increase in taxation."[10] The exchange led newspaperman William March to suggest that the colourful Liberal leader was "throwing what ammunition he has extremely well from the purely partisan point of view," but made him wonder if Hicks could "pierce the not inconsiderable armor of the ponderous, careful Conservative leader, one of whose undeniable traits is a prominent ability to look well before leaping."[11]

By this time Stanfield had gained much the same mastery over provincial finance as Angus L. Macdonald had had. For the next year he forecast a surplus of $270,000 on record revenues of $83 million. He feared, however, that the cushion provided by the health tax was not enough to sustain for long the annual growth in the health plan, which he estimated at 10 per cent. Like Macdonald, he told Nova Scotians not to "make a fetish about holding our debt constant." Had not all recent debentures provided for annual sinking fund payments calculated to permit retirement in twenty years? Opposition finance critic R.M. Fielding complained that hospital tax revenues were being used to support general expenditures, a charge which proved to be unfounded.

Michael MacDonald expressed concern over the takeover of important provincial industries by A.V. Roe, later to become Hawker Siddeley. Their acquisitions included Dosco's steelworks, and within a decade MacDonald's fears proved all too warranted. As the session closed, Hicks and G.I. Smith engaged in a spirited exchange on the use and misuse of criticism. The former charged the government with acting as if constructive criticism should be ignored; Smith told him to stop behaving as if his only duty was to criticize. He accused his opponent of trying to kill Industrial Estates Ltd., "one of the first full-scale efforts, adequately financed," to promote industry in Nova Scotia. If it did not succeed, Hicks would be largely responsible for its failure.[12]

Before the 1960 session began, the *Chronicle-Herald* called for an avoidance of partisanship to permit informed discussion of the plight of the colliery communities in Pictou and Cape Breton counties and of the mounting problems of the municipalities, which were having to tap their main source of revenues, i.e., real estate, to an unconscionable extent. The speech from the throne lacked grandiose announcements, but in typically Stanfield style included a plethora of smaller items such as grants of $200 a mile for the maintenance of town and city streets, a rental scheme for high school texts, free insulin for the needy, and payment of the province's share of school construction costs during the actual building to save the municipalities from outlays for interest.

That set the stage for a Hicks-Stanfield confrontation which was routine in these years. The Liberal leader warned that the public had to look elsewhere than the newspapers to understand the actual state of public affairs. Though not critical of the *Chronicle-Herald,* he said that it took a "view, very much like that of the London Times . . . it is the spokesman . . . for the government of the day." That was true during his premiership and it was still true. The second major paper, the *Cape Breton*

Post, was out-and-out Conservative and it had the right to be so. So, unfortunately, no Liberal daily existed to show that Stanfield had been presiding over the liquidation of the coal industry, or that he had failed in his promise to halt the rising cost of education and relieve the burden of municipal taxation, or that he had stopped pressing Diefenbaker for a fair share in national development.[13]

To Stanfield, Hicks was gloom personified. For the premier, the previous year had been one of outstanding progress and "if this movement towards new industry can maintain its momentum the outlook in this province will be transformed in a few years." Between 1956 and 1959 the provincial per capita production showed increases ranging from $971 to $1,140 per annum. In the same period his administration had given $3.5 million to municipalities, beside which the grants of his Liberal predecessors paled in comparison. As for the Diefenbaker government, it had provided Nova Scotia with support on an unprecedented scale. Admittedly something more would have to be done for Pictou County. "A patchy job . . . will not be adequate"; a diversification of industry there was essential. To that end his government would present proposals to the Rand Commission, recently set up by the federal government to report on conditions in the coal-mining areas.[14] Because Nova Scotians would accept Stanfield's, rather than Hicks's, view of the Nova Scotia situation, he would win the next three elections. As if to confirm the Liberal leader's thoughts on the *Chronicle-Herald,* the newspaper found in the premier's report "barometers of social progress," which were all the more reliable as they came from one who was "generally recognized as a cautious individual [and] who does not resort to rose-colored glasses nor takes a chance on being caught out very far on a limb."[15]

When the premier announced a surplus of $3.5 million for 1958-59, $3.26 million more than expected, Hicks condemned the "unreality" and "inaccuracy" of the estimates and both he and Fielding contended that the surplus should have gone to the municipalities, not to debt retirement. In turn, G.I. Smith accused them of "consummate nerve or utter senselessness" and reminded them of their boasts in the 1949 election of a surplus of $9 million: "People's memories may be bad, but not that bad." Stanfield pointed out the difficulties of a provincial treasurer in not being able to gauge precisely how much money he would receive from Ottawa and prophesied rightly that this problem would continue.

The opposition also questioned the payment of $3,750,000 for 12,000 acres of land held by the Oxford Paper Company of Maine — the so-called "Big Lease" — but Stanfield declared that the land was essential to the Nova Scotia Pulp Company's operations and that expropriation would have been more expensive than purchase. IEL also came under criticism for its failure to provide information to the opposition, but the government refused to let anything be divulged that might damage the relations between the Crown corporation and its clients.

When the Liberals appeared to question Stanfield's integrity they suffered another dose of the medicine generally given them. The incident began with a resolution by Hicks deploring the uncertainty caused by statements of the premier that contradicted those of federal cabinet ministers. G.I. Smith, indignant that the opposition leader had not followed the "normal, decent" course of questioning Stanfield in the house, moved in amendment that the premier had always exhibited a "full measure of candour, exactitude and sense of sound responsibility." Stanfield declared first that he did not like to be called a liar and that he prided himself on what "I consider my sense of integrity"; then he read extensively from correspondence to show that he had been consistent and truthful, and suggested to Hicks that "before he made accusations he should carefully check his facts." When Smith demanded Hicks's resignation for bringing in a quibbling, frivolous, vexatious, and irresponsible motion, Hicks denied that he had ever implied that Stanfield was a liar and accused his opponents of overreacting.[16] He was probably right, but was nonetheless unwise to raise the matter in the manner he did.

The session barely over, Stanfield had an election set for June 7th, only three and a half years after the previous one. According to him, the voters should have a chance to decide which party was to negotiate a new fiscal agreement with Ottawa and deal with the Rand Report on coal. Michael MacDonald announced that his party would campaign on "a planned economy to cope with unemployment." Organized much better than in 1956, he hoped to profit from the party's association with the Canadian Labour Congress. However, even though the CCF nominated thirty-four candidates instead of ten, neither old party gave it much attention.

For sheer vigour, Hicks's campaign could hardly have been bettered. He viewed with "righteous wrath" the record of the Diefenbaker and Stanfield years. In 1957 and 1958 the Tories had swept through the province offering everything conceivable, "promises which without exception have not been kept." When he talked of bargaining more fruitfully with Ottawa than the existing government, Stanfield was flabbergasted. Imagine Nova Scotia being run by a band of Diefenbaker haters like Hicks and Fielding.[17] Later the Liberals played into their opponents' hands by their treatment of Diefenbaker, still highly popular in Nova Scotia. During his visit to Acadia University, where his wife was to receive an honorary degree, they published a cartoon that allegedly "made an offensive and weak minded joke" relating to a supposed personal and physical impairment. This, said Stanfield, was not "the kind of political campaigning most people want." To him irresponsibility was unlimited during the "present trying period in the history of the Liberal party."[18]

Hicks's manifesto declared that the government's intention to introduce new manufacturing industries unrelated to the province's natural resources was "a frantic effort to entice industrial enterprise at any cost." The premier defended IEL and expressed satisfaction that it had brought its first industry to Pictou, but neither party made it a crucial part of the campaign. On the coal industry Hicks conceded that he had no magic formula but insisted that the industry must be saved even if it required a tariff, a quota system, or an embargo on American coal. Stanfield hoped to remedy the situation through co-operative action with the federal government and said little more until a Liberal advertisement quoted Mr. Justice Rand as telling him, "Well, Mr. Premier, you have not really been able to make one substantial suggestion for the improvement of the coal industry." When Hicks refused to withdraw the statement, the Conservatives ran a full-page advertisement under the caption "A Simple Matter of Truth" in which they used Rand's precise words: "you [Mr. Premier] have had difficulty in

introducing new industry to Cape Breton and your experience
. . . has not been such as to allow you to make any concrete
suggestions to date."[19] The Liberals had presented Stanfield
with another opportunity to appear as the personification of
truthfulness.

The leading issue was to be the municipal tax burden,
described by Hicks as the province's "most difficult and
important problem." Stanfield, he said, had magnified it by not
letting the foundation programme develop properly and
permitting the provincial government's share of the costs of
education to become outdated. His party heralded a vital
announcement to be made at the Halifax West high school on
May 17th. There he promised to pay every municipality 10 per
cent of its 1960 property taxes for reimbursement of its taxpayers
up to $50 a person, the money to come from the several millions
that Stanfield had put into debt retirement. "There you have an
issue in this campaign. . . . We do not believe that such
surpluses ought to be accumulated when the pressing needs of
Nova Scotians are left unattended.''

Stanfield replied that no money was "lying around in the
public treasury" to implement a degrading, irresponsible, and
unjust proposal. If the treasury was to be looted in this way,
urgently required public projects would have to be cancelled.
"Such a proposition . . . is [a] calculated insult to the people of
this province — a dangerous under-estimation of their own
integrity and public values."[20] Michael MacDonald described
the proposal as an "attempt to bribe the people with their own
money." Reacting strongly to being called a "looter," Hicks
said Stanfield could "throw as many rabbit punches as he likes.
. . . [He] simply does not understand the problems of the
ordinary people because he has never had to face up to such
problems himself."[21] Stanfield refused a public debate with the
Liberal leader on the subject, saying that he had discussed
matters with him for ten years and if Hicks had anything further
to say "let him say it." Obviously he had nothing to gain from
an oratorical contest with his highly articulate opponent.

At the outset many believed that the Liberals had a chance to
unseat the government, but they appeared to lose ground during
the campaign. The *Canadian Annual Review* suggested that

Hicks's quick mind, "brilliant sorties," and "sharp needling" were unsuited to the provincial hustings.[22] His proposed municipal tax rebate — some called it a last desperate gesture — actually contributed to a loss in his party's credibility partly because of the manner in which Stanfield handled it. As in 1960, the strategy of the Liberals and their advertising agency was questionable. They adopted the slogan, "Bridge the gap," without explaining exactly what it meant, and led Stanfield to wonder "what gap it was they were trying to bridge."[23]

Actually no strategy would have brought Hicks victory in 1960. The Conservatives had performed at least creditably without serious mistakes, for which much of the electorate gave credit to the premier. Little was heard of the party title "Conservative," but much was heard of the slogan: "There'll be more progress with Stanfield." In contrast, Hicks's name did not usually appear in the later Liberal advertisements. The Conservatives summed it up in a major advertisement on the eve of the election: "In the eyes of Canada the name Stanfield stands for the public virtues of Nova Scotia's great tradition of public leadership — integrity and sincerity, firmness and candor. Every 'X' marked for the . . . Progressive Conservative candidate . . . is a vote for Stanfield."

Though the Liberal vote fell from 48.2 to 42.6 per cent, the results were by no means one-sided. The Liberals gained three seats, lost six, and held the Conservatives to twenty-seven seats, only a net gain of three for the government. The Conservative popular vote actually fell slightly from 48.6 to 48.3 per cent, mostly because the CCF staged something of a comeback. Though twenty-nine of its thirty-five candidates lost their deposits, the CCF increased its popular vote from 3.0 to 8.9 per cent. After seven failures by women to win seats since 1920, Conservative Gladys Porter was finally successful in Kings North. The two leading Liberals both lost their seats, Hicks by eight votes in Annapolis East and Fielding by twenty-seven in Halifax Northwest. For the able, articulate Hicks this was the end of his active political career. It had been his misfortune to collide with the man who would become by far the most successful Conservative politician in Nova Scotia history. Some of Hicks's problems resulted from his allowing impetuous action to override better judgment, some from his inability to sublimate an unfortunate public image, and some from his political strategists' failure to match their opponents' skills. However, most of Hicks's problems resulted from his having to contend with Stanfield, who had assumed the highly respected image of his family, and in whom Nova Scotians recognized the qualities they wanted in a leader.

At the session's opening in 1961 a highly optimistic *Chronicle-Herald* lauded proposals that bore the "stamp of progressiveness," including one to attract new industries through preferential interest rates. That did not prevent the new Liberal house leader, Earl Urquhart of Richmond, from delivering a forty-six-page address outlining a multitude of sins. With no little pleasure Stanfield reminded Urquhart that he led a party which had attempted to buy the people with their own money, and called on him to re-establish it as "one of principle."[24] Though admitting that Stanfield had gained a lease on life for three doomed mines on Cape Breton Island, Michael MacDonald called for the complete nationalization of the coal industry to avert disaster.

Though the Liberals cut off the debate on the address in reply precipitately (Smith congratulated them for "realizing they have nothing to contribute"), Stanfield was ready with the public accounts and the budget. For 1961-62 he estimated a surplus of $8,133 in the province's first $100 million budget. However, if he had not almost exhausted the hospital reserve account and raised the gasoline tax by two cents, he would have had to forecast a deficit of $5.5 million. He used the occasion to speak anything but kindly of the municipalities. If they were as hard up as they alleged, why were they building so many large auditoria in schools? Judge Pottier had never considered them necessary and the province had never been prepared to share in their cost.[25] Perhaps he should have been delighted that the rural municipalities themselves were insisting upon modern educational facilities.

When Urquhart described the estimates as unreliable and contended that increased taxes were unnecessary, Stanfield showed that the province's share of the hospital plan would rise to $11.2 million in 1961-62, $1.3 million more than revenues. "It is costly and will grow more costly, but construction should continue until all sections of the province are reasonably well served." As for the increase in the gasoline tax from 17 to 19 cents, it simply ensured that the users of highways paid their full cost.

At the end of February the premier announced a new fiscal agreement with Ottawa that would yield about $2 million more annually than he had anticipated. The tax-rental agreements would be replaced by tax-sharing arrangements in which specific portions of the two income taxes and the estate tax — the so-called standard taxes — would be levied by the provinces and would be supplemented by a system of equalization and stabilization grants. Though by no means fully satisfactory to Nova Scotia, the arrangements came closer than before to meeting the province's continuing demand for grants based on fiscal need.

Despite Stanfield's reputation for caution he took action to modernize and liberalize the liquor laws to an extent that Macdonald had not been prepared to go. Following the report of a royal commission the government sponsored a complete overhaul of the Liquor Control Act. To secure the maximum of concurrence, the bill, in typical Stanfield fashion, was actually drafted by a special legislative committee that followed, with a few modifications, the commission's recommendations. Among other things it provided for the licensing of taverns, beverage rooms, and restaurants to sell beer and wine by the glass or bottle, and the licensing of hotel dining rooms and lounges to sell hard liquor as well. So carefully had the way been prepared that only one member opposed the bill on second reading.

The assembly also approved a bill making Dartmouth the province's third city. The strength of the agricultural lobby manifested itself when Dr. C.H. Reardon's bill to allow the use of coloured margarine was defeated by twenty-seven to thirteen before it even went to committee. However, the government's chief problem remained the coal industry. It reluctantly let the Bayview colliery at Joggins be closed and its 150 miners be laid off because the mine had been an extremely high-cost producer. On behalf of three Cape Breton County mines, Michael MacDonald and a forty-five-man labour lobby asked the government to assume ownership, but Stanfield opposed it, not on doctrinaire grounds, but because it was "beyond the financial resources of this province." Instead the house unanimously adopted his proposal to call on the federal government to make coal competitive and, should all practicable efforts to prevent closures fail, to soften their effect through expenditures to promote employment.

In 1962 Urquhart changed his tack and condemned the government for the same reasons that Stanfield and Smith had damned the Macdonald administration: a failure to maintain industries and to develop new ones on a scale sufficient to absorb laid-off workers. He was engaging in pure hyperbole when he described his twelve proposals as "so extraordinary that they will stimulate new life and interest in our province and its citizens." Michael MacDonald even wondered "how far away we are from the hungry thirties." Later, when he attributed many of the ills of society to the contributions that corporations gave to the old parties' slush funds in order to influence governments more readily, he drew Stanfield's ire. "No corporation has enough money to buy the favor of the Conservative Party of Nova Scotia . . . . We have never in my time accepted any donation with any strings attached." In his view corporations had a negligible political influence in Nova Scotia. "The only vote the boss controls today is his own . . . . We do not intend [however] . . . to attack a corporation, or anything else, simply to create a political issue."[26]

During these years the government was often accused of manipulating the accounts to suit its own purposes. In 1960-61 Stanfield could show a surplus only by transferring $1.23 million from the hospital reserve account to the revenue account. The next year, because of larger payments from Ottawa, he was able to return $1.4 million to the same account. His estimates for 1962-63 indicated that, despite steadily increasing federal funds, he would have to use $1.56 million of reserve money. Clearly he was having to cope with constantly rising expenditures on education, social services, and highways, and the larger federal payments resulting from increases in the gross national product (GNP) were by no means certain to occur at the time or in the amount that he needed them. To Stanfield the great challenge was to provide an adequate standard of essential services without allowing excessive taxation to discourage initiative. At the same time he was confronted by an increasing number of organizations whose propaganda and pressure were unremitting to secure the biggest share possible of the available resources. Obviously they could not all win; indeed, if any one of them got its way completely, all other public services would suffer. Hence, he reconciled himself to "a steady flow of resolutions condemning the inadequacy of this program or that."[27]

After a short lapse Stanfield had reassumed the education portfolio. He met repeated complaints that no one could do justice to finance and education at the same time. Although he did not share this view, he announced his intention to give up direct responsibility for the provincial treasury and place it under a single portfolio, finance and economics, which would have a division working with other departments to assist in the expansion of old, and the development of new, industries.

To implement the Shaw royal commission report, the government sponsored a new election act which introduced limited proxy voting, officially recognized political parties, provided a similar system of registration for rural and urban voters, and reduced the minimum time between the issue of election writs and polling from forty-three to thirty-six days. Attorney General Donahoe carried through a measure, long mooted, for the division of the Supreme Court into trial and appellate divisions. By adding two judges it was possible to have three judges on the appeal side headed by the chief justice of Nova Scotia and six on the trial side headed by the chief justice of the trial division; the act was to become effective only on proclamation. Another measure authorized the government to conclude a land-lease deal with Bowater-Mersey, giving that company access to 280,000 acres of forest lands in order to ensure continuity of supply. Once a bill taking away the government's power to regulate the colour of butter substitutes came before the law amendments committee, representatives of the farmers, margarine interests, and housewives "rolled up their sleeves" and gave it a thorough going-over. The outcome was a compromise: coloured margarine could be sold, but outside the normal colour range of butter.

The most dramatic event of the session developed around charges made by Liberal Dr. C.H. Reardon. After the premier had defended a contract giving the province's travel advertising to Dalton Camp and Associates, Reardon declared that the action was perhaps "the biggest piece of political graft in Nova Scotia since the advent of responsible government." Again demonstrating an unwillingness to let the integrity of himself or his government be impugned, Stanfield had the matter referred to the public accounts committee. There Camp appeared with his records relating to the government but not to his accounts with the Conservative party and was grilled by Liberal members for six hours. Eventually the majority of the committee found Reardon's charges to have no validity. In the house the Liberals sought unsuccessfully to censure the Conservative chairman for not admitting relevant evidence, and to censure Stanfield for giving statements to the house that were allegedly contradicted in committee. Instead the assembly censured Reardon for "reckless, unfounded and completely false charges of graft" against the government and citizens outside the house. Apparently Stanfield felt so strongly that he had even considered an act taking away Reardon's immunity and leaving him open to an action for slander.[28] Sixty-six years earlier the constitutionality of the province's law on members' privileges had been confirmed in a case in which Stanfield's grandfather had been imprisoned for allegedly slandering Liberal assemblymen.[29]

The federal election of June 18, 1962 raised Nova Scotian matters in a variety of ways. Generally the Liberals stressed national issues but in Halifax Lester Pearson went into detail on specific remedies for Maritime difficulties. He stressed particularly the need for thermal plants to sustain the coal industry and the need to extend Canada's jurisdiction over its territorial waters to protect its fishery resources. Leading the newly established New Democratic Party (NDP), T.C. Douglas promised grants to enable the Atlantic Provinces to provide adequate services until a development programme put them in a position where they no longer needed help.

For Nova Scotia Conservatives the past and expected assistance of John Diefenbaker became the major focus of the campaign. "If," said Stanfield, "George Nowlan and his colleagues had, in the 1957-58 campaign, promised the assistance [that they had actually provided], no one would have believed them." A full-page advertisement pictured the province's Conservative candidates headed by John Diefenbaker with the comment: "These men have done more for Nova Scotia in five years than preceding governments in twenty-two years." Despite losses, in Nova Scotia the Conservatives did well when compared with the overall results, which resulted in a Diefenbaker minority government. Though their popular vote fell from 57.0 to 47.3 per cent, they took nine of the twelve seats. The NDP won Cape Breton South, and Allan MacEachen and another Liberal the remaining seats.

In November 1962 the Liberals met in convention to choose a successor to Henry Hicks. When told that "politics had not been kind to him," he disagreed: it had given him nine rich, rewarding years and an opportunity for stimulating experiences. In a close contest for the leadership, the Richmond member Earl Urquhart defeated prominent lawyer and Halifax member Gordon Cowan by 314 to 303. To many it was a case of Halifax being pitted against the rest of the province. However, Urquhart's oratorical abilities were the decisive factor in his choice.

Unfortunately for him, Urquhart started his party leadership at a time when Stanfield was moving towards the zenith of his political power and the public would soon be talking of the "new Nova Scotia" being built during his premiership. Admittedly the coal industry was barely surviving through federal subventions. Admittedly, too, neither Conservative government had been able to secure facilities to take steel beyond the billet stage, a failure that would be disastrous in later years. Nonetheless, the usually restrained Stanfield was talking exuberantly in 1963 of three recent "economic miracles": the construction of the pulp mill at Point Tupper, the agreement on a co-operative abattoir, and the establishment of a Volvo automobile plant on the Halifax waterfront. Profuse in his thanks to the federal government and especially to George Nowlan — "God bless him!" — for their help with Volvo, he declared it to be the first instance of an European car manufacturer setting up a Canadian assembly plant outside of southern Ontario. He also exulted that IEL had helped to establish more than thirty plants of varying size and that the province's annual per capita income had risen by $218 between 1956 and 1961, $41 more than the increase in Canada as a whole.

Despite rapidly escalating costs, Finance and Economics Minister G.I. Smith declared the provincial finances to be healthy in 1963. Like Stanfield before him, he would continue to put money in or take it out of the hospital reserve fund as his objective of balanced budgets dictated. Changes in the foundation programme would cost the province $3 million more in the current year and $4 million more in subsequent years. This demonstrated the Stanfield government's pragmatic approach to the municipalities — to give them assistance step by step as the need arose instead of resorting to some broad overarching plan that might soon become outdated. Smith also had to deal with assistance to the universities. Though the province maintained the Nova Scotia Technical College, the Nova Scotia Agricultural College, and the Nova Scotia Teachers College, it had given little aid to the other institutions since 1881. Recently the province had received an unexpected $2.78 million, which it had put into a special reserve fund for the universities to be divided according to the recommendations of a three-man committee headed by former university president N.A.M. Mackenzie. However, that fund, Smith warned, was likely to meet only a single year's needs. He was a little perturbed too that the province was dependent upon Ottawa for 42 per cent of its funds, a doubling of the proportion in six years. Urquhart, worried about the net debt of $174 million, declared the province's immediate future to be "mortgaged to the hilt." Countering, Stanfield demonstrated serious flaws in Urquhart's statistics and argued that the province had an excellent credit rating both in Canada and the United States.[30]

This session the government acted to put into concrete shape the voluntary economic planning (VEP) which it had announced in 1962. Largely the brainchild of G.I. Smith, the Voluntary Planning Act established a central provincial board to co-ordinate economic plans made by various sectors of industry, all on a voluntary basis, the aim being to provide an overall plan for the provincial economy. Other acts set up a crop insurance agency with limited scope, established family courts in place of juvenile courts in designated areas, provided a provincial water control board to deal more effectively with environmental pollution, and strengthened the functions of the committee on human rights set up in 1962. Urquhart sought to have the voting age reduced from twenty-one to eighteen on the ground that young people had become more mature because of better schools and the impact of radio and television. However, the government would not depart from the Shaw report on elections, which had held that a reduction in voting age would cause confusion between federal and provincial elections and that twenty-one years had traditionally been considered synonymous with maturity.[31]

Most controversy in 1963 centred on the Collection Act, which some described as an imprisonment for debt bill. Liberal J.E. Ahern pointed out that 320 men and six women had been jailed under it in the previous year, and he proposed an amendment requiring that a jailed debtor be granted a hearing before a county court judge within two days. Attorney General Donahoe insisted that no one was confined for debt, but only for refusal to honour an order made under the act, and that the debtor's ability to pay was always taken into account prior to the issue of an order. However, the *Chronicle-Herald* considered it neither proper nor fair to invoke a criminal sanction in a civil matter, especially when other remedies were available. In place of the distasteful practice of imprisoning debtors, it wanted to put more of the burden where it belonged, upon those who involved purchasers in contracts beyond their ability to maintain. In heated exchanges in committee, lawyer W.C. Dunlop demanded incarceration only by judges, not by special examiners inclined to side with a seller. Though Donahoe continued to maintain that no one was jailed for debt,[32] the assembly at least reduced the time from fourteen days to two within which, if the provision was applied, a county court judge would review imprisonment under the act.

Typical of Stanfield's insistence upon full information prior to action was his decision to have a committee appointed to study the Lord's Day Act. One witness called the act an "unsavory relic of a bygone day," and the majority who testified wanted it brought into accord with societal changes that had occurred since its passage in 1906. When the committee was authorized to continue hearings after the session's close, the *Chronicle-Herald* was disappointed that a "raft of open and deliberate violations "would be permitted for another year.

Despite a lengthy agenda, the session lasted only twenty-two days, a record of brevity in modern times. Obviously it was shortened by the members' desire to participate in the federal election. Defeated in a vote of non-confidence, Diefenbaker had an election set for April 18th, a date that allowed Nova Scotian MLAs only eighteen days to campaign. This time Pearson promised a new agency to assist disadvantaged areas, but generally he stressed that Atlantic Canada had the most to gain from an overall Liberal programme designed to reduce unemployment and promote trade. Accordingly, his party's advertisements stressed national issues, asking in particular, "Does Canada want government by the Diefenbaker-Caouette axis?"

Once again the Conservatives campaigned on Diefenbaker as the friend of Nova Scotia. When, in mid-February, the province's coal industry secured a contract to supply Ontario with 2.85 million tons of coal, they lauded Ottawa's new subvention policy. Later, as Diefenbaker whistle-stopped through the Maritimes, he promised to implement the recommendations of the Atlantic Development Board — his government's creation — to raise living standards in the area. Once again Stanfield hailed him as "a man who showed no indecision in connection with the problems of Nova Scotia" and as "the first Prime Minister to recognize the principle of fiscal need." Conservatives in Nova Scotia deeply resented the activities of Judy LaMarsh's "Truth Squad," which was publicizing Diefenbaker's supposed deviations from the truth. When, in Halifax, the squad was forced to ask for police protection, its activities ended. Conservative advertisements stressed the "new spirit . . . in the new Nova Scotia. Let Diefenbaker and Stanfield continue it." Nevertheless the Conservatives' strength in Nova Scotia continued to decline, though not to the same extent as in central Canada. They took Cape Breton South from the NDP, but lost three other seats to the Liberals, for a final standing of seven Conservatives and five Liberals. Their popular vote was 46.9 per cent compared to the Liberals' 46.7 and the NDP's 6.4.

The federal defeat did not prevent Stanfield from holding a provincial election on October 8th, only three years and two months after the previous one. Urquhart dismissed as "hogwash" the premier's argument that, because the Pearson minority government might be defeated at any time, it was desirable to avoid a possible conflict with a federal election. The Liberal leader's position on industrial development became the basic issue of the campaign. Despite elements of validity, it was probably the most misguided approach that a political leader could have adopted under the circumstances of the day. At first he warned of the serious danger of giving public money to wealthy companies while neglecting people who really needed help. Stanfield, though a fine person, was stubborn and his heart was with the "big man." Unaware of the realities of the province, he was creating too many captains of industry. In contrast, the Liberal party would follow a policy of industry dispersal which would let all Nova Scotians share in industrial development.

Meeting criticism, he declared that he would not abandon IEL but simply use public funds to assist all areas, especially those with chronic unemployment. A Liberal advertisement pictured two philosophies of government using two funnels, one upside down. Allegedly the Conservatives stood for gradual development from the top down, hoping that in time it would benefit everyone, while the Liberal approach was to put money into the pockets of low and middle income groups, who would spend it and provide a sound basis for self-supporting industry. Urquhart promised $10 million, in amounts up to $25,000, to establish new and expand old industries, the aim being to balance out the millions being put into big, subsidized industry. "It is time," he said, "that the funnel be tilted a little, so that some of these millions" reach the ordinary people of Nova Scotia.[33]

Stanfield dismissed Urquhart's position as "parish pump politics, practiced by those whose only appeal is to narrow sectionalism." If the Liberals won they would get rid of IEL and bring the momentum of the past seven years to a halt. Attorney General Donahoe pointed out that the government could not tell new industries where to go. "I am not a bit ashamed of getting big industry here, because in the final analysis, big industry employs little people and it employs more of them, and for a longer time, than small industries." Throughout the province the premier declared his intention to "do more of this kind of thing so long as the end result is more and better jobs for Nova Scotians." His manifesto promised to increase IEL's borrowing capacity from $18 million to $50 million, since $40 million in prospective undertakings were already being discussed. Conservative advertisements kept repeating, "New industry means new jobs; a Stanfield government means new industry."[34]

Urquhart's manifesto promised to make his party "the most enlightened . . . this province has ever known" and contained a twenty-point programme headed by immediate medicare for the needy, and eventually universal medicare. Stanfield called it "a curious combination of 'me too' meaningless platitudes and costly promises without price tags on them."[35] However, though Stanfield asked to be judged "not by what we give away but by how we administer the hard-earned tax money," he too had promises not without cost: an even larger highway programme; improved educational facilities, including further assistance to the universities; and eventually a medicare programme. The NDP presented a different face than had the CCF. For the time being at least its direction had passed from its labour base in Cape Breton to academics in Halifax. In that county it nominated five candidates and its chairman, Professor J.H. Aitchison, announced its intention to build the party to the point where it could contest all the seats.

It turned out that the real issue was Stanfield himself.[36] By the end of the campaign his opponents talked of his "obvious deification" by his party. When his supporters suggested that he was of prime ministerial calibre, the *Cape Breton Post* expressed something akin to horror: "But we don't want to lose him in Ottawa, we want to keep him in Province House in Halifax." The *Post* contended that it was disastrous for Urquhart to attack the basics that Stanfield stood for and to seem content to leave Nova Scotia as largely a backwater. To be fair to Urquhart, however, a differently conceived campaign would have availed little, for he was confronting a man who had established himself much as Fielding, Murray, and Macdonald had before him.

The NDP could nominate only twenty candidates compared with the CCF's thirty-four in 1956. Its popular vote fell from 8.9 to 4.1 per cent, and Michael MacDonald, winner in five previous elections, lost his seat. Only two of its candidates, both in Cape

Breton County, polled half the winner's total, and its fifteen candidates on the mainland secured only 4,017 votes. For the Liberals the results were almost as bad as in 1925, their only previous disaster. In that year they had taken 36.3 per cent of the vote and won three seats; in 1963 it was 39.7 per cent of the vote and four seats by majorities of just 311, 193, 44 and 11. Urquhart himself was beaten, no former Liberal executive councillor was elected, and the Liberals were left with only one highly articulate assemblyman. However, he, Peter Nicholson, would be a mainstay of the party for the next fifteen years. Perhaps indicating the reaction of business interests, Halifax County finally gave all its seven seats to the Conservatives. By taking thirty-nine of the forty-three seats and 56.2 per cent of the popular vote, the party came close to matching its landslide victory of 1925.

Urquhart remained unbowed at his party's annual meeting in November, blaming the electoral disaster largely on the press. "Certain daily newspapers were not sympathetic" and, along with weekly and monthly periodicals, "promoted the cause of Toryism." Unless "certain events" brought about a change in plans, "you have not seen the last o' my bonnet and me." For the party generally, unused to defeat on this scale, the situation was traumatic. In a rowdy session delegates attacked the party's constitution, called for a trusteeship to be placed over the provincial party, and asked to have public relations experts hired to organize the party anew and sell it to Nova Scotians. The nomination of Eric Balcom as president for two years was challenged from the floor, something almost unprecedented in the party's history. Cape Bretoner Allan Sullivan was indignant that the delegates were not saying what they really thought. "You are too worried of what the press might report. We should not put up with the same list of the executive year after year." Another Cape Bretoner proposed a two-man committee of Gordon Isnor and ex-judge Kenneth Crowell to direct party reorganization at the grass roots level, but Senator Isnor hesitated to accept further responsibilities.[37] An inconclusive meeting, in effect, left the basic party decisions to be made behind the scenes. In a sense it seemed to confirm Stanfield's joking statement that "Liberals are always bewildered when they find themselves out of office."

Certainly Stanfield had thrived on office.[38] Conservative Ralph Shaw had said earlier that he had the making of another "Abe" Lincoln. "He is going to be hard to elect but if we get him elected they'll never get him out." The better he became known the more his stature grew. His agriculture minister, E.D. Haliburton, pointed out accurately the wide measure of party discipline both in cabinet and caucus in the Stanfield years. At the beginning it was "a sort of parental control. . . . He could transfix us with a level look that made one feel like a naughty boy." In time it came to be complete confidence and loyalty in a man who was establishing the dominance of a once minority party. Haliburton emphasizes that Stanfield was "a catalyst and persuader," not "a Dictator type" who sought to "bulldoze his Executive Council." If he found disagreement in cabinet, he dropped a matter altogether, although he might raise it months later. "I cannot recall that he ever asked the Council to approve any course of action if a single member was dead set against it."

The 1964 session was, in most respects, typical of the Stanfield years. What was different was the existence of a virtual one-man opposition, for though the Liberals numbered four, only Peter Nicholson had the ability to challenge the government on a wide range of issues. Twice in this century the same situation had existed, but Nicholson's position was even more difficult than that of Charles Tanner in the first decade or that of William Chisholm between 1926 and 1928 because, instead of having to deal with a government entrusted with a few million dollars annually he had to confront one spending over $100 million. No one human can keep an effective watch over all the modern governments's wide-encompassing range of functions.

The *Chronicle-Herald* gave gentle support to the speech from the throne: "nothing radical or particularly startling but . . . a better one than might have been expected from a solidly-entrenched government fresh from securing an overwhelming mandate." As to be expected, Nicholson demanded programmes to ease municipal financial burdens and to reduce unemployment. He was especially harsh on government patronage: the "trough is only so large, and the spectacle of the hangers-on and political henchmen of 90% of the members of this House trying to get into it all at once, beggars description."[39] Like Urquhart, Nicholson also wanted to have industry dispersed to areas of chronic high unemployment. The next day Stanfield announced a contract between Deuterium of Canada, 51 per cent owned by IEL, and Atomic Energy of Canada for the building of a $30 million plant at Glace Bay to produce heavy water for Atomic Energy of Canada. It would be a fateful decision for the government and the province.

Different for Stanfield in 1964 was the existence of a Liberal government at Ottawa, which he could now criticize freely. Condemning it for not giving incentives to bring industry to areas of high unemployment, he demanded "more positive inducement, far less timidity." The *Chronicle-Herald* joined him in asking, "Is it impossible . . . for a federal government to encourage openly industry in the Atlantic Provinces?"[40] It feared that the tax incentives announced by Finance Minister Walter Gordon in June 1963 to attract industries to disadvantaged regions might cause them to locate in high unemployment areas in central Canada instead of Nova Scotia.

G.I. Smith also found fault with Ottawa even though fiscal 1962-63 was "one of the most satisfactory the province has experienced" — a small surplus after transferring $5 million to the hospital reserve fund and $2.7 million to current account to pay for normally capital expenditures. His main objection was the fiscal agreement negotiated with the new federal Finance Minister Mitchell Sharp which based equalization on revenues in the two provinces in which the per capita returns from the standard taxes were highest. In his view the result was to divert money from the weaker provinces to others in which the returns from the standard taxes were already above the national average. He also complained that a system of equalization that took into account only the returns from the three standard taxes and natural resources fell far short of full equalization. He was pleased to get an additional $5.74 million, but he regretted that "the principle of fiscal need has [not] yet been properly recognized in federal-provincial financial arrangements."[41]

On its own, without apparent pressure, the government proposed a change in government purchasing in which patronage had long been rampant. The existing purchasing committee was to be replaced by a director of purchasing appointed by the governor in council and subject to scrutiny by the auditor general to whom the director would report all expenditures over $100. The actual purchasing would be done by an agency controlled by the director, who alone could make exceptions. In other matters the cabinet continued to use what Haliburton calls the "total immersion treatment," i.e., using every means at its disposal to collect all the available factual knowledge before making its decisions.[42] The committee on university education headed by N.A.M. Mackenzie submitted a 55-point programme that recommended an additional $1.5 million in grants for the current year and forecast higher expenditures by both the government and the universities if genuine needs were to be met. The *Chronicle-Herald* commended the report except for its recommendation that "all graduate work at the Ph.D. level" should be confined to Dalhousie.[43] Stanfield himself was pleased that on the one-hundredth anniversary of free public schools he could assist universities substantially, and he criticized Nicholson, who opposed university subsidization largely because of the large number of out-of-province students. Agreeing with President Henry Hicks of Dalhousie, the premier contended that well-equipped universities were needed to serve the increasing throng of high school graduates and that a good school of graduate studies would be highly useful, especially in industrial development.

Burgeoning suburban development led the government to appoint W.D. Outhit, Chairman of the Public Utilities Board, to make recommendations on municipal boundaries and with one major exception it followed his proposals. Instead of creating a new permanent and independent board, it let the Public Utilities Board (acting as a municipal board) determine a wide range of municipal questions, including boundaries, representation, size of councils, annexation, and amalgamation. Its conclusions could be reconsidered by the governor in council, whose decision would be final. A province-wide redistribution of municipal seats would be required by the end of 1965 and regularly every six years thereafter always along lines approved by the board. The *Chronicle-Herald* declared that the act "required a measure of political courage on the government's part" because it meant some diminution in local autonomy.[44] One of the board's first and biggest tasks was to deal with the contentious issue of annexation by the city of

Halifax of Rockingham, Fairview, Armdale, Spryfield, and the Halifax watershed area.

In three instances the government used committees of the legislature as fact-finding agencies. One headed by James Harding, which explored the possibility of appointing an ombudsman, found the witnesses unenthusiastic, and unanimously rejected the idea. Basically the committee concluded that more safeguards existed against arbitrary action than were generally realized and that an ombudsman might reduce the effectiveness of the ordinary assemblyman by causing him to lose contact with his constituents. The committee on the Lord's Day Act headed by G.H. (Paddy) Fitzgerald, reconstituted after the election, finally presented a report which, at one stage, caused the *Chronicle-Herald* to have fears of prosecutions for acts that presently went unchallenged. In the end, however, Fitzgerald called the perfected measure "a forward, progressive step to ensure that the law is not universally disobeyed" and the *Chronicle-Herald* declared the law "much improved" and "freer of Sunday restrictions" than was true of any other province. The act allowed the opening of movie theatres and the charging of fees for sporting events after 2 p.m. on Sunday. Subject to local option, licences could be issued to small corner stores, novelty stores, fruit stands, and the like for opening on Sundays.

Public pressure led the government to deal with the fact that both Halifax North and Northwest had no fewer than 60,000 voters. The result was a representation committee headed by G.I. Smith with authority to meet after prorogation. Smith's elaboration of the difficulties indicated that he considered his mandate broad enough to propose a modern system of representation. To what extent, he asked, would it be possible to reconcile the conflict of the two principles that each county should have a member and that representation should be strictly based on population? Could the remaining dual ridings — Colchester, Yarmouth, and Inverness — be made into single seats even though the parties had customarily nominated a Protestant and a Catholic in the last two counties?

Late October brought reports of the projected establishment of new industries accompanied by charges that both the federal and provincial governments were making premature disclosures to promote their political objectives.[45] The rumours were right, for November and December brought definite announcements: the move of Clairtone Sound Corporation from Rexdale, Ontario to Stellarton, the result of a federal incentive grant and an IEL guarantee of $8 million; a railway car order of $9 million for Trenton Industries, a subsidiary of Dosco; and the construction by Scott Paper of a $50 million pulp mill at Abercrombie, near New Glasgow. All three projects were in Pictou County, once dependent upon a coal industry now virtually extinct.

Politically the Liberal party took its first steps in 1964 to rejuvenate itself. Urquhart — shortly to become a senator — announced his resignation in November just before the party was to have its annual meeting. A young "ginger group" headed by R. MacLeod Rogers, son of Norman McLeod Rogers (although they spelled their names differently), secured control of the organization and started the work of rebuilding.

Though the government boasted of continuing economic growth in 1965 — an increase of 49 per cent in manufacturing since 1960 — it met opposition on other grounds. When, in the Stanfield mode, the speech from the throne was a mixture of small programmes, Aitchison dismissed it as "a patchwork of platitudes." Nicholson criticized the addition of five members to the cabinet, making it the largest in provincial history, but his major argument was that the rural citizenry was suffering from the development of pockets of industrial expansion. Stanfield insisted, however, that establishing the two pulp mills would do more to combat rural poverty than anything the previous government had done in twenty-three years. Calling on the province to prepare for a breakthrough, he urged the planning of "a Nova Scotia for the 1970s which will be in the forefront of Canada."[46]

Smith continued to create small surpluses by transferring funds into and out of the hospital reserve as the circumstances required, but he warned that the government might have to increase taxes in 1966-67. When Nicholson replied that the treasury was overflowing, he was told that university assistance, only $1.09 million in 1961, had gone up to $4.5 million and would require much more in the future. On its own initiative the government took action to increase grants to children's aid societies, made large loans to universities for construction purposes, assumed the operating costs of municipal hospitals that met approved standards, and took action to prevent further tax evasion in the use of "marked gas" supposedly intended for farmers and fishermen. Two government activities raised doubts. When Nicholson wondered about the value of voluntary economic planning, Stanfield called it "a great experiment" that was "breaking new ground" and might "encourage our people to think not only in terms of growth but in terms of taking measures themselves to encourage that growth."[47] When foresters, woodlot owners, and lumber operators called the conservation bill of Lands and Forests Minister Haliburton "dictatorial and coercive," he shrugged off the criticism. "They are the most difficult people in the world to get together."[48] Also receiving unfavourable comment was Attorney General Donahoe's announcement that no change would be made in the Collection Act which permitted debtors to be imprisoned under specific conditions. Once again the *Chronicle-Herald* called it "a Dickensian anachronism that can scarcely be boasted about when the government talks about the 'new Nova Scotia' it is building."[49]

Despite broader intentions the redistribution committee contented itself with recommending three new seats for Halifax County. That meant that Halifax's ten seats would have an average population of about 25,000, compared with 16,000 elsewhere, a balance between urban and rural populations which G.I. Smith found reasonable. The *Chronicle-Herald* called the report "good as far as it went," but it also wanted a statutory redistribution every ten years using the federal system of tolerance.[50] To determine the boundaries of Halifax County's ten seats, the government approved a new procedure by leaving it to a Provincial Electoral Commission composed of private individuals.

Following his usual course, Stanfield appointed a committee to study the indemnities of assemblymen and the salaries of cabinet ministers. As a result, the members' indemnities were increased from $3,200 to $4,000, their expense allowances from $1,600 to $2,000, and annual expense allowances were provided for cabinet ministers and the leader of the opposition. Acceding to an earlier request of Premier Robichaud of New Brunswick, the premier also secured unanimous approval for an independent study of Maritime union.

The Union of Nova Scotia Municipalities having requested alternative sources of revenue to obviate the municipalities' almost complete dependence on the property tax, the government had appointed Touche, Ross, Bailey and Smart to consider the request, even though Nicholson complained that it was relying too much on commissions, boards of inquiry, and consultants for financial advice. The recommendations were to reduce the municipal burden by increasing the education grants and by having the province take over completely the care of the mentally ill, the administration of justice, the specialized education of the deaf and dumb, and the registry offices. Later the Union of Nova Scotia Municipalities sharply condemned the government for not implementing the report. Stanfield, like Macdonald before him, was skeptical of the plight of the municipalities as they presented it. As usual he provided some minor assistance, such as assuming the cost of prisoners incarcerated six months or more, and providing additional aid to depressed towns, but his government showed no intention of probing deeply into municipal finance.

Late in July 1965 the Liberals met in convention to choose a successor to Earl Urquhart. Perhaps because the delegates "wilted in the humid sticky atmosphere" or because the heyday of the Stanfield years offered little encouragement to the provincial Liberals, it was a somewhat lacklustre affair. Two academics, including myself, occupied an entire side of the Halifax Forum for much of the afternoon. In a meeting of only two and a half hours, Gerald Regan, MP for Halifax, triumphed over Robert Matheson, a senior Halifax lawyer, by 379 to 201. Regan received large blocs of votes in rural areas, while much of Matheson's support came from Halifax. The winner promised to retire soon from federal politics but would not contest any by-election, preferring to "brush up" on the Stanfield government from the sidelines.[51] Attesting to his promise of vigorous leadership, he was soon taking issue with the government on a wide variety of matters.

Several times during 1965 the government disagreed strongly with Ottawa. In what would be a long drawn-out conflict on the ownership of offshore mineral rights, Stanfield contended that they had been the undoubted possession of Nova Scotia since before Confederation and still remained so, but Prime Minister Pearson decided to let the courts decide the question. A second dispute arose over the federal government's decision to authorize Atomic Energy of Canada to negotiate with Canadian General Electric to supply 400 tons of heavy water a year for ten years instead of discussing a possible contract with Nova Scotia's Deuterium of Canada. Some said that it persisted even more strongly in that course after the Liberals had fared badly in Nova Scotia during the federal election of November 8th.

Pearson had called that election to secure an overall majority, and this time he sought to make a special appeal to Nova Scotia. Early in the campaign he promised to restore the coal industry to an efficient state, and shortly afterwards Labour Minister MacEachen announced an expenditure of $25 million for a new mine at Lingan and the modernization of other mines. Pearson also agreed to discuss the offshore question with Nova Scotia as soon as the courts had made their decision and to replenish the Atlantic Development Board fund when its initial $100 million was used up.

Yet Diefenbaker remained the hero in Nova Scotia. He drew Stanfield's plaudits for promising to have the offshore question settled not by the courts but by a federal-provincial conference in accord with the spirit of Confederation. Late in the campaign Diefenbaker and Stanfield formed a mutual admiration society in western Nova Scotia, the former prime minister re-echoing the sentiment that "the Atlantic Provinces have always been close to my heart," the premier contending that, in building up a new era for Nova Scotia, "the factor that more than anything else encouraged us, lifted our hearts and spirits, was the Diefenbaker government" and its special assistance.[52] To him Diefenbaker's Atlantic adjustment grants were far superior to any aid provided by the Atlantic Development Board as administered by Pearson.

The Conservatives could hardly have fared better at the hands of Nova Scotians. In the civilian vote they led in every seat but Allan MacEachen's Inverness-Richmond, although Antigonish-Guysborough eventually went to Liberal John Stewart by forty-seven votes after he received a majority of seventy-six in the military vote. The Liberal popular vote fell from 46.7 to 42.0 per cent, the largest drop in all of Canada. For the *Chronicle-Herald* it was a Stanfield victory. "In the 1963 provincial election, he established himself as the political master of the province. The master's touch . . . remains."[53] The Conservative gain of three seats in Nova Scotia had foiled by two seats the Liberal hopes of gaining an overall majority. Keith Davey put it this way: "We got creamed by the Stanfield machine. . . . I think Mr. Stanfield was making his bid for the Conservative national leadership and he was successful at that."

After seeing Stanfield in action, I wrote, "He is still awkward in his delivery, and he makes no attempt to appeal to the emotions. Yet his audiences listen in rapt attention even though they forbear to cheer. In him they recognize the man of sincerity, the man of reasonableness and good sense."[54] In reply Stanfield indicated that he had intended to speak only at his party's nominating conventions in Halifax and Colchester-Hants, but having discovered that MacEachen and Regan were anticipating substantial Liberal gains in Nova Scotia and hoping to involve the Nova Scotia government in the defeat, he and his cabinet had "a very direct interest in campaigning, in the interests of self-preservation."[55] He played down, however, his part in the outcome and attributed it more to the backlash against Quebec and to the Pearson government's unpopularity in Nova Scotia. As usual, he was being unduly modest.

Both Nicholson and Aitchison regarded the speech from the throne in 1966 as a "singularly lack-lustre document." Referring to Stanfield's recent statement that "it's not as much fun as it used to be beating the Grits," and to a recent Chambers cartoon showing the premier throwing a ball over his shoulders while bowling and saying, "I'm bored," Nicholson promised to do what he could to "pep up [Stanfield's] appetite during the next seven or eight weeks."[56] When Nicholson called for a full-time minister of education, Stanfield replied that he would "really like to keep hold" of that portfolio. In his turn the premier denounced Ottawa's refusal of tax incentives or rebates to companies for settling-in costs in metropolitan areas. That policy had simply slowed down development in Halifax-Dartmouth, Nova Scotia's most promising growth area. As he saw it, "we must accept some centralization of industry . . . until we develop some centres which generate industrial growth."[57]

By far the most dramatic action in 1966 occurred on a private bill altering the control over Acadia University hitherto held by the United Baptist Convention of the Atlantic Provinces. In the end great credit was given to D.C. MacNeil, the chairman of the private and local bills committee, for securing a *modus vivendi*, which enlarged the Board of Governors and made it more representative, especially by allowing the alumni to appoint as many members as the convention. Although others were satisfied, many members of the convention were strongly opposed to having their historic rights interfered with by legislation.

Once again the prevailing Canadian prosperity and hence larger payments from Ottawa came to the rescue of a Nova Scotia government just as G.I. Smith was contemplating higher taxes. He expected a small surplus in 1965-66 even after using $7.5 million to pay capital items out of current account and adding to the hospital reserve; he forecast another for 1966-67 even though university grants would go from $4.5 million to $6.0 million. Nicholson again criticized Smith for juggling the hospital reserve account, not providing realistic reserves for IEL borrowing, and failing to aid the municipalities when the treasury was overflowing. However, Smith, denying any surplus of funds, declared that Nova Scotia was still unable to provide the same quality of services as other provinces. He was therefore heartened by Mitchell Sharp's budget which, though not ideal, promised that the calculation of equalization would in future "take into account a wider concept of fiscal capacity based on a comprehensive range of provincial revenues." Smith attributed Nicholson's inaccuracies to his having "fallen upon a new and baneful influence," that of Gerald Regan in the galleries of the assembly.[58]

The slightness of the government programme indicated that 1966 would not be an election year, something that Stanfield confirmed in June. Generally well received was a new assessment act which divided the province into sixteen units and sought to equalize and regularize assessment across the province. However, its inclusion of an occupancy tax based on

20 per cent of the assessed value of occupied property caused such a storm of municipal protest that the legislature met in December to make the tax optional. The government kept its promise to share more fully in the costs of education, public health, the administration of justice, and municipal social assistance, while insisting as usual on some degree of local administration and financial participation. When the Liberals demanded larger and more immediate assistance, Municipal Affairs Minister McKeough recited a long list of shared programmes in which the province had increased substantially its share of the cost and declared that his immediate concern was with the four towns that had lost revenue sources through no fault of their own.

Health Minister Donahoe had been having discussions with Ottawa on universal medicare, but because the federal officials calculated the cost at $25 per capita in contrast with Nova Scotia's estimate of $35, no agreement had yet been reached. The government tabled the first plan of the Voluntary Economic Planning Board, in the development of which 2,000 people had participated. Aitchison called it a "shoddy document, showing every evidence of hasty preparation and improper execution," but after Stanfield commented glowingly on the work, the house unanimously approved its goals and philosophy.

Worries about the coal and steel industries continued in 1966. Trade and Industry Minister Manson feared that the Sydney steel plant would die within twenty years if something like a sheet and strip metal mill were not added. He was especially critical of Dosco and its parent company, Hawker Siddeley, for keeping the Sydney plant in a vacuum while plants elsewhere were undergoing expansion. Before the assembly's industry committee the president of Dosco testified that he had no long-term plans for the plant, nor plans to introduce basic steel-producing facilities elsewhere in Canada. Conservative Percy Gaum reminded him that a wire-drawing machine installed at Sydney in 1953 was being transferred to Dosco's rod and bar mill in Quebec, while the one set up in 1937 was being left behind. Meanwhile conditions in the coal industry were reaching crisis proportions. In October the Donald Report recommended that a federal Crown corporation take over the mines and phase them out in fifteen years, during which an area development programme would seek a smooth transition. Late in December Pearson and Stanfield announced a rehabilitation plan for the Cape Breton area based largely on the Donald proposals.

Though its older, basic industries were in decline, the "new Nova Scotia" was enjoying accelerated development: a flour mill in Halifax, a Japanese car assembly plant at Point Edward, a textile plant in Yarmouth, the Anil hardboard plant at East River, a caustic soda plant in the Canso Strait area, and the renewal of seventeen acres of downtown Halifax. The province was also becoming more involved in high technology. By late June Canadian General Electric had decided to build a plant in the Strait of Canso area to produce 5,000 tons of heavy water over the next dozen years. To placate Deuterium of Canada, it was authorized to produce a similar amount. To provide the financing, the government of Nova Scotia purchased the 49 per cent of Deuterium held privately; in September came an announcement that its production would be doubled.

Stanfield himself was largely responsible for keeping one old industry in Nova Scotian hands when he had the legislature convened to prevent Bell Telephone from gaining control of Maritime Telephone and Telegraph (MT&T). Bell maintained that it wanted to prevent American interests from taking it over, but even after Stanfield promised not to let that happen, it had acquired 51 per cent of Maritime's shares. The common belief was that Bell hoped to ensure for its subsidiary, Northern Electric, a monopoly of the cable and wire used by the Nova Scotia company. At Stanfield's prompting, the legislature thwarted Bell by preventing any MT&T shareholder from voting more than 1,000 shares. The Liberals supported the bill, but the NDP favoured expropriation and public ownership. The "widows' stock" would remain under Nova Scotia control.

Late in the year, Stanfield, not to his liking, became involved in the Diefenbaker-Dalton Camp feud when the provincial party association elected as its president a pro-Diefenbaker man over his own choice. Still later, however, at the national association meeting Stanfield was talked of as a future national leader.

Throughout 1966 Regan's barrage of criticism continued. To him little of the year's legislation would meet the province's difficulties and a government which had started out with promise had become old and tired. The speech from the throne in 1967 clearly foretold an election: minimum wages of $1.25 per hour; an arbitration procedure to settle disagreements between the government and its civil servants; an "equitable distribution" of the funds returned by Ottawa from the tax levied on private utilities; and, above all, millions for municipal governments. Per capita grants for the rural municipalities would rise from 26 cents to $1.25, and a municipal services plan would provide assistance for fire and police protection, street lighting, garbage collection, street paving, and sewer and water services. Aitchison declared that many of the things were "long overdue," others quite inadequate. Regan could see merely "patchwork" and "little to indicate long-term planning or permanent solutions." Nicholson perceived a failure to diagnose correctly the problems of municipal governments unless "they are very inept . . . at prescribing the right medicine."[59]

Dismissing these criticisms, Stanfield argued that the proposals would raise markedly the level of basic municipal services. In education alone an additional $7.3 million would be provided to help all municipalities, rich and poor. However, he cautioned that other services were equally important in introducing "intelligent humanity . . . in our politics. . . . It is not our desire to make the dollar almighty in Nova Scotia. We wish to see Nova Scotians living full and well-rounded lives, and not be cramped into any rat race. Nova Scotians wish to make decent livings and we wish to help them . . . into a better future, and not lead them into a blind alley."[60] Both the president of the Union of Nova Scotia Municipalities and the *Chronicle-Herald* generally approved of the grants, but Regan called them "a classic example of election year deceit," which Nova Scotia should have outgrown in the twentieth century.[61]

Small surpluses continued the order of the day as G.I. Smith again used the hospital reserve fund to meet his ends. For 1967-68 he expected both expenditures and revenues to be over $200 million for the first time, the increase in the former being largely used for developmental purposes by IEL, Deuterium, the Fishermen's Loan Board, and the Industrial Loan Board. For the first time the hospital tax was likely to fall short of meeting hospital construction grants, and he expected it to be the last year before a tax increase. Aitchison called the budget "so uninspiring and commonplace that it is hard to believe it is an election budget." Nicholson again accused Smith of playing a game of musical chairs to bring revenues and expenditures into balance. "If he had too much money, he put it in a reserve; if not enough, he takes it out." He also charged Smith with holding a sword over the taxpayer with his comments on the difficulty of holding the tax line any longer. So it was last year, so it would be the next.

The government was not without its difficulties. Criticism of the Workmen's Compensation Board had become so widespread that its chairman W.T. Hayden resigned. Clairtone, it appeared, was a problem in the making. Its president, Peter Munk, indicated that he was satisfied with its performance, but Conservative Dr. McKeough warned that defective products were being returned from all over North America by retail dealers and that the company might soon be in a precarious position. For that statement Regan accused him of inexcusable irresponsibility and of delivering a "potentially crippling blow" to a $10.5 million investment. However, Stanfield had lost none of his enthusiasm for IEL which, he said, had created 2,000 new jobs directly and many more indirectly. He gave much of the credit to the businessmen on the board, especially Frank Sobey: "We cannot buy or hire his type of talent." At the same time G.I. Smith expressed pleasure that the VEP Board had exceeded its goals.

Because everyone was expecting an election, Stanfield found that he had little choice but to announce one earlier than he had intended. As he put it: "Once you get that kind of atmosphere it becomes increasingly difficult for a government to transact business in a normal way."[62] Though he had repeated almost *ad nauseam* that he had no interest in federal politics, this was not enough for the NDP's Aitchison. Since the premier might still be drafted, "nothing less than the equivalent of General Sherman's famous statement that he would not accept if nominated, and would not serve if elected," would satisfy him.

Each party turned to non-Nova Scotians for assistance. The Liberals brought in J.E. (Ned) Belliveau, who had managed successful contests in New Brunswick and Prince Edward Island; assisting the NDP was Cliff Ashfield, formerly of

Saskatchewan; and for the Conservatives Dalton Camp would spend at least half his time in Nova Scotia. The NDP put on a hard-hitting campaign. Aitchison, since 1966 the party leader, called it "ridiculous to charge the cost of education against property"; described the cabinet ministers as incompetent, lacking in energy and vying with each other to make the most stupid statements; and demanded the takeover of Nova Scotian components of Hawker Siddeley, which had closed one mine after another and permitted the steel plant and the Halifax Shipyards to decline to a sorry state. Because the Liberals were completely inept in opposition, he called on Cape Bretoners to elect the full NDP slate. "We are scrappers to a man," and "industrial Cape Breton needs scrappers, not clowns or dummies." T.C. Douglas lambasted the Stanfield government for not taking action to save the coal industry, while David Lewis declared that Cape Breton still suffered from problems which he had seen since as early as 1938.

Regan, never lacking in energy, conducted a wide-ranging offensive. Among other things his twenty-point manifesto promised an increase in old age pensions based on need, the building of an all-weather highway through the Annapolis Valley, long-term housing loans, appropriate action to save the steel industry, and assistance to the McBean coal mine, the last one left in Pictou County. Most of all, he stressed the municipal burden. Though federal equalization had increased by $32 million since 1950, the province had let municipal debt grow from $51 million to $103 million and many municipalities were on the verge of bankruptcy. He would relieve much of their burden by assuming the full cost of education without resort to deficit financing; unlike the Conservatives he would not "let the hoary old wives' tales of finance over-ride the needs of the people."[63] Both Regan and his followers were highly critical of the government's financial record as it related to IEL. Eileen Stubbs of Dartmouth declared that some of the worst monsters had been created under its auspices, partly because it forgot that the only real safeguard was the "blazing limelight" of public opinion. "Mr. Stanfield has tried to cover the province with a cloak of prosperity, but his underwear is beginning to show."

The Stanfield manifesto promised to expand the programme of social and economic development with special emphasis on voluntary economic planning; to pay a larger share of educational costs, especially where capital projects and debt-servicing charges were involved; to improve the municipal services programme; to introduce a housing incentive programme; and to appoint a director to co-ordinate all the government's youth programmes. The premier also held out hopes of developing Bay of Fundy tides. Even the $400 million worth of projects planned or under way were "modest compared to Fundy power . . . if this comes off, the consequences will be beyond calculation." He denied that he had done anything to delay the establishment of the Cape Breton Development Corporation (DEVCO), which was simply awaiting federal legislation, and he described as groundless the rumours that hundreds of workers were to be laid off at the Sydney steel plant.

Most Conservatives boasted of a "new spirit" in the province, but some stressed even more Regan's alleged financial irresponsibility. He must, said Stanfield, have a poor opinion of the intelligence of Nova Scotian voters and "a high opinion of their ability to pay through the nose." The premier also accused him of "a recklessness with the facts sufficient to defy any credibility." One example was his statement that Ontario's last surplus was in 1948; in point of fact it had had surpluses since 1941.[64] G.I. Smith called Regan's manifesto "the best bit of fiction-fantasy since Alice in Wonderland." To him, the "delectable document simply bubbles over with good things for everybody from the cradle to the grave, and never spoils the fun by asking where the money will come from. . . . It even takes away the sting of the old saying that nothing is certain but death and taxes, for this document is built on the central theme that taxes are not certain, but are going to be done away with."[65] In like vein, Tando MacIsaac said that if "a soapmaker advertises he has a new miracle flake to make white whiter than white, I suppose we can't stop a political leader from saying he is a new miracle man who can govern without taxation."[66] The *Dartmouth Free Press* agreed that Regan had "put [his] diagnostic fingers on a sensitive sore spot, namely too heavy taxation on real estate," but wondered if his "proposed cure [might] be worse than the disease."[67]

As Allan Dunlop points out, the Liberals were placed in a very difficult situation. "Stanfield was far too popular to attack and comparing Gerald Regan to the Premier only evoked smiles from most Nova Scotians."[68] Similarly the success of IEL at this stage made it virtually invulnerable to attack. The Conservatives abandoned their manifesto almost the day they released it and instead seized upon the weak chinks in the opposition platform. Once again they made Stanfield the chief issue. Liberals across the province echoed the same lament: "They always mentioned Stanfield. It was always the Stanfield government and very seldom did they mention Conservative or the Conservative candidate. . . . They always had Mr. Stanfield there as their standard bearer and it worked."[69]

The NDP fared almost as badly as in 1963. It polled only 5.2 per cent of the vote, elected no one, and had only one candidate who did at all well — its leader in Cape Breton East. The Liberals did marginally better. They increased their popular vote by 2.1 per cent and elected two more members in a house enlarged by three. Regan won in Halifax Needham, but by a mere 102 votes. As a reward for the vigour of his campaign, it must have been a sorry disappointment. For the Conservatives it was 52.8 per cent of the votes and forty of the forty-six seats.

More and more it had become clear that Nova Scotia was no longer the Liberal province of old. For four consecutive elections its people had voted Conservative, the last two times decisively. Stanfield and Diefenbaker had chanced to appear on the scene at a time when other factors were loosening the attachment to hereditary partisan loyalties. No means exist to measure the change quantitatively, but certainly more people than before were calling themselves Conservatives and many more were not bound by the fierce party attachments of old.

Yet, at the peak of their fortunes, the Conservative suffered the worst possible loss. Robert Stanfield, who as late as June 8th had declared that he would not contest his party's national leadership, announced his candidature on July 19th. Not unexpectedly, the province's opposition leaders, especially the NDP's Aitchison, accused him of breaking faith with the electorate, the more so because the provincial Conservatives had campaigned largely on his name. To Stanfield himself it was simply a case of being persuaded to do his duty to his party and his country. When elected national leader on September 9th, he faced the problem of creating the same image in the vast expanse of Canada that he had in little Nova Scotia. At the time barely a glimmer existed of the difficult legacy that he was leaving to his successor.

In the early stages Stanfield had not found the political struggle easy. Yet, strengthened by his membership in one of the best known and most highly respected Nova Scotian families, he had made considerable headway against Angus L. Macdonald in two general elections. A complex combination of factors had led to his comfortable, although not highly decisive, victory in 1956, the first victory for his party since Confederation at a time when the province was not beset by serious economic difficulties. He had done only marginally better in 1960 when he was still in the process of establishing himself, but by the election of 1963 he had made himself political master of the province much as Fielding, Murray, and Macdonald before him. The hesitant, awkward oratory of the early years had matured into a definite asset. He could not rouse audiences to rapturous applause, but in a higher form of democratic politics he had gotten them to listen and reflect. His successful promotion of industrial enterprise led to his being recognized as the prime mover in building the "new Nova Scotia." Determined to maintain the reputation for integrity which he and his government had built up, he had resisted with vigour all challenges on that score, almost always to the detriment of the accuser.

Considerate and self-effacing, he once embarrassed me, after I had interviewed him on television, by offering to drive me to the bus station. On another occasion, while I sat in a darkened room where a nominating convention was being held in south-end Halifax, he arrived unaccompanied from a convention in the north end and sat in the back, his presence known to only a few. Not until the platform speaker declared that he would continue only until the premier appeared did someone make known his arrival.

Despite partisan rhetoric, nothing illustrates better the lack of meaningful philosophical differences between Nova Scotia's Liberal and Conservative parties than the political attitudes of Angus L. Macdonald and Robert Stanfield. For though the "red Toryism" of Stanfield only became fully evident later on broader federal issues, it was manifested occasionally on the provincial scene, and in matters of government intervention it would be hard to deny that his general approach was further to the left than the right-of-centre liberalism of Macdonald. It is arguable too that Stanfield's caution has been seriously exaggerated. For when a full examination of the facts demonstrated that a particular course of action was both desirable and feasible, he could be counted upon to act without delay. Of one thing there could be no doubt: he had left his party in a position that it had never before enjoyed in Nova Scotia.

CHAPTER 11

Smith and IEL: A Two-Edged Sword

By cabinet agreement G.I. Smith succeeded Stanfield as premier on an interim basis, and in November the party's annual meeting confirmed him as leader without benefit of a convention. R.A. Donahoe, the only likely contender, waived any claim he might have had because of the economic crisis confronting the province. As Dal Warrington pointed out, no fanfare of trumpets greeted "Ike" Smith's accession to office. Though long active and highly respected in Conservative ranks, he was not particularly well known by Nova Scotians generally. Selfless and unassuming, he had worked largely in the Stanfield shadow. Although the most considerate of men, he had become "labelled, rightly or wrongly, as the premier's 'hatchet man,' who could be counted on to do the unpleasant but necessary jobs with a minimum of fuss, leaving his chief free for loftier matters."[1] This happened, wrote Dalton Camp, "because he was always the best-informed man in the Legislature when he debated an issue" and also because he was one of the very few who knew how to debate. "As a consequence, most political arguments with Smith had to end in a kind of overkill."[2]

According to the *Canadian Annual Review*, Nova Scotians had no firm opinions on the leaders at this stage. Smith had "yet to project any great public appeal" or to present "a forceful public image," and the public was indifferent towards Regan, perhaps because of "his over-eager brashness in presenting issues."[3] Many Conservatives thought he should have remained a sports announcer on radio where, they said, he had deservedly won the sobriquet "Gabby." They badly underestimated him.

Smith had been premier barely a month when on October 13th — Black Friday — Hawker Siddeley Canada announced that, because of large operating losses, it would close the Dosco steel plant in Sydney on April 30, 1968. All elements of the community condemned it as an act of social irresponsibility. To keep the plant open, the province had little choice but to buy it, intending to operate it for at least one year beyond the projected shut-down. The stress and overwork of these days left an irreparable mark on the premier's health. Nonetheless, at the Confederation of Tomorrow Conference in Toronto in November 1967, he won favourable publicity for advocating flexibility in dealing with Quebec's demands. Except for the position of the monarch he promised a completely open mind.

From the beginning of the legislative session in 1968, Regan did everything he could to destroy the government's credibility. He declared that the speech from the throne contained "little more than crumbs," he described Donahoe's delay in introducing medicare as "shilly-shallying," and he charged that IEL's failings had led to the province getting involved in managing "a wider variety of industrial operations, than perhaps any state west of the communist block." With great relish he told his opponents that Stanfield would "not be here to re-elect you the next time...it is all right to be elected on someone else's coattails, but you can't govern that way."[4] In reply Smith flayed the federal government for providing only $2 million in assistance to the steel plant and hoped that the flame of its political life would "soon sputter out." Had anyone, he wondered, the same mania for melancholy as Regan. "The more success [IEL] seems to achieve, the more bitter is [his] attack."[5]

Generally the government handled Liberal attacks with ease in 1968. It continued to show a small surplus and promised no increase in taxes unless medicare was introduced during the year. As usual, Nicholson accused it of playing musical chairs with the hospital reserve, but in the end the timing of medicare provoked much more debate than finance in general. Most doctors and a majority of witnesses before the legislature's public health committee wanted it to come into effect as planned on July 1, 1968. However, the *Chronicle-Herald* warned that it would mean a less satisfactory school system and higher taxes, and asked the legislators to make sure that

George Isaac Smith   1967-70

Courtesy of NSIS Photo

"medicare's penalties, obvious and hidden, are understood by the people."[6] Health Minister Donahoe's doubts about the possibility of introducing it in 1968 steadily increased, partly "because the federal government has limited us in the form it takes" and partly because it took considerable time to perfect the administrative machinery. The Medicare Advisory Board headed by R. MacD. Black had reported that to secure the $18 million required in the first year the sales tax would have to be increased to 7 per cent and more items would have to be taxed. More important for the timing, however, was the need to register the 312,000 family units. When Regan suggested that lists were available, Smith indicated that any relevant ones were at least five years out of date. The outcome was that the cabinet, with the approval of caucus, decided not to make a start until April 1, 1969 in order to ensure a sound structure for the scheme.

Among significant bills was one to set up a Crop Insurance Commission to administer a protection plan for farmers; another was to enable county court judges to be appointed as local judges of the Supreme Court and to have jurisdiction under the new federal divorce act. The most important bill was an amendment to the Trade Union Act aimed at reducing work stoppages. Under it the Labour Relations Board could act as a labour court and at its discretion decide whether or not to order employees on a wildcat strike to return to work immediately.

The uncertainty of the economy caused particular concern. When 103 Search and Rescue Unit was scheduled to be moved from Greenwood to Summerside, the premier commented bitterly that Nova Scotia had enough problems of its own without the federal government creating more. Regan declared it wrong to "set up the straw man of the Federal Government, and knock it down . . . and set it up again and again, for the same purpose," but the premier would have none of it. "I propose to say in this House, whatever I feel ought to be said, about the effect of Federal policies on Nova Scotia" and the need for new ones "not only as a right — but as a duty, of any Nova Scotian."[7] When he again chastised the federal government for its niggardly contribution to the province's steel industry, even Regan conceded that it was not doing its share. "It takes courage to stand up and admit it," said Donahoe.[8] Nevertheless, through the Cape Breton Development Corporation, a Crown corporation set up the previous year in conjunction with the provincial government, attempts to rehabilitate the island's economy had begun. In the years to come Devco would in particular oversee the working of the coal mining industry.

With one exception the government had no difficulty in repelling opposition attacks on IEL operations in 1968. Forty-eight of the crown corporation's fifty-six clients were already in production and, though Deuterium was thirty months behind schedule, its long-range prospects still appeared good. With Clairtone the situation was different. Its position had not improved even after IEL took over its operations. Before the legislature's industry committee Frank Sobey put much of the blame on the press, especially Ontario newspapers, which supposedly had never forgiven the industry's loss to Nova Scotia. When, in a five-hour session, Sobey accused Regan of trying to make political capital, the Liberal leader declared it his duty to ask questions even though three cabinet ministers were trying to shut him up. Other witnesses testified that the plunge in coloured TV sales, not a bad ministerial decision, was primarily responsible for the difficulties. By a vote of twenty-nine to three the house expressed confidence in the directors of IEL.[9]

The federal election on June 25th gave Stanfield a chance to show if he was still the political master of Nova Scotia. One Conservative advertisement declared that "there's a sense of confidence and trust in the 'quiet man from Nova Scotia' . . . . The Stanfield philosophy put the province on the road to economic progress and Nova Scotians have not looked back since. Now Canada needs the Stanfield philosophy . . . urgently." Perhaps to counter Trudeaumania, Stanfield put forward his view of an ideal Canada in another advertisement:

A place, not of oppressive regulation but of opportunity.
A place, not of increasing conformity, but of individuality. . . .
A place not like any other on earth.
A place that is our own.[10]

Nova Scotia and the Atlantic area exhibited some evidence of Trudeaumania, especially in the urban districts. However, as Peter Regenstreif reported, the people of this conservative region did not believe that Trudeau possessed the image that a prime minister ought to have, "You know, this business of kissing the girls all the time."[11] Nationally the Liberals won their victory in the three most populous provinces — Ontario, Quebec and British Columbia — where Trudeaumania was dominant and where, to some extent at least, Stanfield was regarded as a throwback to the past. There the Liberals took 136 seats to the Conservatives' twenty-one. In the rest of Canada it was fifty-one Conservatives to nineteen Liberals, and in Atlantic Canada it was twenty-five to seven. Five of these seven Liberal seats were in Acadian New Brunswick, but even there the majorities were small and not a few Acadians said, "I like Stanfield. He didn't do badly in Nova Scotia." The Conservatives took all the seats in Nova Scotia but MacEachen's and polled 55.2 per cent of the vote. Stanfield was still master in his own province.

The last two months of 1968 produced significant political events. Early in November, at a convention in Sydney, former civil servant and broadcaster Jeremy Akerman succeeded J.H. Aitchison as NDP leader and, in effect, took away the direction of the party from the academics in Halifax. Later that month the Smith government still seemed to be riding high when it gained Dartmouth North in a by-election. Yet the signals were mixed. In October, after the Nova Scotia Association for the Advancement of Colored People had a three-hour closed meeting with the premier in which it expressed dissatisfaction over black housing, education, and employment, Smith promised comprehensive human rights legislation in 1969 to remedy their grievances. Yet at a stormy meeting of the Nova Scotia Human Rights Conference in December he was subjected to hostility and abuse by part of the audience.

The opening of the 1969 session brought the surprise announcement that an assembly committee would help to determine how to pay for medicare. The *Chronicle-Herald* under the heading "Medicare: Take 11th Hour Look," demanded answers to several questions before the final plunge. Where, in five years, would the province get the money if, as Trudeau suggested, the federal government reduced its support of medicare? How much of Great Britain's financial and economic problems were attributable to its massive welfare programme?[12]

Regan's response to the government's proposal was a massive onslaught which never ceased until the election of 1970. To him Smith was in full retreat from his responsibilities. Because constitutional authorities held that the cabinet alone had responsibility for initiating taxes, the five Liberal members would under no condition let themselves be "conned" into acting as straw men in this matter, nor would they be quieted on other government misadventures. One example was the Sackville land development scheme of the Nova Scotia Housing Commission, which Regan described as a "scandal-ridden branch of the Tory government." In his view the scheme had become the "playground of some shady speculators" who had operated to cheat the long-time owners of the land and achieve huge middle-men profits. A royal commission was already investigating their activities when Attorney General Donahoe drew Regan's ire by ordering the RCMP to make their own inquiry into possible criminal charges, thereby delaying the release of any findings by the commission. Exasperated, the Liberal leader accused Donahoe of procrastination and of reactionary attitudes, especially on imprisonment for debt. When Regan called him "the worst attorney-general that Nova Scotia has ever had," Donahoe simply replied that "coming from the worst leader of the opposition . . . that's a compliment."[13] Defending his attorney general to the hilt, the premier declared that he presided over the administration of justice with "fairness, honor, dignity, ability and humanity," had brought into being the best of hospital insurance schemes, and was doing the same with medicare.[14]

Not only did the *Chronicle-Herald* continue its opposition to universal medicare, but others inserted advertisements in its pages calling on the premier to abandon the "little pup" lest it become a monster. Witnesses with the same point of view appeared before the committee considering medicare financing and urged that it be restricted to those unable to afford medical services. Dismissing these representations, the committee approved the full scheme and recommended higher liquor, tobacco, and gasoline taxes, as well as raising the health services tax to seven per cent, this tax to be widened to include automobiles and their parts, electric power, telephone services, and hotel accommodation.

The proposed increases brought new critics. Civic officials and labour spokesmen contended that the increased taxes would be inflationary and hurt economic growth. The president of Nova Scotia Light and Power complained about the possible damage to the competitive position of the province's utilities. However, the chief assault came from Regan, who regarded these taxes as making war on the poor. He had a special name for each tax: the increase in the gasoline tax was the "Clairtone tax"; that on liquor was the "Tory patronage tax"; that on motor vehicle fees the "heavy water tax." By holding the floor for almost fifteen hours he delayed the enactment of the taxes several days beyond the anticipated time of passage. When Nicholson asked that cabinet ministers give the speech the attention that it deserved, the premier dropped his newspaper to say that they were. The *Chronicle-Herald* left it to parliamentary experts to decide if Regan's speech constituted a filibuster; certainly he had "displayed great tenacity and physical endurance"[15] and the wide publicity he secured served his political ends much as he had hoped.

Though the government's programme was more substantial than usual in 1969, it did not become the focus of attention. The premier kept his promise to sponsor amendments to the human rights legislation which, he said would make it the best in all of Canada. In particular, it became much easier to get convictions on charges of rental discrimination. The government also took quick action to implement most of the findings of the Green royal commission on election expenses. In future the parties and their candidates would be limited in their election spending and required to report their expenditures. Any candidate who polled one-eighth of the votes in his constituency would be reimbursed a substantial portion of his outlay. Somewhat too optimistically, the *Chronicle-Herald* believed that the mandatory reporting of expenditures would be "an effective guard against the perpetration of corrupt electioneering practices, such as vote buying."[16]

After concluding that members' indemnities and cabinet ministers' salaries were traditionally low in Nova Scotia, the Green commission had recommended a middle scale — one not so low as to require an excessive amount of economic sacrifice, yet not so high as to make a political career an exceptionally attractive avenue to achieving a high income. Continuing in the Stanfield mode the government agreed to increases of no more than half of what the commission recommended, although its bill did provide the leader of the opposition with office facilities, a secretary, and a research assistant, and gave members living twenty-five miles or more from Province House $20 a day during sessions. Regan declared that the time was not right for increases, but one of his members disagreed.

One bill of Education Minister Doucet sought to meet the need for co-ordination in education spending through the setting up of an education assistance committee of five to review all school board budgets and those of local councils. After providing an opportunity for appeal, the committee would make recommendations to the Minister of Education, whose order would establish the education budgets of all boards and councils. Regan called the provisions "a giant step towards dictatorship," but most educational authorities supported the measure.[17] A second Doucet bill resulted from a 150-page master plan of Montreal consultants which declared that the province would reap rich dividends if it amalgamated its school boards and implemented school consolidation. The minister indicated his approval, not because it would mean savings, but because it would permit the development of "a comprehensive school system . . . where each child will have an equal opportunity to develop his potential." Though he considered a substantial reduction of the ninety-four major school boards and 900 boards of school trustees to be "educationally sound and economically desirable," he refused to use compulsion and his amendment to existing legislation simply permitted amalgamation of school boards through mutual consent.[18]

Because of a large increase in equalization grants the new minister of finance and economics, W.S.K. Jones, considered the state of the finances to be healthy even though, if medicare were included, the province's expenditures would reach $300 million during the next year. For Nicholson it was time to take stock when the interest on the provincial debt was approaching $60 million, about the size of the total budget in 1960. However, this was only polite sparring compared to the opposition's massive attack on the government's industrial development programme. Trade and Industry Minister McKeough eventually became so tired of it that he likened Regan and the other faint hearts, cynics, skeptics and "'blues' spreaders," as he called them, to the character in Al Capp's comic strip who travelled the country under his private rain cloud, spreading gloom and doom.

Basically the Liberals, both in the house and its committees, charged the government with pouring money into Deuterium,

Clairtone, and a Digby County strawberry project without any system of review or analysis of operation. To some extent they were joined by the *Chronicle-Herald*, which wondered if the government was worried by the rise in the provincial direct debt from $466 to $725 million. Perhaps, it suggested, the future emphasis should be on labour-intensive industry rather than on "hyper-sophisticated, capital-intensive projects," whose overall benefits seemed "less than the optimum." The newspaper denied resorting to "partisan political rhetoric," but it agreed with Regan that the province's taxpayers, as shareholders in questionable enterprises, ought not to be left largely in the dark.[19]

Both Jerome Spevack of Deuterium and Peter Munk, formerly of Clairtone, spent hours before the industry committee without contributing much that was new. Regan seemed to have better success in the public accounts committee when attacking the Digby strawberry farm's operations. Earlier the provincial auditor had complained of its bookkeeping and the loss to date of $500,000 of public money. Under severe questioning its manager, M.E. Jamerson, testified that an excellent strawberry crop had been lost when "locals" who did not want the project to succeed spread rumours of rotten food and poisonous snakes, and caused 92 per cent of the workers to leave. Regan rightly pointed out the "weird arrangements" between the government and Jamerson, and demanded a full inquiry.

Both IEL and the government struck back. In the industry committee Frank Sobey accused Regan of using Clairtone's difficulties as a "political football," only to have the Liberal leader tell him that "you fellows did such a lousy job of running [it] . . . that almost $9,000,000 was lost last year and now you are blaming the politicians."[20] In reply, the premier promised to support Clairtone "so long as I have the strength," and he denounced Regan and Nicholson for dealing only with the two industries that had not yet succeeded. "I have never said that we never make mistakes. . . . This promise of growth will yet be fulfilled." Condemning even more harshly the attacks on the men who ran IEL, he wondered how the government could attract men of ability under such circumstances.[21] Trying to steer a middle course, the *Chronicle-Herald* declared that it could understand Sobey's desire to take Clairtone out of the political cockpit and, so, if the public were kept informed about its general progress, it should be allowed to operate without harassment.[22]

Turning from industrial development to the Sackville land-assembly scheme and having been told that he could not trespass on matters before the royal commission investigating the project, Regan accused the committee chairman of "plugging all the loopholes" to prevent legitimate questioning. Charged at one stage with not doing his homework, he listed cabinet ministers who had failed in exactly that respect: Donahoe had been unaware that a debtor had languished in prison for five months; Haliburton had known little about rural telephone companies; Akerley had not understood the causes that led to the "strawberry fiasco" at Digby; Harding had been unaware for months of the difficulties at Sackville; and the premier himself had not been reading the monthly reports of Clairtone.[23] However, Regan was also on the receiving end when he objected to a provincial contract given to the Minas Coal and Supply Company, of which Conservative Senator Frank Welch was a principal. Gentlemen of the Liberal persuasion, the premier told him, "think it's a sin for a Conservative to . . . do business with any government, Liberal or Conservative." In fact, they thought that they had not only the divine right to govern, but also the divine right to sell to the government.[24]

Before the legislature met again both old parties had something for which to congratulate themselves. The Liberals considered it a good omen that A. Garnet Brown had retained Halifax Eastern Shore for them in a by-election. The Conservatives were even more delighted that IEL's loan of $50 million had persuaded Michelin Tires (Canada) Ltd. to locate in Nova Scotia rather than Quebec and to build plants in Granton and Bridgewater that would employ 1,300. No less pleasing to them was the announcement, late in December, that the Sydney Steel Corporation (Sysco) had produced a record million tons of steel in 1969, up from 873,413 tons in 1968.

If anything, the speech from the throne in 1970 again contained more specifics than usual, including compulsory automobile insurance, a reduction in the voting age, a board to advise the government on industrial development, and an $84 million programme to modernize the steel plant. Yet Regan

called it "lean fare," and Akerman "all sauce and no grub."
Though the province's net debt had risen from $200.9 million to
$241.9 million, surpluses remained the order of the day, the one
forecast for 1970-71 being the thirteenth in a row. Dr.
McKeough, the new finance minister and a Tory of the left,
dismissed a balanced budget as not "an all in all" and
considered much more important "measures to invest in human
beings . . . to provide the facilities to enable each Nova Scotian
to live, learn and labour as he should wish." Both Nicholson
and the *Chronicle-Herald* expressed concern that spending was
rising annually by about 10 per cent. They wondered if the
outlay on education was becoming top heavy and if too much
attention was being paid to higher and graduate education, and
too little to primary and secondary education and vocational
training.

A contentious item in the government's legislative programme was the proposal to lower the voting age to nineteen.
Everyone wanted it reduced, but some thought that the starting
age should be eighteen as in New Brunswick, Newfoundland,
and the United Kingdom. The *Chronicle-Herald* declared that
the government appeared determined to do good, but in a half-
hearted manner. "We should welcome [the eighteen-year olds] as
partners in democracy in this province." Regan agreed but
appeared more worried that any change might not come into
effect in time for an election in 1970. Hence he made sure that
the bill would not be subject to the waiting period normally
operative before changes in the election act came into effect.[25]
That action may well have resulted in his becoming premier
later in the year. Even more controversial was a proposal to set
up a bilingual community college in southwestern Nova Scotia,
which would replace Collège Ste. Anne at Church Point,
operated by the Eudist Fathers for some seventy-five years. The
bill proposed to make a planning commission fully responsible
for all aspects of establishing the new college. Liberal Benoit
Comeau called this an insult to his constituency of Clare, where
he expected the college to continue to be located, and Liberals
generally believed that Education Minister Doucet had another
location in mind. The minister warned correctly that the
wrangling would prevent quick action.

As forecast, the government took action to set up a five-member Financial Assistance Advisory Board to advise the government on major requests for help and, where it was granted, to offer management advice both to business and government departments. Despite the expectations of the *Chronicle-Herald*, the premier denied that it would act as a watchdog over IEL, which would remain an autonomous body. Regan dismissed the board as simply adding "another step on the hierarchy of bureaucracy."[26]

This year a select committee headed by Conservative Victor Thorpe reached a different conclusion on the office of ombudsman than had the earlier one. Though it believed that the quickest and best way to obtain redress of administrative ills would continue to be through an MLA, the committee concluded, nevertheless, that an ombudsman having powers like those in Alberta and New Brunswick would be an asset. Indeed, it recommended that his usual functions be widened to include the investigation of municipal complaints. Reporting on the previous year's legislation, Education Minister Doucet announced that amalgamated school boards would soon be in operation in Kings County, Northside Cape Breton, and Colchester-Hants, and Health Minister Donahoe pronounced the first year of medicare a success and announced that its cost would rise from $26.7 million to $30.4 million in the second.

More than ever before, Nicholson accused the government of abdicating its own responsibilities to study groups and commissions, and the *Chronicle-Herald* agreed that the government might be falling into the habit of believing that before a decision was made a panel of specialists had to submit a report, the result being to slow down the process of government.[27] In his turn Regan attacked the Voluntary Economic Planning report for being nothing more than a series of graphs which failed to show where the board was going. McKeough called these comments unfair to the people who worked voluntarily in VEP[28] and suggested that the Liberal leader did not like the graphs because they indicated a dramatic growth of the economy.

Knowing where the most political capital was to be made, Regan continued to keep the ills of the industrial development programme before the assembly and public without let up. Apparently fearing that the man whom they once dismissed scornfully as "Gabby" was eroding the government's credibility, the Conservatives interrupted his seventy-minute barrage in the debate on the address in reply with heckling and catcalls. He called the government "a plunger," "a gambler," not "a prudent investor"; warned that the $50 million loan to Michelin Tires was "a lot of eggs to put in one basket"; charged that the "veil of secrecy" supposedly protecting the interests of clients of IEL was, in reality, designed to protect the government; and labelled Spevack, Munk, and Jamerson as members of the Conservative senate of Nova Scotia. Smith, in reply, described the Liberal philosophy as "play safe, think small, do little," at a time when Nova Scotians were finally getting back into the mainstream of Canadian life.[29]

The *Chronicle-Herald* hoped that the appointment of Finlay MacDonald as full-time head of IEL would lead to a better calculated use of its financial resources and asked that he be given time to work into his onerous position before having to appear before the industry committee. However, Regan never ceased his ferreting, whether it was an IEL project or not. When he brought up the strawberry farm again, the *Chronicle-Herald* suggested that to the Conservatives it must have seemed like the Beatles' song, "Strawberry fields forever." In this instance the government had taken its losses and leased the Digby lands to nearby farmers, and it justified the project as a "valuable example of applied research."

Exasperated at being unable to ask questions about the Sackville land deal because the royal commissioner had not yet reported, Regan turned to other so-called "fiascoes." Clairtone provided plenty of grist for his mill. Because IEL was a promoting but not an operating agency, the government had taken Clairtone over, along with its losses to date of $17,921,000. The hope, a remote one, was to establish the company on a small but solid economic base. To this end Clairtone was in the process of moving from its 260,000 square foot plant to a 28,000 square foot one, where it would produce experimentally a new line of solid-state television sets and seek subcontract work.

Regan reserved his harshest language for Deuterium, whose fortunes had gone from bad to worse. The crowning blow was the serious deterioration of the not quite finished plant through salt water corrosion. After the federal government had offered assistance of $41.4 million, the province gave Deuterium of Canada, now divested of Jerome Spevack, the authority to proceed with the plant's rehabilitation. Blaming the Smith government's "hopeless inadequacy" for turning "this plant into a millstone around the necks of the people for several generations" to come, Regan suggested that the venture might cost Nova Scotians $300 million. Once again the premier accused the leader of the opposition of being confused by the facts, afflicted with "funnel vision," and blind to anything but the "bad things in life."[30] Smith estimated the total cost to be $167,500,000, and the net cost to the province as $144,900,000.

The *Chronicle-Herald* expressed its worries about Deuterium more strongly than before. In 1970 the newspaper was having its own difficulties with the Special Senate Committee on the Mass Media headed by Senator Keith Davey. That committee took to heart the criticisms of the *Herald* by Halifax's "boat-rocking" bi-weekly (later weekly), *The 4th Estate*, and treated the *Herald's* publisher and officers sternly in its public hearings. Its final report, devastatingly harsh, found the paper "guilty of uncaring, lazy journalism . . . for years,"[31] especially in its failure to examine critically the development programmes of Stanfield and Smith.

The *Chronicle-Herald* could hardly deny that since 1940 it had seldom been strongly critical of any provincial government and that the Stanfield government had enjoyed an especially favoured existence at its hands. However, it is also true that it had had doubts about the province's development projects even before the Davey committee came into being. Though that criticism became more pronounced after evidence highly unfavourable to the newspaper was placed before the committee, none can be sure if it would have treated the Smith government less harshly but for these hearings. In any case, like Regan, the newspaper steadily expressed increased fears about a small province becoming involved in "sophisticated, highly technical, capital-intensive ventures of high-risk potential" and it wondered, again like Regan, if "Nova Scotia tax dollars should [not] be utilized primarily for the development of Nova Scotia skills and businesses."[32]

Regan and Nicholson went to the point of charging the government with selling out the province to outsiders and allowing the province's capital to enrich foreign companies in far-flung parts of the world. In this instance the *Herald* was unconvinced by what it called Regan's "bogey man." To require outside companies that did well in the province to share some of their profits with Nova Scotians would only repel them altogether.[33] The closing exchanges between the two leaders summarized the session. To Regan, Deuterium was "a financial tiger by the tail," Clairtone "a white elephant," and both demonstrated the government's belief in grandiose schemes to the neglect of the overall welfare of the province. To Smith, his opponent displayed "more and more of his lack of responsibility" every time he spoke. "You don't have to imagine that Nova Scotia is making progress — you can see it,"[34] but Regan's approach was to "draw a blanket around himself, cover his eyes, and let the world go by."

Disquietude had undoubtedly developed among business men and the public generally about the government's development policies. Was "too high a price . . . being paid for too few new jobs"?[35] Throughout 1970 other troubles appeared: a lengthy strike by the United Fishermen and Allied Workers Union to organize seafood plant workers and trawlermen; wildcat strikes in the construction industry that resulted in large increases in industrial wages and building costs; pollution problems caused by the spilling of 1.5 million gallons of bunker oil by the Liberian taker *Arrow* into Chedabucto Bay; and Scott Paper Company's discharge of objectionable effluents into Boat Harbour, a problem compounded by the apparent unwillingness of the responsible minister to recognize that anything was wrong. For most of these troubles the Smith government had been in no way responsible, but a demanding electorate was not likely to make penetrating analyses to assess the blame.

Nevertheless, Smith thought the time appropriate for an election. On September 5th he declared that, though he had never wished or expected or tried to be premier, "I've gotten used to it, and am enjoying it." Taunted often for not possessing a mandate of his own, he had not sought one mainly because of the troubles in the steel industry. Now he wished to put the Smith stamp on the government and its programme. To his colleagues, party insiders, and workers, "Ike" Smith was known for his ability and his unvarying decency. However, it quickly dawned upon party strategists, used to winning elections by selling Stanfield, that the process would be more difficult with a leader not nearly as well known or appreciated by Nova Scotian voters. Hence on September 26th they ran a full-page advertisement of pictures showing Smith in varying aspects of his career with the simple title: "Smith for Nova Scotia." Another ad on October 2nd pictured a smiling "Ike," farm boy, lawyer, soldier, politician, and leader, who had built one of the best highway systems in Canada, managed financial affairs so well that the province was ready for medicare, introduced Voluntary Economic Planning, and saved the Sydney steel plant. A third on October 9th asked the question, "think about it . . . is there anyone you'd rather have as Premier of Nova Scotia than Nova Scotia's Premier Ike Smith?"

Previously Smith had been regarded as one of the best platform speakers in Nova Scotia and certainly one of the hardest hitting, but in this election someone described his approach as "prime ministerial"; another as a "love-in." According to the *Chronicle-Herald*, the premier had "forsaken the stage and turned to the street, gladhanding his way across the province and back again, with a press conference here, a factory tour there, and a friendly smile elsewhere." Harold Shea of the same paper declared that politics had become a parlour game and the election "a dull, lack-lustre affair."[36] A Chambers cartoon pictured Stanfield saying to Dalton Camp, "Let's face it, Dalton — [Ike's] lost that old killer instinct."[37] Only occasionally, as at Digby, did Smith take off the gloves and blast Liberal promises as merely "a lot of words." Had the overwork and worries of the past two years left their telltale mark or was he following a low-profile campaign devised by Camp? One who heard a weary, seemingly worn-out premier at Bridgewater late in the campaign wondered if he was capable of mounting the fire of old.

Smith's manifesto sought to emphasize that he was not participating in "a public auction of promises." Yet he offered the abolition of all poll taxes, an increase in minimum wages to $1.50 per hour, an improvement in the students' loan plan, and the creation of a new branch of IEL to deal with small industries, always stressing that their financial implications had been carefully weighed and that they would require no tax increases. Nevertheless, the *Chronicle-Herald* asked, "Can Nova Scotia, even with financial assistance from various outside sources, afford the reforms which Mr. Smith projects?"[38] Was the Davey committee affecting this newspaper's editorials even before it had published its report?

The premier escaped bitter, harsh criticism, but not so his attorney general, especially at the hands of *The 4th Estate*, which accused him of reflecting "another age and another set of values." While admitting that Donahoe had introduced hospital insurance and medicare, the latter allegedly with reluctance, the newspaper declared that in the administration of justice he had displayed a "dismal, unfeeling, punitive and totally unimaginative attitude" and, "lace curtain Irish," had treated imprisonment for debt in archaic fashion.[39] The article was exaggerated and unfair, but it demonstrated that the government had not been fully alert to possible political liabilities. For though Donahoe was right that the provisions of the Collection Act, if applied as intended, did not constitute an imprisonment for debt law, it was all too easy to make it appear that they did.

In his first election campaign Jeremy Akerman advocated "a brand of softened socialism" which called especially for taxation based on the ability to pay and a free bargaining process not harassed by the government or the press. However, because of the party's lack of financial resources, he seldom ventured to campaign on the mainland and sought mainly to win his own seat.

To many Conservatives the idea that Regan could become premier was out of the question. Some of them declared that the Liberal leadership had fallen into "not very worthy and not very able hands," and that Regan was simply "itching to get in the Senate."[40] To them his well-devised campaign undoubtedly came as a surprise. At the outset Regan declared that, having had his say on fiascoes like Deuterium and Clairtone, he would now develop his policies with a better Nova Scotia in view. He likewise made sure that he could not be accused of spending his way into office. Contending that economic development was a science, not a lottery, he promised "a rational and scientific approach to attracting industry" through a single department of economic growth that would create a consistent policy for all development programmes. Though not opposed to outside entrepreneurs, he felt that past provincial governments had not put a welcome mat before Nova Scotia businessmen, and to that end he promised a new sense of direction with fresh ideas and approaches.[41] Liberal advertisements carried large pictures of "Gerald Regan, the Man for Nova Scotia" with the slogan: "Nova Scotia needs a new direction." On the last two days of major campaigning, Regan caught the public eye in somewhat dramatic fashion — on Friday with hurry-up visits to eight communities between Halifax and Sydney Mines, and on Saturday with a sixteen-hour helicopter trip, stopping at a similar number of places in the Annapolis Valley and along the South Shore, and ending at Fort Needham in his own constituency.

Overall, it was the closest election in provincial history. Despite polling 46.9 per cent of the vote to the Liberals' 46.1 and the NDP's 6.6, the Conservatives won only twenty-one seats to the Liberals' twenty-three and the NDP's two; a shift of only forty-one votes would have given them the most seats. However, in a real sense it was a massive rejection because, compared with 1967, the Conservatives lost nineteen seats while the Liberals gained seventeen.

Seeking to explain the unexpected, *Time* declared that holding office for fourteen years "inevitably saps the vitality of any enterprise," and that "political complacency and misadventures in industrial development eroded [the Tories'] currency."[42] Neither they nor the election prophets had appreciated the appeal of the forty-one-year-old Regan when contrasted with the somewhat shopworn image projected by Smith. Lyndon Watkins suggested that though Regan did not have the charisma of a Trudeau, he did understand where the Conservatives were vulnerable and he had clearly used that knowledge to forge his victory.[43] The two questions Watkins posed for the Conservatives were easily answered. Smith had not called on Stanfield for help because he wanted to win his own election, and if a low-profile campaign was deliberately planned it was a mistake.

Two things about the election puzzled Smith. Before he had always been able to detect the voters' intentions; this time "he had not seen what was coming." Almost as surprising to him was the conduct of the steelworkers, who had elected the NDP's Paul MacEwan instead of Conservative Percy Gaum. Politicians before him had learned that it was not unusual for them to bite the hand that fed them. Smith conceded that it had been a political mistake to give the vote to nineteen-year-olds, and Camp agreed that they had found it difficult to identify with someone of sixty-one years whose experience made him reluctant to give glib and entertaining answers to profoundly complex questions. "Men like Smith are not entertainers and they cannot be glamorized; there is no cosmetic in the [world] which would make Ike Smith a television personality, a charismatic political star, or a clown. He lacks the ego to attempt it and any interest in achieving it."[44]

The election exhibited another feature that would become even more significant in years to come, the growing electoral importance of Halifax County. The Conservatives had won six of ten seats on Cape Breton Island, seven of ten in the eastern counties, and seven of sixteen in western Nova Scotia. "Hence their defeat resulted primarily from the loss of nine out of ten seats in Halifax [County], all but one by large majorities."[45] Several reasons may explain the city's revulsion against the government. Halifax had been the last area to turn to Stanfield and the Conservatives, and hence was likely to be the first to desert them; a mobile, increasing population is more given to pronounced voting swings than a static one; and an urbanized area tends to be more receptive to charges of financial mismanagement than a non-urban one. Certainly Haligonians had had a front-row seat during Regan's arraignment of the government.

The Conservatives were not the only losers in 1970. "In 1967 it was all Robert Stanfield and the new Nova Scotia. Supposedly the province was on the verge of an industrial break-through which, at long last, would end its disadvantaged position in Confederation." IEL, the chosen instrument for this purpose, had "occupied a hallowed place in Conservative party rhetoric." As was the duty of a leader of the opposition, Gerald Regan had led a three-year fight to publicize the failings of the government's industrial programme. In the end IEL stood discredited and forlorn, never to attain anything like its former position.[46]

IEL would have had a diminished role in any case since all the provinces were now in the competition, with industry-attracting institutions of their own. The experience with Deuterium and Clairtone had made it apparent that the normally successful approach of Stanfield and Smith — to gather all the information possible, whether through government officials, task forces or royal commissions, before making policy decisions — would not necessarily work in assessing highly technical or complex business operations where incalculables like the inherent goodness of processes, the expertise of specific entrepreneurs, variations in market demand, and the like came into play.

Though defeated, the Conservatives in their fourteen years of office had provided themselves with insurance against the arguments that had long been used successfully against them. They had paved many more miles of highways than had the Liberals, they had implemented two massive social programmes, hospital insurance and medicare, and they had presented a long series of balanced budgets. It had been G.I. Smith's misfortune to lead the province at a time when a host of circumstances turned against him, starting with the near collapse of a major industry that had been ailing since the First World War. Though beset unrelentingly by difficulties which drained his physical and mental resources, Smith had produced legislative programmes in each of his three years which were little affected by the circumstances. Supposedly he had been somewhat more conservative than his predecessor; yet the evidence does not support it. Despite the reluctance of some members of his cabinet and caucus, he led them undivided to the implementation of medicare. To one like myself, who was privileged to be part of a delegation accompanying him to constitutional conferences, he stood out for his intelligence, ability, industry, and unfailing decency.

CHAPTER 12

Regan: The Fading of Dreams

On election night in 1970 television viewers saw a Gerald Regan whom they had not seen before, a man seemingly surprised by his victory and fearful of the responsibilities to come. That did not last long. However, cabinet-making did present difficulties because only five Liberal members had had legislative experience. Four of these became ministers in a cabinet of only nine members averaging forty-one years in age, compared with the previous cabinet's fifty-one years.

In an attempt to provide modern management and avoid "fumbling fiascoes," Regan acted to modernize the procedures of cabinet government.[1] The result was something resembling Trudeau's privy council and prime ministerial offices. Fred Drummie became deputy minister of the executive council and secretary of the cabinet, Peter Green acted as legislative adviser to the cabinet, and Michael Belliveau was made the research director in the executive council office. In the premier's office Dr. Michael Kirby, the chairman of the party's policy committee over the preceding year and regarded by some as the mastermind of its election victory, became principal assistant; James Robson was appointed press secretary and the premier's executive assistant in his capacity as chairman of the Nova Scotia Power Commission; and David Thompson became the arranger of his day-to-day activities. Undoubtedly Stanfield and Smith had had too little expertise of this kind, but questions immediately arose. Was the new apparatus too elaborate and hence too expensive? More important, how would the deputy ministers, long-time office-holders, loyal to any incumbent government, circumspect in performing their duties, and generally tending to be conservative, get along with newcomers who in some respects were challenging them? How, too, would the opposition react to the appointment of executive assistants to cabinet ministers?

In December, not two months after assuming office, the government presented the house with a heavy legislative programme designed to fulfil some of its election promises. One bill established the office of the ombudsman; another provided builders of new houses with cash grants of $500 and drew immediate criticism for falling short of promises and not making provision for older homes. The most important bill made significant changes in the labour law so as to incorporate some of the philosophy of the premier, himself a labour lawyer; recommendations of the Woods royal commission on labour; and parts of the labour law of other provinces. Workers benefited in the virtual abolition of *ex parte* injunctions in trade union disputes, but some of the new penalties were described as "ferocious." Thinking of the twenty-seven illegal strikes in the previous year, Labour Minister Pace declared that "stern times call for stern measures."[2]

From the outset NDP leader Jeremy Akerman performed so well that before long some observers would call him the best of the assemblymen. Because G.I. Smith was recovering from a heart attack, W.S.K. Jones acted as Conservative house leader. Accusing the government of being preoccupied with political imagery and the scoring of political points, he singled out Highways Minister Garnet Brown as a combination of Spiro Agnew, Martha Mitchell, and Keith Davey. Brown was already finding uncongenial the give and take of parliamentary debate.

Peter Meerburg of the *Chronicle-Herald* was surprised by the government's "uncanny aptness for taking over the reins of office, and projecting an image of vigor." To him the Liberals looked and sounded as if they had always been there. Only once, when accused of a "continent-wide credibility gap," was the premier a little embarrassed. That occurred when Conservative John Buchanan held aloft the tape of a Regan speech in Los Angeles in which he, who had lambasted the Smith government for leading Nova Scotia to wrack and ruin, presented the "picture of a province in which it would be sound to invest."

Gerald A. Regan   1970-78

Courtesy of NSIS Photo

Generally, however, Regan "sat in the premier's chair . . . almost soft-spoken, projecting an air of confidence, but carefully hiding any arrogance," a credit, wrote Meerburg, to the image-makers who had started working on him a year earlier.[3]

Regan started 1971 ebulliently by describing the Fundy tides as "a horizontal Churchill Falls," whose development was inevitable and perhaps imminent because of the "restless advance of technology" and an unquenchable "thirst for electrical energy."[4] This was the beginning of his interest in great projects which in the end would hurt him politically. After a discussion with Baron Edmond de Rothschild, he even prophesied that the time was coming when Nova Scotia would be contributing towards rather than receiving equalization moneys.

In February 1971 Peter Nicholson presented his first budget. Over the next eight years he would have much the same relationship with the premier as that which had existed between Smith and Stanfield. Nicholson's handling of the finances was such that Regan would never again be accused of financial irresponsibility as in the election of 1967. As usual on changes of government, Nicholson blamed his predecessor for prospective deficits in 1970-71 and 1971-72, but Dr. McKeough told him that the use of reserve funds could have prevented them and talked about a "green" budget, a "green" minister, and a government relying too much upon a "quarter million dollars worth of special assistants in the premier's office." When Fred Drummie was described as "a highly paid technocrat of unknown ability," the premier rose in righteous indignation. He was tired of the constant reference to "the whiz kids downstairs. . . . They are worth every cent that they are paid."[5]

This year the government continued to implement its election promises: abolition of the poll tax; reduction of the municipal voting age to nineteen; setting up of the Nova Scotia Amateur Sports Advisory Council; and extension of collection bargaining rights to both inshore and deep-sea fishermen. Developmental plans became a primary concern. In keeping with the premier's high hopes, the government sponsored the establishment of a Tidal Power Corporation backed by a $10 million fund. To accord with his philosophy that resource-based industries deserved more attention, he revamped the departmental machinery. The department of trade and industry disappeared and the department of finance and economics became simply the department of finance. A department of tourism came into being, and economic matters went to a department of development which, among other things, superintended the existing development agencies. Though Regan declared that IEL had left "a millstone for the future," he refused to fight the past and simply tried to operate that institution in accord with the government's general development policies.

Fulfilling another promise, the government appointed the Royal Commission on Education, Public Services and Provincial-Municipal Relations headed by Professor John Graham. Completing unfinished business, it announced that Collège Ste. Anne at Church Point would be phased out as a degree-granting institution but would offer a two-year programme leading to a degree elsewhere. Though it favoured consultation with the other Maritime Provinces on the Deutsch royal commission report favouring union, the Assembly demonstrated hostility to complete union, and before long Regan would say that union was "as dead as a door nail. . . . Integration, yes . . . unification no."

Early in the year G.I. Smith resigned as Conservative leader on medical grounds. At a convention in March three candidates, former cabinet ministers Gerald Doucet and John Buchanan, and the Mayor of Dartmouth, Roland Thornhill, sought to succeed him. Doucet led on the first ballot, but Buchanan was the eventual winner after Thornhill gave him his support. Some commentators perceived a religious split, but the *Canadian Annual Review* dismissed the idea as "one of the most imaginative interpretations of the year."[6] Nonetheless, many delegates left with a sense of bitterness. Under the title "Renewal '71'," Buchanan held more than twenty meetings throughout the province prior to a policy conference in October as part of his preparations for the next general election.

Late in June the legislature met again to deal with problems in the construction industry at Granton, where 800 workers constructing the Michelin plant refused to cross the picket line of seventy-two millwrights. To bring peace to the industry, Pace sponsored a bill requiring pre-start agreements through collective bargaining in contracts valued at $5 million or more. Once an agreement had been secured, picketing would be prohibited. A union not signing the agreement could strike for thirty days but would then be subject to compulsory arbitration. McKeough called the bill "a miscarriage of justice against the labour people"; Akerman asked the premier if he had "the guts to admit that you are making a terrible mistake." Regan maintained that he was simply taking a "giant step" towards giving more people an opportunity to work. If the legislation was ineffective, "we'll be right back in the house in a month or two months." He had the support of the *Chronicle-Herald* which described the bill's critics as "exponents . . . of letting things drift, possibly into industrial chaos."[7] In the end the government made one concession: the compulsory arbitration provisions would lapse within a year.

Generally the year 1971 was good for the government. It reached a favourable agreement with the federal government for the rehabilitation of the heavy water plant at Glace Bay by Atomic Energy of Canada; in October crude oil condensate and natural gas were discovered in considerable quantities off Sable Island; and a by-election victory in Kings West the next month gave the Liberals an overall majority in the legislature. However, in two matters the government did not escape controversy. When the ombudsman found that a highway worker had been dismissed for political reasons, Highways Minister Garnet Brown refused to reinstate him, and Attorney General Pace ruled that the relevant statute did not permit the ombudsman to override ministerial decisions. In taking action to acquire the Nova Scotia Light and Power Company the government argued that the creation of one large power utility would permit "significant economies of scale, with resultant savings to the taxpayers, "but it did not escape criticism for eliminating widely held "widow stock" holdings. Two years later the Nova Scotia Power Corporation, in effect the successor to the Nova Scotia Power Commission, would become responsible for operating all publicly owned energy utilities.

Most of its promises having been fulfilled, the government had few proposals to offer in the speech from the throne in 1972, and Buchanan called it "a flowery production" without substance. G.I. Smith was back to keep ministers on their toes. When the premier complained about members editorializing during question period, Smith called him the worst offender in that respect. Besides, the house was "as much bound by practice and tradition as it is by rules" and it had been the custom to allow the greatest latitude to questioners. Smith also took aim at

Ralph Fiske, the minister of development and a highly successful businessman, for announcing government policy outside the house while it was in session. Fiske apologized but admitted that he would never become a master of house rules.[8]

By far the most serious controversy of the session occurred on McKeough's resolution condemning the levying of taxes without legislative authority. The previous autumn, in concluding a five-year taxation agreement with Ottawa, Nicholson had again agreed to have the federal government collect the province's share of income, estate, and gift taxes, and that had occurred since January 1st without statutory provision. Professor Duncan Fraser declared that "what the McKeough resolution is really concerned about is the preservation of responsible government in . . . Nova Scotia."[9] Not until March 9th did Nicholson start action to legalize the controversial taxes. Meanwhile Buchanan had introduced a bill prohibiting the collection of illegal taxes and imposing fines on cabinet ministers who authorized their collection. Conservative party official Joseph H. Clarke initiated action against Attorney General Pace to recover $35 allegedly deducted from him wrongfully in income tax. After pointing out that retroactive taxes were legal, Pace put the blame on the Diefenbaker government which in 1957 had required the provinces to indicate their approval of taxation agreements by October 1st of the previous year. Nicholson indicated that five provinces were in the same position as Nova Scotia. Eighteen members spoke in a debate punctuated by the interventions of an indignant Regan before the government had its way by twenty-three to twenty-two.

Nicholson's budget also led to protracted controversy. Though the federal government was abandoning estate duties, Nova Scotia decided to continue their use. As a result, the *Chronicle-Herald*, an inveterate opponent of their imposition, published, almost as if it were news, an article from the *Canadian Chartered Accountant* of March 1972 that was highly critical of Nova Scotia's decision. Since the article had been written before the tax had been made more palatable and contained not a few factual errors, the Liberals alleged "yellow journalism" and the publication of "lies" and "inflammatory garbage." However, G.I. Smith objected to "trumped-up questions of privilege" being raised whenever a minister did not like newspaper comment. When the premier repeated the charges of "irresponsible journalism," Conservative Gerald Ritcey shouted: "that's gratitude, [the *Chronicle-Herald*] elected you."[10]

Nicholson's budget, purported to achieve fiscal responsibility, came close to producing a balance, not merely by the retention of estate and gift taxes, but also by a pronounced increase in provincial income taxes. Naturally the *Chronicle-Herald* doubted if the "tax-hungry government" could take much credit for its so-called achievement. Little, in fact, that the government did in 1972 escaped criticism. G.I. Smith declared the bill to set up a department of environment so all-inclusive that it conferred authority "over everything we do — even breathing." The premier's bill to create the Nova Scotia Communications and Information Centre, which put all the government's information services under one umbrella, was denounced as an attempt to establish a Liberal propaganda machine; once again the premier charged the *Chronicle-Herald* with making "vicious" and "irresponsible" statements about its intent. However, a bill to give legal existence to the Council of Maritime Premiers established in 1971 passed without objections or enthusiasm; Regan called it "relatively innocuous," and Buchanan and Akerman expressed indifference.

It was not a happy year for Garnet Brown. Frustrated by what he called procedural wrangles, he engaged in such prolonged exchanges with G.I. Smith that the speaker adopted the unprecedented course of adjourning the assembly for fifteen minutes, not, however, before Brown had declared: "Ike, you're a has been and won't admit it." In December Brown failed in his long fight with the Canadian Union of Public Employees (CUPE) when highway workers voted to recognize that union as their bargaining agent. Two months earlier he had been relegated to the relatively unimportant provincial secretaryship. Most annoying of all, his advocacy of a third national park along the Eastern Shore met opposition in his own constituency.

Continuing the recent history of coal mining, Mines Minister Bagnell announced the closure of the McBean mine at Thorburn and the phasing out of the River Hebert mine.

Elsewhere the economic news was better and the premier maintained his keen interest in great projects. Federal and Maritime provincial officials reached agreement on a study of the tidal project. In August Mobil Oil made a new gas discovery off Sable Island; and in November Regan announced that John Shaheen of New York would build a $233 million oil refinery at the Strait of Canso and that his government would spend $35 million to construct a common-user dock to service it and to assemble the needed land.

In the federal election of October 30th Nova Scotian observers pondered the strength of coattails. Liberals were certain that Stanfield's ironclad grasp on the province would be broken this time, while Conservatives suggested that disillusionment with Trudeau would work in their favour.[11] Stanfield contended that Trudeau's Department of Regional Economic Expansion (DREE) had been a dismal failure in the Atlantic Provinces. The fault, he charged, lay partly in a centralized bureaucracy, but mostly in a fiscal policy which, in attempting to curb inflation, had slowed down the economy in provinces like Nova Scotia that were not responsible for the inflationary spiral. As usual, Conservative advertisements asked the province's voters to make Stanfield the fourth prime minister to come from Nova Scotia. NDP leader David Lewis agreed with Stanfield on the failure of DREE, but Trudeau contended that they were simply trying to destroy confidence in the department. Boasting of Devco's efforts to rehabilitate Cape Breton, Trudeau warned Nova Scotians not to listen to the "preachers of confinement" or to develop a ghetto-like mentality.[12]

How much of it was disillusionment with the Trudeau government and how much Stanfield himself is debatable, but the Conservatives retained ten of the province's eleven seats and Stanfield remained political master of Nova Scotia federally. He might have become the province's fourth prime minister if, in an election in which the Liberals won only two seats more than the Conservatives, he had not lost three seats in the other Atlantic Provinces. Earlier because of Diefenbaker, now because of Stanfield, Allan MacEachen, the province's spokesman in the federal cabinet, was having difficulty in retaining his own seat. As a result his constituency became one of the most highly favoured in all of Canada for the allocation of federal handouts.

For Nova Scotia 1973 did not produce substantial legislative measures, but did produce reasonably prosperous conditions in the earlier months and the certainty of a substantial increase in federal transfer payments. Hence the government decided to spend $5.1 million on a one-time programme to assist persons receiving the Guaranteed Income Supplement and to get out of estate taxes nine months earlier than expected, an action the *Chronicle-Herald* described as belatedly redressing a wrong.

The government also took action to change the department of public welfare to the department of social services; to create the first department of recreation in Canada under Garnet Brown; and to pass a new department of the environment bill to replace the unproclaimed one of the previous year. Early in the session Conservative Dr. James MacLean sponsored a bill which lowered the voting age to eighteen, something his party had opposed in 1970. The government, which approved of the principle, let the bill lie on the table for a few weeks before deciding to go along with it. Though annoyed at the political one-upmanship of his opponents, the premier simply said that "an 18 year-old is as wise to make a voting judgment as the people of any other age group."[13] Perhaps most pleased about the session were the denturists, who at long last won the limited right to make full plates.

Actually the actions of individual members won more attention than legislative proposals in 1973. Conservative Michael Laffin was suspended for two weeks after physically assaulting Paul MacEwan on the house floor for insinuations about his brother. Liberal Walton Cook, who had experienced trouble with the Barristers' Society during the previous session, declared that he would attend only when his legal duties permitted. Alarmed by the power of the bureaucrats and unable to get the Liberal members to do anything about it, he stopped attending caucus and decided to vote as his conscience dictated.[14] Akerman, not at all pleased with the session, described Buchanan as "the next thing to a nightmare" and accused Regan of an appalling lack of leadership in running the house and in keeping his ministers under control. One instance had occurred during the investigation by the industry commit-tee of Garnet Brown's charges that Scott Paper Company was "raping" the forest lands of the Eastern Shore. Three cabinet ministers, and particularly Brown and Fiske, disagreed on the conclusions, and the latter even thought of resigning. The premier used his diplomatic skills to produce a toned-down resolution that all could accept. Fiske declared the differences not unusual: "If you have a bunch of yes men, what's the point."[15] Some Conservatives, though not outspoken like Akerman, were having doubts about the performance of Buchanan as party leader. Their uneasiness increased when his party lost a by-election in Guysborough to Alexander "Sandy" Cameron, who would shortly become minister of fisheries.

For the Liberals the roseate picture of early 1973 changed dramatically during the year as oil prices kept escalating through the actions of the Organization of Petroleum Exporting Countries (OPEC) and as the cost of living mounted. A special session in November was all the more distressing to the government because it knew that it could not provide a remedy quickly in a province that depended upon oil for 90 per cent of its power. To ease the rising cost of living, it took action to remove the sales tax on clothing and footwear, thereby saving the public an estimated $12 million. However, as Akerman pointed out, the poor spent less on clothing than on any other necessity.

To provide some control over the prices of gasoline and fuel oil, the government also secured changes in the Gasoline Licensing Act, which required the oil companies, when raising prices, to provide a detailed justification to the Public Utilities Board. If this board found the increases unjustified, it could rescind them. Buchanan wanted the board's permission before increases took place, but Regan feared any action that might cause the companies to divert oil from the province. On energy in general the premier indicated that the Power Corporation was re-examining the Wreck Cove project in Victoria County which, if proceeded with, would be the largest single hydro undertaking in the province. He opposed the construction of an oil pipeline from Alberta to Nova Scotia, partly because it might delay the development of the province's offshore resources, partly because the oil would be expensive. Above all, he considered large federal subsidies as a necessity for the time being. Stan Fitzner of the *Chronicle-Herald* called the session "cantankerous," a "special" session that had "nothing very much 'special' about it." All it had done was to provide "token respect to an energy crisis."[16]

Even though Fundy power took a back seat in 1973, Regan still talked optimistically of the other great projects. He hoped for a pipeline from the offshore and the bringing of a commercial product to the mainland in four years. He spoke even more eloquently about the oil refinery and the common-user dock at the Strait of Canso, though the first doubts had risen about John Shaheen and complaints were highly vocal about wide variations in payments for expropriated land in the Melfort area. Regan expected investment in the project to reach $2 billion in ten years and hoped to see Nova Scotians become the new Phoenicians.

Almost everyone expected a provincial election in 1974; few expected it on April 2nd even before a spring session of the assembly. At the time the polls were favourable to the provincial Liberals, the possibility existed that the unstable political situation at Ottawa might develop unfavourably for the party, Regan's stature appeared to have been enhanced, and the election would come only two days before the end of a federal-provincial agreement on energy that had kept prices from escalating unduly. The *Globe and Mail* believed that the timing assured Regan a victory, but it added prophetically that he had "chosen the eye of the storm for his election." He might win with an increased majority only to "find that it has given him a future full of trouble."[17] Lyndon Watkins, in *the 4th Estate,* called the timing "morally reprehensible" but astute. Fascinating him was the means Regan had used to convey the message to the electorate. The premier had videotaped an announcement which was deposited at the television stations at 8:30 p.m. on Saturday night for airing within fifteen minutes. As a result, it became the first item on the CBC's national news. This device had also allowed Regan to avoid a news conference where questions might have been asked. "We live in an electronic age, don't we?" remarked a Liberal insider.[18]

In this election none could accuse the NDP of "pie in the sky" promises. The previous summer Akerman had presented a modest programme typical of the democratic left, and during the campaign he added rental control and a Nova Scotia oil corporation to replace the private companies. In contrast with

1970 the NDP had sufficient funds to permit its leader to campaign throughout the province and to import an experienced party organizer.

Buchanan accused the Liberals of trying to buy themselves into power, but the charge might equally have been made against himself. Among other things he promised dental and prescription drug plans, the assumption of full responsibility for primary and secondary education, and aid to fishermen, farmers, and shipbuilders. Listed as major goals were slowing down the escalating cost of living and eliminating the "new level of bureaucracy," especially the information service, or the Liberal "propaganda arm" as he called it. To catch the public eye, more than to woo Sable Island's ten voters, he spent part of a day on the island. Perhaps the premier's harshest criticism came from Dr. McKeough, who declared that as "a master of stereophonics, he can speak out of both sides of his mouth at the same time."

Not at all reticent about his government's record, Regan boasted of 300 accomplishments, of which 64 were listed in advertisements. After emphasizing his government's restoration of fiscal responsibility, he called the Conservative platform "a chronicle of incredibility," which would require $165 million and result in huge tax increases. He himself promised the takeover of all education costs in three years, free drugs for senior citizens, and a 25 per cent reduction in property taxes for the next year, all carefully costed at $35 million, of which $23 million would come from the new equalization grants, $12 million from general revenues, and none from new taxes. He also gave an assurance that, as a result of the recent energy conference, the government could stabilize costs.

The three parties used their leaders to the best advantage. The NDP stressed Akerman's reputation as a growing political force; the Conservatives, the only party with a slogan, proclaimed "Honest it's John" on radio, television, posters, and billboards; and the Liberals pictured Regan as an "efficient, forceful and dedicated leader" who got things done. The Liberals' last advertisement highlighted his whirlwind helicopter trip from Sydney to Yarmouth and back to Halifax on the Saturday prior to the election. Since the campaign produced no overriding issues, Duncan Fraser concluded that the voters had to base their choice "upon the relative images projected by the leaders." Senator Hicks declared that a non-exciting, non-issue-oriented election usually presaged a government victory,[19] and he prophesied correctly.

The Conservative popular vote fell from 46.9 to 38.6 per cent and, though they gained four seats, they lost twelve to the Liberals and one to the NDP, for a total of twelve. "It's back to the drawing board," said Buchanan. The NDP retained its two seats, won Cape Breton Centre from the Conservatives, and raised its popular vote from 6.6 to 13.0 per cent. Next time, declared Akerman, "we'll be going for the jackpot." Though the Liberals' popular vote rose only from 46.1 to 47.9 per cent, their seat total went from twenty-three to thirty-one. Walton Cook's running as an independent in Lunenburg Centre had cost them one seat. The Conservatives' poor showing led to considerable discontent within that party and, though its annual meeting gave Buchanan a vote of confidence in the fall of 1974, dissatisfaction continued.

As some prophets had suggested, it would be a Pyrrhic victory for the Liberals. The energy crisis simply would not go away, and the revenues needed to prevent its doing serious political harm would not be forthcoming. Ever since 1940 the province's finances had been healthy, first because of swollen liquor profits, later because of enormously enlarged transfer payments. Whenever much higher taxes seemed inevitable, a new five-year agreement, providing returns based partly on a GNP growing steadily in good times, had come, more by chance than intention, to the rescue. The Regan government's policies in 1973 and its promises in the election of 1974 had used up most of the new moneys resulting from the 1972 taxation agreement. Henceforth the rate of increase of federal transfer moneys would generally slow down, partly because the economy was often troubled. At the same time the costs of the greatly expanded health, education, and other social services that had been entered into during a boom period would escalate beyond all expectations and cause ministers of finance extraordinary difficulty.

Nevertheless, the government was exuberant during the session beginning in May 1974 — the provincial per capita income had risen to more than 80 per cent of the national average; unemployment was below the average, and so for the moment was the cost of living; a small surplus was in prospect; and the rise in the net direct debt was modest. Health Minister William MacEachern fulfilled one election pledge by sponsoring a pharmacare programme for citizens sixty-five years and over applicable to 74,000 persons, and Municipal Affairs Minister Mooney fulfilled another by initiating a 25 per cent reduction in property taxation for the current year at a cost of about $17 million. Other measures included the establishment of a Nova Scotia Police Commission to oversee the operations and standards of all the provincial police forces; the granting of collective bargaining privileges to teachers; and the creation of the University College of Cape Breton through the combination of Xavier College at Sydney with the Eastern College of Technology.

Late in June the legislature adjourned to permit its members to participate in a federal election in which inflation became almost the only issue. At dissolution Stanfield was ready with his major proposal to implement a ninety-day prices-and-income freeze to counter the rampant inflation psychology. Trudeau campaigned largely on the recent Turner budget which had increased corporation taxes, removed the sales tax on clothing and footwear, and provided larger exemptions for low income earners. For the NDP David Lewis gave up the slogan but not the theme of his earlier "corporate rip-off" campaign. Trudeau heaped scorn on Stanfield's "90 days of wonder and amazement" only to be accused of "calculated deception" for having an even more complicated scheme in readiness as a last resort.

This time the election in Nova Scotia was not mainly oriented towards provincial issues as such although Liberal advertisements boasted of thirty-four programmes that would bring down the cost of living in the Atlantic Provinces, and the Conservatives argued that Stanfield's remedy for inflation would help Nova Scotia in its battle against regional economic disparity. However, Stanfield's basic proposal did not get off the ground, said the *Chronicle-Herald*, because he "failed to sell it, or the electorate refused to be sold on it."[20] He lost two of his seats in Nova Scotia and personally won rather narrowly over Brian Flemming in Halifax. Most disappointing of all was that

Stanfield, who had done more to understand Quebec than any Conservative leader before him, could not in his last two elections win more than three seats in that province. That fact, more than anything else, had prevented him from becoming Nova Scotia's fourth prime minister.

At its resumed sittings the legislature considered a proposal to merge Dalhousie University and the Nova Scotia Technical College. A leading opponent was the *Chronicle-Herald*, which declared that approval of the union would be to cross "an educational Rubicon" since it would mean that the province would have one university, Dalhousie, and a number of affiliated colleges.[21] When Acadia and other institutions also objected, the proposal was doomed to failure. The house approved a compulsory seat-belt law that would not be proclaimed for another dozen years. The Conservatives and NDP resisted unsuccessfully the setting of the ombudsman's salary by the cabinet. Incomprehensibly, Agriculture Minister Hawkins thought it shameful even to suggest that the change might bring the ombudsman under the cabinet's influence. When Labour Minister Walter Fitzgerald complained about the "pussyfooting" attitude of other ministers towards a proposed multi-million-dollar Halifax waterfront development, the premier said simply, "I don't believe every member of cabinet has to have the same priorities . . . it isn't realistic."[22]

After three years' work the Graham Commission presented a 6,990-page report which argued that the fragmented municipal structure was hopelessly inefficient and recommended a reallocation of the functions of the provincial and municipal governments that involved the elimination of seven counties, the redrawing of municipal boundaries, and the reorganization of municipal administrative and financial structures. Apparently the commission felt that the political culture had reached a stage at which the populace would agree that what was theoretically best would actually be best, even if it meant laying rough hands on the existing county structure.

The premier's ebullience of early 1974 seemed to be dissipating towards year's end. The possibility of short-term offshore development had receded, the promised review of the Fundy tidal project had not occurred, John Shaheen had not started his oil refinery, the *Canadian Annual Review* suggested that the common-user dock might be the premier's "Achilles heel"[23], and a new steel complex at Gabarus about which the premier had expressed enthusiasm was less assured.

During the 1975 session a mild recession led McKeough and Akerman to demand a stimulant, not a depressant, to relieve unemployment. However, Nicholson contended that it would be "irresponsible and dangerous" to bring in a deficit budget. He was struggling with a situation in which an increase of $85 million in expenditures on health and education would drive the total up to $910 million, and he was adamant that the province's financial muscle was such that "we can only muster up one Sunday punch" and "now is not the time."[24]

In June the government moved to take over assessment from the municipalities in order to ensure uniformity over the province. It also announced that though it would not adopt the Graham Report it its entirety, it would use the report as a guide in developing policies of municipal reform. For example, it would itself not reduce the sixty-five municipal units to eleven, but it would consider amalgamation whenever individual municipal units requested it. Clearly the commission and the government differed widely on the nature of the changes that the political culture would tolerate.

In November Nicholson had further proposals for restraints in public spending but, recognizing the need to combat unemployment, he also outlined work projects that would provide 2,000 jobs during the winter. As 1975 ended the premier had few grounds for optimism. The Wreck Cove hydro project was receiving heavy criticism from environmentalists and its costs were escalating far beyond estimates. The Shaheen plans appeared to have collapsed; neither Fundy power nor the offshore provided any immediately hopeful signs; Sysco did not appear capable of operating on a profitable basis; and changing conditions in the world steel industry were dampening the prospects for a new steel complex at Gabarus. Worst of all, the premier's credibility suffered when, despite his earlier assurances, an increase in domestic oil prices took place on July 1st.

Early in 1976 the Conservatives settled the problem of leadership, which had become linked with drafting a party constitution providing for a leadership review. The constitution prepared by a special committee, after amendments by the provincial executive, would have required a review within twelve months of an election. At the party's annual meeting in January, some delegates, especially defeated candidate Joseph Stewart of Richmond, demanded an immediate vote on the leadership. Buchanan, who initially stated that votes of this kind tended to cause rifts, later insisted that he must know "whether this party is with me." He found that it was, because more than 80 per cent of the delegates voted by secret ballot against a leadership convention.[25] The constitution as approved provided for a leadership review twelve to eighteen months after an election. A decade later Buchanan would declare that the expression of confidence in him was "a turning point" from which there was "no turning back."[26]

The stage for 1976 was set in late January when the president of the Nova Scotia Power Corporation suggested that power rates might increase drastically. Not unexpectedly the speech from the throne forecast no new initiatives in public spending and demanded that Ottawa adopt policies to deal with serious regional problems such as energy. Buchanan described Development Minister George Mitchell as "a round peg in a square hole," while the *Chronicle-Herald* worried that the growing disparity in energy costs would be "a powerful barrier against new investment" in the region.[27] This was at a time when debate was occurring throughout Canada about the propriety of increased governmental intervention to solve ills. Perhaps in reply to Prime Minister Trudeau's statement that Canada must be changed fundamentally if it was to survive, Nova Scotia's Lieutenant-Governor Clarence Gosse declared publicly that the province's institutions were sufficiently strong to cope with contemporary problems without increasing government controls significantly. Gosse did not escape criticism for the intervention of the Crown's representative in political matters, but the *Chronicle-Herald* called it only "a cautiously low-key departure from the traditional homily."[28]

Despite Nicholson's difficulties he again budgeted for a surplus, though it required increases of 1 and 2 per cent in the health services and corporation taxes, and higher levies on tobacco, alcohol, and telephone calls. Businessmen warned him not to "kill the goose that laid the golden egg." Buchanan was appalled that people already burdened with the highest electric rates in Canada would suffer further from a higher sales tax. When, on March 18th, the president of the Power Corporation reported that the fuel adjustment charge might triple during the year and that a person paying $27.24 a month was likely to be billed $43.72 before long, Regan let loose at the federal officials who condemned Nova Scotia for failing to provide earlier for its future power needs. Nothing in the past, he said, disqualified the province from being assisted with power generation. Akerman gave him little comfort. When "all the sword fencing and all the political huffing and puffing" was over, it was the provincial government that was on the spot: "if [it] comes through, it will gain . . . respect and gratitude. . . . If it fails it can reap the harvest of the wild wind."[29]

The government could find no way to provide quick relief. Offshore drilling had increased, but bringing natural gas to the mainland was a long-term prospect. The same was true of the utilization of tidal power. Montreal Engineering Ltd. reported that, after the development of Wreck Cove, no further sites existed for large-scale hydro production. The government did what it could. It moved to put the Power Corporation under the scrutiny of the Public Utilities Board, but admitted that this action was "as much a reassurance for the public . . . as anything else."[30] The Regan government continued to ask the federal government for relief. It explored the possibility of using coal for power generation now that the high price of oil was making it competitive, but none of its actions did much to inspire public confidence.

Although energy matters dominated the house in 1976, the government also took action to have the province participate in an Atlantic regional lottery and announced major expansions of the Michelin plants at Granton and Bridgewater. Frustrated at times by assembly rules which had not been thoroughly reviewed for many years, the government employed Michael Ryle, a deputy principal clerk of the British House of Commons, as assistant clerk during the session and from him received a thirty-six-page report with recommendations for modernization. However, none of the premier's major projects was showing promise and, though his government received a federal power assistance grant of $63 million in December, it came at a time when the Public Utilities Board was considering an application for a 65 per cent increase in power rates.

Even the *Chronicle-Herald* seemed taken aback in 1977 by a speech from the throne which exhibited "a bit of something for everybody approach" but lacked any large or decisive programme to ameliorate economic difficulties. The provincial auditor was highly critical of $112 million in expenditures authorized without legislative sanction by no fewer than one hundred orders in council. Cautious as usual, Nicholson estimated a small surplus without resort to any increases in taxation except on liquor and tobacco. Although still highly regarded, he received his first strong attack. Calling him hopelessly out of tune with the times, Akerman asked him to resign. Thornhill perceived an underlying thread in the budget, "a thread almost of despair."[31]

In normal times the government's programme might not have seemed run-of-the-mill. The legislature agreed to increase the size of the Supreme Court from ten to thirteen by adding one judge to the appellate and two to the trial division; conferred responsibilities for legal aid upon a Nova Scotia Legal Aid Commission; converted highways to the metric system; established an Advisory Council on the Status of Women; and enacted the province's first Freedom of Information Act. An eight-man committee was appointed to consider the Ryle Report with a view to revising the house rules and procedures. Health Minister MacAskill pressed his colleagues without success to have the seat-belt legislation of 1974 proclaimed. Presaging difficulties for the future was the involvement of Metropolitan Area Growth Investments (MAGI) and hence the government in a cruise-ship operation. After only a single cruise *Mercator I*, in which the investment had been $5 million had ceased operations. The opposition did a good deal of ferreting but learned little.

Overshadowing everything else was the energy question. Gloom prevailed when the Public Utilities Board granted a 47.2 per cent power rate increase. Buchanan prophesied that the outcome would be the failure of the province's economy. A bitterly disappointed Akerman alleged that the board "went through the motions and made it appear as if they were not duped as they were." The president of the Power Corporation scornfully replied that self-appointed experts were as "plentiful as flies in a cow pasture."[32] When the premier declared that power rate increases were occurring elsewhere, the *Chronicle-Herald* told him that "illness is not unique to Nova Scotia but it would be a poor government which did not seek to provide the facilities for combatting the problem."[33] All Regan could do was to announce the start within a year of a prototype tidal-power project on the Annapolis River, and to promise a comprehensive proposal to relieve energy costs.

Clearly Regan's position was deteriorating. Intimations that he might get out of his difficulties by succeeding Clarence Campbell as president of the National Hockey League turned out to be unfounded. According to Buchanan, Conservative polls showed his party ahead of the Liberals in popularity and the premier trailing his own party. When the government finally decided on a by-election in Pictou Centre, the Conservatives increased their majority from 146 to 2,310 and the Liberals barely outpolled the NDP.

Generally the 1978 session was much like that of 1977. The speech from the throne repeated all the possibilities of securing cheaper power, mentioning particularly new initiatives in the use of coal and the province's partnership in the Maritime Energy Corporation. Pitilessly, Akerman told Regan that he had ventured on a misguided course during the previous eight years by dreaming "the impossible dream" and overlooking the province's natural resources. "We must hold everything we have, expand on our indigenous industries . . . and then we can go looking for the dream"[34] by pursuing the Rothschilds and the Shaheens. Despite what Nicholson called "some fuzzy haired" advisers, he refused to venture on deficit financing, and his $1.3 billion budget forecast a small surplus, the seventh in a row.

This year a select committee on redistribution used a new formula. A county having a population of up to 20,000 would receive one member; 20,000-39,999, two members; 40,000-59,999, three; 120,000-139,999, six; and 280,000-299,999, fourteen members. The result was to increase the size of the assembly by six members to fifty-two, four of the additional members to go to Halifax. In a special session in July the house approved the completion of the work by an Electoral Boundary Commission.

A second committee proposed major changes in the house rules, based on the Ryle Report. Among other things the open-ended question period on Tuesdays and Thursdays would become forty minutes on Tuesdays, Wednesdays, and Thursdays; Wednesdays would be "opposition days" in which the leader of a recognized opposition party would have the right to call bills and resolutions of his choice. The speaker anticipated that the changes would permit the house to perform three months' work in two, but their adoption would await the decision of a later session.

This year the government could not escape a barrage of criticism for its participation in MAGI, the outcome of which was to leave on its hands the white elephant cruise ship *Mercator I*, eventually to be tied up in Shelburne harbour awaiting disposition. The energy situation was also steadily worsening. If the Power Corporation's request for a 20 per cent increase in rates was granted, it would mean that Nova Scotians would be paying 140 per cent more for power than they had four years earlier. Buchanan's argument that the government's takeover of Nova Scotia Light and Power was partly responsible appeared to have little merit. In any case the only thing that mattered to the public was the prospective increase.

Probably the premier would have called an election for late 1977 except for his party's poor showing in the Pictou Centre by-election and except for his own polls which, like those of the Conservatives, had shown the Liberals in second place. Throughout 1978 he found the situation no more propitious. Early in the year he tried to minimize the energy problem by pointing out that when other provinces would be struggling with oil at $30 a barrel, "Nova Scotia's tides will still be flowing and the coal reserves would still be there to be tapped."[35] Except for the steady development of offshore fishing resulting from the establishment of a 200-mile economic zone, general economic conditions were also unfavourable. Unemployment, though the lowest in the Atlantic Provinces, was still high at 10.2 per cent. Facing an uncertain future was the Halifax Shipyards, which the government had taken over, not by choice, from Hawker

Siddeley and then sold to a Canadian-Dutch consortium after providing most of the money for the transaction. To counter the general economic malaise, the premier resorted to a refuge of Nova Scotia's politicians and promised his best to wrench the national parties and Canadian business generally from "their blind commitment" to centralization.[36]

Believing that the political climate might get worse before it got better, he had an election set for September 19th. Perhaps underestimating Buchanan, just as the Conservatives had underestimated himself in 1970, he hoped to conduct a campaign that would overcome his low standing in the polls. A delighted Akerman prophesied that it would be the first three-party fight in the province's history. Generally Akerman's approach was pragmatic rather than doctrinaire. Declaring that the old parties were tied hand and foot to big corporations, he made a special appeal to small business. Because much of the old radical left had departed, he had been able to broaden the party membership, helped by his outstanding performance and moderate course in the legislature. Its strong showing in the Pictou Centre by-election led the NDP to expect considerable success on the mainland.

Buchanan's campaign centred on high unemployment, high electricity rates, and the position of the monarchy. Described as next to Diefenbaker the country's most ardent monarchist, he lambasted Ottawa's tinkering with the role of the Queen. Even though supposedly his first priority was to provide jobs, he concentrated on ways to bring energy under control. To that end he promised subsidies for the time being and stabilized rates in the long term. "The past policy of band-aids yesterday, band-aids now and band-aids tomorrow is sheer, inexcusable negligence." Buchanan's course would be to reduce dependence on oil through tidal and solar power, a greater use of coal, and more efficient administration by the Power Corporation.

The Liberals put their chief reliance on the premier, of whom Attorney General Mitchell said when referring to Buchanan, "It's not a question of comparing oranges to apples. It is more like comparing watermelons to grapes."[37] According to a *Chronicle-Herald* reporter, Regan had mellowed somewhat from the brash, fast-talking politician who had become premier in 1970 but was still a master of astute political manoeuvring.

On returning from Ottawa in February he had been besieged by reporters who wanted to know if he had taken his hairdresser and film crew with him. Realizing the possibility of political damage in an election year, he called a news conference at which he appeared wearing a blond wig. The reporters erupted in merriment and the premier easily convinced them that expenditures on hairdressers and the like were necessities for a politician seeking to win re-election in a media-conscious age.[38]

On the hustings Regan had lost none of his old vigour. In particular he promised to emphasize the indigenous resource sector and foresaw a new agency, Fisheries Nova Scotia, which would promote fish sales within the province. Home-owners would be allowed to deduct the first $1,000 paid each year in mortgage interest in calculating their provincial income tax. The first rebate of its kind in Canada, the premier hoped that Ottawa might introduce a similar one. As he knew all too well, his political future depended upon how convincing a case he could make on energy. Hence he promised, as a priority, to "bridge the gap" between dependence on oil and reliance on the new coal-fired generators at Lingan. This was "not a deathbed repentance," he declared, since he had used every conceivable means since 1973 to reduce energy costs. But, try as he might, he could not convince the electors that he could bridge the gap.

The election produced a geographical division of seats the like of which Nova Scotia had never before seen. The Conservatives elected no one on Cape Breton Island; the NDP took four seats in Cape Breton County and the Liberals took the remaining island seats. On the mainland the Liberals won the two eastern and the three western counties but only three other seats — Halifax Needham, Halifax Chebucto, and Cumberland Centre — for a total of seventeen. The Conservatives only won seats in the core of the mainland, but they ensured victory by taking thirty-one of its thirty-four seats.

The NDP added one seat to its total, raised its popular vote from 13.0 to 14.4 per cent, and ran second in Pictou Centre, but its leader was sorely disappointed. As usual, when Nova Scotians wish to defeat a government, they turn to the party most likely to do it. Regan was not surprised. For two years his polls had shown that the energy question might lead to his defeat, and his campaigning did nothing to change these results.[39] Workers of all parties who rang door bells in Halifax knew the outcome long before election day. The county that had elected eight Liberals and two Conservatives in 1974 gave the Liberals only two of its fourteen seats this time.

Conservatives who in 1970 had prophesied dire results from the installation of any government headed by Regan were clearly wrong. His administration had turned out to be a credible one which under normal circumstances might well have won re-election in 1978. More than anything else, the actions of OPEC were responsible for its defeat. In combination with Nicholson, Regan had ensured financial responsibility of the highest order; indeed, to some, balanced budgets became almost a fetish that took precedence over the government's political needs. Apparently Regan went along with Nicholson's determination to produce surpluses, even if it prevented a resort to energy subsidies on a scale that might have saved the government.

Some senior civil servants believed that Regan, "a peripatetic premier," did not spend sufficient time participating in the development of policy, but all agreed that he was a man of ability. When *The 4th Estate* conducted random sampling in 1975, it found a strong feeling that Regan had tended to run "a one-man government, with himself assuming a high profile in the public eye."[40] Even if wholly valid, this perception accounted only minimally for his defeat. The major cause was that the circumstances of the time prevented any of his major dreams, and particularly those relating to energy, from being realized, and he became the first premier since Confederation who, having had one or more electoral victories, later suffered defeat. Premiers such as Angus Macdonald and Robert Stanfield, who had built up highly attractive images of themselves, might have survived the storm, but — as will be shown later — comparatively recent changes in the political culture of Nova Scotia may militate against long tenures in the future.

CHAPTER 13

Buchanan: No Cuts in Services despite Deficits

The Conservatives had been out of office only eight years, and so Buchanan had five assemblymen with previous legislative experience suitable for inclusion in his fifteen-member cabinet. For the moment he took over the finance portfolio and his chief lieutenant, Roland Thornhill, the department of development. When the legislature met in December 1978, heading the agenda was a proposal to create 8,500 new jobs through Task Force Nova Scotia and its twelve divisions. Three departments received new names. Of the change from simply recreation to culture, recreation and fitness, Thornhill said that its reorganization would ensure that it was "more than a mere cheque-writing extension of the government."[1]

At the resumed session in 1979 the premier announced a task force which would examine a thirty-year accumulation of regulations and, among other things, identify those that impeded small business. The department of the provincial secretary, which dated back to the beginning of British settlement and from which most other departments had been broken off, became even more insignificant. In reorganizing his cabinet the premier announced the establishment of the policy board headed by himself to make policy analyses for the full cabinet, and the management board which replaced the treasury board and took over the management and implementation of policies, including their financial supervision. In an accompanying cabinet shuffle Joel Matheson became minister of finance.

Buchanan used the occasion to accuse the Regan government of acting as if provincial moneys were endless and declared that "we are now in a position where we must cut spending." When he blamed his predecessors for a projected deficit of $76.8 million for 1979-80, Peter Nicholson — defeated in the election — declared that before he had left office he had required financial statements from all departments and was convinced that none was "grossly over- or under-spent."[2]

The session adjourned to let the members participate in the federal election of May 22nd in which Nova Scotians heard a great deal about energy and industrial development. NDP national leader Ed Broadbent favoured a complete modernization of Sysco and a shipbuilding policy in which the federal government would assume a major equity position in Halifax Industries Ltd. Prime Minister Trudeau prophesied that "coal will again become king in Cape Breton" and boasted that his government had already given $3 million towards making Fundy power a reality. However, he denied any possibility of the Atlantic Provinces getting jurisdiction over their offshore. The Fathers of Confederation, he said with dubious validity, had decided otherwise 112 years earlier. To him it had made good sense then and still did. In a front-page editorial the *Chronicle-Herald* condemned him for his general constitutional stance and especially for trying to "bulldoze the other parties in Confederation. . . . *the federal government, as a creature of the union of the provinces, and not their creator, has no moral right to assume the role as the lord and master of all things*. The constitution belongs to the people of Canada, not the prime minister."[3]

Long before the election Joe Clark had promised Nova Scotia complete control of its offshore and generous support to modernize Sysco. A mine having been shown to be feasible in the Donkin area, he agreed to help bring it into production. When he also promised to negotiate contracts with industries locating or expanding in Atlantic Canada which would exempt them from federal income taxes until 150 per cent of their investment had been recouped, Development Minister Thornhill said, "I've never been as encouraged by any political statement as by this one."[4]

John M. Buchanan   1978

The results in Nova Scotia were the same as in 1974: nine Conservatives, two Liberals and one NDP. Thus the province made a significant contribution towards producing a Conservative minority government. For Clark it was a very considerable victory to have done as well as Stanfield five years earlier. For

Allan MacEachen it was the continuing story of winning few seats in the province in which he was his party's federal leader.

Throughout 1979 the energy question remained dominant. In March the budget provided an additional subsidy of $18.4 million to keep increases in power rates close to those in the cost of living. However, though the province signed an agreement to build an experimental tidal project on the Annapolis River, and Mobil Oil made significant discoveries of natural gas off Sable Island, prospects of short-term relief for energy consumers were anything but bright. In October the premier unveiled a new $1.2 billion energy policy stressing the reduction of dependence on foreign oil and the use of domestic fuel sources. Provincial initiative led the Clark government to accept a proposal to sink a new coal shaft at Donkin which would provide fuel for two large thermal plants at Lingan.

The legislature ended its 1979 session stormily in December. In April Labour Minister Kenneth Streatch had introduced a bill to satisfy Michelin Tires, not known for its rapport with trade unions. The bill proposed to amend the Trade Union Act so that, in integrated manufacturing facilities that involved two or more factories within a single company, trade union certification would require company-wide, not just single factory, approval. Since Michelin was the only Nova Scotian company fitting that description, organized labour denounced it as the Michelin bill. When Streatch withdrew it in April, Regan called it "the greatest retreat since Napoleon left Moscow."[5]

However, in December it was back, unchanged in principle. To Gerald Yetman and the Nova Scotia Federation of Labour the villain was not Streatch but Thornhill. The latter contended that the bill would promote the labour stability that had become even more necessary now that Michelin would be building a third plant in Nova Scotia and expanding those at Granton and Bridgewater. He did not want to see Nova Scotians become pawns in an international game. The United Rubber Workers could unionize the Michelin employees and, allied with the labour lobby in Washington, ensure that if anyone was out of work because of a weak world rubber market, the rubber workers in Akron and other American cities would be the last to leave the shop floor.[6]

The Nova Scotia Federation of Labour did everything it could to fight the bill; Yetman even vowed not to meet again with Streatch on any subject. After presenting their case, the government forces sat silent while their opponents conducted something of a filibuster. When the bill finally passed by twenty-six to sixteen, Yetman called it "a black Friday for the democratic rights of Nova Scotians."

By years' end Canada was immersed in its second election within a year following the defeat of John Crosbie's budget and especially the proposal to increase the excise tax on gasoline by 18 cents a gallon. Adding to his programme of the last election, Ed Broadbent promised Nova Scotia and Atlantic Canada a national fish-marketing agency similar to the Canada Wheat Board and a change in the Foreign Investment Review Agency to permit a different application to areas where Canadian capital was unavailable. The Liberals, confident of victory if they kept Trudeau under wraps and made no serious errors, avoided specificity in their platform. However, they did promise Nova Scotians that energy would become the core of regional development. By blending the costs of existing domestic, new domestic, and imported crude oil, they would establish a domestic price that would be below the world price and yet permit taxation revenues which could be used for regional development projects.

Well behind in the polls, Prime Minister Clark fought a rearguard action. After singling out his contributions to Nova Scotia's energy undertakings, he warned that the Liberal refusal to transfer offshore resources to the provinces would turn coastal residents into second-class citizens. However, in the election of February 1980, Nova Scotians, like Canadians generally, reacted against his government. The Liberals took Halifax and Southwest Nova from the Conservatives, and Cape Breton — The Sydneys from the NDP, for a final provincial standing of six Conservatives and five Liberals. It was the closest that Allan MacEachen would come to winning a majority of seats in the province and his party actually led in the popular vote, 39.9 per cent to 38.7 for the Conservatives.

Gerald Regan having moved successfully to the federal scene, Benoit Comeau became Liberal house leader in 1980. Finance

Minister Matheson exulted that he had reduced the projected deficit from $76 million to $61.2 million and that he was forecasting a deficit of only $16.2 million for the next year on record spending of $1.8 billion. Because $172 million, or 48.5 per cent of the capital budget, was devoted to resource management, he called it a development budget, but Akerman saw "cause for neither dancing in the streets nor for wearing sackcloth and ashes."[7] The government's proposals to protect the provincial heritage, give the provincial court a chief judge, and establish a judicial council to hear complaints against provincial judges received little opposition. Though the government had produced several drafts of a new freedom of information act, it decided not to proceed until it examined a proposed federal act. At long last the legislature agreed to new rules based largely on the Ryle Report which were designed to streamline the legislative process without impairing the functions of the opposition.

The energy problem remained as intractable as ever. Buchanan stated emphatically that he would oppose any increase in the price of oil until the province could convert largely to coal-generated electricity. When federal Energy Minister Lalonde pointed out the cost would be $500 million over the next seven or eight years and Ottawa did not have that kind of money, the premier declared that a provincial subsidy would prevent any increases to domestic and commercial users in 1980 and 1981. This and similar decisions may have been a principal factor in his future political successes. The government's position on another aspect of the energy question became manifest in its Petroleum Resources Act which claimed total ownership of the offshore. Akerman called it a "terrible risk" to bet everything on "one spin of the wheel," but Buchanan could see no harm in demanding ownership even if the basic problems centred around questions of control such as: Who issues the licences? Who determines pipeline construction from offshore to inshore?[8]

The year 1980 was of considerable significance for all three parties. Thornhill complained bitterly of "intense efforts to destroy my political and personal reputation" through the circulation of letters full of "innuendo and allusions" to members of the media. He had suffered serious financial losses which, after investigation by senior banking officials, were settled for a fraction of the total. Thornhill maintained that the resolution of his difficulties followed conventional banking practices, but the Liberals tried to discover if it took place before or after he had become a cabinet minister and accused Buchanan of being less than forthright about the debt. For the moment at least the incident did not hurt the Conservatives, because in three by-elections in May they gained two seats from the Liberals and cut their majority substantially in the third. Conservative Edmund Morris, the victor by twenty-six votes in Regan's old riding of Halifax Needham, declared: "a win is a win is a win."

To choose a successor to Regan the Liberals met in convention in June and after three ballots chose Alexander (Sandy) Cameron over Vincent (Vince) MacLean by 558 to 356. Some said that Cameron was a Robert Stanfield type of leader, while others contended that he was the choice of the party establishment.

The NDP provided the major dramatics in 1980. Akerman resigned as leader in May. None had performed better than he in the legislature and, though the Cape Breton control of the party had succeeded in electing more members than the academic mainland management that had preceded it, he had been profoundly disappointed by the results in 1978. Some party purists were unhappy for another reason: that the successes had resulted from "manipulative politics" rather than reliance on "even mildly left-wing principles."[9] Akerman's resignation led his constituents to feel that they had been betrayed, the more so when he accepted a high office from the Buchanan government. Paul MacEwan, however, caused the NDP its greatest trouble. Freed from the restraint of Akerman, he made statements and published writings such as *The Akerman Years* in which he and his leader were pictured as having been continually menaced by a conspiracy "out to get them" and determined to undermine the Cape Breton party leadership.[10]

MacEwan went too far for his party's executive when he declared that its lack of co-operation had forced out Akerman, and that Trotskyite elements bent on seizing control were infiltrating the party. In the absence of MacEwan and the executive's Cape Breton members, the executive expelled him from the party on June 15th. The next month the provincial party council presided over by David Lewis rejected his appeal by fifty-six to twelve. Though the NDP assemblymen, by a vote of two to one, allowed him to remain a member of the legislative caucus, the party's leadership convention decided that only a party member in good standing could attend caucus meetings. The convention chose Alexa McDonough, who took 237 of the 320 votes, as its leader. MacEwan's response was to establish the Cape Breton Labor Party, which in the immediate future would seriously hurt the NDP.

The government proposed no significant legislation in 1981, but the "generality, diversity, and length" of the speech from the throne led to rumours of an election despite gloomy economic predictions. The crucial factor was that the party's polls, including that of the.party's national pollster, Allan Gregg, showed the Conservatives well ahead. Apparently Buchanan had learned a basic lesson from the defeat of Gerald Regan. Despite the prophecy of Liberal William Gillis that the province was "heading into fiscal higher-space," Matheson's $2.3 billion budget forecast a deficit of $139.9 million and capital expenditures that would raise the net debt to more than $1 billion. In justification he declared that it would have been "morally and financially irresponsible" to let power rates increase by 15 per cent under the depressed conditions of 1981."[11] Though as part of a bargain the government had agreed to assume responsibility for a Sysco debt of more than $300 million, it secured a revitalization and business plan for Sysco in which Ottawa promised to finance up to 80 per cent of a total commitment of $100 million. The Conservative party thus undoubtedly strengthened itself in Cape Breton.

Education Minister Terence (Terry) Donahoe, son of Richard Donahoe, announced the government's intention to proceed with implementing the major recommendations of the Walker Commission on Public Education Finance. To reduce the large number of educational authorities it would provide incentive grants of $17 million to secure their consolidation. The inducement was such that in a relatively short time all parts of the province except the town of Hantsport came under district school boards. This genuine revolution in educational administration was made possible because, unlike proposals in the Graham Report, it did not clash with the province's political culture.

During the session the Liberals unsuccessfully demanded the resignation of Speaker Arthur Donahoe for not interpreting the new rules as they wished; and they sought to revive the Thornhill affair, but without much success. They also tried to make political capital out of Portland Estates, 500 acres of which had been expropriated by the Regan government and which Buchanan, because of different plans, decided to return in large measure to its original owners. Calling it an exercise in "raw political power," the Liberals accused the government of using public funds to bail out its political friends. The NDP joined the Liberals in condemning the government's Freedom of Information Act as being no better than the Liberal act of 1977. To them its confidentiality clause would allow the government to refuse any information it wished to keep secret.

The most heated debate occurred on the work of the Provincial Electoral Commission, composed of non-assemblymen, which had been charged with eliminating the remaining two-seat constituencies of Yarmouth and Inverness counties. Its five members — three Conservatives and two from the other parties — had no difficulty in dividing Yarmouth but, in creating an Inverness South which had half the population and one-quarter the area of Inverness North, its Conservatives were charged with trying to create a safe seat for William Joseph (Billy Joe) MacLean, the Mayor of Port Hawkesbury. Despite evidence by opposition assemblymen that the division had been prearranged, they could effect only a minor change in the proposal. The Conservatives made little attempt to justify the provisions even though the *Chronicle-Herald* advised them to "take another look."[12]

In announcing an election for October 6th — only three years and seventeen days after the last one — the premier contended that he had completed his 1978 mandate, including building a firm foundation for the future in energy, and that the time had arrived to determine the leadership to deal with new challenges. Alexa McDonough agreed that the principal issue was leadership, but not the kind being sold by the other parties and certainly not "five steady weeks of John Buchanan shaking hands, kissing babies, and handing out long-overdue approval for public projects funded by our tax dollars." She promised to have the Michelin bill repealed and a provincial energy corporation established, but she would not spend her time dreaming up "election goodies"; rather her party would work towards a secure future for all Nova Scotians and a government "free of influence peddling, patronage and cynicism."[13]

Early in the campaign Cameron dealt mainly with the government's record, often in strong language. The Conservatives, he said, wanted a mandate to "complete the rape of your wallet without having to face you in an election for five years."[14] Starting on September 23rd he presented his specific policies in piecemeal fashion: a one-year, $8 million relief programme providing property tax relief; a one-year freeze on residential power rates; and the elimination of provincial operating deficits within ten years. Buchanan's approach was one of unbounded optimism. Using the slogan, "Our Future is Here," he emphasized offshore development and major economic growth. The Conservatives made extensive use of one-quarter-page advertisements lauding the premier for stabilizing power rates, protecting the dignity of senior citizens, and trying to build a world-class hospital at Camp Hill.

For the *Globe and Mail* reporter the campaign was "the dullest, and by all accounts, most cynical . . . in recent memory." Certainly it evoked little enthusiasm, 23,582 fewer voting than in 1978 and the turnout falling from 78.2 to 74.2 per cent, the lowest since 1945. The Liberals were the chief losers, their seats reduced from seventeen to thirteen, their popular vote from 39.4 to 33.2 per cent, the lowest to date since Confederation. Largely because of the MacEwan affair, the NDP lost all its seats in Cape Breton and, adding insult to injury, MacEwan himself took Cape Breton Nova. Overall, however, the party's popular vote reached 18.1 per cent, the highest to date. McDonough herself won Halifax Chebucto, her party's first victory on the mainland, and in Halifax County the party polled 24.9 per cent of the vote, only slightly behind the Liberals.

The Conservatives again failed to win seats in the five counties on the extremities of the mainland, but they had nothing but triumphs elsewhere as they took thirty-seven of the fifty-two seats and 47.5 per cent of the vote. This time they won seven of the eleven Cape Breton seats, including Inverness South. For John Buchanan, who even after 1978 had a few Conservative skeptics, this election created a strengthening of his position beyond any doubt. By this time he had made himself widely known throughout the province and become generally regarded as "a nice guy."

The future declared to be here during the election seemed to have evaporated in 1982. Recession came later to Nova Scotia than other parts of Canada, but "when it arrived, it hit with a vengeance."[15] Both opposition leaders were outraged when the government announced a light legislative programme. To McDonough it was "quite fantastic" for the government to be "sitting back and waiting for prosperity to be thrust upon us. . . . There are no programmes, no legislation, no action."[16]

The opposition continued with its heavy criticism of the province's finances. When it appeared as if the deficit for 1981-82 might reach $187 million, Liberal finance critic Gillis warned that Nova Scotia, already ninth among the provinces, was sliding to the "bottom of the credit ratings." Matheson refused to apologize for deficits resulting from the stabilization of power rates and alleged that recent drastic cutbacks by Ottawa meant, in effect, "a massive shift of the federal deficit to the province." Almost forced into action, he presented a budget with large tax increases: the health services tax went from 8 to 10 per cent; the provincial income tax to 56.5 per cent of the federal; and the corporation tax to 15 per cent. He also imposed additional levies on liquor, tobacco, long-distance calls, and insurance premiums. Even so, escalating costs might produce a deficit of $300 million. Gillis called the budget "a toboggan ride to oblivion." If it "heralds our future, God help all of us."[17] To complaints from the *Chronicle-Herald* the premier replied that the fault lay with the Liberal government of the 1970s which had added new programmes when revenues were buoyant; now the programmes were in place, but not the money to pay for them.[18]

Positive legislation was noticeably absent in 1982. The government failed to strengthen the Freedom of Information Act despite charges that in five years it had not facilitated the release of a single piece of previously withheld information.[19] The opposition complained that much of the Walker Report had been put in place by "blackmail" and "bludgeoning tactics." However, once again it was energy questions which dominated the political scene. In March an agreement was finally reached by which the province would get most of the revenue from the offshore resources, while the federal government retained management control. On the crucial question of electricity rates the Power Corporation asked for a 35 per cent increase in August and received one of 31 per cent in December. A government subsidy that limited the increase for consumers to 17 per cent indicated once again the Buchanan government's continuing sensitivity on this question.

The speech from the throne in 1983 indicated another housekeeping session although a single sentence promised a long-heralded restraint programme through the adoption of a public sector wage and salary policy. Cameron found the speech "morally unacceptable" for its failure to deal with unemployment; McDonough called it "totally lacking in thrust . . . no vision at all." Later, when Gillis condemned the trebling of the provincial debt since 1978, Matheson replied that the "ability to pay is subject to our economic growth which is now stated in terms of billions rather than millions." When Matheson budgeted for a deficit of $248.5 million for 1983-84, Gillis accused him of bringing Nova Scotia to a "rendez-vous with financial disaster." In one hundred years the province had accumulated a net debt of $500 million; in six years Buchanan had more than quadrupled this figure.[20]

To avoid having itself determine the remuneration of the members, the house agreed to allow the speaker to appoint a commission each autumn to review and decide on the indemnities and salaries of assemblymen, cabinet ministers, the speaker, and the leader of the opposition. McDonough criticized the practice, operative only in Nova Scotia, of paying assemblymen a lump sum for membership on a committee, even if it met only once a session or perhaps not at all. For this she drew heckling and boos from both Liberals and Conservatives. Though anything but a momentous session, the assemblymen put 2.6 million words in Hansard and spoke 624,000 words during the unpublished debates on the estimates.

In one matter the auspices looked good for the government during the 1984 session. Seven rigs were operating on the offshore and about 150 gas- and oil-related industries had established themselves within the province. McDonough declared that "the premier and his senior ministers seemed to be so awed by the big boys — the oil barons, the governors and utility officials in the United States, the federal government — that they have lost sight of what they were elected for."[21] Yet the speech from the throne dealt primarily with human resources and improvement of public services. More particularly it promised to tackle social problems such as drunk driving and pornography, and forecast the appointment of two deputy ministers in the labour and manpower, and the education departments to help meet the demands of the workplace. Nonetheless, Cameron complained that 86 of 101 paragraphs in the speech constituted "a history lesson" on earlier government undertakings.

As usual, finance dominated the session. Gillis expressed horror that the annual interest on the provincial debt would reach $354 million, and the Halifax Board of Trade wanted an across-the-board cut of 5 per cent in government spending. However, the government determinedly adhered to its decision not to cut services. Gregory (Greg) Kerr, the new Minister of Finance, forecast total expenditures of $3.2 billion, the largest in history, and only a slightly reduced deficit of $194.3 million. An outraged Gillis declared that "I don't see how in God's name we could do worse." Of the cut in estimated snow removal costs, he said scornfully, "Possibly King John, alias the premier, is going to abolish winter."[22] Buchanan himself told the Halifax Board of Trade that their demands would have serious consequences: closed hospital beds, the elimination of the children's dental programme, and a reduction in the level of services for seniors. "To have done otherwise [than engage in deficit financing] would have been to fail in our responsibilities to Nova Scotians."[23]

Once again the issue of power rates erupted in controversy. "No other issue seems to cut the premier's fuse shorter," wrote one newspaperman, "than the price Nova Scotians pay for electricity."[24] When Cameron argued, despite Conservative contentions, that the costs in Nova Scotia were not close to the national average, Buchanan rushed back to the house to engage him in acrimonious debate. Later both the president of the

Power Corporation and the energy minister announced that no increase in power rates would take place before April 1, 1986, even though the price of coal would rise substantially. That brought charges from the Liberals that the corporation had secured much larger increases than necessary in 1983 in order to build up a slush fund which would obviate increases before the next election. One thing was certain: the political acumen of John Buchanan was not at fault.

A bill of some significance banned extra billing by doctors, and Nova Scotia became the first province to enact such legislation. Another bill let the cabinet designate an Acadian region for educational purposes even if it was within the boundaries of an existing district board. The board of the new region could then devise a curriculum that adhered to provincial regulations on the proportion of instruction to be given in French and English. Once the course of study was approved, the region would be eligible for additional funding. During the session Paul MacEwan told Alexa McDonough to stay out of Cape Breton and not take votes away from his party. "Let the NDP run in the 41 mainland ridings. That's all they're interested in anyway."[25]

By the summer of 1984 John Turner had become the Liberal national leader and prime minister, and had an election set for September 4th. Immediately Brian Mulroney bid a "somewhat tearful farewell" to Central Nova to run in Quebec; and Allan MacEachen gave up his Cape Breton Highlands — Canso seat to become Liberal leader in the Senate. Generally the Nova Scotia campaign followed that in the other provinces. All three leaders agreed that the troubled Nova Scotia steel and coal industries should be kept in operation. Turner also promised the assistance needed to facilitate the early development of the Venture offshore gas field and warned that Conservative energy policies would delay it. Mulroney proclaimed that he would have "no hesitation in inflicting prosperity on Atlantic Canada" and promised to treat the fisheries department as a major portfolio, not manned as "a farm team" like the Liberals, who had given it twelve different ministers since 1968. Nova Scotia joined the rest of Canada in the Conservative landslide. The Liberals won Cape Breton East — Richmond and Cape

Breton — The Sydneys, but the Conservatives took the remaining nine seats, polling 50.8 per cent of the vote to the Liberals 33.6 and the NDP's 15.2. Lawrence O'Neil, who won Allan MacEachen's old seat, declared that he did not want to be the "Patronage King" of the riding.

The Conservatives were riding a tidal wave, and rumours were rife that a provincial election was imminent, especially because the next year might bring a higher deficit and bleaker economic prospects.[26] Forestalled temporarily by the visit of the Queen and the Pope, Buchanan waited twenty-four days before having an election set for November 6th. He vigorously denied that he was taking advantage of the Mulroney landslide: "I've never gone to victory on anybody's coattails but [on] the policies of our party." Once again he argued that an election was needed because his government had fulfilled its mandate; however, somewhat puzzling was his contention that elections should not be "fought on issues . . . [but] on the basis of asking for a mandate to carry out the policies of a government."[27] His opponents promptly replied that the public wanted him to pronounce on many issues, especially the mismanagement of the finances, the offshore, and energy. Buchanan, however, maintained as the general thrust of his campaign his contention that Nova Scotians were at a critical time in their history, that they must adjust to the modern world, and that only the Conservatives could provide the decisive leadership that was needed. On specific questions he promised no tax increases, unconditional support to the traditional Cape Breton industries, complete commitment to Fundy tidal power, and substantial aid to ease traffic problems in the metropolitan areas.

Hopeful that his Cape Breton Labor party would be third in assembly seats, MacEwan got eleven candidates to run under its banner, all but one from Cape Breton, and one more than the number required for status under the Nova Scotia Elections Act. Even more optimistic, Alexa McDonough saw the possibility of her party becoming the official opposition. She complained about the difficulty of contending with the Conservatives, who chose to use mass-marketing methods to sell themselves as a commodity like Pepsi-Cola or McDonald's hamburgers. She was especially critical of grants to large corporations and demanded that the premier announce a programme for small business.

Cameron attacked the management board for not introducing restraint and promised to tackle unemployment by upgrading programmes in fishing, farming, and forestry. A fortnight before election day, perhaps to revive a flagging campaign, he raised an earlier issue having to do with specific assemblymen's expense accounts. Under threats of prosecution he diluted his charges somewhat, but he refused to back down on his contention that the attorney general's department had interfered with an RCMP investigation into the matter. In a televised leaders' debate this topic occupied the first third of the ninety-minute proceedings, but nothing emerged that hurt the government seriously.

The Conservatives won massively, increasing their number of members from thirty-seven to forty-two and their popular vote from 47.5 to 50.6 per cent. The Liberals elected only six members, down from thirteen, and their popular vote fell from 33.2 to 31.3 per cent, the lowest since Confederation. The NDP's popular vote dropped from 18.1 to 15.9 per cent, but it won three seats, all on the mainland. In Cape Breton County, formerly its chief source of strength, its vote fell from 11,639 to 4,709, while the Cape Breton Labor party polled 7,951 votes. MacEwan was elected again through his "remarkable constituency work" and especially his "rendering of basic political favours." Of him one critic wrote: "Politics for MacEwan is not about having the right position on the issues, but about getting elected . . . his is a history of methods and techniques that can make even his strongest supporters squeamish."[28] The NDP made its best showing in Halifax County where it polled 27.6 per cent of the vote to the Liberals' 25.0 and elected two of its members. McDonough could say, "I do not intend to stand alone anymore."[29]

Though conscientious and industrious, Sandy Cameron had failed to capture the popular imagination. The *Chronicle-Herald* faulted the Liberals, who, after hammering away at deficits and debts for five years, "failed to produce any sort of debt-reduction program."[30] Perhaps the party should have remembered that although deficits and debts had been major targets of opposition parties for many years, they had seldom been crucial in elections and never when factors like those in 1984 were present — an improvement, even if small, in the economic climate; no increases in taxation; relative stability in oil prices; the running of a Conservative tide; and a personally popular premier.

This election the Conservatives had concentrated their resources on seats formerly held by Liberals[31] and were perhaps more successful than they had hoped. Except for Cape Breton South and Cape Breton Nova, they had won all of the island's eleven seats. In the seven seats at both ends of the mainland they had lost only the single ridings of Antigonish and Shelburne, even defeating Liberal leader Cameron in Guysborough. However, they had also lost four seats where internal difficulties had existed: Dartmouth East, where the sitting member had been tried but acquitted on criminal charges; Lunenburg East, where the party organization was badly split; Kings South, where the sitting member was not fully accepted by his party; and Sackville, where the expense accounts of the sitting member had become a major issue.

A government at its zenith in November 1984 quickly came down from the heights, and no speech from the throne could have forecast more of a housekeeping session than that of 1985. It emphasized that the resources of every government department and agency would be used to "create the climate in which the private sector can expand to secure permanent jobs." Naturally McDonough accused the government of being afflicted with "private-sector mania and public-sector phobia."[32] The speech also promised action to increase trade and jobs but, after discovering that Thornhill's much-touted Trade Development Authority consisted of little more than the creation of a ministers' committee and a trade council made up of private citizens to advise the government, the opposition lambasted it for introducing nothing new. The only employment it would create, said Liberal house leader Vince MacLean, are "a few jobs for a couple of [Thornhill's] political friends."[33]

After eleven years compulsory seat-belt legislation had finally taken effect at the beginning of 1985. Although both the Regan and Buchanan governments had feared to proclaim it, the public accepted it with hardly a murmur. However, the state of the finances drew its usual round of criticism from the opposition. Kerr continued to insist that under no conditions would the government reduce services. Though revenues would increase because of a reduction in sales tax exemptions, the deficit for 1985-86 was forecast to be $184 million, and during the year the net debt would probably exceed $3 billion. Drawing widespread protests was the "kiddies' tax," which resulted from lowering expenditures subject to sales tax from 50 to 25 cents. Reduced by $15 million were the capital and special grants expected by the municipalities. MacLean called it a "pretty sleazy way" to run the province, but the government contended that it had no choice because of a smaller increase in federal funding, especially in equalization grants.

Because the legislative programme was light, the opposition focussed its attention elsewhere to its advantage. McDonough unleashed her attack on Thornhill, whom she accused of creating thirty-seven additional committee positions in order to find work for the forty-two Conservative members. Later Thornhill admitted that his proposals constituted an error in judgment and proposed a ten-member committee chaired by the speaker to review committee rules and remuneration, a course which the NDP leader had been advocating for some time.[34]

Unable to get satisfactory replies to his charges that counties with Conservative members had received additional highway funds before the last election, MacLean got the chief electoral officer's agreement to investigate a so-called "slush fund." He was even more dissatisfied with the government's treatment of members' expense claims. Finding that much of the overpayment to former Sackville member Malcolm MacKay had been forgiven, he questioned this "exemption from the law." He was no less disturbed to discover that officials of the attorney general's department, after conversations with the RCMP, had decided not to lay charges against Billy Joe MacLean. Told that he himself could initiate action with the RCMP, Vince MacLean eventually did with results favourable to himself. As the premier himself seemed to admit, it was the opposition's session. "I've been 20 years at this business," he said, "and I've seen storms come and go. I've seen hurricanes. I've seen tornados [sic]. There was a bit of wind in this one."[35]

Again, little went well for the government during the 1986 session. Vince MacLean, elected Liberal leader over James Cowan by 1,082 to 721 shortly before the house opened, missed no opportunity to embarrass the government. Gillis charged that Nova Scotia was devoting a larger percentage of ordinary revenues to debt service charges than any other province and that the government had "taken the finances of the province from 'A-OK' in 1978 under the guidance of . . . Peter Nicholson to 'I.O.U.' under . . . John Buchanan."[36] Because of these difficulties the government did nothing to prevent a rise of almost 10 per cent in energy rates on April 1st.

Before budget day the opposition lambasted the government for a leak; McDonough called it "pre-budget striptease." Finance Minister Kerr's prophecies were gloomy: a likely deficit of $245 million for the current year, $233 million for the next, and a provincial net debt of $3.5 billion by April 1987. According to the opposition, the government had lost complete control of finances and the *Chronicle-Herald* demanded "a concrete, credible plan for bringing the growth of the public debt under control."[37] An unapologetic Kerr refused to make excuses for letting the deficit rise "rather than see horrendous disruption" in health and other services.[38] Thornhill scorned the unholy alliance of the Halifax Board of Trade and business interests with their new friend Alexa McDonough on this matter; if the government had cut services, they would likely have called it "that heartless bunch of fiscal reactionaries."[39]

Because financial stringency prevented eye-catching legislation, the government contented itself with bills like those of Lands and Forest Minister Streatch which emphasized forest resource protection and management, and was supposedly "the start of a dynamic new era" in the industry. The opposition was pleased to have it finally recognized that one of its members would chair the public accounts committee and that some of its members might be appointed to the internal economy board which controlled the house's finances.

Generally, however, the opposition sought to damage the government's credibility. It had no doubt that Nova Scotia Resources Ltd., set up in 1982 to acquire a 10 per cent interest in the Venture field, would sustain heavy losses. It lambasted

Minister of Environment Guy LeBlanc for the serious pollution problems at the Rio Algom tin mine at East Kemptville. It alleged that "political strings" were pulled to get a cabinet minister's girlfriend appointed to a senior position at the Art Gallery of Nova Scotia. It finally secured a list of passengers carried on the Nova Scotia government plane only to charge that it was laundered. It made the most of Billy Joe MacLean's resignation from the cabinet in April following a long investigation into his expense accounts which had led to ten charges of fraud and forgery. Vince MacLean pointed out that this was the first instance of a Nova Scotia cabinet minister resigning because he faced criminal charges. To him it indicated "a system of justice for the friends of government and another system for the rest of us." Five of the ten charges, he said, resulted from information which the attorney general's department had on file for twenty-nine months; it had simply been a case of Attorney General Ron Giffin getting "politics mixed up with his job."[40]

The government's difficulties did not end when Billy Joe MacLean pleaded guilty to four counts of submitting forged documents. In October it convened the assembly to pass "An Act Respecting Reasonable Limits for Membership in the House of Assembly" which expelled MacLean as a member and declared anyone convicted of an indictable offence punishable by imprisonment for more than five years to be ineligible for nomination or election to the assembly for five years. Premier Buchanan, a personal friend of MacLean, called it "the most difficult time for me personally in my 20 years of public life." MacLean contested the act's constitutionality in the Supreme Court, which early in January 1987 upheld his expulsion but found the section permitting his five-year exclusion from the assembly to be "paternalistic . . . excessive," and in contravention of Section 3 of the Charter of Rights and Freedoms, which guaranteed the right of all Canadians to be qualified for election.

When the government decided not to appeal, MacLean was re-elected for Inverness South in a by-election in which the Conservatives ran third. To some Nova Scotians the outcome made the province a laughingstock across the country. To them MacLean was hardly a John Wilkes standing up for a principle;

the penalty imposed by the assembly was in no way harsh; and either the charter or its interpretation was at fault. Chief Justice Glube might say that "the citizens of the province should be given credit for having the sense to determine who is a proper member,"[41] but the citizens who determined MacLean's re-election were those of a particular constituency probably moved more by personal considerations than by a higher good. The decision reached earlier for all Nova Scotians through their elected representatives may well have been the proper one. As the premier put it, however, a traumatic experience had ended and the government would no longer be distracted in its work.

Basically the Buchanan government hoped to .improve its public image by dealing effectively with the problems of morality in politics and budget deficits. This began early in February when Terry Donahoe replaced Giffin as attorney general. Admitting that the public had serious misgivings about the administration of justice, he hoped to "pick off, one by one . . . these negative perceptions." The premier called the speech from the throne "a blueprint for economic and social progress," but the opposition labelled it a sedative and the *Chronicle-Herald* wondered why the government had not demonstrated that some "sinew and bone [held] together the . . . flabby body." Vince MacLean drew fire when he described Buchanan's hope to sell coal-generated electricity in New England as "pie in the sky." "Maybe," replied the premier. "But I'll be reaching for that pie in the sky, and when we get it, it will be divided up among Cape Breton miners and their families."[42]

The opposition was not slow to raise the question of political morality. McDonough blamed the Billy Joe MacLean affair on the "corrupting nature" of Tory and Grit practices. Buchanan simply replied that "a bad apple once in a while in the barrel, doesn't make the whole barrel bad."[43] Vince MacLean proposed a package of five bills which, he contended, would "clean up the image of politics," end undue secrecy, and prevent improper interference in the administration of justice.[44] The government's answer was Donahoe's measure which required all MLA's to file annually a disclosure of assets with a designated superior court judge and which provided machinery for prosecution in cases of conflict of interest. Donahoe also indicated his intention to introduce at the next session a bill to depoliticize provincial judicial appointments. He defended vigorously his department against Vince MacLean's accusation that it was not functioning properly when a provincial judge added ten additional counts to the original charge of fraud against Conservative Gregory (Greg) MacIsaac of Richmond in connection with his expense accounts. The original charge, Donahoe pointed out, was an umbrella one from which the others flowed and the judge was not doing the Crown's work.[45]

The critics had their innings when the public accounts indicated a likely deficit of $251 million for 1986-87, substantially more than expected. Gillis, the Liberal chairman of the public accounts committee, declared that spending had been out of control since 1978, and the *Chronicle-Herald* complained about "unhealthy accounts." However, the government was quick with its defence. Because health costs, then $816 million annually, were escalating without let up, Finance Minister Kerr announced that a royal commission would be asked to recommend ways to bring medical expenditures under control. Also, though his 1987-88 budget contained no major tax increases, he promised reductions in the deficit to $185 million, $150 million, and then $120 million over the next three years. MacLean called it "a counterfeit document," McDonough "an exercise in deception," but the *Chronicle-Herald* considered it "a promising start" and "rounding the corner." Buchanan told the Halifax Board of Trade that the deficit was under control, but that he would not cut education and health services under any conditions since his government wanted to have "Nova Scotia recognized globally as a place offering excellence for the quality and life of its people." To reporters he indicated that he was "really not that interested in what the Board of Trade recommends to us."[46]

In the house the cabinet assumed a more aggressive stance than usual. Angered by MacLean's continued criticism of the finances, the premier called him "a little man" with a "vicious" political style, who found grating the government's success in bringing the deficit under control. Throwing caution to the winds, MacLean accused the government of allowing Tories to withhold the payment of sales taxes; later he was proved altogether wrong by the tax commissioner.[47] When McDonough, possibly in frustration, referred to a "perception within

educational circles . . . that . . . some members of the government . . . have personal financial interests in private trade
schools," Giffin called it "one of the sleaziest, most under-
handed" of statements, told her to sit down, and accused her of
grossly violating the rules of the house.[48]

The government's legislative programme provided for the
inclusion of four laymen on the provincial medical board to
ensure a tighter discipline over doctors, and for a stock plan by
which investors in specific Nova Scotia public companies
would be permitted a maximum exemption of $3,000 a year in
declared provincial income. Because of a successful challenge by
Frank Fraser of Canso under the Charter of Rights, the
government had the Civil Service Act amended so that 85 per
cent of the 10,000 civil servants — all but the most senior —
could be politically active. By going directly to the prime
minister, Buchanan got the plan for the modernization of Sysco
that he wanted. The government took satisfaction that the
Public Utilities Board used its earlier legislation — the only act
of its kind in Canada — to reduce substantially the price of
gasoline. It was not unhappy that the federal government had to
assume the major responsibility for action when Hawker
Siddeley decided to close its railway car plant at Trenton.
However, a Conservative backbencher from Pictou County
lambasted the company for taking everything out of Cape
Breton and leaving when the going became difficult, repeating
the action at the Halifax Shipyards, and now doing the same
thing at Trenton. "They don't have the decency, or the
responsibility as a private citizen, to try to find a solution."[49]

Buchanan was elated with a quiet session which in his view
had done highly useful work. MacLean conceded that the
proceedings had not been flamboyant, but attributed it to his
party's concentration on the failure to deal effectively with
unemployment. A disappointed and perhaps franker McDonough pointed to the difficulty of getting "a government on the
ropes that is totally concerned with its own political survival."
Not only had it "all the resources and levers at its disposal," but
it faced "a tiny opposition that's divided four ways."[50]

Nevertheless, Buchanan found it unpropitious to have the
autumn election that he obviously wanted. According to the
polls, he remained the most popular of the three leaders and his

party had improved its position somewhat. However, it was still behind the Liberals, the Conservatives had lost overwhelmingly in New Brunswick, and the federal Conservatives were highly unpopular in Nova Scotia. Distancing himself from the federal party, Buchanan — always a populist of sorts and ever becoming more so — declined to attend a gathering of the élitist federal "500 Club" in Halifax; it was not his style of politics, he declared. The Liberals were not without their problems because the polls indicated that MacLean was the least popular of the leaders. To suggestions that they were seeking to remake his image, they simply replied that they were simply presenting a side of him different from the harsh, critical one which the public normally saw.

Before the session of 1988, Conservative MLA Greg MacIsaac was convicted of fraud in connection with his expense accounts. Also adding to the government's difficulties, although unforeseen, would be its setting up of a commission with broad powers to investigate the imprisonment for eleven years of Donald Marshall, a Micmac, wrongfully accused of murder. Nevertheless, the government thought that it was well prepared for the session. Its legislative proposals — an "environment enhancement program," assistance to senior citizens and small businesses, and recognition of equal pay for work of equal value — seemed to be well conceived. Moreover, prosperity in central Canada and the consequent increase in federal transfer payments allowed a deficit of $64 million less than expected for the previous year and equally favourable prospects for the next. As a result, Finance Minister Kerr avoided any increase in taxation and even proposed one small decrease. However, the government would gain little kudos for its budget or legislative proposals. Instead a host of other matters allowed the opposition and the media to keep it almost continually on the defensive.

In the opening day, Liberal leader Vincent MacLean accused the Buchanan government of "creating and condoning a climate of governing which has brought a sense of shame into this legislature."[51] From then on the opposition parties never let up in their attacks, and through the media dominated the public agenda. Liberal Guy Brown charged the government with making a "sweetheart deal" in its twenty-five-lease of the Joseph Howe Building from Centennial Properties owner Ralph Medjuck, the premier's former law partner. The NDP's John Holm alleged favoured treatment for Conservative Allen Stockall in a loan and in the funnelling of federal offshore development money through the city of Dartmouth for a sewer on Stockall's Portland Estates project. To their accusers the Conservatives were "backward Robin Hoods" who rescued rich developers and ignored poor Nova Scotians.[52]

The opposition and the media were also quick to seize upon the miscues of two cabinet ministers. Originally somewhat misleading about his knowledge of the federal government's granting of four offshore lobster licences, Fisheries Minister John Leefe later admitted that he had talked to federal officials on the subject and even suggested three possible grantees. Attorney General Terry Donahoe, after suggesting that cases involving Indians might be taken away from two judges whose testimony at the Marshall inquiry indicated possible bias against them, later retracted that intention, a course that accorded with the chief justice's wishes.

Donahoe had more trouble with the Roland Thornhill debt-settlement case, resurrected after eight years by a *Toronto Star* article in which Hugh Feagan, the former commanding officer of the RCMP in Nova Scotia, was quoted as saying that political interference prevented the laying of charges against Thornhill. The government suffered two damaging blows as a result. Not wanting to add to the government's other problems, Deputy Premier Thornhill resigned. The attorney general, after urging by the premier, who had talked to Feagan by telephone, obtained a signed letter from the former RCMP officer that retracted the basics of the *Toronto Star* article. However, after seeming to intimate that the letter was Feagan's own and that his departmental officials played no part in its composition, Donahoe later admitted that it virtually consisted of the notes which he had sent to the former RCMP officer. The reaction was immediate and trenchant. The opposition demanded Donahoe's resignation; the *Chronicle-Herald* castigated his efforts at damage control and declared that "dramatically, the Thornhill affair has become the Donahoe affair."[53] Although Donahoe apologized for being "too lawyerish" and giving answers which were "not as straightforward as they might have been,"[54] the entire episode hurt the Buchanan government badly.

The government gained some relief when Ottawa suspended the controversial offshore lobster licences and agreed to ban drilling for oil on Georges Bank until the year 2000. But in other matters there was little comfort. Belatedly, the opposition argued that the Meech Lake agreement's inclusion of fisheries on the agenda of future constitutional conferences might result in the loss of 6,000 Nova Scotia jobs to Newfoundland. Only with difficulty did the government gain approval of the accord in the closing days of the session. The opposition also charged the government with using President Louis Comeau of the Nova Scotia Power Corporation to prevent an increase in electric rates until after an election, and it followed with accusations that Chief Provincial Court Judge Harry How was dabbling in politics.

More telling were the charges of a "grubby pattern" in the administration of justice, supposedly evidenced in part by the department of the attorney general's handling of the prosecution in the Billy Joe MacLean and Greg MacIsaac cases. The powers the government had conferred on the commissioners conducting the Marshall inquiry also brought difficulties. Arguing partly that the broad scope of these powers amounted to a waiver of confidentiality, and partly that the public interest demanded it, Chief Justice Glube ruled that ministers must divulge their discussions in the cabinet room about the amount of compensation to be paid Marshall even if it meant breaking their oath of secrecy. Although the government wanted to avoid creating the impression that it had something to hide, it eventually decided to enter an appeal based on the importance of the principle at issue.

This was only one of three recent cases that had presented the possibility of judicial intervention of great magnitude into provincial politics and government. Some months earlier, Chief Justice Glube had used the Charter of Rights to strike down that part of a provincial act which would have prevented Billy Joe MacLean from serving in the assembly for the next five years; now she had made serious inroads into the principle of cabinet secrecy that had governed the operations of British-style governments for years without serious challenge; further, she had to decide whether appeal court judges must account publicly, at least in a limited way, for their actions. Probably no judge has in so short a time been required to make decisions which could affect radically all three branches of government — legislative, executive, and judicial. Two of the cases raised the question of whether the public interest, in a judge's opinion, required open government: difficult decisions since positive action might be labelled by some as judicial adventurism and might be fraught with danger because of its possible effects on established institutions of proven utility.

As the 1988 session ended, last-minute polling convinced Premier Buchanan that he ought not to call the immediate election that he wanted. Although non-Halifax Conservative members on the mainland wanted to go to the polls, the party's position in the Halifax-Dartmouth metropolitan area was weak. Clearly the session had done nothing to improve the Conservatives' chances. As the *Globe and Mail* put it, "ten years in office are starting to show."[55] Nevertheless, the premier remained the most popular leader and his party's chief asset. To his opponents he was, in the manner of Ronald Reagan, the Teflon premier to whom none of the failings of his colleagues would stick. Likely his aim would be to improve his party's image in preparation for an early fall election prior to a federal one.

CHAPTER 14

Ninety-Two Years of Politics

Some of my later articles have perhaps exaggerated the conservatism of the Nova Scotian political culture and its static character. These writings have not reflected fully the developments since the Second World War and particularly since the mid-1950s, some of which have become clear only in retrospect. Changes in voters' loyalties and their attitudes towards the old parties were apparently concealed for some time after 1945 because Angus L. Macdonald continued to win provincial elections, not so much because he was a Liberal, but because he was "Angus L.," while for similar reasons "Uncle Louis" St. Laurent could easily triumph federally over Drew in Nova Scotia. It seemed extraordinary that Stanfield and the Conservatives could win provincially under non-crisis conditions in 1956, but when they also won the next three, the last two overwhelmingly, it became clear that some sort of revolution had taken place. Subsequent events have demonstrated that Nova Scotia is not the Liberal province it once was and that the Conservatives can now compete with the Liberals on at least equal terms.

How and why these changes occurred will never be known with precision. In my class in Lunenburg Academy in the late 1920s all but two of the twenty-eight students came from Liberal families. Forty years later a few of the twenty-six were actually Conservative workers, and a considerable number did not identify themselves with any party. Admittedly, members of prominent Liberal and Conservative families throughout the province generally appear to have retained their fathers' and grandfathers' party affiliations. Undoubtedly, too, in the rural areas those loyalties may have remained much as they were. However, in larger communities, perhaps because of the solvent of war and the movement of population, the voters entered the postwar era much less bound to the old party ties. Growing urbanization after 1945 may have further weakened the old bonds. A little later because of Stanfield and, to a lesser extent, Diefenbaker many voters never returned to their old loyalties, and the post-1950 Nova Scotia political world became markedly different from the old.

In 1957 I quoted an opinion of Viscount Bryce in the early 1900s that American political parties "continue to exist, because they have existed. The mill has been constructed and the machinery goes on turning, even when there is no grist to grind." At that time I suggested that this was also a reasonably accurate description of Nova Scotia's Liberal and Conservative parties. Since then, however, significant changes have occurred. A one-and-a-half party system is a thing of the past. Because of Conservative electoral successes since the mid-1950s, a dramatic change has occurred in the status of the old parties. The days are gone when the Liberals, in the manner of Angus L. Macdonald, could boast that they had initiated almost all the social legislation and done almost all the road paving. Indeed, the monetary outlay on these services has shifted dramatically in favour of the Conservatives, and the Liberals seem much less inclined to boast of their liberalism. Even more than before the old parties appear to be pragmatic and undistinguishable.

Their dominance, too, is being challenged to a greater degree than before. In the 1984 election Cape Breton County, which since the late 1930s had sporadically elected democratic socialists, became barren ground for the NDP because of Paul MacEwan and his Cape Breton Labor Party. With that party's collapse the NDP may well regain its former position in that county.

Much more important may be the betterment of the NDP's position on the mainland. In 1978 one of its candidates ran second to a Conservative in Pictou Centre and in 1981 its leader Alexa McDonough won Halifax Chebucto, her party's first victory outside of Cape Breton. In addition, her fourteen candidates in Halifax County polled almost as many votes as the Liberal that year. Three years later the NDP won all its three seats on the mainland, but two of its victories — those in Sackville and Kings South — resulted at least in part from the weakness of the Conservative candidates and may not necessarily be repeated. McDonough, however, solidified her position in Halifax Chebucto and her party polled 27.6 per cent of the vote in Halifax County compared with the Liberals 25.0 per cent. Slowly the NDP has also been adding to its vote in many mainland constituencies.

The relationship between the political culture on the one hand and the decision-making and success of the major politicians on the other is highly complex. It brings into play a host of variables which, to be understood fully, need greater exploration in depth than can be attempted here. Obviously George Murray's natural conservatism fitted in nicely with the prevailing attitudes of the times and the *Chronicle's* reference to him in 1906 as "safe, in every sense of the word" remained an apt description throughout his twenty-six years as premier. A.K. Maclean, who might have given the government a genuinely progressive stance, moved to federal politics after serving only two years as attorney general between 1909 and 1911.

Almost all of Murray's undertakings that appeared innovative seemed designed to suit his personal inclinations or to accrue to his political advantage or both. His establishment of a public utilities board, the first in Canada, was intended in large measure to relieve himself and his cabinet of the political responsibility for decisions he found troublesome. This board was, in fact, part and parcel of his general practice of setting up a myriad of boards and commissions, sometimes headed by Conservatives, which effectively reduced cabinet responsibility to an extent probably true in no other province.

Not to be minimized is Murray's record in providing technical education, in which at one time Nova Scotia led all other provinces. During the 1916 election he boasted of a comprehensive programme which included the Nova Scotia Technical College as well as technical and miners' schools: "we have developed a system which will enable every Nova Scotian, boy and girl, to be trained sufficiently to perform his or her work in the best possible manner." However, was this not what should have been expected at a time when the coal and steel industries were the bulwark of provincial industry, a principal source of public revenue, and the major hope of Nova Scotia development?

Despite Murray's contention towards the end of his political career that he had always stood by the workmen and given them "as advanced [labour] legislation as . . . anywhere else," the evidence is that he provided less than was politically possible, although never lagging so far behind public opinion as to endanger himself. Thus his Employers' Liability for Injuries Act of 1900, instead of using the British act of 1897, followed the much less liberal act of 1880. Not until 1910 did the Workmen's Compensation Act adopt the basic principles of the 1897 act, and even then one Liberal backbencher complained that if excluded workmen were taken into account "you have practically nothing left."

Murray's attempt to maintain a balance between the interests of labour and capital was so successful in the case of the latter that many leading businessmen who supported the Conservatives and the National Policy federally looked upon him with favour. In the middle years he must have found highly disturbing the views of Liberal Dr. Arthur Samuel Kendall of Cape Breton County, who described the directors of the coal and steel companies as "Bourbon-like . . . despots [who] . . . aim to set back the hands of the clock"; who was certain that the companies' profits were sufficiently large to increase miners' wages and lower the cost of coal to consumers; and who advocated major social legislation on the ground that the duty of government, and especially of liberalism, was to "regulate the forces of society so that the greatest good may be enjoyed by the greatest numbers." Murray's confrontation with Kendall on the floors of the assembly was minimal, but he may have breathed a sigh of relief when Kendall failed to be re-elected in 1911. In retrospect it may seem strange that the voters of Cape Breton County rejected a member who acted so strongly to protect them against corporate interests.

On matters such as the abolition of the legislative council, Murray willingly "let sleeping dogs lie" as long as the public was quiescent. It was a safe course for anyone who read public attitudes as well as he. It was, of course, not a highly demanding people that he led, and his task was made all the easier because of other factors — his own engaging personality, which made it difficult for people to dislike him; the negativism of his Conservative opponents; and the prosperity of the first two decades of this century resulting first from the burgeoning coal and steel industries, and later from war. When the postwar period introduced a new world that was uncongenial to him, he found it opportune to retire.

In contrast with Murray, Angus L. Macdonald, aided by Conservative bumblings early in his career, quickly developed a mystique that ensured continued political success. Though his immense popular appeal would have permitted a much less cautious approach to governmental matters than Murray's, like Murray he was seldom much out of line with popular attitudes, which he normally gauged with accuracy. Only occasionally did any of his followers express the opinion that he erred on the side of caution. However, in the liberalization of the liquor laws, where he took great care not to alienate Protestants, some thought that he might have gone further without hurting himself politically.

Macdonald's basic credo emphasized that "some things Government can do, some things they must leave to others," and he declared more than once that Nova Scotians approved his manner of applying it. Though his first day in office saw the proclamation of an old age pensions act — Liberals had been demanding it for years — his early years as premier indicated that he was less favourably disposed to major social legislation than Conservative leader Gordon Harrington, a "red Tory" in modern parlance. Later he expressed distaste in private for the federal government's "green book" proposals of 1945 and their promise of a new world with "no unemployment, no financial problems, neither . . . sickness nor death any more." To him they were the product of bureaucrats in "the ivory towers," whose work had not been subjected to proper scrutiny. Though he had little choice but to accept Ottawa's plans for extending old age security benefits in 1951, he feared that they would be inflationary and that he would end up in old age, after careful saving all his life, with "a fixed sum of dollars, which will buy only a fraction of what they will buy today."

Openly he showed no reluctance to denounce those whose demands or actions made unreasonable demands upon the treasury. Once he went so far as to declare that "more ridiculous resolutions [have been] passed in Nova Scotia than would fill a room" and to suggest that their authors should be put in "padded cells." He even lectured severely the miners in his native county of Inverness who seemed to care not a whit about productivity. "A mine cannot be run on a basis like this." Privately he had unkind words for Father Moses Coady and A.B. MacDonald of the "Antigonish Movement," and he reminded them that their progress had been possible because of government moneys and that they should make good their earlier pledges without further assistance. Clearly it irked him to find some of the movement's more radical members denouncing capitalism and labelling him and other Liberals as "enemies to the cause of social justice." After extensive reading he kept saying to the end of his days that the inevitable result of the planned economy of the socialists would be totalitarianism without elections or a parliament, and he was not deterred when David Lewis called him "either dishonest or illogical."

But this was not the Angus Macdonald that most Nova Scotians knew or cared anything about. He was right that they had little desire, and certainly they exerted little pressure, to increase the government spectrum beyond the area that he believed desirable. To them he was the man of progress; the man, who though the most careful of financiers, was willing to double the provincial debt to ensure vastly improved highway and educational systems; and hence the man who played a vital role in providing the infrastructure conducive to provincial development. The personification of "Nova Scotianess" in the public mind, Macdonald has probably been the province's most successful vote-getter.

Unlike Macdonald and like Murray, Stanfield required time to establish his political pre-eminence. Unlike Murray, Stanfield did not inherit a Fielding legacy already in place which, with suitable nurturing, could ensure his continued success. Stanfield had first to wage two unsuccessful elections against an invulnerable Macdonald, and only then did the contests and legislative sessions that followed permit him to demonstrate qualities that Nova Scotians appreciate in a leader and thus gain a political mastery of the province. Like Murray and Macdonald, he readily attuned himself to the feelings and attitudes of the electorate and won from them a similar degree of trust.

By the election of 1960 Stanfield's party's advertisements were already proclaiming that he stood for "the public virtues of Nova Scotia's great tradition of public leadership — integrity and sincerity, firmness and candor." Realizing after his first victory in a normally Liberal province that his position differed from those of Murray and Macdonald, he told his followers that his government had to be "moderate and not bitterly partisan" in order to "increase the respect of those who are non-Conservative." He had two things going for him which previous Conservative leaders had lacked: the name Stanfield for which genuine respect existed throughout the province, and the weakening of party ties after the Second World War. The latter factor combined with the attributes he brought to politics helped to make Nova Scotia a genuinely two-party province.

Like Macdonald, Stanfield made no promises that he could not keep and always strove to keep them. Unlike Macdonald, he lacked great oratorical talents and resisted any attempt to appeal to the emotions. Yet in time "his audiences [listened] in rapt attention even though they [forbore] to cheer. In him they [recognized] the man of sincerity, the voice of reasonableness and good sense." Although his wry sense of humour often passed unnoticed, some of his one-liners are almost classics. Like Macdonald he reacted fiercely to any charges of lack of integrity or graft directed against himself or his government. In the case of Dr. Reardon, he even considered denying a member legislative immunity by statute in order to permit proceedings in the courts. He rejected summarily any suggestion of subservience to special interests. "No corporation," he once said, "has enough money to buy the favor of the Conservative Party of Nova Scotia." Like Macdonald, he dismissed, though perhaps not as emphatically, demands which he considered unreasonable or inappropriate. At times he might have regarded the municipal governments as a badgering pressure group whose demands, if met, would have subtracted substantially from their powers. Rejecting an elaborate overhaul of municipal finance, he simply adopted the gradualist course of periodically providing assistance to a wide variety of municipal services.

Like Murray and Macdonald, Stanfield was generally regarded as highly cautious, a trait not normally politically damaging in Nova Scotia. One writer declared that he seldom "takes a chance on being caught out very far on a limb"; another that he showed "a prominent ability to look well before leaping." But his was not the caution of Murray or Macdonald. If a definitive delineation of the facts on matters of substance showed convincing reasons for change, he was usually not slow to act. In time he was criticized for his extensive use of royal commissions, special legislative committees, and the like, but these devices, revealing citizen attitudes through public hearings, enabled him to modernize liquor laws and the Lord's Day Act with scarcely a political ripple. His own understanding of Nova Scotians led him to conclude accurately that, despite their supposed phobia against direct taxation, they would willingly pay a sales tax — euphemistically described as a health services tax — for otherwise free hospitalization.

Unlike Murray and Macdonald, Stanfield solidified his political position through his role in building "the new Nova Scotia." Beginning with his first session in the legislature he called for industrial development, and his success was such that in 1965 he could call on his compatriots to plan a Nova Scotia for the 1970s which would place it in the forefront of Canada. In his usual style he enlisted the province's leading business talents to promote that development through IEL. Despite IEL's substantial success, it became apparent, that large undertakings requiring scientific expertise introduce incalculables that defy ordinary business principles, and Stanfield was forced to leave two enterprises that later became a nightmare for his successor.

Almost as Angus Macdonald might have done, Stanfield called for "intelligent humanity in our politics" to help "our people into a better future . . . not lead them into a blind alley." An opponent once alleged that he did "not understand the problems of the ordinary people because he has never had to face up to such problems himself," but all the evidence points to the fact that he was thoroughly in tune with his fellow Nova Scotians.

To what extent has a government's financial record played a crucial part in the province's politics? Until very recently politicians have acted as if sizable deficits and tax increases should be avoided at all costs as a major key to political success. Consideration of the financial returns and the estimates has often constituted an inordinate part of the legislative sessions and perhaps of this present volume as well. Yet the conclusion must be that criticism of a government's financial performance has led only occasionally to big political dividends. Over many years Charles Tanner made such criticism a major part of his legislative activities, and his negativism may have led to his becoming one of the big losers in provincial politics. In retrospect, it seems almost ludicrous that an opposition would make financial incompetence its major weapon against so careful a financier as Murray.

Between 1925 and 1933 the Liberals concentrated on the financial records of the Rhodes and Harrington governments which, through little fault of their own, incurred eight successive deficits. In the end, however, it was economic recession, the franchise scandal, and Macdonald's appeal that accounted largely for the Conservatives' defeat. Both Macdonald and Stanfield had many successive years of surpluses, and on the one occasion when the latter imposed a substantial new tax he lost nothing politically because he coupled it with a highly desired service. None would suggest, however, that either man owed much of his success to his handling of the public purse.

The one instance in which finances apparently determined the outcome of an election was the defeat of the Smith government in 1970. Though enjoying surpluses, it lost largely because of misadventures in industrial development. It was left to the Regan government to demonstrate that balanced budgets in difficult times do not ensure political success. Boasts of financial responsibility could not override the failure to 'prevent massive increases in electricity costs; energy subsidies, even if deficit-producing, might have been more politically rewarding. Heeding the lesson, the Buchanan government prevented a soaring in energy bills even if it meant unprecedented increases in both budget deficits and the provincial debt, and a serious deterioration of the province's credit rating. By the end of the legislative session in 1988 the electorate had yet to pronounce whether it agreed with this approach to provincial finances.

Provincial governments in Nova Scotia, like those elsewhere, do their utmost to use the federal government of the day to their advantage. Not surprisingly, the relations have usually been more cordial when the same party holds office both federally and provincially but, at times, as political exigencies or firm personal opinions dictate, a Nova Scotia premier has disassociated himself from the federal government of his own party and been highly critical of its behaviour.

The George Murray era began when William Stevens Fielding, the repealer of 1886, became federal minister of finance in 1896, largely reconciled to the National Policy which he had previously condemned as a menace to Nova Scotia's interests. There followed fifteen years of friendly relations between Fielding and Murray, undoubtedly the most amicable period in Dominion — Nova Scotia relations. For the first and only time National Policy worked strongly to the province's advantage; the coal and steel industries developed enormously and coal royalties became the largest single source of provincial revenue. After 1911 the Borden and Murray governments occasionally had minor differences of opinion, but nothing disturbed the generally prosperous conditions that prevailed until the end of the war.

Then Nova Scotia found a world altered for the worse. The coal and steel industries, bolstered by National Policy for almost two decades, were in a state of decline. The coal industry was finding it harder and harder to compete against cheaper American coal in Upper Canada, and the steel industry was experiencing similar difficulties in competing with new and larger plants in Ontario. Since 1920 provincial politicians have used much of their energy trying to induce federal governments to save the two industries upon which much of the province is dependent. Starting with Besco in 1921 until the virtual takeover of the coal industry by the federal government, and the takeover of the steel industry by the provincial government in the 1960s, charges were common of financial manipulators, mostly outsiders, using watered stock and other corporate devices to milk these industries for their own benefit. Much of federal —

Nova Scotia relations since the First World War has related to troubles in these industries.

The pronounced weakness of these major industries, combined with a general postwar recession, contributed largely to the Maritime Rights agitation, of which E.H. Armstrong was a principal victim. Possessed of a personality that did not endear him to a federal cabinet of his own party, he had the added burden of having to deal with the King government when, in the interest of self-preservation, it was currying favour with western Canada and showing little sympathy for the Maritimes. One of his ministers even complained that "our Federal Gov. is not being a help but rather a hindrance to our political welfare. . . . It would seem as though an unfriendly government were in office."

Conservative Premier Rhodes, who faced Liberal governments at Ottawa during most of his premiership, seemed to relish lashing out at Prime Minister King for disclosing confidential communications between the province's lieutenant-governor and the federal government on the status of legislative councillors. However, because King, after once appreciating the intensity of the Maritime Rights agitation, appointed and implemented most major recommendations of the Duncan Commission, relations between the two governments were generally on an even keel. Conservative Premier Harrington always found the Bennett government at least sympathetic and never more so than in 1932 when a trip to Ottawa resulted in the promise of an increased subvention that would permit the sale of an additional million tons of Nova Scotia coal in Quebec and eastern Ontario.

Angus Macdonald's first period as premier produced no open clash with the King government, although the position which he developed with his friend Norman McLeod Rogers on federal-provincial relations made later conflict almost inevitable. Aspiring to be regarded as a Liberal no less federally than provincially, Macdonald participated vigorously in federal contests. He also avoided public criticism of federal ministers, even when they exasperated him. Once, after he had gone out of his way to defend unpopular federal policies, he was highly annoyed that Fisheries Minister Michaud seemingly accepted the suggestion that he had treated harshly Nova Scotia fishermen who were in distress. Philosophically he wrote: "in this game I suppose everybody feels that he must look out for himself."

None could have been more co-operative than Premier MacMillan in supporting the federal government's war effort. "Suggest what you want and it will be done if it is in our power" was his position. However, he could not agree with a federal government of his own party on financial policy. Though he showed no bitterness, he only reluctantly signed the wartime taxation agreement of 1942, which he considered unfavourable to Nova Scotia, and would have much preferred the adoption of the Rowell-Sirois principles. Rightly he prophesied that the agreement heralded radical changes in federal-provincial relations that would lead to Ottawa's financial dominance, and the 1942 *Journals* preserve his views for posterity.

Macdonald returned to the premiership accompanied by a *Chronicle* editorial telling him that he was the man needed to "hammer into the federal mind that we are against further centralization." In two years of differences with Ottawa he maintained that constitutional changes should come first and taxation arrangements afterwards; that the Rowell-Sirois principle of fiscal need should not be abandoned; and that, though the federal government should have exclusive jurisdiction in the major tax fields, in order to preserve some degree of provincial autonomy it ought to abandon the minor tax fields which it had not used before the Second World War. Publicly Macdonald avoided personalities and contented himself with a clear statement of his constitutional position; privately he feared that the federal authorities hoped to hush up the provinces with a little money and wondered "whether they want provinces . . . or not." With the full support of his cabinet and caucus, he was eventually able to preserve some degree of provincial financial autonomy. However, some of his former colleagues at Ottawa regarded him as a "very sinister fellow" who had held out "for personal reasons and to satisfy personal grudges."

Between 1957 and 1963 it was almost a love affair between the Diefenbaker and Stanfield governments, much of it resulting from the prime minister's genuine desire to assist the have-not provinces. In 1962 a Conservative advertisement boasted that the Diefenbaker government had done more for Nova Scotia in five years than the preceding Liberal ones in twenty-two, and Stanfield declared that if in 1958 Diefenbaker and George Nowlan had promised the assistance which actually came to Nova Scotia, "no one would have believed them."

Within one year after Pearson's Liberals took office in 1963, Stanfield was criticizing them for failing to provide incentives to areas of high unemployment and for not using the Atlantic Development Board to go to the root of the province's economic problems. In the 1965 federal election he was again at the side of Diefenbaker, the man who "encouraged us, lifted our hearts and spirits," and recognized that the Maritimes needed special measures. Believing that MacEachen and Regan were anticipating substantial gains in Nova Scotia and intending to identify the provincial government with the losses, he and his cabinet campaigned actively to protect themselves. Their actions prevented the majority Liberal government for which Pearson had called the election.

As minister of finance and economics, G.I. Smith had congratulated his Liberal federal counterpart Mitchell Sharp for moving towards the full equalization that Nova Scotia had been demanding by including a wide range of provincial revenue sources in calculating equalization grants. However, later, as premier, he scoffed at opposition leader Regan's charge that he was setting up the federal government as a "straw man" again and again for the purpose of knocking him down. Instead Smith insisted that it was "not only . . . a right — but . . . a duty of a Nova Scotian" to condemn federal policies that had a harmful effect on the province. Even Regan admitted that the Pearson government had not assumed its share of the responsibility for the Sydney steel plant, and Smith hoped that the "flickering flame" of that government's life would soon sputter out."

Early in his premiership Gerald Regan secured highly advantageous arrangements from the Trudeau government for the rehabilitation of the Deuterium of Canada heavy water plant by Atomic Energy of Canada. Later federal oil subsidies fell far short of what Regan needed for his political salvation. Perhaps because he realized that the moneys required would be enormous, he did not enter into a public debate with Ottawa.

Clearly John Buchanan has felt much more comfortable in dealing with the Mulroney government than the Trudeau government. Possibly because Nova Scotia provided Mulroney with his first seat in the Commons, Buchanan has more than once gone to him directly when his dealings with other federal ministers have not satisfied him. Certainly that was true in reaching a final agreement on the modernization of Sysco. The Nova Scotia premier was delighted to take advantage of the federal Conservatives' victory in September 1984 to win a massive majority provincially a few weeks later. However, late in 1987, when considering a provincial election, he must have found the low standing of the federal Conservatives in the polls inhibiting. Populist as he is, and fearing public reaction, he also thought it best to shun the gathering of the federal party's elitist "500 Club" in Halifax.

No highly significant generalizations are possible about federal — Nova Scotia relationships. Because Nova Scotia is a have-not province, in which two major industries, once benefiting from National Policy, have declined steadily since 1920, its premiers have gone frequently to Ottawa cap in hand. Complaints of inaction or inadequate treatment have usually been more common when different parties control the two governments. However, whatever party is in power at Ottawa, no provincial government has been reluctant to criticize federal agencies intended to promote development in the poorer provinces. It has been all the less inhibited when it has been able to accuse distant bureaucrats of rendering the agency ineffective through ignorance and red tape. Sometimes strong premiers have pursued personal goals distinct from party considerations. Such was the attempt of Angus Macdonald to preserve a genuine federal system, as was that of Stanfield and Smith to secure full recognition of fiscal need in federal-provincial financial relations.

Between 1882 and 1967 just four men have held the Nova Scotia premiership for sixty-seven of the eighty-five years. During this period other provinces have also had long-serving premiers, but none to match Nova Scotia in their number of election victories and total length of time in office. If John Buchanan were to win again, he would become the fifth man with at least four victories. Does this phenomenon indicate a uniqueness in the Nova Scotia electorate? When one of its premiers becomes generally trusted, is he in an unchallengeable position? Would George Murray have won the 1925 election? Would Angus L. Macdonald have beaten Stanfield in the next election after 1953? Would Stanfield have defeated Regan in 1970? An affirmative answer to the last two questions is probably correct; perhaps the best response to the first question is that Murray would not have let the political situation deteriorate as Armstrong had done. None can answer the general question definitively, but the likelihood is that the Nova Scotia phenomenon is more the result of accidental circumstances than of uniqueness.

The probability of a premier enjoying a continual lease on power may be less in the future. When Gerald Regan became the first premier after Confederation to suffer defeat after winning an election (actually he won two), he was the victim of circumstances which only recent premiers have had to face. Because of a substantial dissolution of old party ties, he could no longer count on the same massive bloc of supporters as his predecessors did. Also crucial is the new situation in Halifax County, which elects more than one-quarter of the assembly and where, because of an increasing and more mobile population, the citizenry is subject to the volatility in voting behaviour that is common to modern urban populations. A final complication for contemporary Nova Scotian politicians, like their counterparts in other democratic jurisdictions, is the great number of pressure groups making demands, often conflicting, on every conceivable subject. Both Macdonald and Stanfield acknowledged the difficulty of dealing with them, and in number and forcefulness they continue to increase. Clearly they make Nova Scotia a much more difficult province to govern. Thus Buchanan in 1988 and his successors thereafter will have to confront relatively new phenomena and difficulties in their efforts to win and retain power.

Epilogue

This short account was written one day after the election of September 6, 1988, which some members of the media declared to be a contest between "sleaze" and "teflon." In other words, could John Buchanan once again cast aside any personal taint for the failings of his administration? An altogether one-sided CBC political panel spoke in terms of twenty-five scandals and some newspeople could hardly restrain their impatience at the opposition's seeming reluctance to press past misdeeds with vigour.

But Liberal leader Vince MacLean, aiming to be regarded as a statesman rather than a street fighter, acted in accordance with his slogan, "It's time for a new start." Treating the past only incidentally, he outlined day by day well-conceived proposals covering every major aspect of the public agenda. To charges that the cost would be hundreds of millions, he replied with an estimate of only $50.6 millions. NDP leader Alexa McDonough took the position that "politics are not about hoopla and hype," and used every opportunity to present her ideas about issues and problem-solving. To deal with the province's economic and social ills, she made proposals estimated to cost $35.4 millions. To her the Liberals could be no more trusted to clean up government than the Conservatives and if Nova Scotians wanted change, only her party could provide it. "This time, Alexa and the New Democrats," went the party slogan.

The master strategist was at work in devising the Conservatives' approach to the election. Because it was staged a week before the Marshall commission was to begin a general probe of the justice system, the government would suffer no electoral harm from its work. Because it was a summer election, the electorate was likely to be somnolent and less critical. "It's an Anne Murray campaign, a Don Messer campaign. It's Nova Scotia on holidays," wrote the *Globe and Mail*. But the crowning point of the strategy was to present the party and government as new and rejuvenated. To demonstrate that change was to take place, four older cabinet ministers announced their resignations on four separate days just before dissolution. The premier played a large part in the selection of the twenty new Conservative candidates, some with impressive credentials, and party advertisements pictured "John Buchanan and Nova Scotia's New PCs." The party slogan became "Strong Leadership for New Ideas," presented in sixteen policy statements which differed little from those of the other parties.

One statement entitled "Ethics and Good Government" promised to establish a public ethics council, appoint an independent public prosecutor, open all government contracts to public tender, and permit a legislative committee to review all major cabinet appointments. Of the past Buchanan said repeatedly: "We don't live in a perfect society . . . one of the tests of leadership is whether you act decisively when a problem occurs . . . we did act decisively when we had problems." To his opponents this was sheer hypocrisy, "an 11th-hour deathbed repentance," but nonetheless the Conservatives made the leadership of John Buchanan foremost in their politicking. Late in the campaign "rockin' rallies" featured big bands, upbeat speeches, and the "blue wave," a group of teen-agers who swarmed about the premier.

Not at their best in this election were the media. In addition to inexcusable inaccuracy, they failed abysmally to place the election in the context of Nova Scotia's political history. In American fashion they sought out momentary eye-catching episodes and gave them interpretations which were highly suspect. The CBC hailed Malcolm MacKay's resignation from the Sackville constituency executive and Conservative party with "Buchanan suffers another blow"; actually the Conservatives were glad to rid themselves of a trouble-maker with little cost to themselves. The media were right that when "Bob" Levy, a leading critic of the Conservatives' use of patronage, accepted a judgeship from John Buchanan, he seriously injured the NDP. But their attempt to couple it with the seizure of marijuana plants from the husband of an NDP candidate was as exaggerated as it was unfair.

The polls, which played a bigger part than in any previous Nova Scotia election, were no less suspect. An Angus Reid poll early in the campaign showed McDonough to be the most popular of the leaders, but a late Omnifacts poll found that 36 per cent of the electorate preferred Buchanan as premier to 24 per cent for McDonough and 20 per cent for MacLean. An early Angus Reid poll indicated a close contest between the two old parties; an Omnifacts poll of August 25 made it even closer and newspeople suggested that the Liberals had gained momentum because of Liberal Guy Brown's revelation of further facts about the lease of the Joseph Howe building and the premier's "opening of Pandora's box" by his statement on ethics in government. Then on September 2, to almost everyone's surprise, came an Angus Reid poll giving the Conservatives a province-wide lead of nine percentage points over the Liberals.

In a very real sense this poll amounted to a roorback since insufficient time remained to check it by conducting another poll. All that MacLean could do was to demonstrate that a Reid poll had been inaccurate in the Manitoba election; that its recent Nova Scotia poll contradicted all the other polls; and that no facts existed to explain it. When the actual results gave the Conservatives 43 per cent of the vote to the Liberals' 40, both MacLean and McDonough wondered if the publication of polls late in the campaign ought to be banned. MacLean might have been on better ground if he had not used an inaccurate poll of his own which put his candidate well ahead of Attorney General Donahoe in Halifax Cornwallis, a contention which the Conservatives quickly refuted with their Decima poll.

The Liberals' increase of 9 per cent over 1984 in their popular vote enabled them to win twenty-one seats instead of six. Eight of their gains came in Cape Breton where only Conservative Brian Young and Independent Paul MacEwan withstood their challenge. The island's failure to enjoy the prosperity of the mainland and the fact that MacLean himself was a Cape Bretoner contributed to these successes. Although the Liberals raised their popular vote in Metro by about 10 per cent, they increased their elected members only from one to three. They also gained four scattered seats elsewhere on the mainland.

From the election's outset the polls indicated that the NDP would not do well outside of Metro. There, however, they appeared to be running second to the Conservatives with the possibility of winning as many as five seats. But, as McDonough pointed out, they were subjected to a not unusual "squeeze"; many voters who wanted to defeat the government turned to the Liberals as offering the best possibility. As a result, the NDP retained only the seat of John Holm in Sackville and that of McDonough, by a scant majority, in Halifax Chebucto. Province-wide the party's popular vote remained at 16 per cent.

By retaining nine of the fourteen seats in Metro and most of their seats on the rest of the mainland the Conservatives won twenty-eight seats and a small majority. But their only gain was the former NDP seat in Kings South and only four of the twenty "new PC" candidates were successful. The bulk of the Conservatives elected were twenty-four incumbents. Making possible the narrow victory was the election of three Conservative Acadians in Yarmouth and Digby counties; the Acadians, normally Liberal, voted to sustain a government which had catered carefully to their needs. Also contributing largely to the Conservative success was the high level of prosperity prevailing generally on the mainland. But in the opinion of friend and foe alike the major factor was John Buchanan. Apparently Nova Scotians will simply not reject a premier whom they have learned to trust over a considerable period of time. Like George Murray in 1916, Buchanan won under extremely difficult conditions in 1988. If Fielding is credited with heading the leaderless Liberals in 1882 as he did from the desk of the *Morning Chronicle*, Buchanan joins Fielding, Murray, Macdonald, and Stanfield all of whom won four or more successive elections. Only history will judge how he ranks in that exalted company.

CHAPTER 1

Endnotes

1. Fielding to Fraser, July 7, 1896, PANS, Fielding Papers, MG2, 487:2:523-4; Jones to Laurier, Sept. 9, 1896 (strictly private and confidential), quoted in C.B. Fergusson, *Hon. W.S. Fielding, vol. 1: The Mantle of Howe* (Windsor: Lancelot Press, 1970), p. 162.
2. See note on J.W. Longley, PANS, MG100, vol. 177, no. 22; Benjamin Russell, "Recollections of W.S. Fielding," *Dalhousie Review*, IX (October 1929), p. 335.
3. Fielding to Murray, Apr. 29, 1896 (private and confidential), Fielding Papers, 487:2:211.
4. J. Murray Beck, *Politics of Nova Scotia, vol. 1, Nicholson to Fielding, 1710-1896* (Tantallon: Four East Publications, 1985), p. 266.
5. *Halifax Herald*, Apr. 10, 1897.
6. Through an error dating back to the 1860s the *Journals* of the House of Assembly (JHA) have wrongly numbered the general assemblies, in the beginning by listing the latter part of the Twenty-First as the Twenty-Second. This volume uses the correct numbering.
7. *Debates and Proceedings of the Nova Scotia House of Assembly* (hereafter Assembly *Debates*), 1899, p. 139.
8. *Ibid.*, 1901, p. 60.
9. *Ibid,* 1900, pp. 74, 77, 154, 158.
10. For comment on the election see esp. *Morning Chronicle*, Sept. 8, 11, 12, 16, 18 and Oct. 1, 2, 3, 1900; *Halifax Herald*, Sept. 7, 10, 13, 14, 20, 23, 27, 30 and Oct. 1, 2, 1900.
11. *Morning Chronicle*, Apr. 4, 1901; *Halifax Herald*, Apr. 5, 1901.
12. *Morning Chronicle*, July 15 and Sept. 11, 13, 30, 1901.
13. *Halifax Herald*, Oct. 3, 1901.

CHAPTER 2

Endnotes

1. Assembly *Debates,* 1903, pp. 142, 144.
2. *Ibid.,* p. 260; *Hubert v. Payson* [1904] S.C.R. 400.
3. *Morning Chronicle,* Mar. 28, 1902.
4. *Ibid., Feb. 20, 1902.*
5. Fielding to Murray (private and confidential), June 23, 1904, Fielding Papers, 448:205-10.
6. Fielding to Laurence (private), Nov. 19, 1904, *ibid.,* 449:1:142-3.
7. Assembly *Debates,* 1905, pp. 12, 23.
8. *Ibid.,* pp. 73, 127.
9. Fielding to Murray (private and confidential), Aug. 30, 1905, Fielding Papers, 452:473-4.
10. Assembly *Debates,* 1906, pp. 67-9; *Halifax Herald,* Mar. 8, 1906.
11. Assembly *Debates,* 1906, pp. 163-82, 193.
12. Fielding to Murray, May 25, 1906, Fielding Papers, 455:718- 9.
13. *Morning Chronicle,* Mar. 10, 1905.
14. See, e.g., *Halifax Herald,* June 2, 1906.
15. *Morning Chronicle,* June 18, 1906.
16. *Ibid.,* Mar. 26, 1908.
17. Assembly *Debates,* 1908, pp. 347-8.
18. *Ibid.,* 1909, pp. 177-78
19. *Ibid.,* pp. 109-13.
20. *Ibid.,* 1910, p. 23.
21. *Ibid.,* pp. 58-70.
22. *Ibid.,* p. 258
23. *Ibid.,* pp. 318-30.
24. *Morning Chronicle,* Feb. 22, 1911; J. Murray Beck, *Government of Nova Scotia* (Toronto: University of Toronto Press, 1959), pp. 166-7.
25. Assembly *Debates,* 1911, pp. 12-13.
26. *Ibid.,* pp. 241, 275, 337, 340-41.
27. *Ibid.,* p. 258.
28. Fielding to Murray (confidential), July 24, 1911, Fielding Papers, 483:717-8.
29. *Morning Chronicle,* Aug. 18 and Sept. 2, 6, 1911.
30. Fielding to Dr. T.B. Flint, Sept. 26, 1911, Fielding Papers, 484:415.

CHAPTER 3

Endnotes

1. *Morning Chronicle,* Mar. 13, 1912; Assembly *Debates,* 1912, p. 588.
2. Assembly *Debates,* 1912, p. 411.
3. *Ibid.,* 1913, p. 32.
4. *Morning Chronicle,* Mar. 15, 1913.
5. *William March, Red Line: The-Chronicle Herald and the Mail-Star 1875 — 1954* (Halifax: Chebucto Agencies Ltd., 1986), p. 101.
6. Assembly *Debates,* 1913, p. 741.
7. *Morning Chronicle,* Mar. 27, 1913.
8. Laurier to Macdonald, July 2, 1913, PANS, E.M. Macdonald Political Correspondence.
9. *Morning Chronicle,* Feb. 14, 17, 1914.
10. *Canadian Annual Review,* 1914, pp. 525-8.
11. Assembly *Debates,* 1915, pp. 196-201.
12. *Halifax Herald,* Feb. 18, 19, 1916.
13. Assembly *Debates,* 1916, p. 119.
14. *Ibid.,* p. 203.
15. *Morning Chronicle,* Mar. 11, 1916; *Halifax Herald,* Apr. 1, 1916.
16. March, *Red Line,* pp. 136-7; *Halifax Herald,* May 24, and June 13, 15, 1916.
17. *Morning Chronicle,* May 23, 1916.
18. *Ibid.,* June 17, 1916; *Halifax Herald,* June 17, 1916.
19. March, *Red Line,* p. 136.
20. *Morning Chronicle,* Mar. 27, 1917.
21. *Ibid.,* Apr. 18, 1917.
22. *Ibid.,* Apr. 12, 24, 1917.
23. Murray to Macdonald, May 3, 1917, E.M. Macdonald Political Correspondence.
24. Murray to Laurier (confidential), June 2, 1917, Fielding Papers, 524:5977; Murray to Fielding, June 2, 1917, *ibid.,* 524:5976.
25. Laurier to D.D. McKenzie, Oct. 13, 1917, E.M. Macdonald Political Correspondence.
26. *Morning Chronicle,* Oct. 24, 1917.
27. *Ibid.,* Nov. 30, 1917.
28. *Halifax Herald,* Dec. 14, 1917.

29. Fielding to Tanner, Dec. 3, 1917, Fielding Papers, 524:5973.
30. *Halifax Herald,* Dec. 19, 1917.
31. Laurier to Macdonald, Dec. 19 (inaccurately Nov. 19) and Dec. 26, 1917, E.M. Macdonald Political Correspondence.
32. For a more extensive discussion see Beck, *Government of Nova Scotia,* pp. 188-90.
33. *Halifax Herald,* Feb. 20, and Mar. 1, 3, 4, 11, 12, 1919.
34. *Morning Chronicle,* Apr. 26, and May 3, 1919.
35. *Ibid.,* May 14, 17, 1919.
36. *Ibid.,* May 7, 8, 1919.
37. *Halifax Herald,* May 5, 1920.
38. *Ibid.,* April 17, 1920; *Evening Echo,* Apr. 30, 1920.
39. *Evening Echo,* Apr. 15, 1920.
40. *Ibid.,* July 6, 1920.
41. *Morning Chronicle,* July 12, 13, 22, 1920.
42. Labourite D.W. Morrison also called himself a veterans' candidate.
43. Mrs. Rogers in Cumberland and Labourite Bertha Donaldson in Pictou became the first women candidates in provincial history.
44. *Halifax Herald,* July 9, 10, 1920.
45. *Ibid.,* July 24, 1920.
46. *Morning Chronicle,* July 26, 1920.
47. *Pictou Advocate,* July 16, 23, 1920.
48. *Halifax Herald,* July 28, 1920.

CHAPTER 4

Endnotes

1. *Eastern Chronicle,* May 24, 1921.
2. *Evening Echo,* Mar. 12, 1921.
3. *Morning Chronicle,* Apr. 22, 1921.
4. Armstrong to Smith, May 7, 1921, PANS, Armstrong Papers, MG2, vol. 36, F6/10186.
5. *Halifax Herald,* May 27, 1921.
6. JHA, 1921, p. 360.
7. *Halifax Herald,* Nov. 9, 1921.
8. See Ernest R. Forbes, *The Maritime Rights Movement, 1919-27: A Study in Canadian Regionalism* (Montreal: McGill — Queen's University Press, 1979), pp. 83-4, 89.
9. *Halifax Herald,* Dec. 7, 8, 1921.
10. *Canadian Annual Review,* 1922, p. 729.
11. *Halifax Herald,* May 30, 1921.
12. *Ibid.,* Mar. 4, 1922.
13. *Ibid.,* Mar. 29, 1922.
14. *Ibid.,* Apr. 7, 1922.
15. *Ibid.,* Apr. 13, 1922.
16. *Evening Echo,* Apr. 27, 1922.
17. *Ibid.,* Apr. 28, 1922.
18. Armstrong to Fielding (personal), Apr. 4, 1922, Armstrong Papers, vol. 10, F2/2947.
19. Pearson to Fielding, June 10, 1921, PANS, Pearson Papers, MG1, vol. 748, no. 9.
20. Irwin to Armstrong (personal), Feb. 11, 1922, Armstrong Papers, vol. 10, F3/3015; *ibid.* (personal), Nov. 29, 1922, F3/3064; *ibid.* (personal), Dec. 11, 1922, F3/3067.
21. Unknown to Tory, Dec. 11, 1922, PANS, MG2, vol. 30, no. 5.
22. Armstrong to King, Dec. 22, 1922, Armstrong Papers, vol. 11a, F6/3605.
23. Tory to Murray (personal), Jan. 18, 1923, PANS, MG2, vol. 30, no. 5; Fielding to Murray (private and confidential), Jan. 19, 1923, Fielding Papers, 498:20-1.
24. Tory to Murray, Jan. 22, 1922, MG2, vol. 30, no. 8.

25. E.R. Forbes, "In search of a post-confederation Maritime historiography, 1900-1967," in David Bercuson and Phillip Buckner, *Eastern and Western Perspectives* (Toronto: University of Toronto Press, 1981), pp. 55, 61.
26. Beck, *Government of Nova Scotia,* p. 201.
27. *Eastern Chronicle,* Jan. 26, 1923; *Halifax Herald,* Jan. 25, 1923; *Manitoba Free Press,* Feb. 17, 1923.
28. Irwin to Armstrong (personal), Jan. 31, 1923, Armstrong Papers, vol. 11a, F5/3563; Tory to Armstrong, Feb. 10, 1923, *ibid.,* F17/3843.
29. *Evening Echo,* Feb. 28, 1923.
30. *Ibid.,* Apr. 23, 1923; *Halifax Herald,* Apr. 23, 1923.
31. *Halifax Herald,* Apr. 7, 9, 1923.
32. McGregor to Armstrong (confidential), Oct. 25, 1923, Armstrong Papers, vol. 11a, F11/3770.
33. Forbes, *Maritime Rights Movement,* p. 54.
34. *Halifax Herald,* Feb. 16, 1924; *Evening Echo,* Feb. 16, 1924.
35. *Halifax Herald,* Mar. 27, 1924.
36. Armstrong to Macdonald (private), Oct. 28, 1924, Armstrong Papers, vol. 11b, F8/4283.
37. *Canadian Annual Review,* 1924-5, p. 333.
38. *Halifax Herald,* Dec. 9, 1924; Armstrong to Blair, Sept. 18, 1924, Armstrong Papers, vol. 23, F/7996.
39. John A. McDonald to Armstrong (personal), Jan. 15, 1925, *ibid.,* vol. 12, F9/4755.
40. Armstrong to Macdonald (personal), *ibid.,* Feb. 13, 1925, F8/4687; Feb. 23, 1925, F8/4694.
41. *Ibid.* (private), Mar. 2, 1925, F8/4699; *ibid.* (confidential), Mar. 25, 1925, F8/4713.
42. *Ibid.* (personal), Feb. 13, 1925, F8/4687.
43. Kelly to Armstrong, Mar. 26, 1925, *ibid.,* F13/4915.
44. See *Halifax Herald,* Apr. 1, 2, 3, 1925.
45. *Evening Echo,* Mar. 10, 25, 26, 1925; *Halifax Herald,* Mar. 28, 1925.
46. Fielding to Armstrong (personal), Mar. 10, 1925, Armstrong Papers, vol. 12, F4/4583; Armstrong to Fielding (personal), Apr. 6, 1925, *ibid.,* F4/4582.
47. JHA, 1925, pp. 227-9; Fielding to Armstrong (personal), June 19, 1925, Armstrong Papers, vol. 12, F4/4580.
48. Rand to Armstrong, Apr. 28, 1925, *ibid.,* vol. 23, F2a/8237; Blanchard to Armstrong, Apr. 30, 1925, *ibid.,* F2a/8253.
49. *Evening Echo,* May 22, 1925.
50. Congdon to Cahan, Feb. 7, 1925, PANS, MG2, vol. 1093, no. 291.
51. *Halifax Herald,* June 12, 1925. For the miners June 11th became Davis Day, which is still observed as a memorial day.
52. C.B. Fergusson Papers, PANS, MG1, box 1857, F2/2.
53. See Armstrong Papers, vol. 23.
54. A.S. MacMillan Private Papers, PANS, doc. 7.
55. King to Armstrong, Nov. 2, 1925, Armstrong Papers, vol. 14, F14/1291.
56. A. Jeffrey Wright, "The Hapless Politician: E.H. Armstrong of Nova Scotia," *N.S. Historical Quarterly,* 6 (Sept. 1976), pp. 259-79.

CHAPTER 5

Endnotes

1. Rhodes to Shipley, June 6, 1925, PANS, Rhodes Papers, MG2, 601:18046.
2. Halifax *Chronicle-Herald*, Dec. 1, 1965.
3. See *Evening Echo*, Sept. 14, 17, 1925.
4. *Halifax Herald*, Sept. 18, 1925.
5. C.B. Fergusson Papers, box 1857, F1/6.
6. *Halifax Herald*, Feb. 13, 14, 1926.
7. *Ibid.*, Mar. 2, 1926.
8. *Ibid.*, Feb. 4, 1927.
9. *Halifax Chronicle*, Feb. 25, 26, 1927; *Halifax Herald*, Feb. 26, 1927.
10. *Halifax Herald*, Feb. 18, 1927.
11. *Daily Star*, Feb. 9, Mar. 11, 1927.
12. *Halifax Chronicle*, Mar. 12, 1927; *Halifax Herald*, Mar. 12, 1927.
13. Forbes, *Maritime Rights*, pp. 162, 176.
14. *Ibid.*, p. 169.
15. *Daily Star*, Mar. 31, 1928. Aged W.H. Owen came from Bridgewater to vote for abolition, but it was too much for him. He died a few days later — forty-six years a councillor and the last link with the Holmes-Thompson government.
16. A.S. MacMillan Papers, doc. 11.
17. *Halifax Herald*, Mar. 16, 29, 1928.
18. *Ibid.*, Sept. 6, 1928.
19. *Halifax Chronicle*, Sept. 28, 1928.
20. *Halifax Herald*, Sept. 21, 1928.
21. *Daily Star*, Sept. 26, 1928.
22. *Halifax Herald*, Oct. 2, 3, 1928; *Halifax Chronicle*, Oct. 2, 1928; Daily Star, Oct. 2, 1928.
23. C.B. Fergusson Papers, box 1857, F1/6.
24. Rhodes to Dennis, Oct. 26, 1928, PANS, Rhodes Papers, MG2, 644:36404; to Lynch-Staunton, Oct. 8, 1928, *ibid.*, 36159; to Wood, Oct. 8, 1928, *ibid.*, 36148.
25. Rhodes to Brittain, Oct. 8, 1928, *ibid.*, 644:36155; to Lynch-Staunton, Oct. 8, 1928, *ibid.*, 36159; to Truman, Oct. 8, 1928, *ibid.*, 36142; to McConnell, Oct. 8, 1928, *ibid.*, 36157; to Wood, Oct. 8, 1928, *ibid.*, 36148; to Webster, Oct. 10, 1928, *ibid.*, 36137.

26. Rhodes to Cahan, Oct. 24, 1928, *ibid.*, 36174.
27. Rhodes to Bilkey, Oct. 12, 1928, *ibid.*, 36184.
28. The gift, anonymous at first, was that of W.H. Chase.
29. *Halifax Herald*, Mar. 7, 1929.
30. *Ibid.*, Apr.23, 1929.
31. *Ibid.*, Apr. 26, 1929.
32. *Ibid.*, Mar. 13, 1929; *Daily Star*, Mar. 13, 1929.
33. Rhodes to Borden (personal), Dec. 20, 1929, Rhodes Papers, 651:39744.
34. Rhodes to Bennett (personal), Jan. 24, 1930, *ibid.*, 39763; to J.T.M. Anderson, Jan. 27, 1930, *ibid.*, 653-40530; to Meighen, Feb. 1, 1930, *ibid.*, 40502.
35. *Halifax Chronicle*, Mar. 26, 1930.
36. *Ibid.*, Mar. 26, 27 and Apr. 8, 24, 1930.
37. *Daily Star*, Apr. 22, 1930.
38. *Halifax Herald*, Apr. 19, 24, 1930.
39. J. Murray Beck, *Pendulum of Power: Canada's Federal Elections* (Toronto: Prentice-Hall of Canada, 1968), p. 198.
40. A.S. MacMillan Private Papers, doc. 12; C.B. Fergusson Papers, box 1857, F2/2 and F1/6.
41. Macdonald to L.D. Currie, Feb. 5, 1926, PANS, Angus L. Macdonald Papers (hereafter ALM Papers), MG2, F1351/3.
42. Much of the account which follows is that of Macdonald. *Ibid.*, F/387.
43. C.B. Fergusson Papers, box 1857, F2/2. Farquhar states that MacMillan was as good as his word: "at his request money poured in from every quarter." *Ibid.*, F1/6.
44. Hanway to Macdonald, Oct. 2, 1930, ALM Papers, F1311/56; MacKay to Macdonald, Oct. 3, 1930, *ibid.*, F1312/59.
45. Macdonald to E.M. Macdonald (private and confidential), Mar. 9, 1936, *ibid.*, F1387/30.
46. *Halifax Chronicle*, Mar. 21, 1931.
47. Beck, *Government of Nova Scotia*, p. 261.
48. *Halifax Chronicle*, Apr. 14, 1931.
49. *Daily Star*, Apr. 29, 1932.
50. *Halifax Herald*, Mar. 24, 1933.
51. *Daily Star*, Apr. 25, 1933.
52. *Halifax Chronicle*, Mar. 24, 1933; *Halifax Herald*, Apr. 26, 1933.
53. C.B. Fergusson Papers, box 1857, F1/6.
54. *Halifax Chronicle*, July 26, 27, 1933; *Daily Star*, July 25, 26, 27, 1933.
55. Walker to Macdonald, Aug. 25, 1933, ALM Papers, F1360/112; MacKeen to Macdonald, Aug. 25, 1933, *ibid.*, F1360/62.
56. C.B. Fergusson Papers, box 1857, F2/2.
57. *Ibid.*, F1/6.
58. Halifax *Chronicle-Herald*, Mar. 25, 1950.

CHAPTER 6

Endnotes

1. Macdonald to Father Stanley Macdonald, Sept. 13, 1933, ALM Papers, F1364/23.
2. *Halifax Herald,* Mar. 3, 8, 1934; *Daily Star,* Mar. 8, 1934.
3. C.B. Fergusson Papers, box 1857, F1/6.
4. *Ibid.*
5. *Halifax Herald,* Mar. 23, 1934; *Daily Star,* Mar. 28, 1934.
6. A.S. MacMillan Private Papers, doc. 16.
7. *Halifax Herald,* Apr. 5, 11, 14, 17, 1934; *Halifax Chronicle,* Apr. 14, 17, 1934.
8. *Daily Star,* May 2, 1934.
9. *Halifax Chronicle,* Apr. 25, 1934.
10. See Beck, *Government of Nova Scotia,* pp. 331-2.
11. *Halifax Herald,* Mar. 15, 1935.
12. C.B. Fergusson Papers, box 1857, F2/1.
13. Beck, *Government of Nova Scotia,* pp. 222-3.
14. C.B. Fergusson Papers, box 1857, F1/6.
15. *Halifax Chronicle,* Mar. 6, 1935.
16. Chisholm to Macdonald, Mar. 12, 1935, ALM Papers, F1375/55; Macdonald to Chisholm, Mar. 29, 1935, *ibid.,* F1375/54.
17. Macdonald to Johnston, Oct. 15, 1935, *ibid.,* F1377/24.
18. Macdonald to Farquhar, Nov. 4, 1936, *ibid.,* F1387/39; Farquhar to Macdonald, Apr. 29, 1936, *ibid.,* F/1387/38.
19. Macdonald to E.M. Macdonald (private and confidential), Mar. 9, 1936, *ibid.,* F1389/30.
20. Macdonald to Father Stanley Macdonald (private and confidential), Mar. 3, 1936, *ibid.,* F1385/81.
21. *Halifax Herald,* July 15, 1936; *Daily Star,* July 15, 1936.
22. *Halifax Herald,* Mar. 4, 5, 1937.
23. *Ibid.,* Mar. 5, 1937; *Daily Star,* Mar. 5, 1937.
24. *Daily Star,* Mar. 18, 1937.
25. *Halifax Herald,* Mar. 9, 1937.
26. *Halifax Chronicle,* Mar. 10, 1937.
27. March, *Red Line,* p. 260.

28. *Daily Star,* June 10, 1937; *Halifax Herald,* June 14, 15, 1937; March, *Red Line,* pp. 261-3.
29. Macdonald to Ilsley, July 6, 1937, ALM Papers, F1403/1; Macdonald to Rogers, July 2, 1937, *ibid.,* F1404/24; Macdonald to Robertson, July 14, 1937, *ibid.,* F1404/18
30. C.B. Fergusson Papers, box 1857, F1/6, F2/2.
31. Macdonald to Alex Johnston, Apr. 20, 1938, ALM Papers, F398/12.
32. *Daily Star,* Mar. 9, 1938.
33. *Halifax Herald,* Apr. 9, 1938.
34. *Daily Star,* Apr. 5, 1938; *Halifax Herald,* Mar. 31, Apr. 5, 1938.
35. Macdonald to Fraser, July 16, 1938, ALM Papers, F397/18.
36. *Ibid.,* Sept. 12, 1938, F397/22. See March, *Red Line,* pp. 288-90.
37. Macdonald to Fraser (private and confidential), Aug. 31, 1938, F397/21.
38. Macdonald to Father Stanley Macdonald, Oct. 17, 1938, *ibid.,* F422/47.
39. Macdonald to Johnston, Feb. 7, 1939, *ibid.,* F405/75.
40. *Ibid.*
41. Macdonald to MacLennan, Apr. 24, 1939, *ibid.,* F406/106.
42. *Halifax Chronicle,* Mar. 2, 1939.
43. *Daily Star,* Mar. 14, 1939.
44. *Halifax Herald,* Mar. 28, 29, 1939.
45. *Ibid.,* Mar. 4, 1939.
46. *Ibid.; Daily Star,* Mar. 7, 1939.
47. See March, *Red Line,* pp. 267-78.
48. Macdonald to Joseph A. Macdonald, July 11, 1939, ALM Papers, F406/20.
49. *Daily Star,* Mar. 8, 1940; *Halifax Herald,* Mar. 8, 1940.
50. Quinan to Macdonald, Apr. 3, 1940, ALM Papers, F414/28; Macdonald to Quinan, Apr. 2, 1940, *ibid.,* F414/29; and Apr. 11, 1940 (private and confidential), *ibid.,* F414/31.
51. Macdonald to MacLennan (personal), Mar. 6, 1940, *ibid.,* F413/71.
52. Macdonald to King (personal and confidential), May 8, 1940, *ibid.,* F412/80.

CHAPTER 7

Endnotes

1. *Daily Star*, Oct. 10, 1940; *Halifax Herald*, Oct. 10, 1940.
2. *Daily Star*, Feb. 27, 28, 1941.
3. *Ibid.*, Feb. 28 and March. 1, 1941; *Halifax Herald*, Feb. 28, 1941.
4. *Halifax Herald*, Apr. 7, 1941.
5. *Ibid.*, Sept. 20, 23, 25, 1941.
6. *Halifax Herald*, Sept. 20, 1941.
7. *Ibid.*, Oct. 25, 27, 1941.
8. MacMillan to Macdonald, Nov. 4, 1941, ALM Papers, F868/3; Macdonald to MacMillan (personal and confidential), Nov. 10, 1941, *ibid.*, F868/4.
9. *Daily Star*, Feb. 24, 1942.
10. *Ibid.*, Mar. 10, 1942.
11. Beck, *Government of Nova Scotia*, p. 333.
12. *Ibid.*, p. 313.
13. *Halifax Chronicle*, Mar. 25, 1943; *Halifax Herald*, Mar. 26, 1943.
14. *Halifax Herald*, Mar. 3, 7, 1944.
15. *Daily Star*, Mar. 29, 1944.
16. Macdonald to MacKeen (personal), Aug. 24, 1943, ALM Papers, F764/1.
17. Macdonald to MacSween (personal), Dec. 13, 1944, *ibid.*, F764/29.
18. *Morning Chronicle*, Feb. 17, 1945.
19. *Daily Star*, Feb. 23, 1945.
20. See Beck, *Government of Nova Scotia*, pp. 341-3.
21. *Halifax Herald*, June 8, 1945.
22. Beck, *Pendulum of Power*, p. 246.
23. Macdonald to MacMillan (personal), Feb. 19, 1945, ALM Papers, F764/42; MacMillan to Macdonald (confidential), Feb. 24, 1945, *ibid.*, F764/41.
24. Macdonald to MacMillan (personal and confidential), Apr. 19, 1945, ALM Papers, F764/50.
25. Patterson to Macdonald (private and confidential), May 4, 1945, *ibid.*, F764/63; Macdonald to Patterson (personal and confidential), May 30, 1945, *ibid.*, 764/62.
26. MacMillan to Macdonald, May 21, 1945, *ibid.*, F764/59; Macdonald to MacMillan, May 26, 1945, *ibid.*, F764/58.
27. C.B. Fergusson Papers, box 1857, F2/2.

28. Macdonald to MacMillan (personal and confidential), June 23, 1945, ALM Papers, F764/70.
29. C.B. Fergusson Papers, box 1857, F2/2.
30. *Ibid.*
31. *Daily Star*, Sept. 1, 1945; *Halifax Herald*, Sept. 1, 1945.
32. C.B. Fergusson Papers, box 1857, F2/2, F1/8.

CHAPTER 8

Endnotes

1. *Ottawa Journal,* Sept. 13, 1945; *Halifax Chronicle,* Sept. 10, 1945.
2. Crerar to Macdonald (personal), Sept. 13, 1945, ALM Papers, box 900, F28a/135.
3. C.B. Fergusson Papers, box 1857, F2/2.
4. *Halifax Herald,* Oct. 3, 1945; *Daily Star,* Oct. 3, 4, 1945.
5. Davis to Macdonald, Oct. 22, 1945, ALM Papers, box 900, F28A/153; Macdonald to Bishop Cody, Nov. 9, 1945, *ibid.,* F28a/108.
6. *Halifax Herald,* Feb. 22, 1946.
7. "Preliminary Statement of the Province of Nova Scotia," JHA, 1946, App. 33, pp. 2-4.
8. Macdonald to Johnston (personal), Feb. 13, 1947, ALM Papers, box 919, F31-1/919.
9. Macdonald to Crerar (personal), Apr. 7, 1947, *ibid.,* box 918, F31-1/164; to John Connolly (personal), Apr. 9, 1947, *ibid.,* F31-1/142.
10. *Daily Star,* May 12, 1947.
11. *Halifax Herald,* Apr. 10, 1947; *Daily Star,* Apr. 15, 23, 1947.
12. Power to Macdonald, May 14, 1947, ALM Papers, box 920, F31- 2/106; Macdonald to Power, Sept. 15, 1947, *ibid.,* F31-2/105; to John Connolly, July 18, 1947, *ibid.,* F31-1/147.
13. He liked particularly J.A. Corry's *Democratic Government and Politics,* both for its examination of federalism and its treatment of individual liberty as an essential ingredient of democracy.
14. Macdonald to Grant Dexter, Nov. 10, 1947, ALM Papers, box 918, F31-1/182.
15. *Halifax Herald,* Mar. 25, 1948.
16. *Ibid.,* Mar. 30 and Apr. 3, 10, 1948; *Halifax Chronicle,* Apr. 3, 1948.
17. *Halifax Chronicle,* Apr. 16, 1948.
18. *Halifax Herald,* Mar. 17, 1948.
19. Halifax *Chronicle-Herald* (hereafter *Chronicle- Herald*), Mar. 12, 1949.
20. *Ibid.,* Mar. 16, 1949.
21. *Ibid.,* Mar. 19, 22, 29, 1949.
22. Geoffrey Stevens, *Stanfield* (Toronto: McClelland and Stewart, 1973), p. 47.
23. Nova Scotia Progressive Conservative Association *Minutes,* pp. 302-10.

24. *Chronicle-Herald,* May 9, 13, 1949.
25. Fielding to Macdonald, n.d., ALM Papers, box 944, F27-10/72.
26. *Chronicle-Herald,* May 10, 26, 1949.
27. Macdonald to Brison, May 2, 1949, ALM Papers, box 944, F27- 10/64.
28. Macdonald to Alex Johnston, July 4, 1949, *ibid.,* F27- 12/68.
29. C.B. Fergusson Papers, box 1857, F2/3.
30. *Ibid.*
31. *Chronicle-Herald,* Mar. 23, 1950.
32. *Ibid.,* Mar. 25, 1950.
33. *Ibid.,* Mar. 28, 1950.
34. *Ibid.,* Apr. 18, 1950.
35. *Ibid.,* May 4, 1950.
36. C.B. Fergusson Papers, box 1857, F2/3.
37. *Chronicle-Herald,* Apr. 14, 17; May 6, 1950.
38. Macdonald to Crerar (personal and confidential), Jan. 15, 1951, ALM Papers, box 964, F31-2/7.
39. *Chronicle-Herald,* Feb. 16, 20, 21 and Mar. 3, 1951.
40. *Ibid.,* Mar. 9, 14, 1951.
41. *Proceedings of the N.S. House of Assembly* (hereafter Assembly *Debates*), 1952, pp. 11, 70.
42. *Ibid.,* p. 365.
43. *Chronicle-Herald,* Mar. 18, 19, 20, 22, 28 and Apr. 2, 3, 1952.
44. Assembly *Debates,* 1952, pp. 846-57, 1021-38.
45. *Chronicle-Herald,* Feb. 10, 11, 1953.
46. *Ibid.,* Feb. 6, 7, 14, 17, 1953.
47. *Ibid.,* Mar. 12, 1953.
48. Macdonald to Crerar (confidential), Mar. 28, 1953, ALM Papers, box 978, F31-2/18.
49. Stevens, *Stanfield,* p. 91.
50. For his account of the election see *Gentlemen, Players and Politicians* (Toronto: McClelland and Stewart, 1970), pp. 109-32.
51. New Glasgow *Evening News,* May 15, 1953.
52. Macdonald's final radio speech, ALM Papers, box 977, F27- 9/24.
53. *Chronicle-Herald,* May 14, 1953.
54. Camp, *Gentlemen, Players and Politicians,* p. 127.
55. *Ibid.,* p. 129.
56. Macdonald to McNair, July 14, 1953, ALM Papers, box 977, F27-12/105; to Grant Dexter, May 29, 1953, *ibid.,* F27-12/10; to Father Stanley Macdonald (personal and confidential), June 9, 1953, *ibid.,* box 978, F31-2/22.
57. A statute in 1946 had permitted the offices of provincial secretary and provincial treasurer to be separated for the first time.
58. Assembly *Debates,* 1954, vol. 1, p. 242.
59. Sec C.B. Fergusson Papers, box 1857, for comments of Jefferson, Connolly, and Hicks.

CHAPTER 9

Endnotes

1. Dalton Camp, *Gentlemen, Players and Politicians,* p. 150.
2. For details of the convention, including accounts of interviews with the candidates, see Allan C. Dunlop, *A Classification of Nova Scotian Elections,* unpublished M.A. thesis, Dalhousie University, 1970, pp. 105-10, 169.
3. Camp, *Gentlemen, Players and Politicians,* p. 152.
4. *Chronicle-Herald,* June 8, 1955.
5. Stevens, *Stanfield,* p. 93.
6. *Chronicle-Herald,* Mar. 9, 11, 16, 1955.
7. Assembly *Debates,* 1955, vol. 3, p. 314.
8. Beck, *Government of Nova Scotia,* pp. 323-5; *Chronicle-Herald,* Apr. 8, 1955.
9. Stevens, *Stanfield,* p. 97.
10. Assembly *Debates,* 1956, vol. 1, pp. 40-1, 151-6, 158- 60.
11. *Chronicle-Herald,* Mar. 27, 1956.
12. *Ibid.,* Sept. 17, 1956.
13. M. Van Steen, "The Rising Tory Star in N.S.," *Saturday Night,* vol. 71, Nov. 24, 1956, pp. 7-8.
14. *Chronicle-Herald,* Oct. 25, 1956.
15. Camp, *Gentlemen, Players and Politicians,* pp. 213-4. Stanfield had been rejected on medical grounds.
16. Cragg to Hicks (personal and confidential), Nov. 13, 1956, PANS, MG2, vol. 1238, no. 8; Cowan to Hicks, Nov. 12, 1956, *ibid.*
17. Notes of Jefferson to Hicks, *ibid.*
18. Beck, *Government of Nova Scotia,* p. 325.
19. See letters of Liberal candidates and party official to Hicks, PANS, MG2, vol. 1238, no. 8; Lunenburg *Progress Enterprise,* Sept. 12, Nov. 7, 1956; *Liverpool Advance,* Sept. 27, 1956.
20. As quoted in *Pictou Advocate,* Nov. 8, 1956.

CHAPTER 10

Endnotes

1. *Chronicle-Herald,* June 11, 1957.
2. *Ibid.,* Apr. 27, May 2, 1957.
3. *Ibid.,* May 1, June 6, 1957.
4. *Ibid.,* May 25, 1957.
5. Roy E. George, *The Life and Times of Industrial Estates Limited* (Halifax: Institute of Public Affairs, Dalhousie University, 1974), p. 6.
6. Assembly *Debates,* 1958, vol. 1, pp. 155-6.
7. *Chronicle-Herald,* Mar. 1, 1958.
8. *Ibid.,* Oct. 22, 1958.
9. *Ibid.,* Mar. 19, 1959.
10. Assembly *Debates,* 1959, vol. 1, pp. 172-211.
11. *Chronicle-Herald,* Feb. 11, 1959.
12. Assembly *Debates,* 1959, vol. 4, pp. 2262-3.
13. *Ibid.,* 1960, vol. 1, pp. 56-7.
14. *Chronicle-Herald,* Mar. 1, 2, 1960.
15. *Ibid.,* Mar. 2, 1960.
16. *Ibid.,* Mar. 15, 1960.
17. *Ibid.,* May 4, 5, 6, 9, 10, 11, 1960.
18. *Ibid.,* May 25, 1960.
19. *Ibid.,* May 28, 1960.
20. *Ibid.,* May 20, 1960.
21. *Ibid.,* May 21, 1960.
22. *Canadian Annual Review,* 1960, p. 21.
23. *Chronicle-Herald,* May 12, 1960.
24. Assembly *Debates,* 1961, vol. 1, p. 186.
25. *Chronicle-Herald,* Feb. 17, 1961.
26. Assembly *Debates,* 1962, vol. 1, pp. 182-3.
27. *Chronicle-Herald,* Mar. 16, 1962.
28. *Ibid.,* Mar. 10, 16, 21, 30, 31 and Apr. 5, 7, 1962.
29. See Beck, *Politics of Nova Scotia,* vol. 1, p. 253.
30. *Chronicle-Herald,* Mar. 6, 7, 1963.
31. *Ibid.,* Mar. 12, 1963.
32. *Ibid.,* Mar. 6, 20, 21, 1963.
33. *Ibid.,* Sept. 14, 18, 20, 21, 24 and Oct. 4, 1963.

34. *Ibid.*, Sept. 13, 20, 26, 28, 30, 1963.

35. *Ibid.*, Sept. 21, 23, 24, 1963.

36. Mary Casey, "N.S. Conservatives Sell the Premier," *Globe and Mail*, Sept. 25, 1963.

37. *Chronicle-Herald*, Nov. 18, 1963.

38. This paragraph summarizes material in E.D. Haliburton, *My Years with Stanfield* (Windsor: Lancelot Press, 1972), pp. 7-8, 20, 38, 40.

39. Assembly *Debates*, 1964, vol. 1, p. 33; *Chronicle- Herald*, Feb. 7, 1964.

40. *Chronicle-Herald*, Feb. 12, 1964.

41. Assembly *Debates*, 1964, vol. 2, p. 581.

42. Haliburton, *My Years with Stanfield*, p. 18.

43. *Chronicle-Herald*, Feb. 25, 26, 1964.

44. *Ibid.*, Mar. 5, 1964.

45. *Canadian Annual Review*, 1964, p. 131.

46. Assembly *Debates*, 1965, vol 1, p. 109.

47. *Ibid.*, vol. 3, pp. 996-8.

48. *Chronicle-Herald*, Mar. 3, 1965.

49. *Ibid.*, Mar. 8, 1965.

50. *Ibid.*, Mar. 29, 1965.

51. *Ibid.*, July 26, 1965.

52. *Ibid.*, Sept. 25, 1965.

53. *Ibid.*, Nov. 9, 1965.

54. J. Murray Beck, "The Electoral Behaviour of Nova Scotia in 1965," *Dalhousie Review*, 46 (Spring 1966), p. 38.

55. Stanfield to Beck, June 3, 1966.

56. Assembly *Debates*, 1966, vol. 1, p. 33.

57. *Ibid.*, pp. 90, 114.

58. *Chronicle-Herald*, Mar. 5, Apr. 2, 1966.

59. Assembly *Debates*, 1967, vol. 1, p. 72.

60. *Ibid.*, pp. 109-10.

61. *Chronicle-Herald*, Feb. 17, 1967.

62. *Ibid.*, Apr. 21, 1967.

63. *Ibid.*, May 12, 1967.

64. *Ibid.*, May 11, 15, 1967.

65. *Ibid.*, May 11, 1967.

66. *Ibid.*, May 22, 1967.

67. Dartmouth *Free Press*, May 25, 1967.

68. Dunlop, *Classification of Nova Scotia Elections*, p. 150.

69. See *ibid.*, p. 151.

CHAPTER 11

Endnotes

1. *Chronicle-Herald,* Feb. 25, 1969.
2. Dalton Camp, "Smith had fought quite a war," *ibid.,* Oct. 23, 1970.
3. *Canadian Annual Review,* 1968, p. 448.
4. Assembly *Debates,* 1968, vol. 1, pp. 71, 80-1.
5. *Ibid.,* pp. 120, 143, 149-50.
6. *Chronicle-Herald,* Mar. 8, 1968.
7. Assembly *Debates,* 1968, vol. 2, pp. 1308, 1313.
8. *Chronicle-Herald,* Mar. 22, 1968.
9. *JHA,* 1968, p. 193.
10. *Chronicle-Herald,* June 22, 1968.
11. Ottawa *Citizen,* May 22, 1968.
12. *Chronicle-Herald,* Feb. 14, 1969.
13. *Ibid.,* Feb. 15, 1969.
14. *Ibid.,* Feb. 18, 1969.
15. *Ibid.,* Apr. 4, 1969.
16. *Ibid.,* Apr. 23, 1969.
17. *Ibid.,* Mar. 8, 1969.
18. *Ibid.,* Mar. 21, 1969.
19. *Ibid.,* Mar. 14, 18, 1969.
20. *Ibid.,* Mar. 26, 1969.
21. *Ibid.,* Apr. 24, 1969.
22. *Ibid.,* Apr. 5, 1969.
23. *Ibid.,* Mar. 15, 1969.
24. *Ibid.,* Mar. 20, 1969.
25. *Ibid.,* Mar. 26, 1970; Assembly *Debates,* 1970, vol 3, pp. 1746-7.
26. Assembly *Debates,* 1970, vol. 3, p. 2309.
27. *Chronicle-Herald,* Apr. 24, 1970.
28. Assembly *Debates,* 1970, vol. 3, pp. 1928-9.
29. *Ibid.,* 1970, vol. 1, pp. 64-5, 96, 134.
30. *Ibid.,* vol. 3, pp. 2470, 2482.
31. *Report of the Special Senate Committee on the Mass Media, vol. 1, The Uncertain Mirror,* 1970, p. 89.
32. *Chronicle-Herald,* Apr. 23, 1970.
33. *Ibid.,* Apr. 7, 8, 1970.

34. Assembly *Debates,* 1970, vol. 3, pp. 2628, 2633, 2635- 6.
35. *Canadian Annual Review,* 1970, pp. 235-6.
36. *Chronicle-Herald,* Oct. 10, 1970.
37. *Ibid.,* Oct. 2, 1970.
38. *Ibid.,* Sept. 24, 1970.
39. *The 4th Estate,* Oct. 1, 1970.
40. *Chronicle-Herald,* Sept. 18, 1970.
41. *Ibid.,* Sept. 25, 26, 28, 1970.
42. *Time,* Oct. 26, 1970.
43. *Globe and Mail,* Oct. 15, 24, 1970.
44. *Chronicle-Herald,* Oct. 23, 1970.
45. J. Murray Beck, "Elections in the Maritimes: The Voters Against Have It," *Canadian Commentator,* Dec. 1970, p. 9.
46. *Ibid.,* pp. 8-9.

CHAPTER 12

Endnotes

1. Assembly *Debates,* 1970-71, vol. 1, pp. 66-7.
2. *Chronicle-Herald,* Dec. 17, 1970.
3. *Ibid.,* Dec. 22, 1970.
4. *Ibid.,* Jan. 14, 1971.
5. Assembly *Debates,* 1970-71, vol. 2, pp. 1665, 1670.
6. *Canadian Annual Review,* 1971, p. 146.
7. *Chronicle-Herald,* June 30, July 7, 1971.
8. Assembly *Debates,* 1972, vol. 1, pp. 161-4.
9. Duncan Fraser, "The McKeough resolution and its implications," *Chronicle-Herald,* Mar. 3, 1972.
10. *Chronicle-Herald,* Mar. 31, 1972.
11. See article of Peter Meerburg, *ibid.,* Oct. 3, 1972.
12. *Chronicle-Herald,* Oct. 3, 1972.
13. *Ibid.,* Feb. 23, 1972.
14. *Ibid.,* Feb. 8, 1973.
15. *Ibid.,* Mar. 29, 1973.
16. Stan Fitzner, "My Line," *ibid.,* Dec. 6, 1973.
17. *Globe and Mail,* Feb. 26, 1974.
18. *The 4th Estate,* Feb. 28, 1974.
19. *Canadian Annual Review,* 1974, p. 200; *Chronicle- Herald,* Mar. 29, 1974.
20. *Chronicle-Herald,* July 9, 1974.
21. *Ibid.,* Nov. 18, 1974.
22. *Ibid.,* Nov. 9, 1974.
23. *Canadian Annual Review,* 1974, p. 205.
24. Assembly *Debates,* 1975, vol. 2, p. 953.
25. *Chronicle-Herald,* Jan. 15, 22, 23, 24, 26, 1976.
26. *Ibid.,* Mar. 18, 1986.
27. *Ibid.,* Feb. 19, 1976.
28. *Canadian Annual REview,* 1976, pp. 212-3.
29. *Chronicle-Herald,* Apr. 7, 1976.
30. *Ibid.,* Apr. 15, 1976.
31. Assembly *Debates,* 1977, vol. 2, pp. 1052, 1061.
32. *Chronicle-Herald,* Mar. 9, Apr. 2, 1977.
33. *Ibid.,* Apr. 9, 1977.

34. Assembly *Debates,* 1978. vol. 1, p. 44.
35. *Chronicle-Herald,* Apr. 8, 1978.
36. *Ibid.,* May 20, 1978; *Globe and Mail,* May 27, 1978.
37. *Chronicle-Herald,* Aug. 18, 1978.
38. *Ibid.,* Sept. 5, 1978.
39. *Ibid.,* Sept. 20, 1978.
40. *The 4th Estate,* Nov. 12, 1975, p. 4.

CHAPTER 13

Endnotes

1. Assembly *Debates,* 1978-9, vol. 1, p. 246.
2. *Chronicle-Herald,* Mar. 17, 1979.
3. *Ibid.,* May 14, 1979.
4. *Ibid.,* May 1, 1979.
5. Assembly *Debates,* 1979, vol. 3, p. 2244.
6. *Ibid.,* vol. 4, p. 3268.
7. *Chronicle-Herald,* Apr. 4, 1980.
8. *Ibid.,* May 3, 1980.
9. Ian McKay, "Left, Right and Centre — Three NDPs in the Maritimes," *The New Maritimes,* 2 (July-Aug. 1984), p. 10.
10. *Ibid.*
11. *Chronicle-Herald,* Apr. 17, 1981.
12. Assembly *Debates,* vol. 5, 1981, pp. 3328-9, 3709-13, 3924-79; vol. 6, 1981, pp. 4633-41; *Chronicle Herald,* May 15 and June 2, 4, 11, 12, 1981.
13. *Chronicle-Herald,* Sept. 4, 18, 1981.
14. *Ibid.,* Sept. 2, 1981.
15. From the report of the Conference Board of Canada, *Chronicle-Herald,* Aug. 11, 1982.
16. *Chronicle-Herald,* Feb. 19, 1982.
17. Assembly *Debates,* vol. 4, 1982, p. 2346.
18. *Chronicle-Herald,* May 14, 1982.
19. See article of Parker Barss Donham, *Globe and Mail,* Feb. 27, 1982.
20. Assembly *Debates,* vol 3, 1983, pp. 1809, 1812.
21. *Chronicle-Herald,* Feb. 27, 1984.
22. Assembly *Debates,* 1984, vol. 2, p. 942.
23. *Chronicle-Herald,* Apr. 10, 1984.
24. *Ibid.,* Mar. 24, 1984.
25. *Ibid.,* Mar. 28, 1984.
26. See article of Peter Moreira, *ibid.,* Sept. 12, 1984.
27. *Ibid.,* Sept. 29, 1984.
28. Patrick Jamieson, "Paul MacEwan and the Strange World of Fourth Party Politics in Cape Breton," *The New Maritimes,* 5 (October 1986), pp. 4, 7.
29. *Chronicle-Herald,* Nov. 7, 1984.
30. *Ibid.*

31. *Ibid.*, Oct. 5, 1984.
32. Assembly *Debates*, 1985, vol. 1, p. 50.
33. *Chronicle-Herald*, Mar. 7, 1985.
34. *Ibid.*, Mar. 19, 1985.
35. *Ibid.*, May 18, 1985.
36. See Bill Gillis, "N.S. credit rating plummeting," *ibid.*, Apr. 2, 1986.
37. *Chronicle-Herald*, Apr. 19, May 1, 1986.
38. Assembly *Debates*, 1986, vol. 3, p. 2022.
39. *Ibid.*, p. 2282.
40. *Chronicle-Herald*, May 1, 1986.
41. *Ibid.*, Jan. 7, 1987.
42. *Ibid.*, Mar. 3, 1987.
43. *Ibid.*, Feb. 28, 1987.
44. *Ibid.*, Mar. 24, 1987.
45. *Ibid.*, Mar. 14, 1987.
46. *Ibid.*, Apr. 11, 28, 1987.
47. *Ibid.*, May 12, 14, 1987.
48. *Ibid.*, May 30, 1987.
49. *Ibid.*, May 14, 1987.
50. *Ibid.*, May 30, 1987.
51. *Ibid.*, Feb. 26, 1988.
52. *Ibid.*, May 6, 1988.
53. *Ibid.*, Apr. 15, 1988.
54. *Ibid.*, Apr. 20, 1988.
55. *Globe and Mail*, Apr. 6, 1988.

Appendix

A

Nova Scotia Ministries
(1896-1988)

Premier	Sworn In	Party
William Stevens Fielding	July 28, 1884	Liberal
George Henry Murray	July 20, 1896	Liberal
Ernest Howard Armstrong	Jan. 24, 1923	Liberal
Edgar Nelson Rhodes	July 16, 1925	Conservative
Gordon Sidney Harrington	Aug. 11, 1930	Conservative
Angus Lewis Macdonald	Sept. 5, 1933	Liberal
Alexander Stirling MacMillan	July 10, 1940	Liberal
Angus Lewis Macdonald	Sept. 8, 1945	Liberal
Harold Joseph Connolly	Apr. 13, 1954	Liberal
Henry Davies Hicks	Sept. 30, 1954	Liberal
Robert Lorne Stanfield	Nov. 20, 1956	Progressive Conservative
George Isaac Smith	Sept. 13, 1967	Progressive Conservative
Gerald Augustine Regan	Oct. 28, 1970	Liberal
John MacLennan Buchanan	Oct. 5, 1978	Progressive Conservative

Appendix

B

Lieutenant-Governors
(1896-1988)

Sir Malachy B. Daly	July 14, 1890
A.G. Jones	Aug. 7, 1900
Duncan C. Fraser	Mar. 30, 1906
J.D. McGregor	Oct. 21, 1910
David MacKeen	Oct. 22, 1915
MacCallum Grant	Dec. 2, 1916
J. Robson Douglas	Jan. 23, 1925
James C. Tory	Oct. 1, 1925
Frank Stanfield	Dec. 2, 1930
W.H. Covert	Oct. 9, 1931
Robert Irwin	May 1, 1937
F.H. Mathers	June 10, 1940
H.E. Kendall	Nov. 30, 1942
J.A.D. McCurdy	Aug. 12, 1947
Alistair Fraser	Oct. 1, 1952
E.C. Plow	Jan. 15, 1958
Henry P. MacKeen	Mar. 1, 1963
Victor deB. Oland	July 22, 1968
Clarence L. Gosse	Oct. 1, 1973
John E. Shaffner	Dec. 23, 1978
Alan R. Abraham	Feb. 1, 1984

APPENDIX

C

NOVA SCOTIA PROVINCIAL ELECTIONS
(1897-1984)

Date	Liberal			Conservative			Independents			Total Vote
Apr. 20, 1897	Candidates 38	Vote 84,000 →		Candidates 36	Vote 67,779 →		Candidates 3	Vote 968 →		152,747
No. of seats 38	Elected 35	55.0%		Elected 3	44.4%		Elected 0	0.6%		

Total candidates
77
Note: Two Liberals elected in Shelburne by acclamation.

Date	Liberal			Conservative			Independents			Total Vote
Oct. 2, 1901	Candidates 38	Vote 78,375 →		Candidates 32	Vote 57,689 →		Candidates 3	Vote 2,147 →		138,211
No. of seats 38	Elected 36	56.7%		Elected 2	41.7%		Elected 0	1.6%		

Total candidates
73
Note: Four Liberals, two in Antigonish and two in Yarmouth, elected by acclamation.

Date	Liberal		Conservative		Independents		Total Vote
June 20, 1906	Candidates 38	Vote 84,359	Candidates 31	Vote 66,638	Candidates 5	Vote 7,423	158,420
No. of seats 38	Elected 32	53.2%	Elected 5	42.1%	Elected 1	4.7%	

Total candidates
74

Note: Four Liberals, two in Antigonish and two in Victoria, elected by acclamation. A Unity Reform candidate elected in Kings.

Date	Liberal		Conservative		Independents		Total
June 14, 1911	Candidates 38	Vote 99,192	Candidates 37	Vote 88,114	Candidates 5	Vote 6,851	194,157
No. of seats 38	Elected 27	51.1%	Elected 11	45.4%	Elected 0	3.5%	

Total candidates
80

Date	Liberal		Conservative		Independents		Total
June 22, 1916	Candidates 43	Vote 136,315	Candidates 43	Vote 131,844	Candidates 3	Vote 2,215	270,374
No. of seats 43	Elected 30	50.4%	Elected 13	48.8%	Elected 0	0.8%	

Total candidates
89

Date	Liberal		Conservative		Labour		Farmer		Total Vote
	Candidates	Vote	Candidates	Vote	Candidates	Vote	Candidates	Vote	
July 2, 1920	40	154,627	31	81,044	12	58,727	17	53,556	347,954
	Elected		Elected		Elected		Elected		
	29	44.4%	3	23.3%	4	16.9%	7	15.4%	
No. of seats									
43									
Total candidates									
100									

Note: In Guysborough Dillon, who ran as a farmer and fisherman, and polled 1,309 votes, is treated as a Farmer.

Date	Liberal		Conservative		Labour		Total Vote
	Candidates	Vote	Candidates	Vote	Candidates	Vote	
June 25, 1925	43	161,158	43	270,544	10	12,260	443,962
	Elected		Elected		Elected		Turnout
	3	36.3%	40	60.9%	0	2.8%	69.1%
No. of seats							
43							
Total candidates							
96							

Date	Liberal		Conservative		Labour		Total Vote
	Candidates	Vote	Candidates	Vote	Candidates	Vote	
Oct. 1, 1928	43	209,380	43	218,974	2	4,862	433,216
	Elected		Elected		Elected		Turnout
	20	48.3%	23	50.6%	0	1.1%	70.9%
No. of seats							
43							
Total candidates							
88							

Date	Liberal			Conservative			CCF			United Front			Total Vote
Aug. 22, 1933	Candidates 30	Vote 166,170	52.6%	Candidates 30	Vote 145,107	45.9%	Candidates 3	Vote 2,336	0.7%	Candidates 3	Vote 2,469	0.8%	316,082
	Elected 22			Elected 8			Elected 0			Elected 0			Turnout 85.9%

No. of seats
30

Total candidates
66

Date	Liberal			Conservative			Labour			Total Vote
June 22, 1937	Candidates 30	Vote 165,397	52.9%	Candidates 30	Vote 143,670	46.0%	Candidates 1	Vote 3,396	1.1%	312,463
	Elected 25			Elected 5			Elected 0			Turnout 79.7%

No. of seats
30

Total candidates
61

Date	Liberal			Conservative			CCF			Total Vote
Oct. 28, 1941	Candidates 30	Vote 138,915	52.7%	Candidates 29	Vote 106,133	40.3%	Candidates 6	Vote 18,583	7.0%	263,631
	Elected 23			Elected 4			Elected 3			Turnout 63.1%

No. of seats
30

Total candidates
65

Date	Liberal			Conservative			CCF			Others			Total Vote
Oct. 23, 1945	Candidates 30	Vote 153,513		Candidates 30	Vote 97,774		Candidates 20	Vote 39,637		Candidates 3	Vote 634		291,558
	Elected 28	52.7%		Elected 0	33.5%		Elected 2	13.6%		Elected 0	0.2%		Turnout 64.7%

No. of seats
30

Total candidates
83

Date	Liberal			Conservatives			CCF			Others			Total Vote
June 9, 1949	Candidates 37	Vote 174,604		Candidates 37	Vote 134,312		Candidates 21	Vote 32,869		Candidates 1	Vote 749		342,534
	Elected 28	51.0%		Elected 7	39.2%		Elected 2	9.6%		Elected 0	0.2%		Turnout 77.7%

No. of seats
37

Total candidates
96

Date	Liberal			Conservative			CCF			Others			Total Vote
May 26, 1953	Candidates 37	Vote 169,921		Candidates 37	Vote 149,973		Candidates 16	Vote 23,700		Candidates 1	Vote 2,065		345,659
	Elected 23	49.2%		Elected 12	43.4%		Elected 2	6.8%		Elected 0	0.6%		Turnout 75.8%

No. of seats
37

Total candidates
91

Date	Liberal			Conservative			CCF			Others			Total Vote
	Candidates	Vote	Elected	Candidates	Vote	Elected	Candidates	Vote	Elected	Candidates	Vote	Elected	
Oct. 30, 1956	43	159,656 → 48.2%	18	43	160,996 → 48.6%	24	11	9,932 → 3.0%	1	1	812 → 0.2%	0	331,396
													Turnout 80.2%
No. of seats 43													
Total candidates 98													

Date	Liberal			Conservative			CCF			Others			Total Vote
	Candidates	Vote	Elected	Candidates	Vote	Elected	Candidates	Vote	Elected	Candidates	Vote	Elected	
June 7, 1960	43	147,951 → 42.6%	15	43	168,023 → 48.3%	27	34	31,036 → 8.9%	1	1	650 → 0.2%	0	347,660
													Turnout 82.1%
No. of seats 43													
Total candidates 121													

Date	Liberal			Conservative			NDP			Total Vote
	Candidates	Vote	Elected	Candidates	Vote	Elected	Candidates	Vote	Elected	
Oct. 8, 1963	43	134,923 → 39.7%	4	43	191,128 → 56.2%	39	20	14,076 → 4.1%	0	340,127
										Turnout 77.9%
No. of seats 43										
Total candidates 106										

Date	Liberal		Conservative		NDP		Others		Total Vote
	Candidates	Vote	Candidates	Vote	Candidates	Vote	Candidates	Vote	
May 30, 1967	46	142,945	46	180,498	24	17,873	2	498	341,814
	Elected		Elected		Elected		Elected		Turnout
	6	41.8%	40	52.8%	0	5.2%	0	0.2%	77.0%
No. of seats									
46									
Total candidates									
118									

Date	Liberal		Conservative		NDP		Others		Total Vote
	Candidates	Vote	Candidates	Vote	Candidates	Vote	Candidates	Vote	
Oct. 13, 1970	46	174,943	46	177,986	23	25,259	2	1,465	379,653
	Elected		Elected		Elected		Elected		Turnout
	23	46.1%	21	46.9%	2	6.6%	0	0.4%	77.3%
No. of seats									
46									
Total candidates									
117									

Date	Liberal		Conservative		NDP		Others		Total Vote
	Candidates	Vote	Candidates	Vote	Candidates	Vote	Candidates	Vote	
Apr. 2, 1974	46	206,648	46	166,388	46	55,902	6	2,220	431,158
	Elected		Elected		Elected		Elected		Turnout
	31	47.9%	12	38.6%	3	13.0%	0	0.5%	77.9%
No. of seats									
46									
Total candidates									
144									

Date	Liberal			Conservative			NDP			Others			Total Vote
	Candidates	Elected	Vote	Candidates	Elected	Vote	Candidates	Elected	Vote	Candidates	Elected	Vote	
Sept. 19, 1978	52	17	175,218 → 39.4%	52	31	203,500 → 45.8%	52	4	63,979 → 14.4%	6	0	2,008 → 0.4%	444,705 Turnout 78.2%
No. of seats 52													
Total candidates 162													

Date	Liberal			Conservative			NDP			Others			Total Vote
	Candidates	Elected	Vote	Candidates	Elected	Vote	Candidates	Elected	Vote	Candidates	Elected	Vote	
Oct. 6, 1981	52	13	139,604 → 33.2%	52	37	200,228 → 47.5%	52	1	76,289 → 18.1%	6	1	5,002 → 1.2%	421,123 Turnout 74.2%
No. of seats 52													
Total candidates 162													

Date	Liberal			Conservative			NDP			Cape Breton Labour			Other			Total Vote
	Candidates	Elected	Vote	Candidates	Elected	Vote	Candidates	Elected	Vote	Candidates	Elected	Vote	Candidates	Elected	Vote	
Nov. 6, 1984	52	6	129,310 → 31.3%	52	42	209,298 → 50.6%	52	3	65,876 → 15.9%	14	1	8,322 → 2.0%	4	0	630 → 0.2%	413,436 Turnout 67.5%
No. of seats 52																
Total candidates 174																

Appendix

D

Federal Elections in Nova Scotia (1896-1984)

	SEATS						POPULAR VOTE								
	L		C (or PC)		CCF (or NDP)		L		C (or PC)		CCF (or NDP)		SC		Others	
1896	10	50.0%	10	50.0%			49,176	48.8%	50,772	50.4%					737	0.7%
1900	15	75.0%	5	25.0%			54,384	51.7%	50,810	48.3%						
1904	18	100.0%					54,783	52.9%	46,131	44.5%					2,647	2.6%
1908	12	66.7%	6	33.3%			56,638	51.0%	54,500	49.0%						
1911	9	50.0%	9	50.0%			57,462	50.8%	55,209	48.8%					351	0.3%
1917	4	25.0%	12	75.0%			54,038	45.5%	57,436	48.4%					7,281	6.1%
1921	16	100.0%					136,064	52.4%	83,928	32.3%					39,801	15.3%
1925	3	21.4%	11	78.6%			93,110	41.9%	125,283	56.4%					3,617	1.6%
1926	2	14.3%	12	85.7%			99,581	43.5%	122,965	53.7%					6,412	2.8%
1930	4	28.6%	10	71.4%			127,179	47.5%	140,503	52.5%						
1935	12	100.0%					142,334	52.7%	87,893	32.1%					43,540	15.9%
1940	10	83.3%	1	8.3%	1	8.3%	142,514	50.6%	112,206	39.8%	17,715	6.3%			9,217	3.3%
1945	9	75.0%	2	16.7%	1	8.3%	141,911	45.7%	114,214	36.8%	51,892	16.7%			2,650	0.9%
1949	10	76.9%	2	15.4%	1	7.7%	177,680	52.7%	126,365	37.5%	33,333	9.9%				
1953	10	83.3%	1	8.3%	1	8.3%	176,554	53.0%	133,498	40.1%	22,357	6.7%			794	0.2%
1957	2	16.7%	10	83.3%			176,891	45.1%	197,676	50.4%	17,117	4.4%	473	0.1%		
1958			12	100.0%			160,026	38.4%	237,422	57.0%	18,911	4.5%				
1962	2	16.7%	9	75.0%	1	8.3%	178,520	42.4%	198,902	47.3%	39,689	9.4%	3,764	0.9%		
1963	5	41.7%	7	58.3%			195,007	46.7%	195,711	46.9%	26,617	6.4%	401	0.1%		
1965	2	16.7%	10	83.3%			175,415	42.0%	203,123	48.6%	38,043	9.1%			1,249	0.3%
1968	1	9.1%	10	90.9%			127,962	38.0%	186,026	55.2%	22,676	6.7%			293	0.1%
1972	1	9.1%	10	90.9%			129,738	33.9%	204,460	53.4%	47,072	12.3%	1,316	0.3%	501	0.1%
1974	2	18.2%	8	72.7%	1	9.1%	157,582	40.7%	183,897	47.5%	43,470	11.2%	1,457	0.4%	458	0.1%
1979	2	18.2%	8	72.7%	1	9.1%	151,078	35.5%	193,099	45.4%	79,603	18.7%			1,829	0.4%
1980	5	45.5%	6	54.5%			168,304	39.9%	163,459	38.7%	88,052	20.8%			2,427	0.6%
1984	2	18.2%	9	81.8%			154,954	33.6%	233,713	50.7%	70,190	15.2%			1,735	0.4%

Notes: In 1917 the Conservative totals include all Unionists and hence Fielding.
In 1921 Progressives polled 31,897 votes (12.3 per cent of the popular vote).
In 1935 Reconstruction candidates polled 39,175 votes (18.0 per cent of ...

INDEX

Abbott, Douglas 209-10, 222
Aberhart, William 182
Acadia University 289
Acadian Recorder 8, 47, 60
Acadians 105, 360, 394
Advisory Council on the
    Status of Women 340
Ahern, J.E. 275
Aitchison, J.H. 278, 284, 288, 290,
                                    292-4, 296, 304
Akerley, I.W. 309
Akerman, Jeremy 304, 310,
    316, 322, 326, 328, 330-3, 337, 339-41,
                                    343-4, 352, 353
Allan, Ann 154-5
Amalgamated Mine Workers
    (AMW) 158
Anderson, C.W. 170-1
Antigonish movement 176-7, 380
Armstrong, E.H. 42, 44;
    cabinet minister, ... 51, 54, 62,
                    74-6, 82, 84-6, 89, 91-3;
    premier, ... 95-113, 116, 139, 385;
    judge, ... 113-14
Armstrong, W.B. 123
Ashfield, Cliff 293-4
Assembly, House of
    indemnities, ... 37, 86, 91,
                    259, 285, 306-7, 358;
    independence, 16-7, 30, 132, 168, 367;
    redistribution, ... 38-9,
    46, 59, 105-6, 131-2, 144, 165-6, 212-4,
        217, 242-4, 283, 285, 341-2, 355;
    rules, ... 339, 342, 352, 355
Atlantic Development Board   . . 276, 387

Bagnell, Glen 328
Baillie, J.M. 41, 43, 45
Balcom, Eric 279
Baptist convention 289
Barnjum, F.J.D. 109-10, 127

Barnstead, A.S. 56, 123
Baxter, J.B.M. 116
Bay of Fundy tidal power 295, 324,
        329, 332, 337, 339, 341-2, 348, 350
Beazley, Charles 236
Beazley, R.G. 102
Bell, Dr. John 80
Belliveau, J.E. 293
Belliveau, Michael 321
Bennett, R.B. 134, 137-8, 163, 180
"Big Lease" 30, 109, 264
Bill 66 . . . . 244-5, 251-2, 255
Bissett, Harold 167, 187
Black, P.C. 83, 115,
    158, 173-4, 178-9, 181, 183, 192, 200, 233
Black, R. MacD. 230, 242, 302
Black, T.R. 28
Blanchard, Hiram 13
Blanchard, Percy 108
Blanchard, Prescott 139
Bligh, F.P. 60, 120, 125, 129
Blois, Fred 181, 192, 194, 196-7
Bluenose 87
Boak, Sir Robert 19-20
Board of Vendor
    Commissioners 77, 96, 122
Boer War 16
Bonusing bill 55
Books, free school 137, 141, 146,
                                        162, 215
Borden, Sir Frederick 7, 28, 50, 57
Borden, Sir Robert 18, 22, 38, 49-50,
                    55, 69, 87, 133-4, 384
Bourassa, Henri 49
Bracken, John, ... 197, 200
British Empire Steel
    Corporation (Besco) 76, 85-6,
    88, 97-8, 99-100, 103-4, 106, 110, 127,
                                        137, 384
British preference 137
Broadbent, Ed 348, 351

Brodie, Douglas 191
Brown Garnet 309, 322, 326, 328, 330
Brown, Guy 370-1
Buchanan, John 322;
　Conservative leader, ... 325-8, 330-1,
　　　　　　　333-4, 338-9, 342-3;
　　premier, 347-73, 383-4, 388, 391-4
Buckingham, Duke of, ... 108
Butts, R.H. 58, 125, 142
Byng, Viscount 121
Byrne, T.I. 142

Cabinet pensions, ... 222-3, 256;
　salaries, 35, 86, 259, 285, 306, 358;
　secrecy, ... 372-3
Cahan, C.H. 22, 130
Cahan, J.F. 130
Calder, R.L. 68
Cameron, Alexander (Sandy) 331,
　　　　　　353, 356, 358-9, 362-3
Cameron, D.A. 72, 95-6, 100, 105,
　　　　　　　　　　　　128, 138
Cameron, Bishop John 166
Campbell, C.A. 40
Camp, Dalton 230-3, 239-40, 242,
　　　　　248-9, 272, 294, 299, 315, 318
Canada Temperance Act 30, 35,
　　　　　　　　　　　　　37, 59
Canadian Labour Congress 265
Cantley, Thomas 136
Cape Breton Development Corporation
　(Devco) 295, 302, 329
Cape Breton Hospital 247, 251
Cape Breton Labour Party 354, 356,
　　　　　　　　　　360-2, 376
Cape Breton Post 262-3, 278
Cardoza, Victor 252
Carroll, W.F. 147-8, 150
Chambers, Robert　145-7, 163, 170-1, 315
Chisholm, Christopher P. . 34, 39, 44, 48
Chisholm, Colin 246
Chisholm, Sir Joseph 162
Chisholm, William 84, 93, 95-6,
　105, 111, 118, 120-1, 125, 127-8, 132-3,
　　　　　　　　　　　　135, 138
Chronicle-Herald (Halifax) 213,
　222-3, 226, 231, 247, 256, 260, 262-3,
　268, 275, 280-3, 285, 288, 292, 300-1,
　304-6, 308, 310-13, 315-16, 322, 327-8,
　330-1, 335-6, 338, 340-1, 343, 348, 355,
　　　　　357, 362, 365, 367-8, 371
Church, C.E. 10, 21
Churchill, Winston 191
Civil Service Act 160-1, 369
Clairtone Sound Corporation 284,
　293, 303, 308-9, 312, 314, 316, 319
Clark, Clifford 223
Clark, Joe 348, 351

Clarke, Joseph H. 327
Coady, Father Moses 177, 380
Coal 15, 25-6, 34, 53, 55,
　76, 91-2, 99-100, 103-4, 106-7, 110,
　115, 121, 143, 145, 158, 176, 195, 198,
　208, 210, 226, 235, 257, 260, 262-6,
　268-70, 276, 287, 290, 302, 328, 348,
　　　　　　　　　　　　　384-5
Cockfield Brown 249-50, 252
Collection Act 275, 285, 316
Collège Ste. Anne 310, 325
Colonial Standard (Pictou) 31
Comeau, Benoit 310
Comeau, J.W. 128, 220
Comeau, Louis 372
Confederation of Tomorrow
　Conference 300
Conflict of Interest legislation 367
Congdon, H.S. 98, 102, 109
Connolly, Harold 111, 118, 139,
　150, 167, 195, 202-3, 205, 209, 222,
　　　　　232, 237, 239-40, 242, 247
Conscription issue 67-71
Conservatives leadership 12-13,
　22, 28, 33, 38, 47, 53, 65-6, 91, 106,
　108-9, 138, 165, 167, 187-8, 207, 216,
　　　　　299, 325, 331, 334, 337-8, 373;
　see elections (federal) and elections
　　　　　　　　　　　(provincial)
Cook, Walton 330, 334
Cooperative Commonwealth Federation
　(CCF) 150, 164, 180-2, 191-2,
　196, 200, 207, 211-12, 214, 217-19, 226,
　　232-3, 250-1, 260, 265, 267, 278
Costs and Fees Act 66, 96
Council of Maritime Premiers 328
Covert, Frank 215
Cowan, Gordon 273
Cowan, James 365
Cragg, E.J. 138
Crerar, T.A. 68, 87, 205, 211, 223, 230
Crosbie, John 351
Cross, Austin 252
Crowell, Horatio 61, 80, 124-5
Crowell, Kenneth 279
Cunningham, Russell 207-8, 210-11,
　213-14, 217, 223-4, 226, 232, 245, 250
Currie L.D. 139, 168, 192, 195, 198,
　　　　　201, 203, 209-10, 214

Daily Star (Toronto) 371
Dalhousie University 336
Daniels, O.T. 51, 59-60, 64, 67, 77, 93
Dartmouth 269
Dartmouth Free Press 295
Dauphinee, Wilfrid 231, 246, 252
Davey Committee on the
　Mass Media 313, 316

Davis, F.R. 153, 174, 178, 208
Davis, William 110
Dawson *Report,* 199
Dawson, R. MacG. 195
Dennis, Agnes 171
Dennis, William 54, 56, 60, 66, 78
Dennis, William Henry 56, 78, 88,
    108, 130, 170-2, 180, 218
Dentistry bill 133
Department of
    Culture, Fitness and Recreation 347;
    Development, ... 324-5;
    Environment, ... 328, 330;
    Highways, ... 72-3, 119;
    Municipal Affairs, ... 144, 160;
    Provincial Secretary, ... 72-3, 347;
    Recreation, ... 330;
    Regional Economic Expansion, 329
DeRothschild, Baron Edmond 324, 341
Deuterium of Canada 281, 287,
    291, 303, 307, 312-14, 319, 326, 387
Deutsch Commission 325
Diefenbaker, John 253, 256-60, 265,
    272-3, 276, 287, 329, 376, 386
Digby strawberry project 308-9, 312
Dingman, Howard 176
Distillery, Berwick 141-2
Dominion Atlantic Railway 42
Dominion Coal Company 9, 14, 26,
    43, 46
Dominion Iron and Steel
    Company 14, 25, 26, 46, 74, 76, 95
Dominion Steel and Coal Company
    (Dosco) . . 127, 137, 143, 176, 290, 300
Donahoe, Arthur 355
Donahoe, R.A. 187, 242, 248, 256,
    259, 271, 275, 277, 285, 290, 299-301,
    305, 309, 311, 316
Donahoe, Terence 354, 367-8, 371-2, 393
Donald *Report* on Coal 290
Donaldson, Bertha, fn. 43 398
Donkin 348, 350
Doucet, Gerald 307, 310-11, 325
Douglas, J.C. 56, 63, 115
Douglas, J. Robson 102
Douglas, T.C. 294
Doull, John 138, 143
Doyle, E.C. 138
Drew, George 200, 210, 233, 375
Drummie, Fred 321, 324
Drummond, Robert 71
Drysdale, Arthur 21, 28
Duff, William 71, 138-40, 174
Duncan *Report* 124-5, 131, 137-8,
    145, 154, 160, 385
Duncan, Sir Andrew Rae 116,
    121, 143
Dunlop, Allan 295

Dunlop, W.C. 275
Dunning, C.A. 137
Duplessis, Maurice 210
Dwyer, Michael 153, 158, 161

Eastern Chronicle 83
Eastern Extension 19, 22
Education 32, 34-5,
    78, 119, 123, 191-2, 196, 210, 214, 215,
    224, 229, 246, 252, 255, 271, 307, 310,
    311, 354-5, 357-8, 360
Elections, federal 1900, 17-8; 1904,
    28-9; 1911, 49-50; 1917, 69-71; 1921,
    87-8; 1925, 115-18; 1926, 121-2; 1930,
    137-8; 1935, 163-4; 1940, 182-3; 1945,
    199-200; 1949, 218-19; 1953, 233; 1957,
    256-8; 1958, 259-60; 1962, 272-3; 1963,
    276; 1965, 287-8; 1968, 303-4; 1972,
    329; 1974, 335-6; 1979, 348-50; 1980,
    351; 1984, 360-1
Elections, provincial 1897, 12-14;
    1901, 21-3; 1906, 32-4; 1911, 47-8;
    1916, 64-6; 1920, 78-82; 1925, 108-13;
    1928, 127-31; 1933, 146-51; 1937, 170-
    2; 1941, 190-2; 1945, 205-7; 1949, 215-
    18; 1953, 230-3; 1956, 247-53; 1960,
    264-8; 1963, 276-9; 1967, 293-6; 1970,
    314-19; 1974, 332-4; 1978, 343-5; 1981,
    355-7; 1984, 361-3; 1988, 391-4
Elections, regulation of 271, 306
Electoral lists 77, 130, 142-3,
    146-51, 158, 162, 271
Electoral Franchise Act 142-3,
    146-51, 153, 158
Electric Tramway Company,
    Halifax 54, 56-7, 60-1
Employers' Liability for
    Injuries Act 17, 35, 43-4, 378
Energy question 331-4, 337-42, 345,
    350-2, 358-60, 369, 387
Estate taxes 327-8, 330
Evening Echo (Halifax) 84, 91, 106,
    107, 108
Expense accounts,
    assemblymen's 362, 364, 366, 368,
    370
Explosion, Halifax 70-1

Farmer — Labourites 84, 89, 91,
    97, 111
Farmers 78-82, 84, 111
Farquhar, George 118, 130, 135, 143,
    147, 154-5, 165, 171-2, 176
Feagan, Hugh 371
Federation of Labour, N.S. . . 73-4, 350-1
Fielding, R.M. 213-14, 217, 229,
    234, 243-4, 262-3, 265, 267

Fielding, W.S. 7-12, 184, 202,
          380, 384, 394;
   Minister of Finance,
   1896-1911, ... 17, 19, 21, 28-30,
          32, 38, 40, 45, 47-50;
   on conscription, ... 68-70, 87;
   Minister of Finance, 1921-5, ... 92-4,
          98, 107-8, 117-18
Finances 11-12, 14-15, 17, 19, 27,
   29, 30-6, 39, 42, 53-4, 58-9, 61-3, 66,
   71, 76-7, 90-1, 96, 100, 106, 118-19,
   122-3, 126, 128, 131-2, 137, 141, 143-4,
   155-6, 162-3, 165, 169, 175, 178, 181,
   188-9, 192-4, 196, 208, 212, 214-15,
   222, 224-5, 234, 243, 256, 261-4, 274,
   284-5, 289, 292-3, 300-1, 307, 309-10,
   324, 327-8, 334, 337, 338-41, 345, 348,
   352, 354, 356-9, 363-5, 367-8, 370, 383-
          4
Finlayson, Duncan 30
Finn, R.E. 44, 85-6, 134, 177, 182-3
Fishing rights 47, 54, 56
Fiske, Ralph 327, 331
Fitzgerald, G.H. 283
Fitzgerald, Walter 336
Fitzner, Stan 331
Fitzpatrick, M.H. 13, 18
Flemming, Brian 335
Flemming, Hugh John 230
Forbes, Ernest 94, 98, 124-5
Forestry 119, 157, 365
Forget interests 44
Forrest, W.D. 148
Fourth Estate, The 313, 316, 332, 345
Foundation programme,
   see Pottier Report
Franchise 11, 19, 26, 31, 41, 67, 71-2,
   77, 142-3, 146-51, 165, 167, 275, 310,
          330
Fraser, Alistair 239
Fraser, C.F. 216
Fraser, Donald F. 175-6
Fraser, Duncan 327, 333
Fraser, Duncan C. 7
Fraser, Frank 369
Fraser, James A. 83, 104, 121-2, 175
Fraser, J. Fred 143
Fraser, L.W. 187-92, 196-8, 206-7, 231
Freedom of Information Act 340,
          352, 355, 357

Gabarus 337
Gas, natural 329, 339, 350, 359
Gasoline Licensing Act   156-7, 187, 331
Gaspereau water power 57
Gaum, Percy 290, 318
Georges Bank 372
"Gerrymander" of 1925 105-6

Giffin, Ronald 366
Giles, T. A. 218, 224, 229
Gillis, Clarence (Clarie) 181, 183,
          200, 233
Gillis, Neil 120
Gillis, William 354, 357-9, 365, 368
Globe and Mail (Toronto) 176, 210,
          332, 356, 373, 392
Glube, Chief Justice Constance 367,
          372-3
Gordon, Robert 132
Gordon, Walter 281
Gosse, Clarence 338
Gouin, Sir Lomer 93
Graham, John 325
Graham Report 336-7, 355
Graham, R.H. 67, 76, 101, 148
Grand Trunk Pacific, ... 29
Grant, H.R. 37, 53, 63, 101, 175
Grant, MacCallum 91
Green Commission Report, ... 306
"Green book" proposals, ... 208, 223-4
Green, Peter 321
Gregg, Allan 354
Gypsum 224, 226

Haliburton, E.D. 280, 282, 285, 309
Halifax and Southwestern
   Railway 21, 26-7, 29, 32, 59
Halifax Board of Trade 359, 365, 368
Halifax by-election (1930) 133-5
Halifax Chronicle 122, 124, 126-7,
   129, 134-6, 139, 143, 146, 148, 158,
   163, 170-1, 176-8, 180, 190, 205, 213
Halifax County . . 318, 345, 356, 389, 394
Halifax-Dartmouth Bridge 217, 226, 242
Halifax Daily Star . . . 122, 129-30, 135-6,
   146, 150, 167, 179, 190, 211, 213
Halifax Herald 18, 27, 29, 31, 56,
   63-7, 69-74, 76, 78, 81, 85-9, 95-7, 99-
   102, 104-7, 110-11, 116, 128-30, 136,
   148-50, 160, 167, 170-80, 183, 190-1,
          195, 199, 213
Halifax Industries Ltd. 348
Halifax Mail 31, 60, 173, 175, 213
Halifax Relief Commission 71
Halifax Shipyards 342, 369
Hall, W.L. 41-2, 45, 47, 54, 56, 58,
   66, 71-2, 74, 77, 80, 82, 91, 106, 108-9,
   115, 122, 132, 143
Hantsport 354
Hanway, J.A. 140
Harding, James 283, 309
Harrington, Gordon 383, 385;
   cabinet minister, . 115, 119, 123, 137;
   premier, ... 138-50;
   opposition leader, ... 154, 156-8,
          160-3, 165, 167-73

Harris, Robert 135
Hawker Siddeley 262, 290, 295,
300, 342-3, 369
Hawkins, Charles 252
Hawkins, W.J. 336
Hayden, W.T. 293
Hayes, Joseph 92
Hepburn, Mitchell 182
Herridge, W.D. 182
Hicks, Henry 219, 282, 334;
cabinet minister, ... 219-20, 222, 224,
229, 235, 235, 237, 239-40;
premier, ...241-52;
opposition leader, ...256, 258,
260-8, 273
Hill, Hector 240
Holm, John 371, 394
Holt, Gundy and Co. 127
Hospital insurance 255, 259, 305
How, Harry 372
Howard, John 56
Howe, Joseph 8, 33, 148, 165, 202,
221, 236-7
Hubert v. Payson 26-7
Hudson's Bay Railroad 38

Ilsley, J.L. 111, 122, 139, 164,
174, 184, 199, 209
Independent Labour Party of
Cape Breton, ... 79
Independent Labour Party of
Nova Scotia, ... 79, 81-2
Industrial development 227, 234,
249, 255, 258, 265, 270, 277-8, 288-9,
291, 297, 300, 307-9, 317, 325, 382
Industrial Disputes Investigation
Act (IDIA), ... 103, 106
Industrial Estates Limited
(IEL) 258, 262, 264, 273, 277, 281,
284, 293-4, 296, 300, 302-3, 308-9, 312,
315, 318, 325, 382
Industrial Peace Act 106, 119
Industry committee 308-9, 330
Intercolonial Railway (ICR) 29,
86-8, 98, 102, 109, 124
Inverness mine 130, 167, 180-1, 195,
223, 226, 228, 380
Inverness South 355, 357, 366
Irwin, Robert 92-3, 95
Isnor, Gordon 137, 141, 279

Jamerson, M.E. 308, 312
Jefferson, H.B. 147, 160, 170, 220,
237, 250
Jenkins, Freeman 250
Jerome Barnum Associates 261
Jenks, Stuart 114
Johnston, Alexander 164, 209

Jones, A.G. 7
Jones, C.H.L. 128, 136
Jones, Harry 158
Jones *Report* 159-62
Jones, W.S.K. 307, 322
Jost, A.C. 132
Joy, John T. 47-8

Kaulback, R.C.S. 56
Kempt, Sir James 91
Kendall, A.S. 35-6, 39-40, 42-3,
46, 48, 378
Kerr, Gregory 359, 365, 368, 370
Killam, I.W. 127
Kinley, J.J. 90, 100, 128, 132,
138-40, 174
King-Byng affair 121
King, W.L. Mackenzie 87-8, 93, 97,
103, 113, 116-18, 120-1, 137-8, 163-4,
182, 199, 201, 205, 209, 219, 385
Kirby, Michael 321

Labourites 81-2, 84, 89, 90-1,
106, 111
Labour Relations Board 302
Laffin, Michael 330
Lalonde, Mark 352
Lands, Crown 17, 56, 170, 172
LaMarsh, Judy 276
Lapointe, Ernest 114
Laurence, F.A. 30
Laurier, Wilfrid 7, 16, 32, 37-8, 49,
58, 68-70, 87
LeBlanc, B.A. 105
LeBlanc, Guy 366
Leefe, John 371
Legislative council 11, 19-20, 32, 38,
46, 61, 86, 89, 96, 102, 105, 111, 119-
20, 123, 125-7, 130, 378-9
Levy, Robert 392
Lewis, David 211, 294, 335, 354, 380
Lewis, John L. 91
Liberals leadership, ... 8-10, 92-3,
138-40, 187, 197, 200-2, 239-40, 273,
286, 353, 365; see elections, provincial
and elections, federal
Lingan 287, 344, 350
Liquor agents, ... 228-9, 231-2;
government sale, ... 122, 131, 133,
135- 6;
interests, ...173;
liberalization of laws, ...212, 222,
269, 379, 382;
revenues, ...141, 175, 178, 188,
192, 194, 196, 198, 208, 210, 215
Liquor Commission, N.S. 135,
141, 145
Liquor Control Act 135-6, 269

Livingstone, "Red" Dan 97
Lobster licences, offshore 371-2
Logan, Hance J. 88, 139-40
Longley, J.W. 8, 10-11, 16-17,
                                    19, 28-30, 71
Lord's Day Act 275, 283, 382

MacAskill, M.C. 340
McBean mine 208, 328
McCurdy, F.B. 50, 104, 108, 110, 139
McCurdy, W.R. 60
MacDonald, A.B. 176-7, 380
Macdonald, Angus L. 239, 242, 244,
          249, 253, 286, 297, 345, 379-83, 385-6,
                                    388-9, 394;
          Liberal leader, . . 139-40, 142, 147-51;
          premier (1933-40), ...153-85;
          federal cabinet minister
                (1940- 5), ...192, 197, 199-202;
          premier (1945-54), ...205-37
MacDonald, Dan Lewis 230
MacDonald, Donald 191-3, 197
MacDonald, Douglas 181, 188, 191
Macdonald, E.M. 69, 102-3, 113, 116
Macdonald, Hugh John 18
Macdonald, John A. 84
MacDonald, John A. 84
McDonald, John A. 84, 103, 153, 172
Macdonald, J. Welsford 154
MacDonald, Michael 207-8, 215,
          232, 250, 260, 262, 264, 266, 268-70,
                                    278
Macdonald, Sir John A. 49, 260
Macdonald, Stanley 166
MacDonald, Vincent C. 102
McDonough, Alexa 354-65, 368-9,
                                    391, 393-4
MacDougall, I.D. 88, 139
Mace 161
MacEachen, A.J. 260, 273, 287, 304,
                          329, 349-51, 361, 387
MacEachern, William 335
MacEwan, Paul 318, 330, 353-4,
                          360-2, 376, 393
McGibbon, D. Lorne 57
MacGillivray, A.J. 91, 111
McGregor, R.M. 67-8, 89, 98, 100-1
"Machine" rule 109, 111, 115, 118,
                                    123, 128
McInnes, Hector 74, 136
MacIsaac, A.A. 295
MacIsaac, Gregory 368, 370, 372
MacIsaac, J.L. 111, 118
Mack, Jason M. 28, 86
MacKay, A.H. 78, 119
MacKay, Malcolm 364, 392
MacKay, R.A. 140
MacKay, William 10, 12-13

McKeen, David 5
MacKeen, H.P. 150, 197
Mackenzie, A.W. 248
McKenzie, D.D. 19, 30
McKenzie, D.G. 84, 89, 95, 99,
                                    111, 131
Mackenzie, N.A.M. 274, 282
McKeough, J.T. 290, 293, 307, 310,
                          324-5, 327, 333, 337
McKinnon, A.H. 195, 226, 228
McLachlan, J.B. 79, 88-9, 97-100,
                                    150, 163, 180
Maclean, A.K. 40-1, 50, 67, 89, 377
MacLean, N.J. 330
MacLean, Vincent 353, 363-70,
                                    391, 393
MacLean, William Joseph
          (Billy Joe) 355, 364, 366-7, 372
McLeod, Daniel J. 22, 26
McLeod, Donald B. 111, 118, 121
McLeod, Philip 58
MacMillan, A.S. 126, 138-9;
          highways administrator, ...83, 95;
          cabinet minister (1925), 105, 113, 115;
          opposition critic (1928-33), ...140-2,
                                    144-6, 148;
          cabinet minister (1933-40), ...153,
          156-7, 161, 169-70, 175, 178-9, 184;
          premier (1940-5), ...187-203, 386
McMullen, T.G. 13, 18
MacNeil, D.C. 289
McNeil, Jane 86
MacQuarrie, J.H. 153, 157, 168, 173,
                                    193-5, 220
McRitchie, Donald 81-2, 87, 107,
                                    109, 128, 137
Mahoney, J.F. 122-4, 133-4
Mail-Star (Halifax) 213
Management Board 347, 362
Manion, R.J. 182-3
Manson, Edward 255, 290
March, William 261
Margarine 215, 269, 271
Maritime Rights 75, 86, 88, 98-9,
          102, 104, 107, 110, 113, 115-16, 124-5,
                                    137, 256, 385
Maritime Telephone and Telegraph
          Company 291
Maritime Union 286, 325
Marshall, Donald 370
Marshall inquiry 370-2, 391
Mathers, F.H. 130, 184
Matheson, Joel 347, 351-2, 354, 357-8
Matheson, Robert 286
Medicare, universal 290, 300-2,
                                    304-6, 311
Media 392
Medjuck, Ralph 371

Meech Lake agreement 372
Meerburg, Peter 322
Meighen, Arthur 87-8, 110, 116,
                           118, 121, 134
Mercator I 340, 342
Mercury Fisheries 243, 246-7
Mersey Paper Co. 127-8, 136, 141
Metropolitan Area Growth
    Investments (MAGI) 341-2
Mewburn, S.C. 68
Michaud, J.E. 177, 385-6
Michelin bill 350-1, 356
Michelin Tires 309, 325, 339, 350-1
Minister of Education 217, 219
Mitchell, George 338, 343
Mooney, Fraser 335
Morning Chronicle (Halifax) 18, 27,
    33, 36, 45, 53, 56-8, 63, 66, 69, 75, 87,
                           377, 394
Morris, Edmund 353
Morrison, Bishop James 166
Morrison, D.W. 90, 97, 111
Morrison, G.M. 79
Mothers' allowances 134, 167, 194
Mulroney, Brian 360, 388
Municipal affairs supervision 178, 194-5
Municipal finance 225, 245-6, 249,
    251-2, 266, 274, 286, 289-90, 292, 294,
                        325, 336, 354-5
Munk, Peter 293, 308, 312
Murdoch, James 103-4
Murphy, G.H. 134, 138, 150, 242
Murphy, J.R. 196
Murray, George H. 102, 111, 113,
    180, 202-3, 377-82, 389, 394;
    political background, ... 8-9;
    premier (1896-1923), ... 10-95

National Government 182-3
National Policy 8, 13, 15, 22, 26, 37,
    48, 94, 96, 99, 104, 107, 110
National Thrift 229, 235, 378,
                           384, 388
Naval Bill 58
"New Deal", Bennett 163, 165
New Democratic Party (NDP) 343-5,
    349, 353-5, 355, 360, 376-7;
    elections, ... 276-9, 293-4, 296,
    316-17, 332-4, 341, 343-5, 351, 355-6,
                           361-2;
    leadership, ... 304, 353-4
Nicholson, Peter 279-80, 284, 286,
    288, 293, 300, 306-8, 311, 314, 324,
    327-8, 337-8, 340-1, 345, 348, 365
Nova Scotia Association for the
    Advancement of
    Colored People 304

Nova Scotia Communications
    and Information Centre 328
Nova Scotia Economic Council 160
Nova Scotia Housing
    Commission 305
Nova Scotia Iron and Steel
    Company 25
Nova Scotia Legal Aid
    Commission 340
Nova Scotia Light and
    Power Company 198, 326, 342
Nova Scotia Police Commission 335
Nova Scotia Power Commission 74, 141,
                           198, 326
Nova Scotia Power Corporation 326,
    331, 338-9, 341-3, 358, 359-60, 372
Nova Scotia Pulp Ltd. 258
Nova Scotia Research Foundation .. 208
Nova Scotia Resources Ltd. 365
Nova Scotia Sanitorium 17, 25, 154
Nova Scotia Steel and Coal
    Company (Scotia) 25, 42, 44,
                       74, 76, 146, 158
Nova Scotia Technical College 34,
                     36, 168, 336, 377
Nowlan, George 172, 187, 218-19,
                     233, 256, 272, 387

Offshore resources 286-7, 336, 348,
                       352, 356, 358
O'Handley, Alexander 128-9
O'Hearn, W.J. 93, 95-6, 99-101, 115
Old age pensions 36, 84, 126, 131,
    137, 141, 147, 153, 167, 194, 223
Ombudsman 283, 311, 322, 326, 336
O'Neil, Lawrence 361
Ottawa Journal 205
Outhit, W.D. 282
Owen, W.H. 19, 90, 120, 125

Pace, Leonard 322, 325-7
Parsons, Albert 41, 58, 131, 172
Parties, political 296-7, 375-7;
    see Conservatives, Cooperative Com-
    monwealth Federation, Farmers,
    Farmer-Labourites, Labourites, Lib-
    erals, New Democratic Party, Pro-
    gressives, Reconstruction party
Paton, V.J. 114
Patronage 30, 39, 115, 119-20, 130,
    153-5, 222, 256, 280, 281-2, 309
Patterson, George 34
Patterson, Malcolm 201, 235
Pearson, G.F. 57, 92, 156
Pearson, L.B. 260, 272, 276, 287, 291, 387
Petroleum Resources Act 352
Pictou Advocate 82

Pipes, W.T. 20, 28, 30-1, 34, 40
Policy Board 347
Political culture 336, 375, 377, 389
Polls, public opinion 111, 393
Portland estates 355, 371
Pottier, V.J. 229, 268
Pottier *Report* 242, 244-5, 251-2
Power, C.G. 211
Presbyterians 101
Pressure groups 196, 211, 270-1,
                                    381-2, 389
Probate court 11
Progressives 87-8, 98
Prohibition, see temperance
Protection 87, 107, 110, 116, 137
Provincial Auditor 19, 26, 39, 118-19
Provincial Electoral
   Commission 285, 342, 355
Provincial Exhibition 26
Provincial Highway Board 73,
                        76-7, 83, 95, 119, 187
Provincial Medical Board 369
Provincial Workingmen's Association
   (PWA) 42-3, 46
Public accounts committee 225-6,
                                    228-9, 365
Public archives 131, 133
Public Utilities Board 39, 54,
            126, 156, 194, 196, 282, 331
Pulpwood export 136, 151
Purchasing, government 39, 119,
                                222, 281-2, 309
Purdy, Gordon 183, 211

Quebec 288, 300, 336

Railways 12-3, 20-1, 25-8, 32-3,
                        36-7, 42, 55-6, 59
Ralston, J.L. 76, 82, 130, 184, 199
Rand, Ivan 265
Rand Commission 263-4
Rand, William 108, 112
Reardon, Dr. C.H. 269, 271-2, 381
Reconstruction party 163-4
Reciprocity 45, 47-50
Redden, A.W. 125
Regan, Gerald 350-1, 353-4, 383, 387,
                                         389;
   Liberal leader, ... 286-319;
   premier, ... 321-45
Regenstreif, Peter 303
Retiring Allowances Act 235
Rhodes, E.N. 50, 106, 163, 383, 385;
   Conservative leader, ... 108-10;
   premier, ... 115-38
Richardson, A.R. 84, 91, 97, 111
Roads 12-3, 34, 54-5,
   72-3, 75-7, 83, 119-20, 147, 157, 161-2,

169-70, 192, 195, 202, 218, 228, 248-9,
                                    255, 319
Robert, E.A. 56-7
Robertson, Struan 61
Robertson, Wishart 202
Robichaud, Louis 286
Robson, James 321
Roe, A.V. 262
Rogers, Grace McLeod 81, 116
Rogers, Norman McLeod 116, 159,
                              164, 183, 385
Rogers, R. MacLeod 284
Romkey, Gordon 129, 233
Ross, Hugh 158
Rowell, N.W. 68
Rowell-Sirois Commission 170, 173
Rowell-Sirois *Report* 193, 208, 386
Royal Canadian Mounted Police . . . 146
Rule of the road 90, 96
Rural electrification 168, 194, 196-8, 202
Rural high schools 214, 220, 224-5,
                                    227, 234
Rural telephones 55
Russell, Benjamin 8, 28, 148
Rutledge, J.E. 195, 211, 215, 243
Ryle, Michael 339
Ryle *Report* 342, 352

St. Laurent, Louis . . . 218-19, 233, 257-8,
                                         375
St. Margaret's Bay 83, 96
Saturday Night 176
Scott Paper Company . . . 284, 314, 330-1
Seat-belt legislation 340, 363
Secession 96-7, 108
Senate 16
Sexton, F.H. 35
Shaheen, John 329, 332, 336-7
Sharp, Mitchell 289, 387
Shaw, Ralph 280
Shaw *Report* 271, 275
Shipbuilding 66, 71, 190
Sifton, Clifford 68
Smith, A.B. 206-7
Smith, G.I. 383, 387-8;
   opposition critic, ... 218, 221-22,
                  225-9, 234, 243, 245-7, 252;
   cabinet minister, ... 256, 262-4, 274,
               281, 283-5, 289, 292-3, 295;
   premier, ... 299-319;
   opposition member, ... 322, 325-8
Smith, Robert 90
Snider case 103
Sobey, Frank 293, 303, 308
Social Credit 163, 182-3
Spevack, Jerome 308, 312
Stairs, John F. 10, 12-3, 21-2
Stamps, postage 11

Stanfield, Frank Sr. 58, 61, 106,
        108-9, 119, 123, 140, 218
Stanfield, Frank Jr. 200, 216, 233
Stanfield, Robert L. 315, 317-9, 345,
        375-6, 380-2, 386-9, 394;
    provincial party leader, ... 216-53;
    premier, ... 255-98;
    national party leader, ... 303-4, 329,
        335-6
Steppanski, Richard 142
Stevens, Geoffrey
    (newspaperman) 216, 245, 248
Stevens, Geoffrey (politician) . . 222, 239
Stevens, H.H. 163-4
Stewart, J.D. 116
Stewart, J.J. 34
Stewart, John 287
Stewart, Joseph 338
Stockall, Allan 371
Strait of Canso causeway 195, 217,
        226, 242
Streatch, Kenneth 350, 365
Stubbs, Eileen 294
Sullivan, Allan 279
Supreme Court 271, 340
Sydney Daily Post 61, 101, 110
Sydney Post Record 234
Sydney steel works . . . 234, 290, 300, 302,
        309, 315, 337, 348, 354, 387

Taggart, H.L. 89
Tanner, Charles 12-13, 18-19, 22,
    25-8, 31-3, 35, 37-8, 41, 53-7, 59-60, 62-
        6, 70, 80, 280, 383
Tariff Advisory Board 124
Technical education 34, 36, 61;
    see Nova Scotia Technical College
Temperance 27-8, 30-1, 35,
        37, 40-1, 53, 59, 63, 75, 77, 101
Temperance Act, Nova Scotia 53,
        59, 63, 101, 122, 133
Temperance Alliance, Nova Scotia . . 28,
        37, 40
Tenure of Office bill 119, 123, 126
Terence Bay 176-7
Terris, Archibald 90, 111
Thompson, David 321
Thompson, J.S.D. 166
Thornhill, Roland 325, 347-8, 350,
        352-3, 355, 363-5, 371-2
Thorpe, Victor 311
Tidal Power Corporation 324, 350
Time 317
Tory, J.C. 55-6, 63, 75, 77-8, 84,
        89-90, 92-3, 95, 99, 102

Tramways and Power Corporation,
    Nova Scotia 60-1
Trade unions 169, 210-1, 215,
        302, 322, 325-6, 350-1
Trawler, steam 141, 174, 178-9
Treasury Board 39
Trudeau, P.E. 303, 329, 335, 338,
        348, 351, 387
Tuberculin testing 126-7, 129
Tufts, Evelyn 176-7
Tupper, Sir Charles 8-10, 17-18
Turner, John 335, 360

Uhlman, Harold 252
Union Government 68-70, 79-80
United Church of Canada 101
United Farmers of Nova Scotia 78-82
United Farmers of Ontario 78-9
United Mine Workers 42-3, 46,
    91, 97, 100, 103, 143, 158, 180-1, 214
Unity Reform 33
Universities 274, 282
University College of
    Cape Breton 335
Urquhart, Earl 268, 270, 273, 275-80,
        284, 286

Victoria General Hospital . . . 12, 41, 168
Vital statistics 36
Voluntary economic planning 274, 285,
        290, 293, 311, 315
Volvo 273

Walker, J.A. 115, 126-7, 129, 133, 150
Walker Report 354-5, 357-8
Warrington, Dal 299
War-time Elections Act 69
Watkins, Lyndon 332
Waye, Forman 84, 90-1, 95, 97,
        99-100, 105, 111
Welch, Frank 309
Western lands 75, 77-8, 131
White Commission 160
Whitman, George 19
Whitney, Henry M. 14
Whitney Syndicate 9, 12, 26, 32
"Whity-Brown" party 21
Wickwire, H.H. 72-3, 75, 77,
        83, 90, 93
Wilcox, Charles 13, 16-19, 38-9, 41
Winters, R.H. 239, 258
Wolvin, R.M. 106, 127
Woman's Christian Temperance Union
    (WCTU) 63, 67
Women's suffrage 67, 71, 77

"Woodpecker election" 172
Woodsworth, J.S. 182
Workmen's Compensation Act 35,
    43-4, 62, 74, 119, 126, 168, 255,
    293, 378

Wreck Cove 337, 339
Wright, A.J. 114

Yetman, Gerald 350
Young, Brian 393